HUMAN INFORMATION PROCESSING
Measures, Mechanisms, and Models

Proceedings of the XXIV International Congress of Psychology
of the
International Union of Psychological Science (I.U.Psy.S.)
Sydney, Australia, August 28–September 2, 1988

Selected/Revised Papers

Volume 2
(For further volumes see back of the cover)

Published for the
International Union of Psychological Science (I.U.Psy.S.)

Human Information Processing

Measures, Mechanisms, and Models

Edited by

Douglas VICKERS

and

Philip L. SMITH

Psychology Department
University of Adelaide
Australia

1989

NORTH-HOLLAND
AMSTERDAM · NEW YORK · OXFORD · TOKYO

NORTH-HOLLAND

ELSEVIER SCIENCE PUBLISHERS B.V.

Sara Burgerhartstraat 25

P.O. Box 211, 1000 AE Amsterdam, The Netherlands

Distributors for the United States and Canada:

ELSEVIER SCIENCE PUBLISHING COMPANY INC.

655 Avenue of the Americas

New York, N.Y. 10010, U.S.A.

```
Library of Congress Cataloging-in-Publication Data

International Congress of Psychology (24th : 1988 : Sydney, N.S.W.)
   Human information processing : measures, mechanisms; and models /
edited by Douglas Vickers and Philip L. Smith.
      p.   cm. -- (Proceedings of the XXIV International Congress of
Psychology of the International Union of Psychological Science
(I.U.Psy.S.), Sydney, Australia, August 28-September 2, 1988 ; v. 2)
   "Published for the International Union of Psychological Science
(I.U.Psy.S.)"--Ser. t.p.
   Includes bibliographical references.
   ISBN 0-444-88520-X
   1. Human information processing--Congresses.   I. Vickers, D.
(Douglas)  II. Smith, Philip L.  III. International Union of
Psychological Science.  IV. Title.  V. Series: International
Congress of Psychology (24th : 1988 : Sydney, Australia).
Proceedings of the XXIV International Congress of Psychology of the
International Union of Psychological Science (IUPsyS), Sydney,
Australia, August 28-September 2, 1988 ; v. 2.
BF20.I614  1988 vol. 2
[BF444]
150 s--dc20
[153]                                                  89-25519
                                                       CIP
```

ISBN: 0 444 88520 X

ISBN set: 0 444 88509 9

Printed in The Netherlands

FOREWORD

The XXIV International Congress of Psychology was held in Sydney, Australia in August/September 1988, as an official activity of Australia's Bicentennial Year.

In undertaking the task of organising the Congress on behalf of the International Union of Psychological Science (I.U.Psy.S.), the Australian Psychological Society (A.P.S.) was acutely aware of the responsibilities it was assuming. In particular, the Society recognised that to be judged a success, the Congress must serve as a milestone in the development of psychology as a discipline, and in the recognition of the I.U.Psy.S. as the international body of psychology.

The response of the international community of psychologists to the invitation to participate in the scientific program was most gratifying. In all, the program included a total of 2,500 individual and symposium contributions covering all the major areas of psychology. Authors from over 50 countries contributed.

The present volume of Proceedings is one of nine volumes containing selections of written versions of Congress presentations. The task of selecting papers to appear in the Proceedings was an unenviable one, as it was impossible to include all worthy papers. The principal selection criterion was quality, i.e., judged contribution to the body of scientific psychological knowledge.

Secondary, but important, criteria were balance and represent-ativeness. We sought to achieve both a reasonable balance across the major areas of psychology, and adequate representation of authors from the various participating countries.

An important decision taken by the Editorial Committee was to ask Volume Editors to provide laser printed copies of their volumes. In order to achieve this goal, Volume Editors requested authors to submit their papers on disk. If authors were unable to accede to this request, it was necessary for Volume Editors to key the papers into a word-processor.

Given the present state of the art of desk top publishing, Volume Editors were required to expend enormous effort and overcome countless technical problems. We trust the final form of the volumes is sufficient recompense for their efforts.

In each of the centres where the work of compiling the volumes was undertaken, the required facilities were made available, and unpaid work on a grand scale was undertaken.

We wish to record our grateful thanks to the Psychology Departments in the following universities: University of Adelaide, Flinders University, La Trobe University, University of Newcastle, Macquarie University, University of Melbourne (Institute of Education), University of New South Wales, and Wollongong University Department of Learning Studies. It is impossible to thank individually all those persons whose contributions were crucial to the enterprise. I must, however, make one exception and record thanks to Louise Kahabka of the School of Psychology, University of New South Wales.

S. H. Lovibond
Sydney, 1989

PREFACE

This volume consists of a selection of papers, presented at the XXIV International Congress of Psychology in Sydney in September, 1988, which report research on various aspects of the processing of information by human beings. The papers collected here reflect orientations ranging from the broadly ecological to the highly abstract and formal. Their substantive concerns encompass questions of perception, action, and the mechanisms which mediate between them, and the papers are characterised generally by a close relationship between empirical findings and theoretical issues. The papers have been arranged into five main groups. The first (Sections 1-3) is concerned primarily with the mechanisms by which external events are registered and represented by the sensory and perceptual systems, and with the mechanisms responsible for the adaptation and control of physical movements, i.e., with the input and output of information. The second (Sections 4,5) is concerned with attempts to model the elementary processing of stimulus representations, particularly in tasks in which performance is timed. The third (Section 6) comprises an examination of computational models of the processes involved in memorising, recognizing, and recalling information. A fourth - small - group (Section 7) is concerned with the modelling of more molar decision behaviour. Finally, the fifth group (Section 8) is predominantly concerned with attempts to derive measures which have explicit relationships to a theoretical account of elementary cognitive activity.

A reading of these papers will reveal a considerable amount of cross-reference, both explicit and implicit. For example, sequential decision models are applied and tested in the areas of psychophysical discrimination, recognition, and behavioural decisions, and provide a theoretical basis for the measures of intellectual ability examined in the last group of papers. Some common themes also emerge, such as the advisability of investigating aspects of information processing systematically over wider contexts, the need to examine adaptive responses to changing stimulus situations, and the desirability of considering more flexible, albeit more complex, configurations of elementary cognitive processes. These more ambitious and comprehensive theoretical endeavours, often made possible only by recent increases in available computing power, promise to provide a useful stimulus to further theoretical development.

Compiling this selection of papers has provided us with an interesting and suggestive perspective of current research in human information processing across a broad spectrum of different, though related, problem areas. In producing this volume for a wider readership we are indebted to Richard Pank for his dedicated assistance in grappling with the problems of reformatting mathematical text.

Douglas Vickers

Philip L. Smith   Adelaide, July 1989

TABLE OF CONTENTS

SECTION 6

COMPUTATIONAL MODELS OF REPRESENTATION, RECOGNITION, AND RECALL

SECTION 7

DECISION MAKING

SECTION 8

MEASURES OF INDIVIDUAL DIFFERENCES IN INTELLECTUAL ABILITY

SECTION 1
SENSORY MECHANISMS

Human Information Processing: Measures,
Mechanisms, and Models. D. Vickers and P. L. Smith (eds.)
© Elsevier Science Publishers B. V. (North-Holland), 1989

SPATIAL AND TEMPORAL FREQUENCY CHANNELS IN THE HUMAN VISUAL SYSTEM

Helen Paulucci

University of Wollongong

This study examined the effects of varying spatial and. temporal frequency on the sustained and transient subsystems of the human visual system. In a 2AFC experiment, subjects were required to detect and identify one of two possible stimuli from one of two possible intervals. Stimuli were sinusoidal gratings (range 0.6 - 16.0 c/deg), which could be varied temporally from 0 - 16 Hz. The data were analysed with respect to the hypothesis that perfectly discriminated stimulus pairs are processed by separate channels in the visual system. The results are discussed in terms of two possible models of the sustained and transient subsystems. One model hypothesizes that a continuum of receptive field sizes underlies the subsystems. The other model hypothesizes that discrete mechanisms underlie the subsystems. The results tend to support the discrete model.

1. INTRODUCTION

Current theories of spatial frequency processing favour the idea that the visual system contains a number of channels, each of which is tuned to a different range of spatial frequencies. A channel might be thought of as a 'filter', selecting only certain types of information from a complex stimulus and ignoring information lying outside its selective range (Blakemore and Campbell, 1969; Braddick, Campbell and Atkinson, 1978). It has been proposed further that distinct mechanisms (or channels) underlie the processing of stationary and moving stimuli. The different mechanisms have come to be labelled the "sustained" and "transient" mechanisms or subsystems.

The sustained mechanism is believed to be primarily responsible for analysing the fine detail (higher frequency components) of visual stimuli. It prefers stimuli with either no, or a very low, motion component. The transient mechanism, which is believed to be responsible for the perception of temporally modulated stimuli, is not sensitive to high spatial frequencies, but prefers low and medium spatial frequencies. It is much poorer at resolving spatial details, and is thought to be a motion or flicker detector. However, the two systems may not function as discretely as was first hypothesized. There is evidence that the sustained system can transmit some information about motion, and that the transient system can transmit some spatial frequency information (Anderson and Burr, 1985; Lovegrove, Martin and Slaghuis, 1986; Thompson, 1983; Wilson, 1980).

Watson and Robson (1981) employed a discrimination task to investigate the number of spatial channels operating at different temporal frequencies. When test stimuli (sinusoidal gratings) were stationary, there appeared to be seven spatial channels available. Each channel was centred on a particular spatial frequency, and channels were separated from each other by approximately one octave. When the test stimuli were modulated at 16Hz however, there appeared to be only two channels available, each much more broadly tuned than the channels available at zero modulation.

What mechanisms might underlie the psychophysical findings? Two are proposed:

The first, Model 1, proposes that a continuum of receptive field sizes exists in the visual system. In this model, as the width of receptive fields varies from narrow to broad, differences in the time constants of excitatory and inhibitory responses are analysed by the visual system in a way that accounts for the psychophysical data. For example, low frequency sine-wave stimuli, by exciting both narrow excitatory receptive field centers and broader inhibitory surrounds, have threshold levels which are the product of these antagonistic processes. High spatial frequency stimuli "do not stimulate the antagonistic surrounds of the receptive fields" (Kelly, 1977, p.115), and so have threshold levels which are the result of different processes than for low spatial frequencies. The evidence supporting this model is largely physiological (Kelly and Burbeck, 1984).

The alternative, Model 2, argues that distinct mechanisms underlie the sustained and transient subsystems. Evidence which suggests that the sustained subsystem can inhibit the transient subsystem, and vice versa, supports the idea that different mechanisms underlie these subsystems (Breitmeyer, 1978). Psychophysical data, such as specific reading disability data (Lovegrove et al., 1986; Martin and Lovegrove, 1987, 1988), may also be interpreted as supporting this model. Further evidence comes from physiological data which indicate the existence of cortical cells with bandwidths which correspond to psychophysical channel bandwidth estimations (Kelly and Burbeck, 1984).

The experiment reported here sought to investigate whether there would be a sudden change between there being many (e.g. six or seven) to being few (two or three) spatial frequency channels available as the temporal frequency of the stimulus was increased, or whether there would be a gradual reduction in the number of channels. A sudden change in the number of spatial frequency channels available would be taken as support for Model 2, which hypothesizes that different mechanisms underlie the sustained-transient subsystems. However, a gradual change in the number of channels available would support Model 1, which hypothesizes a continuum of receptive field sizes underlying the sustained-transient dichotomy.

This experiment is based on work by Watson and Robson (1981), and attempts to replicate as far as possible their procedure, which measured spatial frequency discriminations at two extreme temporal frequencies (0Hz and 16Hz). However it also examines the effects of intervening temporal frequencies (2, 4 and 6Hz) on the number of spatial frequency channels available.

Watson and Robson hypothesized that stimuli are detected by labelled detectors, so that an observer can distinguish a response by one detector from that of any other detector (at detection threshold). In this model, each detector is assumed to have a specific threshold, so that a stimulus is detected whenever that threshold level is reached. Thus, if two stimuli were processed by the same labelled detector, the observer would not be able to tell the two stimuli apart, but, if two stimuli were detected by different labelled detectors, then the identity of each detector would unambiguously identify each stimulus. In this case, each of the two stimuli would be correctly identified whenever it was detected (Watson and Robson, 1981).

2. METHOD

2.1 Subjects

Initial threshold levels were determined from 6 subjects (3 men, 3 women, age range 22-40 years). All had normal (or corrected to normal) visual acuity. Two of these subjects were employed in the main (detection/discrimination) experiment.

2.2 Apparatus

The stimuli were vertical sinusoidal gratings, the contrast of which could be varied. The gratings were counterphased sinusoidally and were of varying spatial frequencies. Stimuli were displayed on a Tektronix 608

X-Y display with a P4 phosphor, and were generated by an Innisfree Picasso CRT Image Generator which was interfaced with an IBM-compatible PC. The presentation of stimuli and the recording of subjects' responses were controlled by computer.

The X-Y display was occluded with a circular occluder, the diameter of which subtended a visual angle of 4 degrees at a viewing distance of 1.14m. The face of the X-Y display was surrounded by a rectangular screen (0.8m by 0.7m) which was matched in hue and space average luminance with the X-Y display. The luminance of both the X-Y display and the surround were set at 28.0 cd/m2, as measured by a Tektronix J16 1 deg. narrow angle luminance probe.

Subjects responded by pressing labelled response keys. They were restrained with a chin rest, and viewed the stimuli binocularly. Both the threshold determinations and the main experiment were run in a darkened room, with an ambient room luminance of less than 1cd/m2.

2.3 Procedure

2.3.1. First Stage. Threshold levels of the stimuli for the detection-discrimination experiment (Second Stage) were determined by a combination of the method of limits and the two-alternative forced choice (2AFC) up-down reversal method described by Wetherall and Levitt (1965). These threshold levels were used to determine contrast levels for stimuli in the main detection/discrimination experiment, and should not be confused with the threshold levels which are calculated from the results obtained there. Table 1 gives the spatial frequencies used in the main experiment. Threshold measures were obtained for each base spatial frequency at each of 0, 2, 4, 6 and 16Hz. Four contrast levels of each stimulus were used in the main experiment.

Table 1

Spatial frequencies compared in the detection/ discrimination experiment

Base frequency (c/deg)	Test frequency (c/deg)			
0.6	0.8	1.0	1.2	1.5
1.5	2.0	3.0	4.0	
4.0	5.0	6.0	7.0	
7.0	10.0	12.0	14.0	
12.0	16.0			

These contrast levels were: one step below threshold, threshold, one step above threshold, and two steps above threshold (3dB steps). Contrasts used for each condition were based on the average threshold as determined from the six subjects.

2.3.2   Second Stage.   Detection and discrimination thresholds were determined using the procedure outlined by Watson and Robson (1981). This involved a 2AFC procedure, where on any trial one of two possible stimuli was presented in one of two intervals, and at one of four possible contrast levels. Within each condition, each stimulus appeared 50% of the time, so that each stimulus appeared 20 times at each contrast level. Subjects were required to indicate, using the response keys, in which interval the stimulus appeared, and which of the two possible stimuli it was.

Stimulus duration was 500 msec, interstimulus interval was 50msec, and intertrial interval was 50 msec. In each block, the choice of stimuli, the contrast level, and the interval in which the stimulus was presented was selected randomly by the computer.

Each condition consisted of 4 blocks (occasionally 3 blocks) of 40 trials. Before each new condition a familiarization session was employed, which consisted of a single block of 10 trials in which the stimulus pairs were presented at three contrast levels, all of which were well above threshold. The order in which conditions for the detection/discrimination task were presented was randomised across subjects.   The order of presentation of trials within a session was also randomised.

2.3.3   Analysis of detection and identification thresholds.   Separate detection and identification thresholds were determined for each stimulus from the data for each session.   To estimate the detection and identification thresholds, a logistic regression model (Everrit and Dunn, 1983), was fitted to the data for each stimulus in each condition.   This model predicts performance using a function of the form

$$\log [P / (1 - P)] = A + B \times C \tag{1}$$

where P represents the proportion of correctly detected or identified responses, A is the intercept of the fitted function, B is the slope of the fitted function, and C is stimulus contrast. The estimate of threshold level was then given the contrast level which corresponded to an 82% correct level of responding. As in Watson and Robson's analysis, it was assumed that two perfectly discriminated stimuli would be identified as often as each was detected. In this case, detection and identification thresholds should be equal, and so the ratio of these two thresholds is a measure of whether the two stimuli were perfectly discriminated. The statistical test of the hypothesis that correct detection leads inevitably to correct identification is described in Appendix 1.

Procedures for applying Watson and Robson's statistical test were not available. However, using available software (GLIM) (Baker and Nelder, 1978), it was possible to fit a model, expressed by Equation (2) of Appendix 1, which satisfied assumptions (i) to (iii) listed therein. In this model, assumption (ii) concerning detection guess rate was modified. Rather than assuming that guessing was equally likely across intervals, it was assumed that there may be an interval bias for detection responses, analogous to the stimulus bias for identification responses. (Subsequent data analysis, which is not reported in this paper, supported this notion.)

3. RESULTS

Table 2 below shows the estimated difference in spatial frequency separation required, for each base frequency at each temporal frequency, for both stimuli to be perfectly discriminable at threshold.

Results were more consistent for Subject AP than for Subject LS. Figures in brackets represent the first reliable separation for LS for that condition. Results for LS should be treated with caution, as those cases where there are figures in brackets show that for that condition, LS could perfectly discriminate either very small separations, or could discriminate a very small separation but could not discriminate the next smallest separation.

4. DISCUSSION

The results of fitting the model in Equation (2) indicated that channel bandwidth estimates for temporal frequencies of between 0 and 6Hz were generally around one octave. However, at 16Hz, channel bandwidth was mostly greater than one octave. Given the qualification that the data were noisy, the results in general show support for a model in which there is a sudden change in the number of spatial frequency channels available as temporal frequency increases, with the change occurring somewhere between 6 and 16Hz. Table 2 indicates that for temporal frequencies between 0Hz and 16Hz, the difference in spatial frequency required for two stimuli to be perfectly discriminable at threshold is no more than 1.5 octaves, and often less than or equal to 1 octave. It should be noted however, that the results for both subjects,

Table 2.

Difference in spatial frequency required before both stimuli are perfectly discriminable.

Base frequency c/deg	Temporal frequency Hz	Difference required +	
		Subject AP	Subject LS
0.6	0	1.5	0.8 (1.2)
	2	>1.5	0.8
	4	1.5	1.0
	6	1.5	0.8 (1.0)
	16	1.5	>1.5
1.5	0	2.0	4.0
	2	4.0	2.0 (3.0)
	4	3.0	2.0 (3.0)
	6	2.0	2.0 (3.0)
	16	>4.0	2.0 (3.0)
4.0	0	5.0	>7.0
	2	7.0	6.0 (7.0)
	4	>7.0	6.0
	6	>7.0	>7.0
	16	>7.0	>7.0
7.0	0	12.0	10.0 (>14)
	2	10.0	10.0
	4	12.0	14.0 (>14)
	6	10.0	12.0 (>14)
	16	>14.0	12.0
12.0	0	>16.0	>16.0
	2	>16.0	16.0
	4	>16.0	>16.0
	6	>16.0	>16.0
	16	>16.0	16.0

+ indicates the minimum spatial frequency value required for perfect discrimination. Those cases where a > symbol appears indicate that a greater separation than was tested was needed for perfect discrimination to occur.

and particularly those for LS, did not show a consistent pattern across the temporal or the spatial frequency range.

The results do not provide support for Model 1, in that there is no evidence of a gradual change in the number of channels available as temporal frequency increases for either AP or LS (at least not between 0 and 16Hz).

The results, although tentative, suggest that more detailed quantification of the changes in spatial and temporal interactions between 6 and 16Hz is warranted, because a change in the number of channels available in the visual system must occur somewhere in that range.

ACKNOWLEDGEMENTS

For their assistance with this work, I would like to thank Professor W.J. Lovegrove and Dr. P.E. Pattison, both of the University of Wollongong.

Correspondence concerning this paper should be addressed to Dr Helen Paulucci, Department of Psychology, University of Wollongong, P.O. Box 1144, Wollongong, N.S.W. 2500

APPENDIX 1

Watson and Robson's statistical test is based upon the following response model:

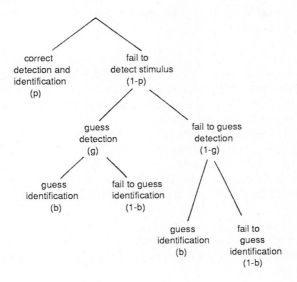

Figure 1: Watson and Robson's (1981) response model. (Pattison, personal communication).

The model was tested against a saturated model in which no particular structure to the detection and identification responses is assumed. The test was conducted for each condition and, when significant, indicated that the reduced model of Figure 1. was unable to fit the data. Watson and Robson interpreted such a lack of fit as evidence for a difference between detection and identification responses, and as support for a 'two mechanisms', or two detectors, rather than a 'one mechanism' account. The model of Figure 1. assumes that:

(i) if a subject fails to detect (and therefore identify) a stimulus, detection and identification responses are independent;

(ii) the rate of guessing detection is fixed at g (which is set to 0.5), and is independent of both the stimulus presented and the interval in which it is presented;

(iii) the rate of guessing identification (the stimulus bias (b)) depends on the stimulus presented but is independent of the interval in which it is presented; and

(iv) all of these features occur independently of the contrast at which a stimulus is presented.

The details of the test of the model are as follows. For each condition, a log-linear model of the following form

$$I R \times B = D R \times I + C \tag{2}$$

where IR represents the identification response, B the identity of stimulus, DR the detection response, I the interval of presentation, and C the contrast, was fitted to data from trials in which correct detections and identifications were not made. The model may be interpreted as specifying a relationship between identification responses and the identity of a stimulus, and between detection responses and the interval of presentation of the stimulus, but as imposing quasi-independence on all other factors. However, it should be emphasised that these relationships are assumed to hold only where both correct detection and correct identification are not observed (i.e., for cases of correct detection and incorrect identification, incorrect detection and correct identification, or incorrect detection and incorrect identification) (Pattison, personal communication).

Whether or not the model fits is assessed by the G^2 statistic, where G^2 is a likelihood ratio criterion, and is given by

$$G^2 = 2 \Sigma \text{ observed} \times \log (\text{observed} / \text{expected}) \tag{3}$$

(Everitt and Dunn, 1983).

REFERENCES

Anderson, S.J., & Burr, D.C. (1985). Spatial and temporal selectivity of the human motion system. Vision Research, 25, 1147-1154.

Baker, R.J. & Nelder, J.A. (1978). The GLIM system: Generalised linear interactive modelling. Rothamsted Experimental Station, Harpenden, Herts, England.

Blakemore, C., & Campbell, F.W. (1969). On the existence of neurones in the human visual system selectively sensitive to the orientation and size of retinal images. Journal of Physiology, 203, 237-260.

Braddick, O., Campbell, F.W., & Atkinson, J. (1978). Channels in vision: Basic aspects. In R. Held, H.W. Leibowitz, & H-L. Teuber (Eds.), Handbook of sensory physiology: Vol. 8 Perception (pp. 3-38). Heidelberg: Springer-Verlag.

Breitmeyer, B.G. (1978). Disinhibition in metacontrast masking of vernier acuity targets: Sustained channels inhibit transient channels. Vision Research. 18, 1401-1405.

Everitt, B.S., & Dunn, G. (1983). Advanced methods of data exploring and modelling. London: Heinemann Educational Books.

Kelly, D.H. (1977). Visual contrast sensitivity. Optica Acta, 24(2) 107-129.

Kelly, D.H., & Burbeck, C.A. (1984). Critical problems in spatial vision. CRC Critical Reviews in Biomedical Engineering. 10(2), 125-177.

Lovegrove, W., Martin, F., & Slaghuis, W. (1986). A theoretical and experimental case for a visual deficit in specific reading disability. Cognitive Neuropsychology, 3(2), 255-267.

Martin, F., & Lovegrove, W. (1987). Flicker contrast sensitivity in normal and specifically disabled readers. Perception, 16, 215-221.

Martin, F., & Lovegrove, W. (1988). Uniform field flicker masking in control and specifically-disabled readers. Perception, 17, 203-214.

Thompson, P. (1983). Discrimination of moving gratings at and above detection threshold. Vision Research. 23, 1533-1538.

Watson, A.B., & Robson, J.G. (1981). Discrimination at threshold: labelled detectors in human vision. Vision Research, 21, 1115-1122.

Wetherall, G.B., & Levit, H. (1965). Sequential estimation of points on a psychometric function. British Journal of Mathematical and Statistical Psychology. 18, 1-10.

Wilson, H.R. (1980). Spatiotemporal characterization of a transient mechanism in the human visual system. Vision Research, 20, 443-452.

Human Information Processing: Measures,
Mechanisms, and Models, D. Vickers and P.L. Smith (eds.)
© *Elsevier Science Publishers B.V. (North-Holland), 1989*

THE VISUAL DETECTION OF SPATIAL BEATS

David. R. Badcock

University of Melbourne

A spatial beat pattern is produced by adding together two sinusoidal gratings with similar spatial frequencies (bar widths). The resulting pattern is a set of bars whose contrast varies across space. This contrast variation is called a spatial beat and it is interesting because it cannot be directly detected by the conventionally defined visual channels. Three experiments will be presented that examine the visual salience of beat stimuli. It will be shown that the human visual system's ability to detect spatial beats requires a change in many current conceptions of the processes involved in coding images. Our sensitivity to such patterns cannot be explained by arguing that the visual system uses the motion signals obtained from a set of spatial-frequency tuned channels. The postulation of non-linearities before the spatial frequency tuned filters does not overcome the inadequacies of the earlier models. Two interval forced-choice techniques are employed to measure the sensitivity to beat displacements; to test whether beat detection depends on the amplitude of distortion products, and whether sensitivity to beat displacements is affected by adding sinusoidal components with the same spatial periodicity as the beat to the pattern.

1. INTRODUCTION

There are many models of the human visual system but most make very similar assumptions about the nature of processing in the first few stages (Marr, 1982; Watson, 1983; Wilson, 1978; Van Santen & Sperling, 1984). Most models argue that the early stages of the visual system are composed of a collection of channels operating in parallel. These channels are thought to differ in the spatial frequency that produces the optimal response and can respond to only a limited range of spatial frequencies on either side of the optimum (Blakemore & Campbell, 1969; Tolhurst, 1973; Watson & Robson, 1981). Many of these models can be summarized as shown in Figure 1. The system outlined in this figure is composed of an initial linear transduction phase which provides signals for a set of spatial frequency tuned channels. These channels operate in parallel and carry independent messages to a decision process.

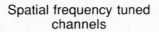

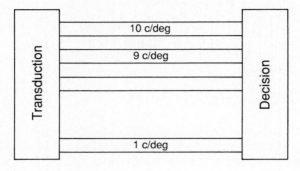

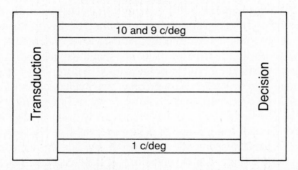

Figure 1: A rudimentary model of the visual system. An initial transduction phase converts light energy into signals appropriate for filtering by parallel channels selective for different ranges of spatial frequency. Perceptual decisions are based on the output of these channels. The upper and lower panels differ in order to show that the range of spatial frequencies processed by a given channel is unclear.

Estimates vary widely as to the range of spatial frequencies that can stimulate a particular channel, but the largest estimates are approximately two octaves (Braddick, Campbell & Atkinson, 1978; Henning, Hertz & Hinton, 1981; Watson & Robson, 1981). This selectivity for spatial frequency is an important feature of the models listed above.

In this paper a series of experiments will be presented which show

a)

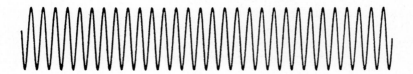

b)

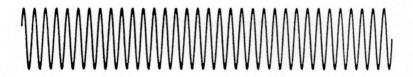

c)

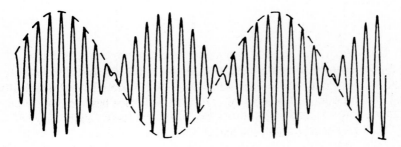

Figure 2: The upper and middle panels show the luminance profile of two sinusoids of similar spatial frequency. The lower sinusoid has the highest frequency. The bottom panel shows the luminance profile produced combining the upper two. The perceptual attributes are prominent; the high frequency variation in luminance (the carrier) and the periodic variation in the contrast of the narrow bars (the beat).

that some visual stimuli are processed in a way that is incompatible with the suggestion that the visual system can only use movement signals from channels sensitive to limited spatial frequency ranges. The stimuli employed are called spatial beats. Beats were produced by adding together two sinusoidal gratings with similar spatial frequencies.

The luminance profiles of the constituent sinusoids and the beat are depicted in Figure 2. The waveform for the combined stimulus (Fig 2; lower panel) has a periodic variation in contrast, the frequency of which is equal to the frequency difference between the two constituent components. Thus a grating composed of 30 and 32 c/deg components exhibits a beat of 2 c/deg. The important feature of the beat for the current discussion is that it is not represented by power in the Fourier domain. That is a Fourier analysis of the compound grating would reveal power centred on both the component spatial frequencies but nowhere else[1]. Thus the beat itself must be detected by making an inference based on the output of the spatial frequency tuned channels that detect the component sinusoids.

The beat pattern is described by

$$L(x) = L_m \{1 + C [\sin(2\pi f_1 x + z_1) + \sin(2\pi f_2 x + z_2)]\} \qquad (1)$$

which clearly shows the two component sinusoids. The mean luminance is specified by L_m, the spatial frequencies by f_1 and f_2 and the phases by z_1 and z_2. The contrasts of the two components were equal ($C = 0.25$) in all but one of the experiments to be reported. The important features of the beat pattern are more easily described by rewriting the equation as

$$L(x) = L_m \{1 + 2C [\cos(2\pi[f_1 - f_2]x/2 + [z_1 - z_2]/2)$$

$$\times \sin(2\pi[f_1 + f_2]x/2 + [z_1 + z_2]/2)]\} \qquad (2)$$

In this form the cosine function represents the envelope of the luminance profile and the sine function represents the narrow bars in the pattern (what we will call the carrier). The periodic variation in the contrast of the profile has a frequency equal to twice that of the envelope since both positive and negative envelope values produce contrast variations in the carrier. It is this latter periodic variation in contrast that is referred to as the beat. For convenience Eq. 2 can be rewritten in a form that is not mathematically equivalent to Eq. 1. to show the beat and the carrier by multiplying the elements of the arguments of the cosine function by 2. This gives

$$L(x) = L_m \{1 + 2C [\cos(2\pi[f_1 - f_2]x + [z_1 - z_2])$$

$$\times \sin(2\pi[f_1 + f_2]x/2 + [z_1 + z_2]/2)]\} \qquad (3)$$

It is important to remember that the beat is a variation in contrast that is periodic but has no power in the spatial frequency domain at the same spatial frequency. The channels tuned to the spatial frequency of the beat are unable to detect it. All information must come from the channels detecting the two component sinusoids.

2. EXPERIMENT 1

In the first experiment to be reported, the sensitivity of observers to beat movement was measured (Badcock & Derrington, 1985). This sensitivity was compared with the threshold for detecting the movement of the component sinusoids alone. In both cases only one component was moved. In the beat pattern, however, a second, stationary component was also present.

If the beat characteristics are detected indirectly by monitoring the channels detecting the component sinusoids then the movement signal within a channel can be expected to be constant at threshold. In fact examination of Eq. 3 shows that three possible outcomes are reasonable.

The first is that the thresholds will be identical when expressed in terms of component movement. This is the prediction just outlined and while it seems reasonable it is in fact very unlikely to be the result. The two component spatial frequencies used to form the beat pattern were either 28 and 30 c/deg or 30 and 32 c/deg. These spatial frequencies are so similar that they are likely to be processed by the same spatial frequency channel (Braddick et al., 1978; Watson & Robson, 1981; Graham, 1980).

The second possible outcome is based on the suggestion that both components are processed by the same channel. Examination of Eq. 3 (or Eq 2) shows that the carrier corresponds to the average frequency of the two components and thus indicates the signal that a channel detecting both components would receive. The phase shift of the carrier is given by $(\Delta z_1 - \Delta z_2)/2$ (where Δz indicates the change in phase of the indicated component). If only one component is moved then the phase shift of the carrier will be half that of the component movement. Therefore a channel detecting both beat components would require a component to move twice as far for the same performance level than when that component was presented alone. This outcome would be the one favoured by models in which movement detection requires the localization of zero crossings (Marr, 1982) and also by models that argue that motion signals must come from the spatial frequency tuned channels outlined in Fig. 1.

A third outcome is suggested if 'beats' can be detected directly. Eq. 3 shows that the beat moves through the same phase angle as does the moved component, but since the beat frequency is much lower than the component frequency the beat will move a much larger distance. Thus if the beat can be detected directly then the threshold component displacement should be much smaller than when the component is presented alone. It should be re-emphasized at this point that a spatial-frequency channel tuned to the beat frequency will receive no signal from a beat pattern.

The experiments were conducted using a Joyce Electronics display monitor (P4 phosphor) with a mean luminance of 160 cd/m². The screen subtended 2.3 degrees horizontally by 1.5 degrees vertically at the 7.5m viewing distance. The entire experiment, including signal generation, was controlled by an LSI 11/73 minicomputer. The vertical grating patterns were presented in a 1.6 sec Gaussian temporal envelope and the 30 c/deg component was displaced at the midpoint of the Gaussian. The observer had to press one of two buttons to indicate whether the grating had moved to the left or the right. Forty trials were conducted within a session, for each of four displacements in either direction. Two sessions were conducted for each condition. A probit analysis (Finney, 1952) was then performed to derive a threshold estimate.

2.1 RESULTS AND DISCUSSION.

The observers were very poor at detecting movement of the 30 c/deg component when it was presented alone. Observer AMD's threshold was -103.7" (± 31.1") while DRB's was 1262" (± 4574.3"). Performance was much better in the other two conditions for both of the observers. The threshold with the 30 + 28 c/deg compound grating was -18.1" (± 1.38") for AMD and -18.7" (± 1.44") for DRB. The 30 and 32 c/deg compound produced thresholds for AMD and DRB of 17.15" (± 1.28") and 26.93" (± 2.5") respectively.

In both conditions the beat frequency was 2 c/deg and the results suggest that the beat movement must have been detected directly and not via the signal from the 30 c/deg channel, since performance was substantially better with the beat patterns. The direction of beat movement also differs with the two beat patterns. Eq. 3 (and Eq.2) predicts this difference. The beat should move in the same direction as the displaced component if the spatial frequency of that component is the higher of the two; however the beat should move in the opposite direction if the displaced component's spatial frequency is lower. The difference in perceived direction obtained indicates that the movement signal is unlikely to have come from the channel centred on 30 c/deg since the direction of component movement is the same with both patterns.

These results pose serious problems for models which use as their initial processing stage a set of narrowly tuned (less than 3 octaves) spatial-frequency selective channels, since the movement signals within those channels can not support the performance obtained.

3. EXPERIMENT 2

There is, however, a relatively simple process that could allow the models mentioned to detect beat patterns directly. A quadratic non-linearity in the visual system prior to the stage at which spatial-frequency filtering occurs would give rise to a visible distortion product at the beat frequency (Burton, 1973). A distortion product could be detected by the spatial-frequency tuned channels and could produce the performance measured in the previous experiment.

Several authors have suggested that the visual system may subject the luminance distribution of an image to a logarithmic transformation prior to spatial frequency filtering (Cornsweet, 1970; Burton, 1973; Nachmias & Rogowitz, 1983). Such a transformation would produce a distortion product at the beat frequency (Derrington & Badcock,1986). The second experiment demonstrated that the presence of beat patterns is not detected by detecting distortion products at the beat frequency.

Derrington and Badcock (1986) have shown that the amplitude of a quadratic distortion product at the difference frequency (the distortion product with the highest contrast) is proportional to the product of the contrasts of the two components. Thus if beats are detected by detecting the contrast of internally generated distortion products, then the contrast required in one component will be inversely proportional to that of the other component at the beat detection threshold. This strong prediction is only likely to hold if the presence of a beat is determined by detecting a distortion product at the difference frequency.

In this experiment a two-interval forced-choice procedure was employed using the equipment described above. A 10 c/deg grating was presented in both intervals while a 9 c/deg grating was presented in only one of the intervals. When both components were present a beat could be seen, providing the components had adequate contrast. The observer's task was to indicate the interval in which the beat had been presented.

The contrast of the 9 c/deg grating required for 75% correct detection was measured for a range of contrasts of the 10 c/deg component. The assumption that non-linearities are detected leads to the prediction that the thresholds should decrease as the contrast of the 10 c/deg grating increases. The dashed lines in Figure 3 show the expected results[2].

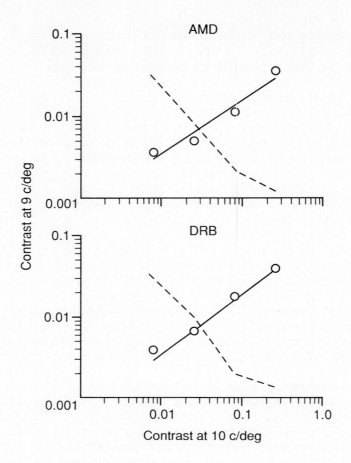

Figure 3: Data points show the contrast required, in the 9 c/deg component of a 9 + 10 c/deg compound grating, to produce a detectable beat at 1 c/deg, plotted as a function of the contrast of the 10 c/deg component. Each point is the mean of 4 estimates; average standard error was 0.05 log units. Dashed lines show performance predicted under the hypothesis that the beat is detected by detecting a distortion product at 1 c/deg. Solid lines show performance predicted under the hypothesis that the beat is detected when it produces a detectable contrast increment. (Figure from Derrington & Badcock (1986) Vision Res. 26, p. 347, and used with permission)

An alternative outcome is also quite likely. The contrast change required to detect an increment in contrast depends on the initial contrast (Legge & Kersten, 1983; Badcock, 1983). For the range of contrasts employed in the current experiment the contrast change increases as the starting contrast increases. The solid line in Figure 3 shows the expected results. This line was derived by measuring the contrast increment detection function for each observer using a 10 c/deg sinusoid as the stimulus (Derrington & Badcock, 1986).

The data for the two observers are shown in Fig. 3. The results do not fall on the line predicted by the detection of distortion products but instead fall on the contrast increment detection prediction line.

Thus the detection of the presence of beats was not mediated by the detection of distortion products. However in the first experiment, observers were required to detect beat *movements* not the *presence* of beats.

4. EXPERIMENT 3

The third experiment to be described determined whether beat displacements are detected by detecting the movement of distortion products (Badcock & Derrington, 1988).

In this final experiment the observers were required to indicate the direction of movement of a beat. The size of the displacement which produced 75% correct detection was ascertained using a staircase procedure (Findlay, 1978).

In order to nullify the signal provided by an internally generated distortion product (should one exist) a stationary sinusoid with the same spatial frequency as the beat was added to the pattern. This extra sinusoid should combine with a distortion product generated internally. The movement at the beat frequency would then be predicted by the vector sum of the two sinusoids (one internal, one external). If the external sinusoid is stationary and has a high contrast relative to the internal distortion product, then the resulting movement will be very small, thus producing poorer performance.

The results are plotted in Figure 4. It can be seen that adding a sinusoid at the beat frequency had very little effect on performance. However it did cause some deterioration. It was therefore important to determine how much deterioration should have been expected. To do this it was necessary to first assume that a distortion product existed and then to determine the contrast of the internally generated component. The spatial frequency of this component would be 1 c/deg and the performance it produced is indicated in Fig 4 by the performance obtained

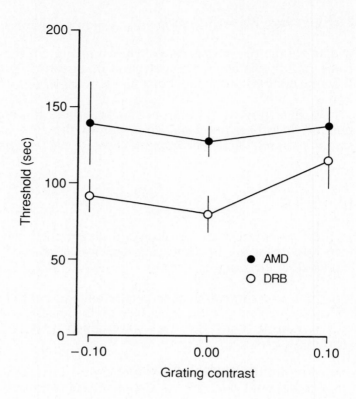

Figure 4: Effect of adding a static grating on thresholds for discriminating the direction of motion of a beat pattern. Threshold displacement is plotted as a function of the added contrast of the static pattern. The grating was added in cosine phase with respect to the beat. Error bars are ± 2 s.e.m.. (Figure from Badcock & Derrington (1988) and used with permission)

when the third component was absent (i.e. had a contrast of zero). By determining the contrast of a 1 c/deg grating required to produce the same performance level, an indirect estimate of the contrast of the internal component would be obtained.

These contrast estimates were then used to calculate the vector sum of the internal component and the added sinusoid of 10% contrast. The change in performance expected by adding a stationary sinusoid was calculated and is shown in Figure 5. Separate predictions were generated for the on- and off-centre cell pathways as these could each generate distortion products (Derrington, 1987). Performance was much better than predicted for three of the four conditions, indicating that distortion products generated by quadratic non-linearity cannot explain the data.

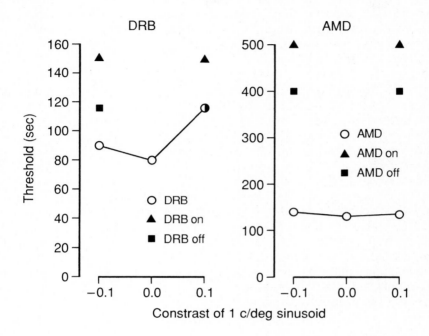

Figure 5: The lines indicate data replotted from Fig. 4. Also included are the predictions of the level of performance expected on the basis of distortion products in either the on- or off-centre pathways. Performance is much better than predicted in all but one case.

5. GENERAL DISCUSSION

The set of experiments presented suggests that a revision of the notion of the role of spatial frequency selective channels, is required. The first experiment demonstrated that the ability of observers to detect beat movements is too good to be based on movement signals from the spatial frequency tuned channels that detect the two component sinusoids. The two subsequent experiments show that early non-linearities also fail to explain the detection. Thus the channels tuned to the beat frequency cannot detect the beat movement.

Our more recent work has been aimed at generating a model to explain beat detection (Badcock & Derrington, 1988). The simplest way to explain the data is to argue that the spatial-frequency tuned channels do not provide the movement signals used in detecting beat displacements.

The receptive field profiles of these detectors at the retinal, lateral geniculate nucleus and striate cortex levels are restricted in space (Shapley & Lennie, 1985) and the spatial frequency tuning is a by-product of the relative sizes of their centres and surrounds. Those units that are selective for the carrier frequency in beat patterns, will vary in their response magnitude depending on whether they are centred on a high or low contrast part of the pattern.

When beats are displaced the bars of the pattern change in contrast. Thus the *location* of the highest contrast bars will alter (although the bars themselves need not move). A system that monitored the location of the most active channels could detect beat movements. Such a system would not be limited by the motion sensitivity of the high spatial frequency channels but it would be limited by their contrast sensitivity and also the precision with which activity peaks could be localized. The variation in activity in high spatial-frequency tuned channels would be relatively independent of the presence of low spatial frequency sinusoids, since these alter the local contrast but have less effect on the location of local activity peaks. The location of the contrast peaks is largely determined by the position of the beat. Thus the lack of interaction between beat patterns and low frequency sinusoids in the current experiments can easily be explained by a system that codes the location of maxima in local-contrast estimates.

Another consequence of this model is that experiments that depend on the contrast threshold rather than the location of contrast maxima could and do show interactions between low spatial frequency sinusoids and beat patterns (Henning, Hertz & Broadbent, 1975; Nachmias & Rogowitz, 1983).

In summary it may be more useful to think of the spatial frequency tuned channels as local contrast detectors and to argue that our visual system monitors the contrast at particular locations than to think of these channels as mechanisms designed to extract amplitude and phase. Such a reinterpretation is helpful in explaining the current experiments and also those which examine the coding of spatial phase (Badcock, 1984a; 1984b; 1988).

FOOTNOTES

1. Our patterns are limited in spatial extent and therefore some spectral spread is present. The spectral spread can be described by a sine function $([sin(x)]/x)$ with a central lobe of 0.87 c/deg in the first two experiments and 0.57 c/deg in the third and fourth.

2. Since the amplitude of the distortion product is proportional to the product of component contrasts one would expect a slope of -1 for the prediction line in Fig. 3. The line deviates from this slope because we have corrected the predictions to allow for the masking effect of a 10 c/deg sinusoid on a 1 c/deg sinusoid. The amount of this masking was determined for each observer in a control experiment (Derrington & Badcock, 1986).

CORRESPONDENCE

Correspondence concerning this paper should be addressed to David. R. Badcock, Department of Psychology, University of Melbourne, Parkville, Victoria, Australia 3052

REFERENCES

Badcock, D. R. (1983) Some aspects of 'spatial phase' coding in man. D. Phil. Oxford University.

Badcock, D. R. (1984). Spatial phase or luminance profile discrimination? Vision Research, 24, 613-623.

Badcock, D. R. (1984). How do we discriminate relative spatial phase? Vision Research, 24, 1847-1857.

Badcock, D. R. (1988). Discrimination of spatial phase changes: contrast and position codes. Spatial Vision, in press.

Badcock, D. R., & Derrington, A. M. (1985). Detecting the displacement of periodic patterns. Vision Research, 25, 1253-1258.

Badcock, D. R., & Derrington, A. M. (1988). Detecting the displacements of spatial beats: no role for distortion products. Vision Research, in press.

Blakemore, C., & Campbell, F. W. (1969). On the existence of neurones in the human visual system selectively sensitive to the orientation and size of retinal images. Journal of Physiology. London., 203, 237-260.

Braddick, O. J., Campbell, F. W., & Atkinson, J. (1978). Channels in vision: basic aspects. In R. Held, H. W. Leibowitz, & H. L. Teuber (Eds.), Handbook of Sensory Physiology. (pp. 3-38). New York: Springer.

Burton, G. J. (1973). Evidence for non-linear response processes in the visual system from measurements on the thresholds of spatial beat frequencies. Vision Research, 13, 1211-1225.

Cornsweet, T. N. (1970). Visual Perception. New York: Academic Press.

Derrington, A. M. (1987). Distortion products in geniculate x-cells: a physiological basis for masking by spatially modulated gratings? Vision Research, 27, 1377-1386.

Derrington, A. M., & Badcock, D. R. (1985). Separate detectors for simple and complex grating patterns. Vision Research, 25, 1869-1878.

Derrington, A. R., & Badcock, D. R. (1986). Detection of spatial beats: non-linearity or contrast increment detection? Vision Research, 26, 343- 348.

Findlay, J. M. (1978). Estimates on probability function: a more virulent PEST. Perception and Psychophysics, 23, 181-185.

Finney, D. J. (1952). Probit analysis. London: Cambridge University Press.

Graham, N. (1980). Spatial-frequency channels in human vision: detecting edges without edge detectors. In C. S. Harris (Ed.), Visual Coding and Adaptability. (pp. 215-262). Hillsdale: Erlbaum.

Henning, G. B., Hertz, B. G., & Broadbent, D. E. (1975). Some experiments bearing on the hypothesis that the visual system analyzes patterns in independent bands of spatial frequency. Vision Research, 15, 887-899.

Henning, G. B., Hertz, B. G., & Hinton, J. L. (1981). Effects of different hypothetical detection mechanisms on the shape of spatial-frequency filters inferred from masking experiments: I. Noise masks. Journal of the optical Society of America, 71, 574-581.

Legge, G. E., & Kersten, D. (1983). Light and dark bars: contrast discrimination. Vision Research, 23, 475-484.

Marr, D. (1982). Vision. San Fransisco: Freeman.

Nachmias, J., & Rogowitz, B. E. (1983). Masking by spatially modulated gratings. Vision Research, 23, 1621-1629.

Shapley, R., & Lennie, P. (1985). Spatial frequency analysis in the visual system. Annual Review of Neurosciences, 8, 547-583.

Tolhurst, D. J. (1973). Separate channels for the analysis of the shape and movement of a moving visual stimulus. Journal of Physiology. London., 231, 385-402.

Van Santen, J. P. H., & Sperling, G. (1984). Temporal covariance model of human motion perception. Journal of the optical Society of America, A1, 451-473.

Watson, A. B. (1983). Detection and recognition of simple forms. In O. J. Braddick, & A. C. Sleigh (Eds.), Physiological and biological processing of images. New York: Springer.

Watson, A. B., & Robson, J. G. (1981). Discrimination at threshold: labelled detectors in human vision. Vision Research, 21, 1115-1122.

Wilson, H. R. (1978). Quantitative characterization of two types of line- spread function near the fovea. Vision Research, 18, 971-981.

Human Information Processing: Measures,
Mechanisms, and Models. D. Vickers and P.L. Smith (eds.)
© Elsevier Science Publishers B.V. (North-Holland), 1989

BINOCULAR INTERACTIONS AS A FUNCTION OF RETINAL DISPARITY

Hideko Fukuda

Kobe Women's University

Kazutaka Kani

Shiga University of Medical Science

Yuji Okamoto

Hyogo College of Medicine

Three experiments were conducted to investigate the effect of varying degrees of disparity on binocular summation and binocular inhibition. In Experiment 1, very small flashes were used to assess detection performance over a range of disparity levels from $0'$ to $42'$ horizontally.   Binocular summation was found at $0'$ and $6'$.   In addition, binocular inhibition was indicated at $30'$ and/or over. This inhibitory effect was further studied: using as inhibitory stimuli a continuous spot in Experiment 2 and a pair of long-lasting slits in Experiment 3, increment detection was measured in relation to the disparity between a target flash and the inhibitory stimuli when viewed dichoptically. Two types of binocular inhibition were suggested: one type which is found in a broad area ($30'$ or more), and is activated by even weak stimuli, and another type which works at very small levels of binocular separation, and is activated by strong stimuli.

1. INTRODUCTION

The two eyes have been found to interact cooperatively when the respective stimuli are identical or highly similar spatially and temporally, and to interact competitively when the stimuli display dissimilarities exceeding certain bounds.   Binocular summation is a typical manifestation of the former phenomenon.   Thorn and Boynton (1974) showed that binocular summation does not occur when the stimuli to the respective eyes are separated by more than 100 msec or are delivered to noncorresponding retinal areas (4 degrees disparate). Westendorf and Fox (1977) studying binocular detection at three different degrees of disparity (the retinal corresponding point (0′), within the fusional range (6′), and outside of the fusional range (20′ - 25′)), showed that binocular summation occurs at disparity levels of 0′ and 6′.

In this study we investigated binocular performance over a wide range of disparity, in order to provide additional basic data on binocular interaction. Experiment 1 examined the effect upon binocular summation of successive 6′ increments in disparity up to 42′. Experiments 2 and 3 were further investigations of binocular inhibitory effects observed during the course of Experiment 1.

As target stimuli we selected very small spots whose diameters were smaller than the excitatory diameter of the human monocular receptive field. The size of excitatory diameters suggested by human spatial summation experiments is 5′ or 6′ at the retinal eccentricity of 2 degrees (Inui, Mimura and Kani, 1981).

2. EXPERIMENT 1

2.1 Method

2.1.1 Apparatus and stimuli.

The experiment was conducted with a fundus haploscope, composed of two infrared television fundus cameras and two perimeters, one for each eye. The fundus images and the stimuli were positioned conjugate to each other, appearing as overlapped images on the television monitors. This equipment enabled us to check the retinal position of the stimuli presented, and to discard those trials in which fixation was not maintained. Each background, target, and fusion stimulus was presented in Maxwellian view through a 1.5mm-diameter artificial pupil. The subject's head was fixed with a chin and forehead rest. A block diagram of the apparatus is shown in Figure 1; further details are contained in the report on the fundus haploscope by Inatomi, Kani, and Abe (1983).

The displays consisted of high contrast photographic transparencies. Identical 30 degrees white backgrounds with a retinal illuminance of 5.6 trolands (3.2 cd/m2) were presented to both eyes continuously. Black fusion stimuli subtending 10 degrees visual angle provided a binocular fixation cross and monocular nonius markers to facilitate accurate eye alignment (see Figure 2). The targets were 2.7′ diameter light flashes of 100 msec duration. The standard position of the flashes was set at a point 2 degrees from the fovea on the 135 degrees meridian. From this point, the position of left eye flash was shifted rightward by means of micromanipulators to produce binocular disparities. Disparities used in this experiment ranged from 0′ to 42′ in increments of 6′. The target intensity could be altered using two types of neutral density filter sets. One was a Kodak Wratten No.96, comprising a set of discrete filters adjustable in steps of 0.1 log units; the other was a circular wedge filter mounted on a stepping motor (0.72 degrees step), by which luminance could be controlled over a 2 log unit range in steps of 0.02 log units.

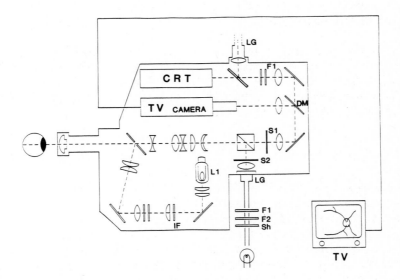

Figure 1. Schematic diagram of fundus haploscope (optical pathway for one eye). L1: light source for observation of the fundus, IF: infrared filter, F1: a set of Kodak Wratten No.96, F2: circular wedge filter, Sh: shutter, DM: dichroic mirror (only infrared rays can be reflected), LG: light guide, S1: fusion stimulus, S2: spot or slits.

2.1.2 Procedure.

Prior to each experimental session the subjects were dark-adapted for 10 min, then adapted for a few minutes to the background luminance. During this time fusional adjustments were made. The intensity of the stimulus presentation was set at the test flash luminance which yielded approximately 40% detection levels for each eye. Binocular detection performance was measured in conditions of horizontal retinal disparity. Detection performance in every condition tested was measured with a temporal four-alternative forced choice procedure. The subjects initiated

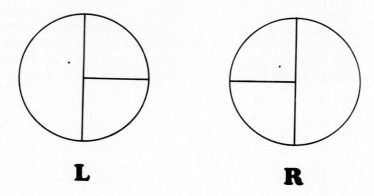

Figure 2. Fusion stimuli for the left (L) and right (R) eye. Binocular fusion cross served as fixation point. Small spots denote the target flash.

the individual trials by pressing a switch when they were able to see a complete fixation cross in the binocular fusion ring. Following a 500 msec delay, a series of four 1 sec tone bursts separated by 500 msec were presented to the subject. Feedback was provided following each trial. Each session contained 50 or 25 trials for each level of disparity, and four or more sessions were conducted for each subject.

2.1.3. Subjects.

One male (KK) and two females (AI, MT) served as subjects. KK was one of the authors and a highly trained subject. Visual acuity in all subjects was 20/20, or was corrected to that level or better in each eye by rotating the focusing knob of the fundus haploscope. All had good stereopsis as assessed by the ability to see large-disparity random-dot sterograms.

2.2 Results and Discussion

Figure 3 shows the binocular and monocular increment detection performance for subject KK. The two lines in Figure 3 represent the two probability summation estimates used to judge detection performance under conditions of binocular stimulation. The lower line is the probability estimate obtained by the measurement of monocular performance at the point of retinal correspondence (R0 & L0 in Figure 3). The upper line is the estimate obtained by integrating the right eye detection rate with that of the left eye at a disparity level of 30′ (R0 & L30; hereafter called Estimate R0-L30). These probability summation estimates were derived from the integration model of signal detection theory (Green & Swets, 1966).

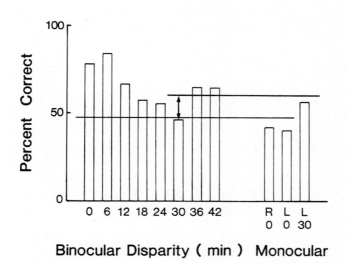

Figure 3. Percentage of correct monocular and binocular detections as a function of binocular disparity for subject KK. Lower line indicates probability summation prediction based on each monocular performance at the retinal corresponding points (R0 and L0). Upper line is the prediction based on R0 and L30.

The results indicate that binocular summation occurs when binocular disparity is small. Detection performance at 0′ and 6′ disparity levels was significantly greater than would be expected from a probability summation model (0′: χ^2 (1, N=50)=16.8; 6′: χ^2 (1, N=50) = 24.5, both p <.01). These results were confirmed in the two other subjects.

The striking feature of Figure 3 is the reduced binocular performance at the disparity level of 30′. The detection performance at this level was significantly lower than the prediction in Estimate R0-L30 (χ^2(1, N=50) = 5.4, p <.05). This result strongly suggests the action of binocular inhibition.

Experiment 1 revealed a clear summation effect at the retinal corresponding point and at a horizontal disparity level of 6′. These findings are consistent with those obtained by Westendorf & Fox (1977). This experiment also indicated the presence of binocular inhibition at large levels of disparity. The data for subject KK recorded in Figure 3 show apparent inhibition occurring at a disparity of about 30′. This finding, however, was far from uniform; in some sessions, inhibitory effects appeared only at the higher disparities of 36′ or 42′. (The results of individual sessions were not pooled in order to avoid obscuring effects.) The variety of results concerning the onset of inhibition (or suppression) suggested the need for further investigation of this phenomenon. This was done in Experiments 2 and 3.

3. EXPERIMENT 2

The situation in Experiment 1, where an identical small flash was presented simultaneously to each eye, is suited to the study of cooperative or excitatory interactions, but is less appropriate for the examination of inhibitory interactions at small degrees of disparity. Fiorentini (1972) suggested that inhibitory mechanisms may take a longer time to build up to full activity than excitatory mechanisms. In Experiments 2 and 3, therefore, inhibitory stimuli of longer duration were used.

The purpose of Experiment 2 was to determine detection performance when a small dot was shown in the presence of a steady spot at various levels of binocular disparity.

3.1 Method

The steady spot which served as an inhibitory stimulus was presented continuously to the right eye, while the target spot for the left eye was shown for 100 msec. The intensity of the inhibitory spot was 0.5 log units above the threshold. The target luminance yielding about 50% detection for the left-eye monocular viewing condition was selected as the flash intensity. Subjects were KK and MT.

3.2 Results and Discussion

Figure 4 shows the results for subject MT. The graph shows two inhibitory troughs. One trough occurs at the disparity levels of 0′ and 6′, the same levels which displayed distinct binocular summation in Experiment 1. Another decline in performance took place at about 30′ of disparity, in the same manner as in Experiment 1. The results obtained in this experiment showed some variation from session to session, but this variation itself might reflect the property of binocular inhibition.

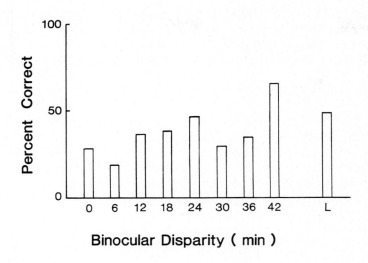

Figure 4. Percentage of correct flash detections in the presence of a contralateral steady spot as a function of binocular disparity for subject MT.

4. EXPERIMENT 3

Ikeda (1975) suggested that a spot might not be able to fully inhibit another spot. In order to exclude the possibility of such a spot-to-spot effect, Experiment 3 was conducted with a pair of slits as the inhibitory stimulus. The increment threshold for a spot flash in the presence of a pair of long-lasting inhibitory slits was measured as the distance between the spot and slits increased.

4.1 Method

The inhibitory stimuli presented to the right eye were a pair of rectangular slits measuring 16.2′ in height x 2.2′ in width; their distances apart were 7.5′, 12.0′, 15.0′, 32.0′, 44.0′, 52.0′, and 62.0′. The slits were set at three intensity levels: threshold, 0.5 log units above threshold, and 1.0 log unit above threshold for each subject. In this paper these three levels are called threshold-slits, 0.5-log-slits, and 1.0-log-slits, respectively. Increment thresholds were determined by the PEST procedure (Parameter Estimation by Sequential Testing), of Taylor & Creelman (1967). The target spot was positioned to appear at the center of the two slits when viewed binocularly. The retinal locus of the spot was set at the 'standard position' used in Experiment 1.

Following a 790 msec delay from the onset of the inhibitory stimuli, the target spot was presented for 200 msec; 10 msec after cessation of the target stimuli, the inhibitory slits were turned off. Hence the total duration of the slits was 1 sec. Subjects were KK and AI.

4.2   Results and Discussion

Figure 5 shows the binocular inhibitory effect at the increment threshold for subject KK. The ordinate denotes the sensitivity to targets in the presence of threshold-slits, 0.5-log-slits, and 1.0-log-slits. The retinal illuminance of a target spot presented in the absence of slits was 25.7 trolands; the degree of sensitivity under this condition was defined as 0 dB. The abscissa indicates the distance between the center of the spot and the inner side of either slit. Open squares, filled circles, and open circles represent sensitivity measured in the presence of threshold-slits, 0.5-log-slits, and 1.0-log-slits, respectively. The curves obtained with 0.5-log-slits and threshold-slits are similar to each other. That is, at a separation of 3.75′ the sensitivity values obtained with threshold-slits and 0.5-log-slits were equal to or insignificantly lower than the value obtained without slits. Sensitivity then decreased up to 7.5′ separation, following which it remained steady to at least 31′ of separation. Although both curves showed similar patterns, as mentioned above, the inhibition effect with 0.5-log-slits was greater than that with threshold-slits: the former reached the significance level at 6′ of separation ($t = 9.37$, df = 24, p <.01), while the latter did so at 7.5′ of separation ($t = 1.71$, df = 41, p <.05). Unlike these two curves, the one obtained with 1.0 - log - slits showed a great sensitivity reduction of 3.6 dB at the separation of 3.75′, although the following flat section was similar in configuration to the other two.

The results obtained in Experiment 3 indicate that there exists a large binocular inhibition area. A pair of slits was selected as the inhibitory stimuli since this allowed the comparison of the dichoptic data obtained in this study with the monoptic data assembled in an earlier study by one of our authors (Kani, Inui, Haruta, and Mimura, 1983). This earlier study showed that the field size of lateral inhibition is about 16′ at an eccentricity of 2 degrees, using the same slits and spot size as in the present experiment. Walker (1978) showed that lateral inhibition between orientation-sensitive channels is primarily confined to those monocularly driven detectors that derive their sensory input from the same eye. These results suggest that binocular inhibition is distinctly different from lateral inhibition.

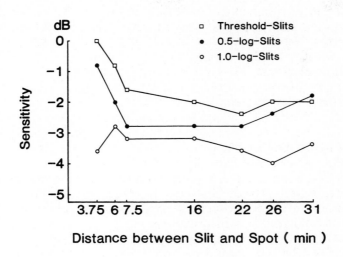

Figure 5. Increment sensitivity for a spot flash in the presence of contralateral inhibitory slits for subject KK. The parameter is slit intensity.

Figure 5 suggested another important possibility, that is, two kinds of binocular inhibition might exist: one type which is found in a broad region, and is activated by even a weak inhibitory stimulus (e.g., threshold-slits), and another type which works at very small levels of binocular separation, and is activated by strong stimuli like 1.0 - log - slits. The latter type might be related to a spread of suppression by binocular rivalry (Hochberg, 1964; Kaufman, 1963). This possibility is indirectly supported by the subjects' statements: they reported that spots presented at very small separations were sometimes detected very clearly, as if rivalry alternations were taking place, while those presented at wider separations were usually quite faint.

Our finding of a large binocular inhibitory area brought to mind certain results obtained in neurophysiological experiments. In their study of the cat striate cortex, Bishop and his colleagues demonstrated that the receptive field of a simple striate neuron is roughly circular, with a centrally located long narrow excitatory region and much larger inhibitory sidebands (about 2 degrees across) to either side of the central region (Bishop, Coombs, and Henry, 1973; Joshua and Bishop, 1970). Similar inhibitory sidebands were demonstrated by tuned excitatory neurons in the study of monkey striate cortex (Poggio and Fischer, 1977; Poggio and

Talbot, 1981). Neurophysiological data has, to date, been obtained from cats and monkeys by means of rather large stimuli (e.g., 4 degrees x 0.14 degrees moving slit), while the psychophysical data in the present study were obtained from human subjects with a very small spot (2.7′). Therefore direct comparisons of our results with those of the neurophysiological studies is not entirely appropriate, although the latter provide interesting suggestions regarding the physiological mechanisms for human binocular interactions.

ACKNOWLEDGEMENTS

The work reported here was supported in part by Grant-in Aid for Scientific Research (No.63304049) to KK and by Grant-in-Aid for Encouragement of Young Scientist (No.61710094, No.62710092) to HF, both from Japan Ministry of Education.

Correspondence should be sent to Hideko Fukuda, Department of Psychology, Kobe Women's University, Higashisuma, Kobe 654, Japan.

REFERENCES

Bishop, P. O., Coombs, J. S., & Henry, G. H. (1973). Receptive fields of simple cells in the cat striate cortex. Journal of Physiology, 231, 31-60.

Fiorentini, A. (1972). Mach band phenomena. In D. Jameson, & L. M. Hurvich (Eds.), Handbook of Sensory Physiology. VII/4. Visual Psychophysics. New York: Springer, 188-201.

Green, D. M., & Swets, J. A. (1966). Signal detection theory and psychophysics. New York: Wiley.

Hochberg, J. E. (1964). Contralateral suppressive fields of binocular combination. Psychonomic Science, 1, 157-158.

Ikeda, M. (1975). Visual Psychophysics. Tokyo: Morikita (in Japanese).

Inatomi, A., Kani, K., & Abe, K. (1983). Fundus haploscope. In P. Henkind (Ed.), Acta: XXIV International Congress of Ophthalmology, Philadelphia: Lippincott, 920-923.

Inui, T., Mimura, O., & Kani, K. (1981). Retinal sensitivity and spatial summation in the foveal and parafoveal regions. Journal of Optical Society of America, 71, 151-154.

Joshua, D. E., & Bishop, P. O. (1970). Binocular single vision and depth discrimination. Receptive field disparities for central and peripheral vision and binocular interaction on peripheral single units. Experimental Brain Research, 10, 389-416.

Kani, K., Inui, T., & Haruta, R., & Mimura, O. (1983). Lateral inhibition in the fovea and parafoveal regions. Documenta Ophthalmologica Proceedings Series, 35, 391-396.

Kaufman, L. (1963). On the spread of suppression and binocular rivalry. Vision Research, 3, 401-415.

Poggio, G. F., & Fischer, B. (1977). Binocular interaction and depth sensitivity in striate and prestriate cortex of behaving rhesus monkey. Journal of Neurophysiology, 40, 1392-1405.

Poggio, G. F., & Talbot, W. H. (1981). Mechanisms of static and dynamic stereopsis in foveal cortex of the rhesus monkey. Journal of Physiology, 315, 469-492.

Taylor, M. M., & Creelman, C. D. (1967). PEST: Efficient estimates on probability functions. Journal of Acoustical Society of America, 41, 782-787.

Thorn, F. & Boynton, R. M. (1974). Human binocular summation at absolute threshold. Vision Research, 14, 445-455.

Walker, P. (1978). Orientation-selective inhibition and binocular rivalry. Perception, 7, 207-214.

Westendorf, D. H., & Fox, R. (1977). Binocular detection of disparate light flashes. Vision Research, 17, 697-702.

Human Information Processing: Measures,
Mechanisms, and Models. D. Vickers and P. L. Smith (eds.)
© Elsevier Science Publishers B. V. (North-Holland), 1989

VISUAL-KINAESTHETIC INTERMODAL RELATIONS

Victor J. Manyam and Judith I. Laszlo

University of Western Australia

Processes mediating the establishment of intermodal relations and, of intersensory integration are examined. Sixty adults were required to explore a standard, two-dimensional, heptagon under one of three presentation conditions: vision, kinaesthesis, or vision plus kinaesthesis, with twenty subjects per condition. Subjects were required to recognize the standard from amongst transforms under intra- and cross-modal conditions in a within subjects design. Results indicate that the availability of congruent, bisensory information during perception of a complex shape does not allow for more accurate recognition of that shape, over unimodal perception, when recognition is based on either of the input modalities. Instead, the data, indicate that the recognition performance of the bimodal groups was visually based. Vision was the dominant modality; intermodal communication between vision and kinaesthesis was shown to be accompanied by symmetrical and significant loss of information. No support was found for the establishment of an integrated, amodal representation of shape parameters. Rather, the results suggest that sensory information is encoded and retained in a modality specific form.

1. INTRODUCTION

There is a substantial body of literature devoted to the issue of intersensory integration (for reviews see Freides, 1974; Walk and Pick, 1981; von Wright, 1970). The literature is not clear, however, as to precisely what is meant by the term integration. The term has not been operationally defined. The use of cross-modal matching and cross-modal transfer studies implies that what is being investigated is intersensory equivalence. In such studies, a subject is typically required to explore a standard stimulus object with information from one sense modality and subsequently recognize or form a match for that object on the basis of information from a different modality. Implicit in the use of such a paradigm is one of two assumptions. Either the way in which information is encoded in each sensory system is different and the task for the subject is to translate information from the code of one modality into that of another, or else sensory information is coded in the same way irrespective of modality and sensory systems are equivalent and interchangeable. Whatever the case, the results of cross-modal matching and transfer studies have been equivocal with respect to the question of intermodal equivalence and have not demonstrated an isomorphism or any consistent relationship between sensory systems (see Walk and Pick, 1981).

If integration is to be considered as a process mediating multimodal perception, then, taking the term literally, integration would involve the convergence of information from different sense modalities to form a single system or unit, i.e. an amodal or supramodal store. Such a process should result in the synthesis of a more comprehensive or representative percept than would be available from unimodal input. Furthermore, such an integrative process could occur only if each sense modality provided qualitatively different information, perhaps by sampling different parameters of the same stimulus object (Goodnow, 1969, 1971; Pick and Pick, 1966). If sensory systems differed only in quantitative terms, then integration would be irrelevant.

If integration, as defined, does occur then at least equivalent performance with each modality would be expected, since perceptual subsystems would have access to the same integrated store of sensory information.

Studies of cross-modal performance, which generally include intra-modal conditions, have shown intra-modal comparisons to be superior to cross-modal conditions. Transfer or translation of information is sometimes shown to be symmetric (e.g. Diewert and Stelmach, 1977; Marteniuk and Rodney, 1979; Newell, Shapiro and Carlton, 1979), and in other studies (e.g. Connolly and Jones, 1970; Freides, 1975; Jones and Connolly, 1970; Millar, 1972) asymmetric, with the direction of asymmetry not always being consistent.

If translation is the process that mediates cross-modal functions, then the translation of sensory information from the code of one modality into that of another must depend on specifying the relationships or correspondences between the two modalities, a process analogous to the establishment of a bilingual dictionary. The nature of the relationships between modalities must be established before translation can occur, and correspondences between modalities, specific to a task, can be established only if the two sources of information are simultaneously available and congruent during the performance of that task.

The present study was designed to investigate the formation of intermodal relations between vision (V) and kinaesthesis (K). In addition to the usual intra- (V-V, K-K) and cross-modal (V-K, K-V) groups a condition was included which allowed for an examination of the effects of congruent bimodal (VK) sensory input during exploration of a standard stimulus shape on subsequent recognition of that shape, where recognition is based on unimodal (VK-V, VK-K) sensory information, in a within subjects design.

If bimodal presentation allows for an integration of bisensory information, then subsequent unimodal recognition should be superior to corresponding performance in intramodal conditions (i.e. VK-V>V-V; VK-K>K-K). If, however, bimodal presentation allows for a more accurate specification of intermodal relations, then unimodal recognition, following bisensory presentation, should be no worse than corresponding intramodal recognition performance.

2. METHOD

2.1 Subjects

Sixty undergraduate students from The University of Western Australia participated in the study. They ranged in age from 18 to 43 years with a mean age of 22.3 years. No attempt was made to equate subject numbers on the basis of sex or handedness as these factors were not found to be significant variables in previous studies with a similar task (Laszlo and Bairstow, 1980). Twenty subjects were randomly assigned to each of the three experimental groups.

2.2 Apparatus

The stimuli used were seven-sided, linear, nonsense shapes generated according to Method One of Attneave and Arnoult (1956). Five standard shapes were constructed and two transforms of each standard were produced, thus giving a total of 15 stimulus shapes. Transforms were achieved by moving each of the vertices of each standard shape a fixed distance in a randomly determined north-south, east-west direction (see Fig. 1). Each shape was drawn on 6mm square graph paper, then traced onto a 55cm x 63 cm masonite board.

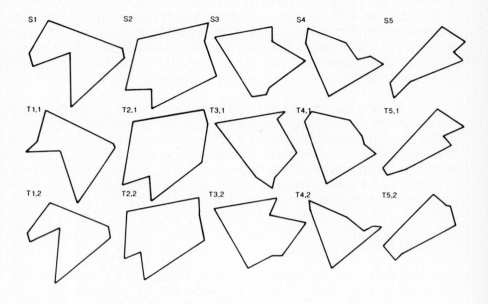

Figure 1: Stimulus forms, orientated for presentation. Sn refers to standard shapes, Tn,n refers to transforms.

A stencil of each shape was constructed with a 1 cm gap separating the inner and outer sections of the shape.

The apparatus on which the shapes were presented consisted of a platform on which the inner and outer sections of each shape could be mounted such that a moveable stylus could fit within the gap between the inner and outer sections. The stylus assembly was constructed in such a way that the stylus could be moved freely within, and be guided by, the 1 cm slot outlining the shape. On the subject's side of the platform was a pair of doors which could be closed to prevent the subject from observing the experimenter changing shapes between trials. A pair of goggles with opaque lenses was used to obscure vision during kinaesthetic conditions.

2.3 Procedure

The task for the three experimental conditions involved the presentation of a standard shape followed by the standard itself or by one of the two transforms of the standard. On each trial a subject was required to judge whether the two consecutive shapes were the same or different from each other. Each of the five standards was presented four times to each subject. The standard was paired with itself on two trials and once with each of its transforms, thus giving a total of 20 trials per subject, with a maximum of 10 "same" and 10 "different" correct responses. The order of presentation of the stimulus pairs was randomised for each block of 20 trials such that each of the 20 subjects within any condition received a different random order of stimulus pairs.

In the first condition (VK) subjects received both visual and kinaesthetic information during exploration of the standard shape. The comparison judgement was based on either visual or kinaesthetic information i.e. ten comparisons for each subject were based on visual information and ten were based on kinaesthesis. In the second condition (V), standard exploration was based on vision while comparisons were based on either vision or kinaesthesis i.e. a within subjects intra- and inter-modal design. The third condition (K) was essentially identical to the second, except that standard exploration was based on kinaesthetic information.

Instructions to subjects in the first condition were as follows: "I am going to close these doors then place a shape on this platform. The shape is defined by a slot and this stylus fits within the slot. When I open the doors I want you to hold this stylus in your preferred hand and move it around the shape twice. While doing that I want you to watch your hand as you move it around the shape and also pay attention to what the shape feels like and what it looks like. When you've done that I am going to close these doors, take the first shape off the platform and put a second shape on. On some trials I will ask you to pull the goggles over your eyes, I will then open the doors, ask you to hold the stylus and move it around the shape twice. On other trials I will ask you to just look at the second shape after I open the doors. In either case, I want you to tell me whether the second shape is the same as or different from the first. There will be a total of 20 comparisons to be made. Do you have any questions?

All the shapes I will present are seven-sided, closed, linear figures. They are all the same relative size, so don't rely on size as a criterion for sameness or difference. All the shapes will be presented in the same orientation i.e. I won't present you with a first shape in one orientation then represent it as a second shape turned upside down or side-on etc".

The instructions to subjects in the second and third conditions were, for the most part, identical to those for the first condition, with the following exceptions. In the second condition (V), subjects were asked to watch the experimenter's hand as he held the stylus and moved it around the standard shape twice. Subjects were told that they should have a good idea of what the shape looked like after the completion of two circuits. In the third condition (K), subjects were asked to wear the goggles and when the doors were opened they were to hold the stylus and move it around the shape twice. They were then told that at the completion of two circuits they should have a good idea of what the shape felt like. The rest of the instructions for the second and third conditions were identical to those for the first.

The procedure described in the instructions was carried out for each of the 20 comparison pairs for each subject. The subject's response was recorded after each trial on a scoring sheet on which the random order of presentation of comparison pairs for each subject was listed.

3. RESULTS

Performance scores for recognition in terms of number correct, were averaged for each of the ten visual and ten kinaesthetic trials over the twenty subjects in each condition and are presented graphically in Fig. 2.

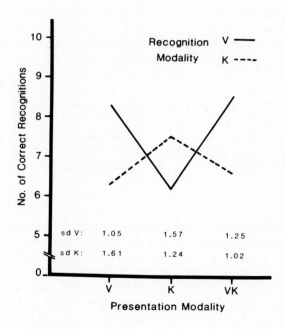

Figure 2: Graphic representation of correct visual and kinaesthetic recognition scores for the three experimental conditions including standard deviations for each condition.

The averaged data was then subjected to a 3 (presentation conditions) by 2 (recognition conditions) analysis of variance (ANOVA) with repeated measures on the recognition factor.

Results of the analysis gave a significant main effect for presentation conditions ($F(2,57)=6.35$ $p<.01$), indicating that recognition performance, irrespective of the modality on which it is based, is dependent on modality of presentation. The main effect for recognition conditions was also significant ($F(1,57)=28.3$ $p<.05$) suggesting that accuracy of recognition is dependent on the modality on which recognition is based. A significant presentation by recognition conditions interaction ($F=(2,57)=26.95$ $p<.01$) suggested that accuracy of visual and kinaesthetic recognition performance within any condition depends on modality of presentation.

In order to determine the relative ordering of group responses, the means of the scores of the six recognition groups were subjected to a Newman-Keuls, multiple comparison test (Ferguson, 1981). Results of the analysis are presented in Table 1.

Table 1

Results of Newman-Keuls MULTIPLE COMPARISON TEST

	Vk	Kv	Kvk	Kk	Vv	Vvk
Vk		N.S.	N.S.	0.01	0.01	0.01
Kv			N.S.	0.01	0.01	0.01
Kvk				0.05	0.01	0.01
Kk					0.05	0.05
Vv						N.S.

Upper case letters refer to recognition modality. N.S. refers to nonsignificant comparisons. Cells with 0.01 and 0.05 refer to significant differences with $p<0.01$ and $p<0.05$ respectively.

4. DISCUSSION

Analysis of cross-modal recognition performance did not reveal any significant cross-modal asymmetry.   Unimodal kinaesthetic recognition following visual exploration was not significantly different from visual recognition following kinaesthetic input. The recognition performance of each of these groups was, however, significantly worse than the performance of the intramodal kinaesthetic group, which in turn, was significantly worse than the performance of the intramodal visual group. These findings support the assertion (Freides, 1974; 1975; Pick, 1970) that vision is more proficient at processing the parameters of extra-personal space than is kinaesthesis, and also suggest that communication between modalities is limited by a transfer or translation function that results in a significant loss of information. The degree of loss does not seem to be modality dependent since communication in either direction resulted in an equivalent or symmetrical loss.

Communication between two sense modalities should be limited by the less proficient modality for the type of information being processed. Kinaesthesis is an egocentrically referenced source of sensory information which is received sequentially and has to be integrated over time. In terms of spatial parameters, kinaesthesis can provide information only on the spatial location of limbs relative to each other and relative to the body. Vision, on the other hand, is externally referenced and provides holistic information on the spatial location of external objects relative to each other and to the limbs and body of the individual. Thus, more spatial information is acquired and is available for processing in the visual than in the kinaesthetic system.

If the limited capacity of the kinaesthetic system was the only factor affecting visual-kinaesthetic communication, then cross-modal recognition involving these modalities would be expected to be no worse than intramodal kinaesthetic recognition. However, the present results show that both V-K and K-V recognition was significantly worse than unimodal kinaesthetic performance. This suggests that the comparative process necessary for recognition is accompanied by a loss of information, irrespective of the modalities involved.

The bisensory condition was included to test the hypothesis that the simultaneous availability of congruent visual and kinaesthetic reafference would lead to the synthesis of a more comprehensive, integrated representation of the standard stimulus. Alternatively, bisensory exploration of the standard may provide an opportunity for more accurate specifications of intermodal correspondences or relations. The obtained results do not provide support for either of these alternatives.

Visual recognition following congruent VK input was not significantly different from visual recognition following visual exploration. Kinaesthetic recognition following bimodal input was not significantly different from corresponding recognition following visual input. The scores of both these groups were, however, significantly worse than the recognition performance of the intramodal kinaesthetic group. Thus, the visual and kinaesthetic recognition scores following bimodal presentation of the standard did not differ significantly from corresponding recognition following visual input, i.e. the recognition performance of the bimodal group was apparently visually based. This was despite the fact that instructions to subjects emphasised that they should have a good idea of what the standard shape looked and felt like and despite the fact that subjects did not know prior to each test trial which sense modality would be required for recognition.

Taken together, the results of the present study argue against the establishment of an integrated amodal representation of stimulus parameters when congruent, bisensory information is available. Further, the results do not support the assumption that bisensory input would allow for an accurate specification of correspondences between congruent modalities. Apparently, when vision and kinaesthesis are available simultaneously for the performance of a task, parallel processing of both sources of information does not occur. At the level of attention demand and conscious experience i.e. perception, the visual system has the dominant role in the processing of extra-corporeal spatial information (Freides, 1974; Pick, 1970) and has priority over kinaesthesis for access to attention.

Apart from differences in information capacity between vision and kinaesthesis, other work has shown that the two sensory systems differ in the way in which spatial information is encoded both between and within modalities (Diewert, 1975; 1976; Keele and Ells, 1972; Laabs, 1973; Lee and Magill, 1985; Posner, 1967; Posner and Konick, 1966). A consideration of these differences and the fact that different aspects of movement may be differentially encoded, argues against a simple translation device analogous to a simple 'look-up' table of visuomotor correspondences mediating intermodal communication. Indeed, the terms translation and integration may be misleading metaphors to describe the process.

What then is the process that mediates the establishment of intermodal relations? That such relationships are not innate is obvious from the fact that continued growth of the body, including receptor and effector organs, must result in a systematic change in the relationship between vision and kinaesthesis during development.

Additionally, visual-kinaesthetic relationships have been shown to be modifiable in adults in studies on adaptation to sensory rearrangement and mirror drawing tasks.

Although objects are perceived as phenomenal entities, sensory systems are known to detect features, not objects. Visual perception is thought to involve differential processing and encoding of object properties such as shape, size and texture (Jeannerod, 1986), while movement perception involves differential processing of location, direction, distance and amplitude. Thus, the phenomenal identification of objects across modalities may involve, as Gibson (1966) asserts, a supramodal perceptual process which abstracts perceptual invariants or allows for the detection of 'higher-order' relations between modalities.

In conclusion, for the task examined in the present study, the evidence indicates that congruent, bimodal presentation of complex spatial information does not lead to the establishment of an integrated, amodal representation at a sensory level. Nor does intermodal communication depend on transfer or translation of sensory information between modalities. Rather, the evidence suggests that sensory information is transduced, transmitted, processed and stored in a modality specific form. Intermodal equivalence is determined by the degree to which equivalent perceptual qualities are detected across sensory modalities and limited by the fact that each sense modality is adept at processing particular kinds of information (Freides, 1974). Thus, sensation, i.e. the object of a sense experience, is encoded in a modality specific form, but perception, which involves interpretation of the sense datum, is amodal.

ACKNOWLEDGEMENTS

The study was supported by University of Western Australia Research Grants; NO.ISF14.0020.84MT. and ARGS NO.A28215977R.

Correspondence concerning this paper should be sent to Victor Manyam, Department of Psychology, University of Western Australia, Nedlands, W.A 6009.

REFERENCES

Attneave, F., and Arnoult, M.D. (1956). The quantitative study of shape and pattern perception. Psychological Bulletin, 53, 452-471.

Connolly, K. and Jones, B. (1970). A developmental study of afferent-reafferent integration. British Journal of Psychology, 61, 259-266.

Diewert, G.L. (1975). Retention and coding in motor short-term memory: A comparison of storage codes for distance and location information. Journal of Motor Behavior, 7, 183-190.

Diewert, G.L. (1976). The role of vision and kinaesthesis in coding of two dimensional movement information. Journal of Human Movement Studies, 3, 191-198.

Diewert, G.L. and Stelmach, G.E. (1977). Intra-modal and inter-modal transfer of movement information. Acta Psychologica, 41, 119-128.

Ferguson, G.A. (1981). Statistical Analysis in Psychology and Education. 5th Ed. New York: McGraw-Hill.

Freides, D. (1974). Human information processing and sensory modality: Cross-modal functions, information complexity, memory, and deficit. Psychological Bulletin, 81, 284-310.

Freides, D. (1974). Information complexity and cross-modal functions. British Journal of Psychology, 66, 283-287.

Gibson, J.J. (1966). The Senses Considered as Perceptual Systems. Boston: Houghton Mifflin.

Goodnow, J.J. (1969). Eye and hand: Differential sampling of form and orientation properties. Neuropsychologia, 7, 365-373.

Goodnow, J.J. (1971). The role of modalities in perceptual and cognitive development. In Minnesota Symposia on Child Psychology. Volume 4. Ed. J.P. Hill. Minneapolis, M.N.: University of Minnesota Press pp. 3-28.

Jeannerod, M. (1986). Mechanisms of visuomotor coordination: A study in normal and brain-damaged subjects. Neuropsychologia, 24, 41-78.

Jones, B. and Connolly, K. (1970). Memory effects in cross-modal matching. British. Journal of Psychology, 61, 267-270.

Keele, S.W. and Ells, J.G. (1972). Memory characteristics of kinaesthetic information. Journal of Motor Behavior, 4, 127-134.

Laabs, G.J. (1973). Retention characteristics of different reproduction cues in motor short-term memory. Journal of Experimental Psychology, 100, 168-177.

Laszlo, J.I. & Bairstow, P.J. (1980). The measurement of kinaesthetic sensitivity in children and adults. Developmental Medicine and Child Neurology, 22:454-464.

Lee, T.D. and Magill, R.A. (1985). On the nature of movement representation in memory. British Journal of Psychology, 76, 175-182.

Marteniuk, R.G. and Rodney, M. (1979). Modality and retention effects in intra- and cross-modal judgements of kinaesthetic and visual information. British Journal of Psychology, 70, 405-412.

Millar, S. (1972). The development of visual and kinaesthetic judgements of distance. British Journal of Psychology, 63, 271-282.

Newell, K.M., Shapiro, D.C. and Carlton, M. J. (1979). Coordinating visual and kinaesthetic memory codes. British Journal of Psychology, 70, 87-96.

Pick, A.D. and Pick, H.L. (1966). A developmental study of tactual discrimination in blind and sighted children and adults. Psychonomic Science, 6, 367-368.

Pick, H.L. (1970). Systems of perceptual and perceptual-motor development. In Minnesota Symposia on Child Psychology. Volume 4. ed. J.P. Hill. Minneapolis, MN: University of Minnesota Press pp. 199-219.

Posner, M.I. (1967). Characteristics of visual and kinaesthetic memory codes. Journal of Experimental Psychology, 75, 103-107.

Posner, M.I. and Konick, A.F. (1966). Short-term retention of visual and kinaesthetic information. Organisational Behavior and Human Performance, 1, 71-86.

von Wright, J.M. (1970). Cross-modal transfer and sensory equivalence - a review. Scandinavian Journal of Psychology, 11, 21-30.

Walk, R.D. and Pick, H.L. (Eds.) 1981. Intersensory Perception and Sensory Integration. New York: Plenum Press.

Human Information Processing: Measures,
Mechanisms, and Models. D. Vickers and P. L. Smith (eds.)
© Elsevier Science Publishers B. V. (North-Holland), 1989

THE PERCEPTION OF STIFFNESS: A NEGLECTED ASPECT OF KINAESTHESIA

Lynette A. Jones and Ian W. Hunter

McGill University

The perception of stiffness was examined in normal human subjects using a matching procedure. An external mechanical system, composed of two electro-magnetic linear motors under computer servo control, was used to generate a range of stiffness amplitudes. Each linear motor was connected to the wrist, and subjects were instructed to adjust the stiffness of one motor (connected to the matching arm) until it was perceived to be the same as that of the other motor (attached to the reference arm). The stiffness of the reference motor was set at one of eight different levels ranging from 0 N/m to 6260 N/m. The psychophysical function relating physical to perceived stiffness was linear, and the accuracy with which subjects matched the stiffness of the two motors was comparable to that reported for force and displacement. These findings indicate that sensory information about muscle forces and limb movements can give rise to a perception of stiffness.

1. INTRODUCTION

Three variables have typically been examined in psychophysical studies of the proprioceptive system: the perception of limb position, movement, and force (Clark & Horch, 1986; McCloskey, 1978). The focus of much of this research has been on defining the sensory origin of these perceptions and assessing the relative contributions of afferent signals arising from receptors in muscles, tendons, joints, and the skin to kinaesthesia. Contrary to early predictions that sensory receptors in the muscle spindle were reserved solely for the purpose of servo-controlling movement (Merton, 1964), the results from a number of experiments have demonstrated quite conclusively that afferent signals emanating from muscle spindles are involved in the perception of limb position and movement (Goodwin, McCloskey & Matthews, 1972; Jones, 1988; Roll & Vedel, 1982). Sensations of force, however, appear to be centrally mediated, presumably via internal neural correlates (i.e., corollary discharges) of the descending efferent command (Jones, 1986; McCloskey,1981).

The experimental paradigm that has been used to study the influence of these various afferent signals on kinaesthesia has been the contralateral limb-matching procedure. The subject is required to match the position or movement made by one limb, called the reference limb, by making a movement of the same amplitude with the other limb, or by aligning the positions of the two limbs. Although the procedure sounds very simple, it is interesting to note that minor variations in the instructions given to subjects can alter the matching relation obtained. For example, Soechting (1982) has shown that the error in matching limb orientation is significantly smaller than that obtained when subjects are asked to match joint angles.

In studies of force perception, the subject is usually required to match the perceived magnitude of forces generated by the reference limb by producing perceptually equivalent forces with the contralateral limb. Under normal conditions, the forces generated by two corresponding muscle groups are matched quite accurately (Jones & Hunter, 1982), and subjects appear to scale forces perceptually with respect to the maximum strength of the muscle (Cafarelli & Bigland-Ritchie, 1979).

Other psychophysical methods have been used to measure the absolute thresholds for detecting movements passively imposed on the limb and for perceiving changes in limb position (Clark & Horch, 1986). Because most proprioceptive stimuli arise as a consequence of voluntary muscle activity, the objective of many of these studies has been to determine differential thresholds (Ross & Brodie, 1987). These experiments have demonstrated that, under appropriate conditions (e.g. imposing extremely slow limb movements), sensory thresholds provide an extremely useful means of studying the dissociation between the perception of movement and limb position (Clark, Burgess,Chapin, & Lipscomb, 1985).

The division of the kinaesthetic system into these three components, namely, the perception of force, limb movement and joint angle, is somewhat artificial in the context of normal motor performance. Recent studies indicate that there are complex interactions between sensory signals conveying force, movement, and position information that often result in kinaesthetic errors known as force-movement illusions (Jones, 1988; Matthews, 1982; Rymer & D'Almeida, 1980; Watson, Colebatch & McCloskey, 1984). For example, the forces generated during the course of a limb movement can influence the perceived amplitude of the movement and, as a consequence, the final position of the limb is overestimated (Rymer & D'Almeida, 1980; Watson et al.,

1984). The external forces acting on a limb must be taken into account during movements (Worringham & Stelmach, 1985), and so it is not surprising to find that the perceived position of a limb may vary as a function of force. In this context it is interesting to note that position information has much less influence on the perception of force than do force cues on perceived limb position (Watson et al., 1984).

These findings can be interpreted as indicating that human subjects are sensitive to changes in stiffness, and that the perception of position is influenced by the stiffness of the limb, that is, the dynamic relation between the angular position of a joint and the torque about it (Hunter & Kearney, 1982). The sensitivity of human subjects to changes in the stiffness of their own limbs or to variations in the stiffness of a mechanical system connected to the body (e.g. a steering wheel) has not been extensively investigated, despite early interest in this issue in the human operator field (Howland & Noble, 1953).

Limb stiffness increases with the force of contraction (Hunter & Kearney, 1982) and when the antagonist muscle is co-contracting with the agonist (Humphrey & Reed, 1983). In order to examine the perception of stiffness independently of force, it is necessary to decouple force and stiffness which does occur during co-contraction. However, it appears that subjects require considerable training before they can reliably control the level of co-contraction in two muscle groups (Jones & Hunter, 1987), and there seems to be an upper limit to the magnitude of forces that can be generated simultaneously by the agonist and antagonist muscles (Hunter, Kearney, & Weiss, 1983). For these reasons, an external mechanical system was used in the present experiment in preference to the subject's own neuromuscular system, so that stiffness could be controlled precisely.

The objective of the experiment was to examine the sensitivity of the human proprioceptive system to changes in stiffness using a novel mechanical system in which stiffness was generated actively by servo-controlling high-performance linear motors connected to the forearms of subjects.

2. METHOD

2.1 Subjects

Eight healthy normal adult subjects (four men and four women) participated in the experiment. Their ages ranged from 25 to 39 years.

2.2 Apparatus

Subjects were seated in an electrically adjustable chair mounted in an experimental rig (1 m square at the base and 2 m high) constructed from square-bar aluminium struts. Attached to the base of the rig were two foot plates one of which was rigid, and the other could be moved bi-directionally by rotating the foot about the ankle axis. An angular position transducer attached to the movable plate signalled the position of the foot.

Two electromagnetic linear motors were bolted to the rig and powered by custom-built 15 A current amplifiers. An aluminium rod and cuff connected to the translation stage of each motor, was used to clamp the motor to the subject's wrist. An LVDT (linear variable differential transformer) displacement transducer (100 mm linear range) was mounted on each motor with its movable core mechanically coupled to the translation stage. Displacement signals were used together with current for real-time control of the stiffness (K) of the motors, via the Micro VAX computer's D/As (digital to analogue converters), associated power amplifiers and servo-system.

A displacement servo-controller with its loop-gain under computer control set the zero position of the motors, and the loop-gain of the servo-controller determined the stiffness of the motor. The output from the angular position transducer attached to the left foot-plate on which the subject's foot rested was recorded on-line and used to adjust the stiffness of the motor attached to the matching arm. A schematic diagram of the equipment and servo-system used in the experiment is shown in Figure 1.

2.3 Procedure

Subjects sat in the chair with each elbow joint resting in a moulded plastic support, whose position was adjusted until the angle between the upper arm and forearm was 90 degrees. During the experiment, subjects were blindfolded to prevent them from using visual cues regarding the extent of forearm movement to facilitate the perception of stiffness.

On each experimental trial the stiffness of the reference motor connected to the right arm was randomly set at one of eight different amplitudes ranging from 0 to 6260 N/m, and each of these values was presented five times. Subjects were instructed to perturb their arms (in the sagittal plane) in order to perceive the stiffness of the two motors, and then to adjust the stiffness of the matching motor attached to the left arm until it was perceived to be the same as that of the reference motor.

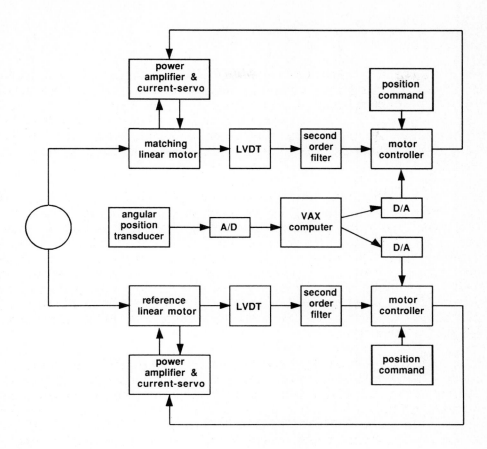

Figure 1. A schematic representation of the recording system.

The stiffness of the matching motor was controlled by rotating the left foot (about the ankle axis). Subjects were given 10 seconds to adjust the stiffness and the loop-gain of the servo-controller of the matching motor was recorded in the final 1 s of this interval.

3. RESULTS

The mean of the five matching stiffness amplitudes recorded at each reference stiffness was calculated for all subjects. The psychophysical function for stiffness is shown for a typical subject in Figure 2. The relation between the reference and matching stiffness is linear (variance accounted for is 96%), and for this subject the slope of the least-squares regression line fitted to the data was 0.86. For all subjects the relation between the reference and matching stiffness was linear, with the variance accounted for by the regression line ranging from 91% to 96%.

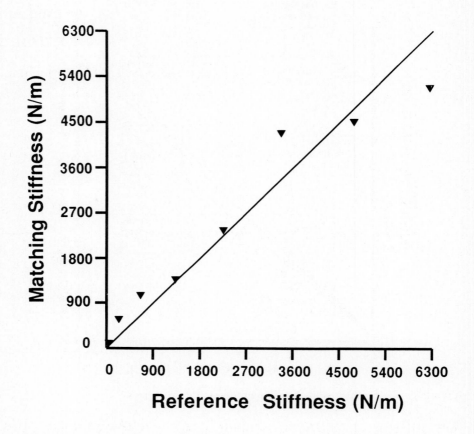

Figure 2. Relation between the stiffness of the reference motor connected to the right arm and the matching stiffness (set by the subject) of the motor connected to the left arm for a typical subject. The data are the means of 5 trials at each reference stiffness. The line of equality is shown.

The sensitivity of subjects to changes in stiffness was compared to that reported for force and displacement. Data from previous experiments on the perception of elbow flexion forces (Jones & Hunter, 1982), and of the position of the forearm (Erickson, 1974) were used to calculate the slopes of the respective matching functions. The slope of the function for force is 0.84, for position 0.95, and for the group data in this experiment the slope for stiffness is 1.01. The three matching relations are shown in Figure 3. These findings indicate that the accuracy with which the stiffness of two motors is matched parallels that reported for force and position.

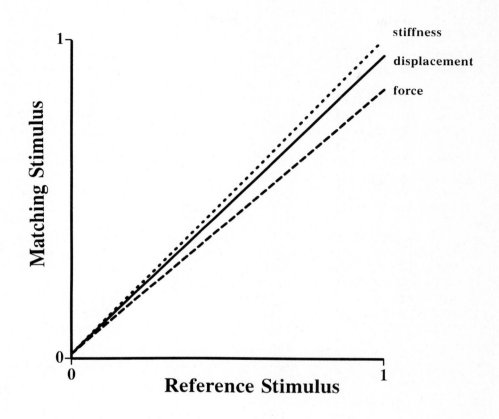

Figure 3. A comparison of the matching functions for stiffness, force (from Jones & Hunter, 1982) and position (from Erickson, 1974).

4. DISCUSSION

The results indicate that subjects perceived changes in the stiffness of the external mechanical system coupled to their arms, and that they were able to control the stiffness of the matching motor with an impressive level of accuracy, given the novelty of the experimental task. The absence of any saturation in the psychophysical function derived from the extensive range of stiffness intensities used in this experiment demonstrates the considerable sensitivity of the human proprioceptive system to this particular mechanical variable. In order to judge the relative stiffness of the two motors, subjects presumably used cues related to the forces generated by the elbow flexors and extensors, and the extent of movement of their forearms. Information about both of these variables is required to perceive stiffness.

In this experiment, the perception of stiffness was examined in the context of control. The matching paradigm was used in preference to numerical scaling (i.e. magnitude estimation), because it does not appear to be as susceptible to the biases that influence numerical estimates of stimulus magnitude (Jones, 1986). In addition, it appears that subjects often experience difficulty in making relative magnitude judgements of some mechanical variables (e.g. the inertia of two objects), even when they can readily indicate that the two objects differ with respect to the property in question (Kreifeldt & Chuang,1979). Results from pilot studies suggested that a similar situation could arise when estimating stiffness because it is also an unfamiliar dimension in terms of mapping onto a verbal domain (i.e. compliance-stiffness).

The sensitivity of the human proprioceptive system to the diverse range of mechanical stimuli that the neuromuscular system encounters in its interactions with the environment has only begun to be analyzed experimentally. On the basis of this research we have started to discover the stimuli to which this system is the most and least sensitive. These studies are not only of intrinsic interest but are also critical for understanding the perceptual constraints on motor performance.

ACKNOWLEDGEMENTS

This research was supported by grants to the author (LAJ) from the Faculty of Graduate Studies and Research, McGill University and from the Medical Research Council of Canada.

Correspondence concerning this paper should be addresses to Lynette A. Jones, Ph.D. Physical & Occupational Therapy, McGill University, 3654 Drummond St., Montreal, PQ Canada H3G 1Y5.

REFERENCES

Cafarelli, E.W. & Bigland-Ritchie, B. (1979). Sensation of static force in muscles of different length. Experimental Neurology, 65, 511-525.

Clark, F.J., Burgess, R.C., Chapin, J.W. & Lipscomb, W.T. (1985). Role of intramuscular receptors in the awareness of limb position. Journal of Neurophysiology, 54, 1529-1540.

Clark, F.J. & Horch, K.W. (1986). Kinesthesia. In K. Boff, L. Kaufman, & J. Thomas Eds.), Handbook of perception and human performance (Vol. 1, pp. 13-1 - 13-62). New York: Wiley.

Erickson, R.P. (1974). Parallel "population" neural coding in feature extraction. In F.O. Schmitt, & Worden, F.G. (Eds.), The Neurosciences: Third study program (pp. 155-169). Cambridge, Ma.: MIT Press.

Goodwin, G.M., McCloskey, D.I. & Matthews, P.B.C. (1972). The contribution of muscle afferents to kinaesthesia shown by vibration induced illusions of movement and by effects of paralysing joint afferents. Brain 95, 649-660.

Howland, D. & Noble, M.E. (1953). The effect of physical constants of a control on tracking performance. Journal of Experimental Psychology, 46, 353-360.

Humphrey, D.R. & Reed, D.J. (1983). Separate cortical systems for control of joint movement and joint stiffness: Reciprocal activation and coactivation of antagonist muscles. In J.E. Desmedt (Ed.), Motor control mechanisms in health and disease (pp. 347-372). New York: Raven Press.

Hunter, I.W. & Kearney, R.E. (1982). Dynamics of human ankle stiffness: Variation with mean ankle torque. Journal of Biomechanics, 15, 747-752

Hunter, I.W., Kearney, R.E. & Weiss, P.L. (1983). Variation of ankle stiffness with co-contraction. Society for Neuroscience Abstracts, 9, 1226.

Jones, L.A.(1986). Perception of force and weight: Theory and research. Psychological Bulletin, 100, 29-42

Jones, L.A. (1988). Motor illusions: What do they reveal about proprioception? Psychological Bulletin, 103, 72-86.

Jones, L.A. & Hunter, I.W. (1982). Force sensation in isometric contractions: A relative force effect. Brain Research, 244, 186-189

Jones, L.A. & Hunter, I.W. (1987). Effects of antagonist activation on sensations of muscle force. In G.N. Gantchev, B. Dimitrov & P. Gatev (Eds.), Motor control (pp. 105-109). New York: Plenum.

Kreifeldt, J.G. & Chuang, M.C. (1979). Moment of inertia: psychophysical study of an over-looked sensation. Science, 206, 588-590.

Matthews, P.B.C. (1982). Where does Sherrington's muscular sense originate? Muscles, joints, corollary discharges? Annual Review of Neuroscience, 5, 189-218.

McCloskey, D.I. (1978). Kinesthetic sensibility. Physiological Reviews, 58, 763-820.

McCloskey, D.I. (1981). Corollary discharges: Motor commands and perception. In
    V.B. Brooks (Ed.), Handbook of physiology: The nervous system. Motor
    control (Vol. 2, pp. 1415-1447). Bethesda, MD: American Physiological
    Society.

Merton, P.A. (1964). Human position sense and sense of effort. Symposium of the
    Society for Experimental Biology, 18, 387-400

Roll, J.P. & Vedel, J.P. (1982). Kinaesthetic role of muscle afferents in man, studied by
    tendon vibration and micro-neurography. Experimental Brain Research, 47,
    177-190.

Ross, H.E. & Brodie, E.E. (1987). Weber fractions for weight and mass as a function of
    stimulus intensity. Quarterly Journal of Experimental Psychology, 39A, 77-88.

Rymer, W.Z. & D'Almeida, A. (1980). Joint position sense: The effects of muscle
    contraction. Brain, 103, 1-22.

Soechting, J.F. (1982). Does position sense at the elbow reflect a sense of elbow joint
    angle or one of limb orientation? Brain Research, 248, 392-395.

Watson, J.D.G., Colebatch, J.G. & McCloskey, D.I. (1984). Effects of externally
    imposed elastic loads on the ability to estimate position and force. Behavioural
    Brain Research, 13, 267-27

Worringham, C.J. & Stelmach, G.E. (1985). The contribution of gravitational torques to
    limb position sense. Experimental Brain Research, 61, 38-42.

Human Information Processing: Measures,
Mechanisms, and Models. D. Vickers and P.L. Smith (eds.)
© Elsevier Science Publishers B.V. (North-Holland), 1989

PHONOLOGICAL RECODING, MEMORY PROCESSING AND VISUAL DEFICITS IN SPECIFIC READING DISABILITY

William Lovegrove and Karen Pepper

University of Wollongong

Frances Martin and Brian Mackenzie

University of Tasmania

Don McNicol

University of New England

This study aimed at determining the relationships between aspects of visual processing, phonological recoding and working memory in normal and specifically disabled readers. All measures used had previously been shown individually to distinguish between control and specifically disabled readers. Fifty-eight disabled readers and sixty-two controls were tested. A factor analysis revealed four factors. The first reflected global poor performance and was interpreted as being a general measure of abilities related to intelligence. Factor two was the most interesting as it showed a link between phonological recoding and the visual measures used. The third factor measured aspects of phoneme segmentation ability but was not very robust. The measures of working memory (factor four) investigated did not appear to relate to either the visual or the phonological recoding measures. The finding that the visual processing and phonological recoding measures load on the same factor suggest that visual deficits may contribute to phonological errors.

1. INTRODUCTION

Many studies have now demonstrated a range of visual deficits in children defined as specifically-reading-disabled (SRD). These include measures of low-level visual processing suggesting a deficit in the transient visual subsystem (Lovegrove, Martin & Slaghuis, 1986) and measures of higher-level perceptual processes also consistent with a transient subsystem deficit (Williams, 1987). The research by both these groups was performed within a framework assuming the existence of two complementary subsystems in the visual system. One of these, the sustained, is primarily involved in information extraction during eye fixations while the other, the transient, has a major role in guiding eye movements and integrating information across fixations. Lovegrove et. al. argue that a large number of specifically disabled readers manifest an insensitivity in their transient system while their sustained system appears to function normally. Consequently SRDs may experience difficulties in integrating information from successive fixations. The recent work by Williams and colleagues has shown that SRDs and controls also differ on a number of higher-level perceptual tasks in a way which is consistent with a low-level transient deficit.

Hulme (1988) has argued that it is most unlikely that such visual deficits are causally related to reading disabilities. A major component of Hulme's argument is that the major types of errors made by disabled readers are phonological in nature and are unrelated to visual processing. The latter conclusion is perhaps a little premature given the absence of clear information about how visual input is converted to a phonological code in reading. The question raised by Hulme could more easily be answered by an investigation of the relationship between vision and phonological recoding in good and poor readers. This is one of the aims of the present study.

As mentioned above, several researchers have shown that SRDs have difficulty in aspects of phonological recoding. One of the most consistent and important findings concerns the inability of SRDs to pronounce nonsense words which are presented in written form. It has been shown often that SRDs are worse than controls in pronouncing nonsense words which tap grapheme-to-phoneme conversion ability (Firth,1972). Furthermore SRDs have difficulties in recognizing (or analysing) the phonemic components of spoken words (Treiman & Baron, 1978).

Another area where SRDs and controls have been compared is in memory capacity. There is substantial evidence that SRDs experience problems with aspects of memory processes. Jorm (1983) summarized these problems as follows:

"There is fairly consistent evidence that retarded readers have adequate long-term memory for non-verbal material and for the semantic aspects of verbal material. However, they appear to have difficulty in the storage and retrieval of phonological aspects of verbal material in long-term memory. Furthermore, this difficulty appears to be related to the failure of retarded readers to adequately utilize the articulatory loop. Although there is no evidence that one causes the other, a plausible theoretical account would be that problems in storing phonological coding information in long-term memory give rise to slowness of retrieval once learning has taken place. Furthermore, slow retrieval of phonological information could in turn give rise to problems in utilizing the articulatory loop." (p. 334).

In his discussion of memory and specific reading disability, Jorm (1983) concludes that a large amount of evidence suggests a difficulty for disabled readers in working memory. In particular, he suggests a problem in the articulatory loop within the theoretical framework proposed by Baddeley and Hitch (1974). The function of the articulatory loop has been described in the following terms:

" ...the articulatory system was seen as serving the primary function of an output buffer for speech responses and the additional function of providing temporary storage in reading and arithmetic." (Hitch, 1978, p. 189).

Jorm also sees this as linking memory processing with phonological recoding because of the involvement of the articulatory loop in phonological coding. It has not, however, been shown explicitly that there is a link between poor phonological recoding and poor working memory within SRDs. This issue is also investigated in the current study.

At this stage it is not known how or if these three deficit areas relate to each other, and how or if they causally relate to specific reading disability. They may or may not be related problems. The current investigation will attempt to provide a preliminary answer to this issue.

The general rationale of this study was to select measures of visual processing, phonological recoding and working memory known from a number of separate previous studies to differentiate between controls and SRDs. These measures were then to be taken from a large number of subjects from both groups to determine the relationships between the measures within a given sample. Such an approach should go some way to answering the questions outlined above.

2. METHOD

2.1 Subjects

Complete sets of data were collected for 58 SRDs and 62 controls. Subjects were selected by the normal procedures used in this laboratory with the main criterion being normal intelligence (WISC-R) accompanied by a two-year reading lag as measured by the accuracy sub-test of the Neale Analysis of Reading Ability. Subject details are shown in Table 1. The Neale Gap score refers to the gap (in years) between the subject's chronological age and reading age on the accuracy subscore of the Neale Analysis of Reading Ability (1966). For controls this was .25 and for SRDs 3.25 years.

Table 1

This shows selection details for the two groups. The Neale Gap score is the difference between the subjects' chronological age and reading accuracy age.

SUBJECT DETAILS

	Age	WISC-R Full-scale IQ	Verbal IQ	Performance IQ	Neale Gap
Controls					
Mean	12.3	107	106	107	.25
SD	.3	10	11	11	.54
SRDS					
Mean	12.6	100	96	104	3.20
SD	.4	10	10	11	.60

2.2 Procedure

In general terms we used three measures of transient processing, three measures of phonological recoding and two measures of short-term memory. The transient measures chosen were the duration of visible persistence at 2 and 12 cycles per degree, sensitivity to a 2 cycle per degree grating flickering at 6 and 20 cycles per second and sensitivity to a 2 and 8 cycle per degree grating flickering at 20 cycles per second. Each of these measures has previously been shown to differentiate between SRDs and controls (Lovegrove, Heddle and Slaghuis, 1981; Martin and Lovegrove, 1987).

Three measures of phonological recoding were used. The first was a sentence verification task based on Baron (1973). Subjects were required to judge whether short phrases make sense or not. Three sorts of phrases were used:

Meaningful phrases--I HAVE NO TIME

Phrases which sound meaningful--I HAVE NOE TIME or I HAVE KNOW TIME

Meaningless phrases--I HAVE BLOO TIME or I HAVE BLUE TIME

Sentences of the second type appear to tap the tendency to convert print to speech in tasks where no print-to-speech conversion is explicitly required. It was assumed that SRDs would do this more than controls.

The second measure of phonological recoding was the reading of non-words aloud (Firth, 1972). It involves asking subjects to read aloud letter strings such as JENB or FELLY. These letters obey the rules of English orthography and skilled readers are in good agreement about their correct pronunciations. Because these letter strings are unfamiliar, the requirement to read them aloud simulates the problems confronting a reader who encounters a new word and must pronounce it.

The third measure of phonological recoding was derived from Trieman and Baron (1978). Subjects were to judge which two of three spoken syllables sounded most alike. Of the three syllables /bi/ (as in BIT), /ve/ (as in VET), and /bo/ (as in BOAT), /bi/ and /ve/ are similar overall but have no segment in common. On the other hand /bi/ and /bo/ share the segment /b/. Trieman and Baron (1978) found for children who had not yet properly learned to read, those who classified on the basis of common segments were able to read more isolated words than those who classified on the basis of overall similarity. The task would thus seem to tap some of the segmentation abilities which lie at the basis of successful print-to-speech conversion.

Two basic types of task were used to assess the extent to which the articulatory loop is used to hold information in working memory and the efficiency with which this is done. The first type of task presents verbal information visually so that the subject can choose to represent it in memory visually or in an articulatory form. The particular task used has previously been used with controls and SRDs by Mann, Lieberman, Mark, Fowler and Fischer (1979) and involves letters which are acoustically similar such as DCPBTV or dissimilar letters such as SFRWMC. In addition a set of visually similar letters such as THXYLK was also included. It has been found (Mann et al., 1973) that performance in controls falls off significantly more than SRDs in the acoustically similar condition. This has been interpreted as suggesting that controls more than SRDs code such materials in short-term memory in an acoustic/articulatory form.

The second task was derived from Mann, Lieberman and

Shankweiler (1980) and asks children to recall spoken sentences composed of rhyming words (PAT'S BAD CAT SPAT AT THE RAT THAT SAT ON THE FLAT MAT) or nonrhyming words (PEG'S BROWN DOG BIT AT THE BONE THAT FELL ON THE CLEAN FLOOR). It has been shown that both reading groups perform equivalently on rhyming sentences but good readers were superior with sentences which did not rhyme. Mann et al. suggested that this result was due to the failure of the poor readers to make effective use of phonemic coding in working memory.

Subjects were tested individually and required four sessions of 40 to 45 minutes each. All of the measures used have been used before and because of space limitations full procedural details are not included here. Further details of procedures used can be obtained from the references cited.

3. RESULTS

The raw data from the various experiments were reduced in a number of ways as outlined below before being entered in the principal components analysis.

3.1 Visible Persistence

The difference between the duration of visible persistence at two and twelve cycles per degree was used as this had previously been shown to differentiate between the groups. Means and standard deviations for each group are shown in Table 2. Although the difference was greater for the control group than for the SRDs as predicted, this difference did not reach significance (t (116)= 1.29, p > 0.05), thus failing to replicate previous studies (Lovegrove et al., 1981).

3.2 Flicker Sensitivity Measures

Means and standard deviations for each group in each condition are shown in Table 2. The results of the two flicker sensitivity tests were submitted to an analysis of variance. For the first test, (2 cyc/deg grating flickering at 6 cyc/sec or 20 cyc/sec), there were significant main effects for the reading group factor (F(1,114) = 5.0, p < 0.05), and the flicker condition factor (F(1,114) = 36.7, p < 0.01). There was no significant interaction. For the second test, (2 cyc/deg or 8 cyc/deg grating flickering at 20 cyc/sec), there were significant main effects for the reading group factor (F(1,114) = 16.6, p < 0.01), and the flicker condition factor (F(1,114) = 183.7, p < 0.01). There was also a significant interaction between these two factors (F(1.114) = 14.0, p < 0.01).

Average thresholds for the two conditions in each Experiment were entered into the factor analysis.

TABLE 2

Means and standards deviations for Controls and SRDs on each of the measures used.

CONDITION	SRD GROUP	CONTROLS
Measure of Transient Processing 1		
Visible Persistence: Diff. 12 cyc/deg - 2 cyc/deg		
Mean	44.40	60.90
(SD)	(62.60)	(76.80)
Measure of Transient Processing 2		
Flickering Grating: 6 cyc/sec		
Mean	0.006	0.004
(SD)	(0.006)	(0.002)
Flickering Grating: 20 cyc/sec		
Mean	0.015	0.011
(SD)	(0.014)	(0.003)
Measure of Transient Processing 3		
Flickering Grating: 2 cyc/deg		
Mean	0.015	0.011
(SD)	(0.014)	(0.003)
Flickering Grating: 8 cyc/deg		
Mean	0.085	0.051
(SD)	(0.063)	(0.017)
Measure of Phonological Recoding 1		
Sentence Verification		
Mean	8.70	3.50
(SD)	(3.90)	(3.50)
Measure of Phonological Recoding 2		
Nonwords		
Mean	101.90	134.20
(SD)	(14.80)	(10.50)
Measure of Phonological Recoding 3		
Segment Comparison:Segment Similarity		
Mean	10.10	11.70
(SD)	(2.50)	(2.50)

Overall Similarity

Mean	4.80	5.10
(SD)	(2.20)	(2.20)

Anomalous

Mean	3.10	1.30
(SD)	(1.90)	(1.40)

Measure of Short-term Memory 1
Short-term Memory: LettersDiff. between Visually Dissimilar and   Visually Similar
Letters

Mean	4.20	6.20
(SD)	(5.20)	(11.50)

Diff. between Auditorily Dissimilar and Auditorily Similar Letters

Mean	7.40	6.20
(SD)	(6.00)	(11.50)

Measure of Short-term Memory 2
Short-term Memory: Sentences Diff. between Non-rhyming and Rhyming Sentences

Mean	5.90	6.20
(SD)	(10.70)	(11.50)

3.3 Sentence Verification Task

The number of errors in the condition which sounds meaningful but which is spelled incorrectly was used here. The data are shown as Phonological Recoding Measure 1 in Table 2. SRDs made significantly more errors where they accepted as correct those sentences which sounded correct but were spelt incorrectly (t (116) = 7.52, p < 0.001). Thus they were converting print to speech when this was not necessary, and doing this poorly.

3.4 Reading Regular Nonwords Aloud

The number correct was the score used. Table 3 shows that SRDs performed at a much lower level than controls. A t-test showed this difference to be significant (t (116) = 13.56, p < 0.001).

3.5 Segment Comparison

Three measures were used for each subject: the number of similar phoneme classifications, the number of overall similarity classifications and the number of anomalous classifications. Results are shown in Table

2 as Phonological Recoding Measure 3. There were significant differences between the groups in the common-phoneme condition (t (116) = 3.3, p < 0.001), and in the anomalous condition (t (116) = 5.63, p < 0.001). Results for each of the three conditions were used in the factor analysis.

3.6 Visual versus articulatory coding in STM.

Two measures were used for each subject. The first was the difference between the neutral stimulus condition (the condition in which the letters were neither visually nor auditorily similar) and the visually-similar stimulus condition, and the second was the difference between the neutral and the auditorily-similar stimulus conditions. The data are shown in Table 2 as Measures of Short-Term Memory 1. There were no significant differences between the groups in either condition. (Visually-similar stimulus: t (116)= 1.89, p > 0.05; Auditorily-similar condition: t (116)= 1.85, p > 0.05 .) The two difference scores were used in the factor analysis.

3.7 Memory For Spoken Sentences

The differences between the score for sentences with words which did not rhyme and those which did rhyme was used as the measure of this ability. Means and standard deviations for each group are shown in Table 2 as Short-Term Memory Measure 2. This measure also failed to differentiate between the two groups (t (116) = 0.14, p > 0.05).

3.8 General Ability Measures

3.8.1 Intelligence.

Both the full-scale WISC-R scores and the difference between the Performance and the Verbal IQs were included in the factor analysis. In terms of a number of sub-typing studies, the majority of SRDs would have a positive score on this measure. A minority would have a negative score. Means and Standard deviations for each group are shown in Table 1. Subjects' ages are also shown in that Table.

3.8.2 Reading Score.

The accuracy score on the Neale Analysis of Reading Ability was used. The difference between each subjects' chronological age and reading age was also included. The data are shown in Table 1.

3.9 Factor Analysis

A four-factor solution principal components analysis was performed on the data. This accounted for 57.3% of the variance. Details are shown in Table 3.

Table 3

General Summary of Factor Analysis

Factor	Eigen value	% variance	cum. % variance
1	3.4	22.8	22.8
2	2.1	14.2	37.1
3	1.8	12.1	49.2
4	1.2	8.2	57.3

3.9.1 Description of Factors.

Table 4 shows the measures weighting on Factor 1. This factor appears to be a measure of general poor reading ability. The intelligence weighting indicates that low intelligence correlates strongly with this factor as does poor reading and poor phonological recoding. One interpretation is that poor reading and phonological recoding are a result of generally poor IQ scores.

Table 4

Measures Loading on Factor 1

Measure	Loading
Full-Scale IQ	-.56
Woodcock Nonsense Words Test	-.70
Sentence Verification	.56
Anomalous Segmentation	.40
Age	.60
Neale Gap	.83
IQ Difference	.68

Conversely the low IQ scores could reflect poor reading ability which in turn results from poor phonological recoding. Probably there is some truth in both of these interpretations with the first being the most likely.

Table 5 shows the measures loading on Factor 2. This factor suggests some link between transient system processing, phonological recoding and poor reading. One possibility is that each of these reflects some general immaturity but it should be noted that IQ does not weight on this factor. Another possibility is that there is some causal link between the three.

Table 5

Measures Loading on Factor 2

Measure	Loading
Woodcock Nonsense Words Test	-.35
Sentence Verification	.53
Anomalous Segmentation	.35
Neale Gap	.34
STM Visual Difference	.37
Flicker Sensitivity 1	.79
Flicker Sensitivity 2	.89

The transient problem may result from either poor phonological recoding or from poor reading. Given the low-level at which transient processing occurs it is unlikely that it is much influenced by phonological recoding. Furthermore the evidence on environmental effects on the visual system makes it unlikely that the poor transient processing results from poor reading. It is possible that the transient problem in some way yet to be specified contributes to problems in phonological recoding and to reading difficulties. This makes sense where the phonological recoding problem is presented in written form (the Woodcock Nonsense word test and the Sentence Verification task) but not when the task is presented orally (the Phoneme Segmentation task).

It is also possible that both the phonological recoding difficulty and the transient system insensitivity both reflect a general difficulty with temporal discrimination across senses. Some evidence for this is found in the auditory work of Tallal (1980) who has shown that SRDs differ from controls in terms of their ability to resolve rapidly-presented auditory stimuli. This and the other possibilities require further research. What the current data do indicate is that phonological recoding and measures of transient system processing are not independent as has been suggested recently by Hulme (1988).

Table 6 shows the measures loading on Factor 3. This factor is weighted on only by the two negatively correlated measures of phoneme segmentation.

Table 6

Measures Loading on Factor 3

Measure	Loading
Common Phoneme	-.95
Segment Similarity	.86

The direction of the weighting indicates that this factor is negatively correlated with "mature" or normal phonological recoding. Because there are only two items on this factor, it is probably unreliable and little will be said about it.

Table 7

Measures Loading on Factor 4

Measure	Loading
Anomalous Segmentation	-.49
STM Visual Difference	.66
STM Auditory Difference	.60
STM Rhyming Difference	.53

Table 7 shows the measures loading on Factor 4. This factor primarily reflects articulatory loop functioning in short-term memory. Each memory measure weights here and in each case the weighting reflects "normal" memory processing. Normal in two cases refers to the greater fall-off in performance with auditorily-similar material as is commonly found in normal readers. In the other case it refers to a fall off in performance when the stimuli are visually similar. Good performance on the phoneme segmentation task also weights here. The major significance of this factor is the independence of this "memory" processing factor from the measures of reading ability, phonological recoding and transient functioning.

4. DISCUSSION

Perhaps the most predictable finding of this study is the

importance of phonological recoding measures in the overall analysis. This is consistent with the large number of studies referred to in the introduction arguing for a causal link between phonological recoding and reading ability.

In terms of the original aims of the study Factor 2 provides the most important information. It shows a relatively strong link between phonological recoding, transient processing and reading ability. As discussed above, there are a number of interpretations of this but the most parsimonious one is that the three are causally linked, with the transient processing difficulty feeding into the higher levels of processing. A somewhat surprising result is that the flicker sensitivity measures and the visible persistence measures are not related according to the factor analysis. This suggests that, whereas flicker sensitivity primarily measures transient system activity, the slope of the visible persistence by spatial frequency function is a measure of sustained system activity. This possibility is reinforced by a six-factor solution showing that persistence weights heavily on the same factor as the discrepancy between verbal and performance IQ's in the direction of performance being better. That factor seems to measure general visuo-spatial abilities.

As only two highly correlated measures weighted on Factor 3, it is difficult to argue about the likely significance of this finding and we will say no more about it.

Factor 4 is of interest in showing that the aspect of memory we measured is independent of phonological recoding. In terms of Jorm (1983), there was reason to believe that these measures would be closely linked to phonological recoding measures. That they are not suggests that these tasks primarily measure articulatory loop functioning concerned with response output. In comparison the phonological recoding tasks used are more concerned with input measures.

This paper provides a preliminary answer to two questions. First it shows a statistical relationship between measures of transient processing, phonological recoding and reading ability. Second it has not shown a link between measures of articulatory loop functioning in working memory and phonological recoding and reading as anticipated by Jorm (1983). The data, however, leave a number of related issues unresolved. The first concerns the failure to show differences between the two groups on the segmentation task. It is possible that this is a problem for beginning readers but not for children with a mean age of 12.6, as was the case for our SRDs. A related problem concerns the memory measures used in this study. They were based directly on studies which had previously shown differences between normal and poor readers. Nevertheless we failed to find such differences. Again this raises the question of whether these differences are restricted to younger age groups or whether they reflect different selection procedures used in different studies. Both of these results question the generality of these widely cited findings to all children with reading difficulties. The current data are also being separately analysed into subgroups and this analysis will provide a partial answer to this question. There is some evidence that only some SRDs manifest short-term memory difficulties (Torgenson & Houck, 1980)

The data reported go some way towards showing a relationship between phonological recoding, reading ability and transient system processing. They fail to substantiate earlier claims about working memory and reading abilities and speculations about phonological recoding and working memory. The exact nature of the relationship between phonological recoding, reading ability and transient system processing will need to be clarified by further research.

CORRESPONDENCE

Correspondence concerning this paper should be addressed to William Lovegrove, Department of Psychology, University of Wollongong, P.O Box 1144, Wollongong, Australia.

REFERENCES

Baddeley. A & Hitch, G. (1974). Working memory. In G.A. Bower (Ed.), The psychology of learning and motivation. vol. 8. New York: Academic Press.

Baron, J. (1973). Phonemic stage not necessary for reading. Quarterly Journal of Experimental Psychology, 25, 241-246.

Conrad, R. (1964). Acoustic confusions in immediate memory. British Journal of Psychology, 55,75-84.

Firth, I. (1972). Components of reading disability. Unpublished Ph.D. thesis: University of New South Wales.

Fox, B. & Routh, D. (1983). Reading disability, phonemic analysis, and dysphonic spelling: A follow-up study. Journal of Clinical Child Psychology, 12, 28-32.

Hitch, G. (1978). Developing the concept of working memory. In G. Claxton (Ed.). Cognitive Psychology: New Directions. London : Routledge & Kegan Paul.

Hulme, C. (1988). The implausibility of low-level visual deficits as a cause of children's reading difficulties. Cognitive Neuropsychology. (in press).

Jorm, A. (1983). Specific reading retardation and working memory. British Journal of Psychology, 74, 311-342.

Lovegrove, W., Heddle, M., Slaghuis, W. (1980). Reading disability: Spatial frequency specific deficits in visual information store. Neuropsychologia, 18, 111-115.

Lovegrove, W., Martin F., & Slaghuis, W. (1986). A theoretical and experimental case for a visual deficit in specific reading disability. Cognitive Neuropsychology, 3, 225-267.

Mann, V. A., Lieberman, I.Y. & Shankweiler, D. (1980). Children's memory for sentences and word strings in relation to reading ability. Memory and Cognition, 8, 329-335.

Martin, F.& Lovegrove, W. (1987). Flicker contrast sensitivity in normal and specifically disabled readers. Perception, 16, 215-221.

Neale, M.B. (1966). The Neale Analysis of Reading Ability. London: Macmillan.

Shankweiler, D., Liberman, I.Y., Mark, L.S., Fowler, C.A., & Fischer, F.W. (1979). The speech code and learning to read. Journal of Experimental Psychology : Human Learning and Memory, 5, 531-545.

Tallal, P & Stark, R. (1981) Speech acoustic-cue discrimination abilities of normally developing and language-impaired children. Journal of the Acoustical Society of America, 69, 568-574.

Torgesen, J. & Houck , D. (1980) Processing difficulties of learning-disabled children who perform poorly on the digit-span test. Journal of Educational Psychology,72, 141-160.

Trieman, R., & Baron, J. (1978). Segmental analysis ability : development and relation to reading. In T. G. Waller and G.E. Mackinnon (Ed.) Reading Research : Advances in theory and practice. vol. 2. New York : Academic Press.

Wechsler, D. (1974). Wechsler intelligence scale for children-revised. New York : The Psychological Corporation.

Williams, M. (1987). Visual search in good and poor readers. Clinical Vision Sciences, 4, 367-371.

Woodcock Reading Mastery Tests, (1973). Minnesota :American Guidance Service, Inc.

SECTION 2

PERCEPTUAL PROCESSES

Human Information Processing: Measures,
Mechanisms, and Models. D. Vickers and P. L. Smith (eds.)
©Elsevier Science Publishers B.V. (North-Holland), 1989

MECHANISMS OF ORIENTATION ILLUSIONS

Peter Wenderoth, Rick van der Zwan and Syren Johnstone

University of Sydney

In a series of recent studies, it has been demonstrated that direct and indirect tilt illusions have different determinants. Variation in the relative spatial positions and spatial frequencies of inducing and test components affects direct but not indirect effects, and a square frame surrounding the entire display eradicates indirect but not direct effects (Wenderoth and Johnstone, 1987; 1988a). In addition, reducing the duration of the illusory display monotonically increases direct effects but indirect illusions appear not to peak at the shortest duration (Wenderoth and Johnstone, 1988b). All of these differences suggest that the direct effect arises early in visual processing, perhaps in V1 visual cortex, but that the indirect effect occurs at a higher level in extrastriate cortex. These data are reviewed briefly and some experiments are reported which were designed to test whether similar differences can be found between direct and indirect tilt aftereffects and between direct and indirect effects induced by two-dimensional stimuli, namely orthogonal crossed gratings (or plaids). The generality of mechanisms underlying one- and two-dimensional illusions and aftereffects is discussed.

1. INTRODUCTION

The research described in this paper aims to show that direct and indirect orientation illusions have different determinants, and that these differences generalise both to one-dimensional tilt aftereffects and to two-dimensional tilt illusions. First, therefore, we present a descriptive framework within which this variety of effects can be understood.

1.1 Definition of terms

A circular, vertical test grating will appear tilted if it is surrounded by another grating or by a pair of orthogonal gratings (a plaid), provided that the inducing grating or plaid is itself tilted at a particular orientation. In the case of a single inducing grating, tilts between 0-50 deg. from

vertical cause the test grating to appear tilted in the opposite direction
while larger inducing tilts reverse the effect. Subjects compensate for
these illusions when setting to apparent vertical, and results obtained in
this way, by Over, Broerse and Crassini (1972), are shown by the solid
symbols in Figure 1. In the case of an inducing plaid which, when
vertical, has one component grating vertical and one horizontal, the
angular function of the tilt illusion is more complex: it resembles the
angular function of the illusion induced by a tilted square outline frame,
which can be regarded as part of a complete plaid pattern. The angular
function of the rod and frame illusion obtained by Beh, Wenderoth and
Purcell (1971) is shown by the open symbols in Figure 1; and the
similarity of the plaid angular function to the rod and frame function was
demonstrated recently by Wenderoth, Johnstone and van der Zwan
(1989).

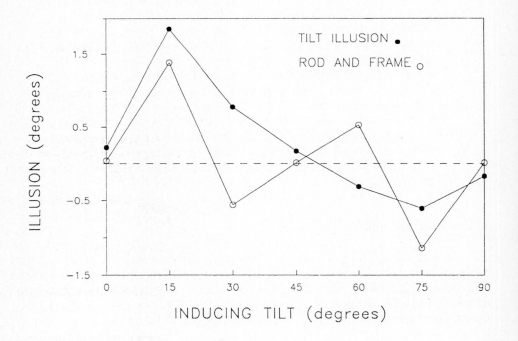

Figure 1. Angular functions of the tilt illusion (filled symbols) and the rod-and-frame
illusion (open symbols). See text for sources.

A descriptive account of the two angular functions in Figure 1 can be given by reference to Figure 2. A single inducing grating, represented by a single bar in Figure 2A, has two axes of mirror symmetry, one aligned with the grating's orientation (dashed line 1) and one orthogonal to it (2). The former may be termed a main line axis and the latter a virtual axis (Howard, 1982). A plaid or square frame, represented by the cross in Figure 2B, has two main line axes (1,2) and two virtual axes (3,4). Assume that a truly vertical test grating appears tilted away from whichever inducing axis of symmetry is closest to vertical. In that event, the solid circle function in Figure 1 occurs because as the grating (Figure 2A) tilts clockwise (CW) from vertical, axis 1 is nearest vertical and the test grating appears tilted CCW. At larger inducing tilts, axis 2 is closer to vertical and so the test grating appears tilted CW. The initial main line axis effects are larger, and persist beyond 45 deg., possibly because actual line axes have stronger effects than virtual line axes (Wenderoth, 1977; Wenderoth et al., 1989). A similar account can be given of the open symbol function in Figure 1 with reference to Figure 2B.

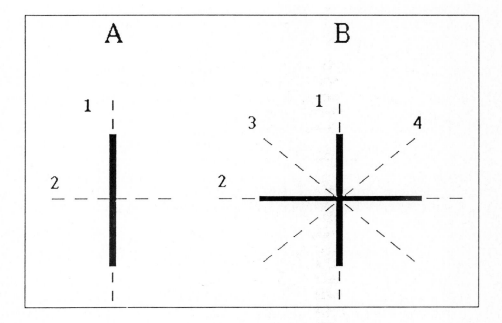

Figure 2. A. Axes of symmetry of a 1D stimulus, one main line (1) and one virtual (2). B. Axes of symmetry of a 2D stimulus, two main line (1,2) and two virtual (3,4).

A version of this descriptive hypothesis was first expounded by Beh et al. (1971) to account for the rod and frame angular function but it clearly applies equally to the simple tilt illusion. Thus, main line effects correspond to what Gibson and Radner (1937) termed direct effects, and virtual axis effects correspond to their indirect effects (Wenderoth et al., 1989). Thus, in Figure 1, direct effects are represented by the positive peak for the 1D illusion (solid symbols) and by the first positive and last negative peak for the 2D illusion (open symbols). Indirect effects are represented by the 1D negative peak and by the two central, and smaller, 2D peaks. Finally, if an observer adapts to a 1D inducing stimulus which is subsequently replaced by a test grating, a tilt aftereffect (TAE) occurs, and this TAE has the same angular function as the 1D tilt illusion (TI) (Figure 1), as shown by Gibson and Radner (1937), Morant and Harris (1965), Muir and Over (1970), and Mitchell and Muir (1976). We are currently studying 2D TAEs, but that work is at a preliminary stage.

1.2 Evidence for different determinants of 1D direct and indirect effects

An influential theory of the TAE and the TI is that of Carpenter and Blakemore (1973), which asserts that the effects are due to lateral inhibitory interactions between populations of orientation-selective neurones in V1 visual cortex. According to this view, a single line or grating in the visual field will maximally excite cells tuned to its orientation, will excite cells tuned to nearby orientations (but less so, depending upon the proximity of their orientation preference), and will inhibit cells tuned to more remote orientations. The single line or grating will be perceived in its correct orientation because this is signalled by the most active cells, which are those tuned to the orientation of the stimulus. If, however, two lines or gratings are simultaneously present, say one vertical and one tilted 10-15 deg., the inhibitory flank set up by each stimulus will subtract from the excitatory peak of the other, causing the net pair of excitatory peaks to shift apart. Since, according to the theory, the perceived orientations depend upon the most active neurones, the stimuli will repel each other perceptually, accounting for repulsion, or direct, TIs.

Direct TAEs are then simply explained by the proposition that, after adaptation, the inhibition is tonic and so affects the test stimulus despite the physical removal of the adapting stimulus. This inhibition theory can be regarded as a contemporary version of Koehler and Wallach's (1944) satiation theory, in which perceived contours were held to induce electrical currents which caused a build up of resistance, with subsequently presented contours being repelled from the resistance sites.

A problem for these theories, old and new, is to explain indirect effects. Inhibition and satiation are repulsion mechanisms and are not able to account easily for remote attraction effects. O'Toole and Wenderoth (1977) suggested a model in which disinhibition could explain indirect effects, but this has not been tested directly. Wenderoth, O'Connor and Johnson (1986) measured TIs using line length variations which, based upon neurophysiological evidence, should have maximised the opportunity for indirect effects to occur, if their mechanism was disinhibition, but indirect effects were not obtained.

There is now convincing evidence that direct and indirect effects have different mechanisms, so that any complete theory of these tilt effects cannot be couched in terms of a single mechanism. This paper first reviews some recently published evidence on TIs, then presents some new data on 1D TIs and TAEs and 2D TIs and finally discusses a theory to explain the effects with suggestions for some future experiments.

1.2.1 Spatial Modulation of Direct and Indirect TIs.

Different kinds of stimulus displays traditionally have been used to study the TI and TAE: a single, short-arm acute angle (e.g. Koehler and Wallach, 1944; Blakemore, Carpenter and Georgeson, 1970; Lennie, 1972; Carpenter and Blakemore, 1973; Virsu and Taskinen, 1975; Wenderoth and Johnson, 1985; Wenderoth et al., 1986); a central, circular test grating surrounded by an annulus inducing grating (e.g. Georgeson, 1973; Tolhurst and Thompson, 1975; Wenderoth and Johnstone, 1988a); an inducing grating with a single test line (e.g. Gibson and Radner, 1937); and relatively long inducing and test lines which intersect at their centres (e.g. Muir and Over, 1970). Indirect effects have not been obtained with the first of these paradigms but occur reliably with the others.

Wenderoth and Johnstone (1988a) used the second display, a central test grating surrounded by an annulus. They noted that direct TIs and closely related Zollner illusions are reduced markedly when inducing and test components do not abut (Wallace, 1969; Virsu and Taskinen, 1975; Tolhurst and Thompson, 1975) or when they differ in spatial frequency (Georgeson, 1973; Ware and Mitchell, 1974). These results were consistent with the view that direct effects arise from V1 lateral inhibition, because V1 neurones frequently are tightly tuned to spatial position and frequency. Thus, introducing gaps or frequency differences between inducing and test stimuli would reduce the overlap between induced and tested neurones, thus reducing the TI or TAE. The question asked by Wenderoth and Johnstone was whether these manipulations would similarly reduce indirect TIs. The basic stimulus display consisted of a 1.5 deg. diameter, 3 cycle/deg test grating surrounded by an inducing grating which filled the remainder of a 9 deg. diameter circular mask placed over a CRT screen. In Experiment 1, the width of the annulus gap between test and inducing stimulus was 0, 0.5 or 1.5 deg. Inducing and test gratings had the same frequency. Whereas increasing gap size caused direct TIs to fall linearly from 2.2 to 1.1 deg., indirect effects were all of the order of -0.7 deg. and were unaffected by gap size. In Experiment 2, both gap size (0 or 1 deg) and inducing spatial frequency (3 or 0.5 cycles/deg) were varied. Direct effects were large (about 2 deg.) only under abutting and same frequency conditions. When the gap or the frequency difference or both occurred, direct effects fell to 0.5-1.0 deg. Indirect effects, averaging -0.43 deg., were not systematically affected by either manipulation. In Experiment 3, the thickness of the now always abutting and 3 cycle/deg inducing annulus was varied. Its thickness was 0.25, 0.5, 1.0 or 3.75 deg. As thickness increased, direct TIs increased markedly at first, then more slowly, showing linear and quadratic trends. The direct TIs for the thinnest and thickest annulus were 0.27 deg. and 1.59 deg., respectively. The corresponding indirect effects, on the other hand, were-0.55 deg. and -0.62 deg., with no significant trend at all.

These results seemed naturally to lead to speculation that whereas direct effects might arise largely in V1, indirect effects could arise later in extrastriate cortex, for the following reasons. A number of authors (e.g. Allman, Miezin and McGuinness, 1985; Maunsell and Newsome, 1987) have drawn attention to the fact that both striate and extrastriate neurones can exhibit not only a classic receptive field (CRF) but also a total receptive field (TRF). The CRF is defined as the retinal area within which the cell's response can be elicited with an appropriate stimulus. The TRF includes much more remote or distal areas which do not influence the cell when they alone are stimulated but which modulate the cell's response to its best stimulus in the CRF. In addition to the TRF, which could be due to feedback from higher extrastriate cells on to lower cells, it has also been reported that extrastriate cells often show little spatial selectivity. Thus, Peterhans and von der Heydt (1987, p.P4) reported that "activity in V2 is more related to object concepts and less to local stimulus features such as luminance and connectedness", and Desimone, Moran, Schein and Ungerleider (1985) suggested that cells in V4 and inferotemporal cortex (IT) might be concerned with global processing and constancy: they noted that "the sensitivity of most IT neurones to shape appears to be based on a global property of the shape rather than on the size or location of local contours."(p.449). Since indirect TIs seemed unaffected by gaps or annulus thickness, an extrastriate locus where global processing is the rule seemed possible.

Finally, we recalled that Gibson and Radner (1937) obtained their direct and indirect TAEs with no vertical or horizontal reference lines visible. Koehler and Wallach (1944) claimed that indirect effects, but not direct effects, disappeared when truly vertical or horizontal edges were present. Could this reflect broad spatial influences of the kind reported with TRFs or extrastriate receptive fields? To establish whether the same phenomenon occurred with the TI, Wenderoth and Johnstone (1988a) surrounded the 1.5 deg. diameter test grating with a 1 deg. thick inducing annulus. This whole display could be centrally embedded in a light vertical, or near vertical square, 4.5 deg. on a side, on a darker background. The presence of the square had no effect at all on direct effects; but it eradicated, or markedly reduced indirect effects, from -0.79 to -0.20 deg., a reduction of 75%.

Wenderoth and Johnstone concluded that direct and indirect TIs have different determinants and speculated regarding an extrastriate locus of the indirect effect. In addition, since gaps, frequency differences and annulus thickness all reduced but did not eliminate direct effects, it was suggested that a small proportion of the direct effect might also arise at a higher level.

1.2.2 Temporal Modulation of Direct and Indirect TIs.

Wolfe (1984) reported that direct TAEs increased dramatically in magnitude when test stimuli were very short flashes. Similar results were found with the direct TI by Calvert and Harris (1988) who simultaneously reduced both the test and inducing duration. In a series of experiments, using flash durations between 25 msec and 1600 msec, Wenderoth and Johnstone (1988b) found that both direct and indirect TIs were larger at short durations. However, while the direct TI seemed to decrease monotonically with duration, the trend was less clear for the indirect TI, with some suggestion of a decrease at the shorter durations. Wenderoth and Johnstone (1988b) took this to be consistent with an extrastriate locus for the indirect effect, with the longer latency of the maximum reflecting later extrastriate processing. Wenderoth and Johnstone also tested the effect of introducing the surrounding frame and found that at all four flash durations used (25, 100, 400 and 1600 msec), the direct effect was unaffected but the indirect effect reduced by 0.67. Again, these data suggested smaller indirect effects at the shortest (25 msec) duration.

With this background, we present seven experiments. These were designed to test: whether 1D direct TIs continue to increase monotonically down to flash durations as short as 10 msec and whether indirect effects decline (Experiments 1 and 2); whether 1D TAEs tested under identical conditions are similar in trend and magnitude (Experiments 3 and 4); whether a surrounding frame selectively eradicates indirect but not direct TAEs, as it does with the TI; and, finally, whether spatial position and spatial frequency differences selectively affect 2D direct but not indirect TIs, as is the case with the 1D TI.

2. EXPERIMENTS 1 AND 2

Experiments 1 and 2 were designed to measure direct and indirect TIs at durations shorter than the minimum 25 msec used in previous experiments. The aim was to attempt to establish whether direct TIs continued to increase at shorter durations; and whether indirect TIs did indeed become smaller again at the shortest durations.

2.1 Apparatus

Stimulus displays were presented on the flat screen of a Tektronix 608 display monitor (P31 phosphor) interfaced with an Innisfree ("Picasso") Image Generator and a PDP-11/23 minicomputer. Subjects used the outer pair of three microswitches to indicate whether the test grating appeared tilted left or right of vertical. The display was viewed in a dark, windowless cubicle adjacent to the experimenter's room. The latter contained all of the stimulus generating equipment, a slave Tektronix 608 display to allow monitoring of the subject's display, and an intercom to allow two-way communication with the subject. The subject's head rested in a padded chin- and forehead rest which also had padded temple screws, and which was situated 57 cm from the display such that 1 cm on the screen subtended 1 deg. of visual angle. All external cues to vertical were removed by draping the area between the headrest and the screen with black cloth to form a rough viewing tunnel; and a matt black aluminium mask mounted on the face of the display restricted the visible screen area to a 6.75 deg. circular area.

The image generator was modified so that it could be controlled by the minicomputer via a custom designed interface which allowed up to three screens to be interleaved at a rate of 188 Hz. A specially written program allowed these separate screens to be constructed by a software-controlled menu.

2.2 Stimuli

The 0.6 deg. circular test grating had a spatial frequency of 5 cycles/ deg., and, when presented alone, was centered on a background luminance of 2.8 cd/m2. The light and dark sinusoidal bars had luminances of 10.4 cd/m2 and 2.1 cd/m2 respectively, measured on a low frequency grating by sweeping across the grating with a Tektronix J16 1 deg. digital luminance probe. Michelson contrast, defined as
[(L max - L min) / (L max + L min)], was 0.67. The inducing grating was confined to a 1 deg. thick annulus, outside diameter 2.6 deg, which was interleaved with the test grating on test trials to produce the percept of a single, non-flickering compound display. The inducing annulus also had a spatial frequency of 5 cycles/deg and a contrast of 0.67. Between trials,

the entire screen was blanked at 6.8 cd/m2 which sufficed to eradicate afterimages.

For both direct and indirect TIs, there were 6 exposure durations of the combined test and inducing fields (test conditions) and each of these was paired with a similar exposure duration of the test grating alone (pretest conditions). The durations chosen were a linear series: 10, 20, 30, 40, 50 and 60 msec. The actual durations were slightly larger than these because they were achieved by presenting a sequence of screen images where, at an interleaving rate of 188 Hz, each image had a duration of 5.32 msec. We arbitrary selected the longer option. Thus, frame multiples of 2, 4, 6, 8, 10 and 12 gave exposure durations of 10.6, 21.2, 31.9, 42.6, 53.2 and 63.8 msec.

2.3 Procedure

Each subject was run under either the direct or the indirect TI conditions, using single staircases which were grouped and randomly interleaved. Thus, there were three blocks of trials: Block 1 contained staircases for the pretests and tests for the 10 and 20 msec flashes; Block 2 for the 30 and 40 msec flashes, and Block 3 for the 50 and 60 msec flashes. For each subject, however, the ordering of Blocks 1-3 was random; and within each block the four staircases (2 test, 2 pretest) were randomly interleaved. There was a short, approximately 2 minute, rest between blocks, and the entire session lasted about one hour. For direct effects and indirect effects, the inducing gratings were always tilted 15 and 75 deg., respectively, clockwise of vertical. All points of subjective vertical (PSV) to the left of true vertical were signed negative and those to the right were signed positive, so that direct and indirect effects (test minus pretest) were signed positive and negative, respectively.

The starting position for any staircase was randomly chosen but was confined to ± 10 deg. from vertical. Step size initially was 2.12 deg. Each staircase was run for 10 reversals and after the first two, step size was reduced to 1.06 deg. The PSV was estimated by averaging the peaks and valleys of the last 6 reversals. Subjects were instructed to make an accurate judgement and to respond only after stimulus offset, by pressing one of the outer switches to indicate whether the test grating had appeared tilted left or right of vertical. A small, light fixation dot appeared 1 sec prior to stimulus onset both to warn the subject of the impending flash and to maintain central fixation. After each response, there was a 500 msec interval before the next fixation point onset.

2.4 Subjects

Subjects were volunteers from an Introductory Psychology course and received nominal course credit for participation. There were 15 subjects in Experiment 1 (direct effects) and 23 in Experiment 2 (indirect effects).

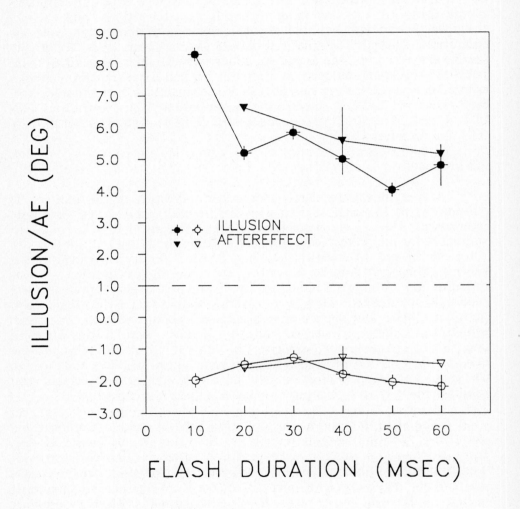

Figure 3. Direct (Experiment 1) and indirect TIs (Experiment 2) as a function of stimulus duration (combined circle and square symbols). Direct (Experiment 3) and indirect TAEs (experiment 4) as a function of test flash duration (inverted triangles).

2.5 Results

The mean illusions are shown by the combined cross and circle symbols in Figure 3, solid symbols for direct and open symbols for indirect effects. The direct TI at the 10 msec duration was 8.33 deg., consistent with Wolfe's (1984) TAE result in which 4/5 of his subjects obtained TAEs greater than 5 deg. at that duration, effects too large to be measurable with his technique.

A treatments by subjects analysis of variance with planned orthogonal contrasts (Winer, 1962, Ch.4) showed that direct TIs decreased with exposure duration both linearly, with $F(1, 70)=104.2$, $p<0.0005$, and quadratically, $F=30.69$, $p<0.0005$. Together, these trends accounted for 81% of the treatments sum of squares. For indirect TIs, on the other hand, neither linear nor quadratic trend was significant, with $F(1, 110)=1.19$ and 2.49, respectively, $p>0.05$ in both cases. Nevertheless, the mean indirect TI over all exposures was -1.80 deg., much larger than those usually obtained in experiments using long duration stimuli. It is interesting to note that although indirect TI trends were nonsignificant, there appeared to be a slight dip in magnitude around 20-30 msec, as noted in previous data. Before discussing these data further, let us consider Experiments 3 and 4 which deal with TAEs with short test durations.

3. EXPERIMENTS 3 AND 4

Prior to conducting Experiment 3 (direct TAE) and Experiment 4 (indirect TAE), pilot studies were conducted to ascertain task difficulty. Initially, we used the same display as Experiments 1 and 2, except that the inducing stimulus was a complete 4.5 deg. diameter circular grating rather than an annulus. One of us (PW) adapted for 2 min. to a +15 deg. grating which was followed immediately by a short test flash. This in turn was followed by a 6 sec adapting "top-up", another test flash, another "top up", and so on. Under these conditions, it proved impossible to see, let alone judge, the test flash. Accordingly, the task was made easier in three ways. First, adapting stimuli and test flashes were always separated by a 500 msec blank interval, as used by Wolfe (1984), although we used a light (6.8 cd/m2) rather than a dark interval. Second, the diameter of the test stimulus was increased from 0.6 to 1.0 deg.. Third, relatively long test flashes, 20-60 msec, were used. We, and volunteer subjects, were then able to do the task.

3.1 Procedure

Subjects first adapted for 2 min to either a +15 deg. (Experiment 3) or a +75 deg. (Experiment 4) tilted grating, and were instructed to move their eyes roughly circularly around the grating to avoid build-up of afterimages. However, to ensure ease of judgement, a small fixation dot was present at the centre of the inducing grating, and, 10 sec before adaptation offset, subjects were instructed to fixate it in readiness for the test flash. Test flashes were replaced with 6 sec top-up adaptation stimuli during which central fixation was constant. Three test flash durations were used: 21.2, 42.6 and 63.8 msec. Each of these adapting conditions was preceded by a pretest session in which only test flashes were presented, separated by 10 sec fixation. In both test and pretest conditions, single staircases began randomly + or - 10 deg. from vertical and continued for 10 reversals, the last 6 of which were used to estimate the PSV. Between the three sets of adaptation sessions, subjects remained in the dark for 5 min, to allow dissipation of TAEs prior to the next condition.

3.2 Subjects

Subjects were from the same population as in previous experiments. Because it was clear at once that direct effects were large and comparable to those obtained with flashed TIs, only 5 subjects were run in Experiment 3. Fifteen subjects completed Experiment 4.

3.3 Results

The results, shown by the inverted triangles in Figure 3, indicate that the TAE data clearly were comparable to those of the TI. Analysis of the direct effect data, as previously, showed that the linear trend was significant, with $F(1,8)=5.46$, $p<0.05$, accounting for 94% of the treatments sum of squares. In the case of indirect effects, neither the linear nor the quadratic trend was significant, with $F(1,28) = 0.1$ and 0.5, respectively, $p>0.05$.

3.4 Discussion

Experiments 1 and 2 showed that, even at the very shortest durations, direct TIs continue to increase, whereas indirect TIs, although they are large at shorter durations, show no consistent trend. Second, Experiments 3 and 4 showed that short duration TAEs have magnitudes comparable to TIs, with direct TIs also showing an increase at shorter durations, while indirect TAEs exhibit no consistent trend. To emphasise both the similarity of short duration TIs and TAEs, and to show consistency with previous data, the results of Experiments 1-4 have been superimposed on those of Wenderoth and Johnstone (1988b) to produce Figure 4. Further work is needed to clarify the precise nature of the function relating the indirect effect magnitude to exposure duration.

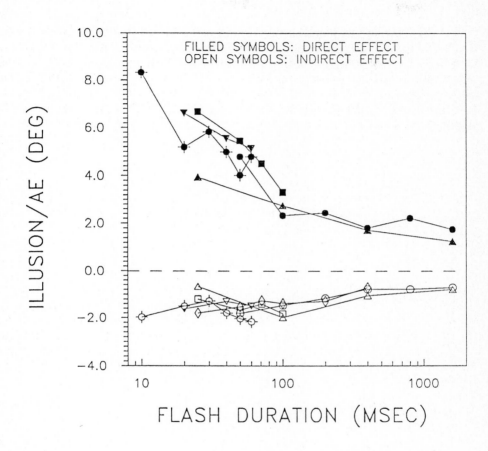

Figure 4. Data from Experiments 1-4 superimposed on those of Wenderoth and Johnstone (1988b). Symbols for Experiments 1-4 data are common to those in Figure 3.

4. EXPERIMENTS 5 AND 6

The fact that TAEs similar to TIs occur at short durations allows a further question to be addressed. First, since a surrounding square frame reduces indirect but not direct TIs, is the same true of TAEs, as would be expected if TIs and TAEs share common mechanisms? Second, does the frame, if it has this effect, influence the TAE at input (during adaptation) or output (during test)? Experiments 5 (direct TAE) and 6 (indirect TAE) were designed to address these questions.

4.1 Procedure

All procedures and stimuli were identical to those in Experiments 3-4 with the following exceptions. First, test flash duration was always 63.8 msec. Second, in some conditions, a square luminance frame surrounded either the adapting stimulus or the test stimulus. This frame was a square, 5 cm on a side, internal luminance 3.0 cd/m2 on a background 1.3 cd/m2. Each subject completed four conditions: square in adapt only; square in test only; square in both; and square in neither.

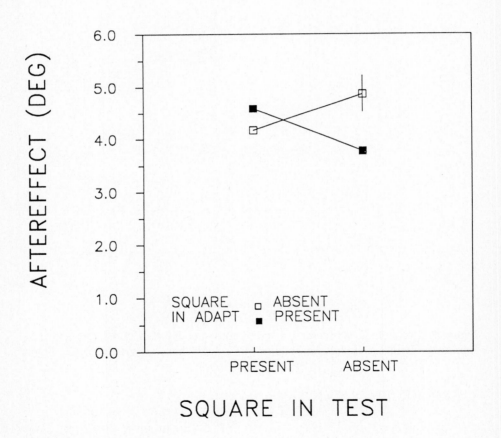

Figure 5. Direct TAE as a function of the presence or absence of surround frame in adapt and test conditions, Experiment 5.

4.2 Subjects

Subjects were drawn from the same population as previously, with 21 in Experiment 5 and 29 in Experiment 6.

4.3 Results

The mean TAEs are shown in Figures 5 (direct TAEs) and 6 (indirect TAEs).

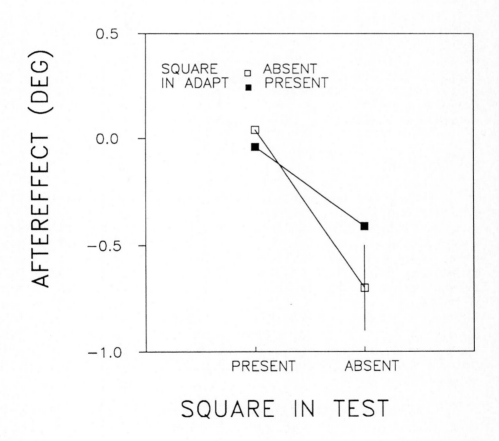

Figure 6. Indirect TAE as a function of the presence or absence of surround frame in adapt and test conditions, Experiment 6.

Planned contrasts analyses, as previously described, were used to test the main effects of the presence or absence of the frame during adaptation, its presence or absence during the test and the interaction. Degrees of freedom for all contrasts were F(1,60). For direct effects, neither main effect was significant, with F=0.99 and 0.02, respectively, p>0.05. The interaction was significant, F=5.05 and p<0.05. However, all four mean TAEs were clearly large and significant: there was no suggestion that the frame reduced TAEs in the manner previously found for indirect TIs. In the case of indirect TAEs, on the other hand, the main effect of the presence or absence of the frame during adaptation was not significant, F(1,84)=0.28 and p>0.05, but the main effect during test was significant, F=7.47 and p<0.01. The interaction was not significant, with F=0.79 and p>0.05. When the square was absent in the test, the overall mean TAE was -0.55 deg. When it was present in the test, the TAE reduced to zero. Because there appeared to be some suggestion of an effect of the square in the adaptation condition only, we wondered whether the short fixation of the adapting stimulus may have resulted in the carryover of an afterimage of the frame to the test. Experiments to test this idea are in progress, but it is clear from the data that the overwhelming effect of the frame is in the test condition.

5. EXPERIMENT 7

This experiment is the first of a planned series designed to test whether the differential effects of spatial and temporal variables on 1D direct and indirect effects applies equally to 2D illusions and aftereffects. Two inducing plaid orientations were used: one in which a main-line axis of symmetry was 15 deg. from vertical (direct effect) and one in which a virtual axis was 15 deg. from vertical (indirect effect). Thus, the orientations of the component gratings were 15 deg. CW and 75 deg. CCW for the direct effect; and 60 deg. CW and 30 deg. CCW for the indirect effect. Note that in both of these cases the axis nearest vertical is 15 deg. CW, so that in this experiment both direct and indirect effects were expected to be positive, using the convention that CW settings are positive and the illusion is defined as test minus pretest measure of subjective vertical.

There were eight conditions in the experiment: 2 levels of spatial separation between the test grating and surrounding plaid (abutting and 2 deg. annulus gap); by 2 levels of spatial frequency (same: test grating 5 cycles/degree, inducing components each 5 cycles/degree); by 2 plaid orientations (direct, indirect). If the 2D TI behaved as the 1D TI (Wenderoth and Johnstone, 1988a) then the prediction was that gaps and spatial frequency differences would reduce direct but not indirect effects.

5.1 Apparatus and stimuli

All aspects of apparatus were as in previous experiments. Sinusoidal plaid inducing annuli were produced by interleaving, or alternating between, the orthogonal gratings at a rate of 188 Hz (5.3 msec per frame) so that the subject perceived a non-flickering plaid. The dimensions of the stimulus displays in the abutting conditions were as in Experiments 1 and 2. In the gap conditions, the 0.6 deg. diameter test grating was surrounded by a 2 deg. thick blank annulus (inside diameter 0.6 deg., outside diameter 4.6 deg.) which in turn was surrounded by a 1 deg. thick plaid annulus (outside diameter 6.6 deg.). Luminances and contrasts were as in previous experiments, except that plaid contrast increased from 0.67 to 0.75 at the points of grating superposition.

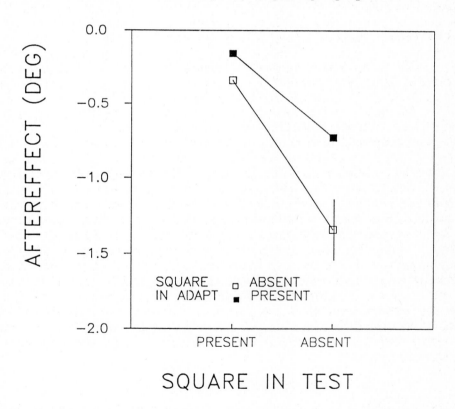

Figure 7. 2D direct effects, Experiment 7, as a function of same (5 cycles/ deg.) or different (5, 2.5 cycles/ deg.)test and inducing spatial frequency. Filled symbols: test and inducing stimuli abut. Open symbols: 2 degree gap. Error bar shows – 1 standard error.

5.2 Procedure

The method of adjustment was used and each subject was tested under all 8 conditions. In each condition, two pretest settings to judged vertical were followed by four test settings and the test minus pretest means defined the illusion. In every case, the starting position was random within ± 10 deg. of vertical. The central test grating was rotated CCW or CW by the left and right microswitches, at a speed of 5.9 deg. /sec in apparently smooth 1/3 deg. steps.

5.3 Subjects

There were 24 subjects, drawn from the same subject pool as before.

5.4 Results

The mean obtained illusions are shown in Figure 7 (direct effects) and Figure 8 (indirect effects).

All means were positive as expected. A subjects by treatments analysis of variance with planned orthogonal contrasts was carried out. For every contrast, the degrees of freedom were (1,161). In the case of direct effects in the abutting condition, the illusion was larger in the same frequency condition (+3.04 deg.) than in the different frequency condition (+1.85 deg.), with F=10.44, p<0.005. With gaps, the means in the respective frequency conditions (+1.37 deg. and +1.4 deg.) were not significantly different, with F=0.006, p>0.05. Overall, the abutting mean (+2.45 deg.) exceeded the gap mean (+1.39 deg.), F=16.59 and p<0.0005. None of these contrasts was significant for the indirect effect, but this may have been a type II error: the overall mean gap illusion (+0.58 deg.) appeared larger than the abut effect (+0.12 deg.) with F=3.11 and p<0.10; and tests of single means showed that one mean, that in the gap/different frequency condition (+0.74), was different from zero, with t(23)=2.85 and p<0.01. It should be noted that Johnstone and Wenderoth (1989) recently reported that 2D indirect TIs only occurred in gap and not in abut conditions.

5.5 DISCUSSION

The data in Figures 7 and 8 closely resemble those obtained by Wenderoth and Johnstone (1988a) with the 1D illusion: all of the tests of direct effects described above parallel their results. With the indirect 1D effect, Wenderoth and Johnstone found no consistent effect of spatial frequency differences or gaps on the illusion. Here, with 2D indirect effects, we find a suggestion of larger effects in the gap conditions, and the largest effect in the gap/different frequency condition. These trends need further testing to establish if they are robust.

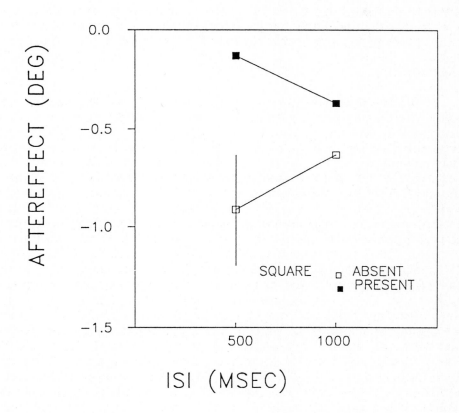

Figure 8. Indirect effects, Experiment 7. Conventions as for Figure 7.

6. GENERAL DISCUSSION

The primary aim of the research presented here was to test the generality of Wenderoth and Johnstone's (1988a; 1988b) findings with the 1D TI that gaps between inducing and test stimuli reduce direct but not indirect effects; that spatial differences have similar effects; and that reducing test flash duration monotonically increases direct but not indirect effects. Experiments 1-4 showed that direct and indirect 1D TIs and TAEs were comparable in magnitude at short test flash durations and that the TAE, like the TI, exhibits a monotonically increasing direct effect but not a monotonically increasing indirect effect, as duration decreases. Experiments 5 and 6 demonstrated that a square frame surrounding the entire display markedly reduces indirect but not direct TAEs, as Wenderoth and Johnstone (1988a;b) found with the TI. These experiments also indicated that the major effect of the frame is on the test stimulus, not the adapting stimulus. Finally, Experiment 7 has shown that gaps and spatial frequency differences have very similar effects on 2D direct and indirect TIs to those on 1D TIs.

We have argued previously that the indirect effect arises at a higher level in the visual system than the direct effect because it is less dependent upon spatial similarities between the inducing and test components of the display, as are single cell responses in some cortical areas beyond V1, and because it appears not to peak at the shortest flash duration. The data of Experiments 1-4 do not appear to show that indirect TIs and TAEs decrease at the shortest duration, but they do show that there is no monotonic increase. It might be, as Wenderoth and Johnstone (1988b) suggested, that indirect effects arise from more sustained rather than transient mechanisms and thus show less temporal modifiability.

Turning now to the effect of the surrounding square frame, the data of Experiments 5 and 6 show that the frame selectively reduces indirect, not direct, TAEs just as it does in the case of the TI. The experiments also suggest strongly that the frame has its effect in the test, not during adaptation, so that it has a response effect rather than modifying the nature of neural adaptation at input. The fact that the remote frame contributes to the judgement of the test grating in the case of the indirect but not the direct effect may reflect the more global nature of receptive field mechanisms involved in the indirect effect. That the indirect effect may relate more to judgemental biases than to neural modification during adaptation is perhaps consistent with the view of Wenderoth and Johnstone (1988a) who attempted to relate indirect TIs to Allman et al.'s (1985) suggestion that TRFs may provide the basis for perceptual constancies. Thus, Wenderoth and Johnstone (1988a, p.310) speculated that

> ....the indirect effect could be seen as arising from such global mechanisms involved in orientation constancy. Under normal circumstances, a rich collection of cues to vertical and horizontal ... is available in the visual field so that orientation coding errors are minimised. However, under impoverished conditions in the laboratory, when the inducing stimulus is the sole reference orientation, errors occur. This could explain why the surrounding frame ... removed

indirect effects by providing the global orientation mechanisms with additional orientation data.

The fact that the frame in Experiment 6 had its effect mainly in the test phase rather than the adapting phase can be regarded as consistent with the constancy mechanism. On the other hand, the fact that the direct TAE persists despite the presence of the frame in the test, suggests that the direct effect produces more local neural modification. When Koehler and Wallach (1944) first observed that indirect TAEs failed to occur when truly vertical edges were visible they concluded : "In view of this difference between 'direct' and 'indirect' effects we hesitate to believe that the latter phenomenon is a figural after-effect in the sense in which we are using this term" (pp.311-312). Our previous experiments had suggested different mechanisms for the direct and indirect TI. The experiments reported here reinforce that view, show that the same conclusion can be drawn regarding the direct and indirect TAE, but also reinforce Koehler and Wallach's claim that the indirect TAE (and presumably the TI) is not attributable to the same kind of local neural adaptation or inhibition as the direct TAE because the latter effect cannot be overridden by remote cues to orientation presented in the test.

The fact that in Experiment 7, gaps and frequency differences seemed to affect 2D direct and indirect TIs in a manner very similar to their effects on 1D illusions suggests a range of additional experiments. We are presently investigating direct and indirect effects induced by briefly flashed plaids, using spatial parameters similar to those in Experiment 7. One reason for this is to examine the relative contributions of real and virtual axes of symmetry as a function of flash duration; another is to attempt to replicate the finding in Experiment 7 that 2D indirect TIs were largest with gaps and frequency difference.

Finally, Morant and Harris (1965) attempted to explain the asymmetry of the TAE angular function (larger direct than indirect effects; zero crossing beyond 45 deg.) by the sum of two processes: a pure "satiation" or direct repulsion effect, which peaks at 15 deg. inducing tilt, and falls eventually to zero at 90 deg.; and a Gibson and Radner (1937) "normalisation" process, in which small but equal direct and indirect effects occur with zero effect at 45 deg. inducing tilt. We have noted (Wenderoth and Johnstone, 1987,1988a) that gaps between test and inducing stimuli reduce direct TIs to the magnitude of indirect TIs. Consequently, we have reformulated Morant and Harris' proposal (Wenderoth and Johnstone, 1987) by suggesting that the TAE and TI angular functions are composed of purely repulsion V1 lateral inhibitory effects and smaller but equal direct and indirect extrastriate global constancy effects. To test this, we intend to measure the TI and TAE angular functions with gaps between test and inducing stimuli, predicting a function with symmetrical direct and indirect effects with a 45 deg. zero crossing. It can then be asked additionally whether a surrounding frame will reduce these more global components, both indirect and direct, a result which would be consistent with the reformulated Morant and Harris theory.

ACKNOWLEDGEMENTS.

This research was supported by the Australian Research Grants Scheme, Grant #A78515620 and Australian Research Council Grant #A78831871, to the first author. Invaluable assistance with all aspects of computing facilities was provided by Senior Systems Analyst Mr. John Holden.

CORRESPONDENCE

Correspondence should be addressed to Peter Wenderoth, Department of Psychology, University of Sydney, Australia. 2006

REFERENCES

Allman, J.M., Miezin, F., McGuinness, E. (1985a). Stimulus specific responses from beyond the classical receptive field: Neurophysiological mechanisms for local-global comparisons in visual neurons. Annual Review of Neuroscience, 8, 407-430.

Beh, H., Wenderoth, P. & Purcell, T. (1971). The angular function of a rod-and-frame illusion. Perception & Psychophysics, 9, 353-355.

Blakemore, C., Carpenter, R.H.S., Georgeson, M.A. (1970). Lateral inhibition between orientation detectors in the human visual system. Nature (London), 228, 37-39.

Calvert, J.E. & Harris, J.P. (1988). Spatial frequency and duration effects on the tilt illusion and orientation acuity. Vision Research, in press.

Carpenter, R.H.S. & Blakemore, C. (1973). Interactions between orientations in human vision. Experimental Brain Research, 18, 287-303.

Desimone, R., Schein, S.J., Moran, J. & Ungerleider, L.G. (1985). Contour, colour and shape analysis beyond the striate cortex. Vision Research, 25, 441-452.

Georgeson, M.A. (1973). Spatial frequency selectivity of a visual tilt illusion. Nature (London), 245, 43-45.

Gibson, J.J. & Radner, M. (1937) Adaptation, after effect and contrast in the perception of tilted lines: I. Quantitative Studies. Journal of Experimental Psychology, 20, 453-467.

Johnstone, S & Wenderoth, P. (1989) Spatial and orientation specific integration in the tilt illusion. Perception, in press

Koehler, W. & Wallach, H. (1944). Figural-aftereffects: An investigation of visual processes. Proceedings of the American Philosophical Society, 88, 269-357.

Lennie, P. (1972). Mechanisms underlying the perception of orientation. Unpublished Doctoral Dissertation, University of Cambridge.

Magnussen, S. & Kurtenbach, W. (1980). Linear summation of tilt illusion and tilt aftereffect. Vision Research, 20, 39-42.

Maunsell, J.H.R. & Newsome, W.T. (1987). Visual processing in monkey extrastriate cortex. Annual Review of Neuroscience, 10, 363-402.

Mitchell, D.E. & Muir, D.W. (1976). Does the tilt aftereffect occur in the oblique meridian? Vision Research, 16, 609-613.

Morant, R.B. & Harris, J.R. (1965). Two different aftereffects of exposure to visual tilts. American Journal of Psychology, 78, 218-226.

Muir, D. & Over, R. (1970). Tilt aftereffects in central and peripheral vision. Journal of Experimental Psychology, 85, 165-170.

O'Toole, B.I. & Wenderoth, P. (1977). The tilt illusion: Repulsion and attraction effects in the oblique meridian. Vision Research, 17, 367-374.

Over, R., Broerse, J. & Crassini, B. (1972). Orientation illusion and masking in central and peripheral vision. Journal of Experimental Psychology, 96, 25-31.

Peterhans, E. & Heydt R. von der (1987). The whole and the pieces - cortical neuron responses to bars and rows of moving dots. in Seeing Contour and Colour Proceedings of Satellite symposium of 2nd World Congress of Neuroscience, Manchester, UK, August 1987.

Tolhurst, D.J. & Thompson, P.G. (1975). Orientation illusions and aftereffects: inhibition between channels. Vision Research, 15, 967-972.

Virsu, V. & Taskinen, H. (1975). Central inhibitory interactions in human vision. Experimental Brain Research, 23, 65-74.

Wallace, G.K. (1969). The critical distance of interaction in the Zollner illusion. Perception & Psychophysics, 5, 261-264.

Ware, C. & Mitchell, D.E. (1974). The spatial selectivity of the tilt aftereffect. Vision Research, 14, 735-737.

Wenderoth, P. (1977) An analysis of the rod-and-frame illusion and its variants. In Day, R.H. & Stanley, G. S. (Eds.) Studies in Perception, (pp.95-141). Perth: University of Western Australia

Wenderoth, P. & Johnstone, S. (1987). Possible neural substrates for orientation analysis and perception. Perception, 16, 693-709.

Wenderoth, P. & Johnstone, S. (1988a). The different mechanisms of the direct and indirect tilt illusions. Vision Research, 28, 301-312.

Wenderoth, P. & Johnstone, S. (1988b). The differential effects of brief exposures and surrounding contours on direct and indirect tilt illusions. Perception, 17, 165-176

Wenderoth, P., Johnstone, S. & van der Zwan, R. (1989) Two dimensional tilt illusions induced by orthogonal plaid patterns: Effects of plaid motion, orientation, spatial separation and spatial frequency. Perception, in press

Wenderoth, P., O'Connor, T. & Johnson, M. (1986). The tilt illusion as a function of the relative and absolute lengths of test and inducing lines. Perception & Psychophysics, 39, 339-345.

Wolfe, J.M. (1984). Short test flashes produce large tilt aftereffects. Vision Research, 24, 1959-1964.

Human Information Processing: Measures,
Mechanisms, and Models, D. Vickers and P. L. Smith (eds.)
© *Elsevier Science Publishers B. V. (North-Holland), 1989*

NATURAL AND ARTIFICIAL CUES, PERCEPTUAL COMPROMISE AND THE BASIS OF VERIDICAL AND ILLUSORY PERCEPTION

R. H. Day

Monash University

A general theory of perception based on the resolution of stimulus ambiguity by natural and contrived references is proposed. The argument begins with an assumption and an observation. The assumption is that perception has evolved in the interest of accurately representing external states of affairs to the mobile observer. The observation is that due to movement and postural changes the pattern of stimulation at the receptors - the proximal stimulus - is equally representative of two or more states of affairs. The central thesis is that natural perceptual references are involved in resolving ambiguous stimulus patterns to a close representation of the actual state of affairs. Natural references are present in the environment and in the signalled motion and posture of the observer. Thus, for example, perceived distance serves to resolve the ambiguous retinal stimulus for size. Similarly, perceived head orientation serves to resolve the ambiguous binaural stimulus for auditory - source location. Spatial "norms" can be regarded as special instances of natural references. Experimental manipulation of references can give rise to three broad classes of non-veridical (illusory) perception. If references are changed from their natural to an artificial form, then resolution of object properties change accordingly. If they are removed, then perceptual instability occurs, and if two or more are present and in conflict, then the resolution is a compromise between them.

1. INTRODUCTION

This paper is concerned primarily with the basis of human perception and what makes it work in the right way and in the wrong way. However, it is not concerned with the machinery of perception i.e., with the neural structures and processes by means of which the properties of objects, situations and events are encoded, transmitted, held in store, and realized as conscious representations. Rather, the aim is to propose a general theoretical scheme - a conceptual framework - in terms of which to explain normal veridical perception and those distortions of perception called illusions which have intrigued us for so long. The theory, as it will be referred to, while not about neural structures and processes, will, bear on what they do and, therefore, point to what the neurophysiologists could usefully start looking for.

Before turning to the task of setting out the general theory itself it is necessary to make clear what is meant by the terms perception and theory, to comment briefly on the sorts of facts on which the argument is based, to make a point about perception as a biological process, and most of all, to acknowledge a debt to earlier labourers in the vineyards of perceptual theorizing.

By perception is meant the representation in consciousness of states of the self and of external states. States of the individual include postures, actions, and internal processes. External states include objects, events, scenes, and extended spaces. By veridical perception is meant an exact or a close accord between the physical and the represented state of affairs, and by illusory perception a discrepancy between them. It is to be stressed that although what is proposed bears mainly on external situations, it is intended that the argument apply equally to states of the self - an aspect of human perception which is usually given scant attention.

What is intended by the term theory? This question has been clearly stated by O'Neil (1969) in his *Fact and Theory: An Aspect of the Philosophy of Science*. O'Neil makes the point that:

> *the only scientific point of theories is the service they perform in respect of facts - rounding the available facts out into a coherent picture, suggesting a pattern or order amongst them or explaining them or anticipating and so providing leads to the observation of further facts.(p. 179).*

In O'Neil's terms, what is being attempted is a rounding out of a large number of seemingly diverse facts into a coherent picture so as to reveal a pattern amongst them.

The facts to be considered come mainly from experiments that have been undertaken by the author and his collaborators on illusory effects. It is worth noting that to start the argument with illusory perception and grope from there toward the basis of veridical perception is contrary to a view once expressed by Gibson (1959). He said of his own attempt to account for the facts:

The theory to be presented is concerned in the first place with veridical perception and only in the second place with illusions and errors. It presupposes that if a satisfactory explanation of the former can be given, an explanation of the latter will be easy. (p. 459)

While not dissenting here from that view, it can be suggested that the opposite standpoint is equally sustainable - that if a satisfactory explanation can be found for perceptual illusions an explanation of veridical perception will follow.

The third introductory point concerns the biological perspective in formulating a general theory of perception. It can be assumed that the function of a perceptual system, including the conscious representations to which it gives rise, is, along with other biological systems, primarily the adaptation and survival of the individual in a physical and social environment. While this point may seem glaringly obvious and so hardly worthy of comment, it is seldom adverted to. It is contended that it is one of the keys to a complete understanding of the nature of human perception. We perceive primarily to adapt and survive in our ecological niche.

The last point is an acknowledgement. No theory stands by itself; a good deal of what is argued here derives from the views of Gibson (1959,1962), not a little from those of Koffka (1935), some from Helson (1964), and some from Brunswick (see Hammond, 1966). What these four pioneers in the business of conceptualizing human perception had to say was far from wrong. It can be argued, however, that their views were limited. What is proposed here represents an attempt to remove the limitations of these earlier attempts in order to achieve a more general synthesis.

The general theory to be proposed can be described as cue-based. Its central theme is that we (and presumably other species) perceptually access objects, situations and events associated with the external environment and self-induced activity by way of cues. Cues are defined as spatio-temporal patterns of energy generated at the sensory receptors, by features and events in the external world, and by self-induced activities. Thus, for example, an approaching vehicle will give rise to a spatio-temporal pattern at the visual and auditory receptors, as will adopting a new posture produce a spatio-temporal energy pattern at the tactile, kinesthetic and vestibular receptors. These patterns of energy are almost always spread over time as well as over space, since our own activities move them about at the receptor surfaces.

It will be argued, by reference to recent experiments by the author and his collaborators on perceptual illusions, that situations and events associated with the world and the self can be correlated with one cue or many, that cues can be *contrived* in the absence of the state of affairs that normally gives rise to them, and that, when cues for a particular state of affairs are in conflict, a process which will be called perceptual compromise occurs. It is to be noted that the idea of perceptual compromise is central to the argument. It is regarded as a primary basis of both normal veridical perception and of illusory perception.

This cue-based argument about the nature of perception accords well with developmental and cross-cultural data. It also offers a solution to some perceptual enigmas of long standing, such as the moon illusion. It also matches up with neurophysiological data on the early processing of stimulus features such as movement, orientation, and colour.

1.1 Single and Multiple Cues

A few years ago we began a series of experiments on illusory contours - the appearance of edges where none occur in physical terms (see Day, 1986, 1987). We originally thought that the effect is due to the induction of various types of contrast that "fill up" regions defined by partially delineated borders. We argued that one form of contrast enhances physical luminance and another reduces it (Day & Jory, 1978). When these opposed forms of contrast occur on opposite sides of a partially delineated border an illusory edge is seen (Day & Jory, 1978). But the explanation was wrong; it was wrong because we later found strong illusory contours occurred along a line of corners in a figure in which there was no differential induced contrast.

Our subsequent work led us to the view that the representation of edges is not cued by a *single* property of the stimulus - such as a step-function difference in luminance or wavelength - but by many properties. These include step-function differences in density, two- and three-dimensional corners, ridges, overlay, movement of one part of a random-dot region relative to another, and depth from retinal disparity in random-dot stereograms. These cues can occur alone or together to give rise to the appearance of a contour. It has been suggested (Day, 1987) that other perceived features, such as form, movement, and transparency are also associated with multiple cues. For example, apparent shape in Johannson's moving-point-light displays (Johannson, 1977, 1978) is determined by the kinetic relationships between the moving points.

The idea of multiple cues correlated with a particular physical feature is not new. It has long been accepted that different cues are correlated with depth and egocentric distance and these are traditionally grouped into the categories of binocular, oculomotor, movement, and pictorial cues.

There is no question that there are *some* features of the world and of the self that are correlated with only one cue. The point to be emphasised is that many are correlated with more than one cue. This is a key point in comprehending the relationship between veridical and illusory perception.

1.2 Natural and Artificial Cues

The next point to be made about cues is that they can be contrived in the absence of the physical features with which they are *naturally* correlated. The classical instance of such contrivance is Wheatstone's (1838) invention of stereograms and the mirror stereoscope with which to view them. Essentially what Wheatstone did was to contrive the binocular-disparity cue for depth in the absence of real depth by means of flat stereograms and so confirmed that it is a cue to depth. Julesz's (1960, 1971) work well over a century later was essentially in the same spirit. He showed that the separate stereograms do not have to be recognizable forms or scenes. The cue is an average disparity between the left and right stimulus patterns at the retinae.

The contrivance of cues in the absence of depth itself did not begin with Wheatstone in 1838. Artists from early in the fifteenth century had used linear perspective to convey an appearance of depth and, as Haber (1980) has reminded us, Dürer, Alberti, and Leonardo da Vinci had all written treatises about it. By way of example, Haber reproduced Canaletto's "Piazza San Marco". It marvellously demonstrates the principle and the effectiveness of linear perspective as a cue. Aerial perspective has also been contrived to produce a similar appearance of extended egocentric distance. A point to be emphasised is that there is no *essential* difference between Wheatstone's (1838) contrivance of binocular disparity and the earlier contrivance by artists of linear and aerial perspective and overlay.

Contrivance of cues is not confined to visual perception. The binaural cues of interaural time and intensity differences have long since been reproduced by mechanical and electronic means to generate the effect of an external source in a particular direction from the listener. Likewise, centrifugation can generate the vestibular cues normally associated with gravitation. There are numerous other instances.

The point to be made most strongly is that by means of artifice the impingent spatio-temporal patterns of energy that are naturally generated by particular features of self-induced activity and of external states of affairs can be contrived in the absence of the states themselves. Thus a distinction can be drawn between *artificial* cues which give rise to illusory perception in the absence of the feature which they represent and natural cues which they copy and which give rise to veridical representations. Artificial cues have for long been part of the stock-in-trade of the artist as well as an important weapon in the armory of the experimental psychologist.

Other but less well known instances of illusory effects resulting from contrived feature cues are illusory contours, in which several edge cues are contrived, apparent movement involving the contrivance of the displacement cue to movement, and apparent transparency for which the cues have been analyzed and then contrived by Metelli (1974).

1.3 Illusions of Misalignment and Perceptual Compromise

To explicate the process of perceptual compromise I shall turn to three series of experiments concerned with the Morinaga, Arc-Chevron and Poggendorff illusions. The Morinaga and Poggendorff effects are fairly well known. The Arc-Chevron effect is not. We came across it by chance a few years ago, and a report of our experiments on it is soon to be published (Day, Jee & Duffy, in press).

In its original form, the Morinaga illusion is the apparent misalignment of physically aligned apexes of oppositely directed angles as shown in Figure 1A. However we quickly showed (Day, Bellamy & Norman,1983) that the effect occurs also with oppositely placed straight lines and other elements, as is also shown in Figure 1B.

Let us consider first what we mean by alignment in physical terms. It is the coincidence of lines, dots, or other elements with a particular axis. The three apexes and the three line ends in Figure 1 fall on the same vertical axis. The cues for alignment are the coincidence of the elements with that axis. Contrariwise, those for misalignment are the non-coincidence between elements and axis. Now, as shown in Figure 1C, in the Morinaga figure there are *two* axes, the axis of alignment, the vertical, and the "axis" or midline of the figure, which is inflected. Whereas the apexes are aligned in the vertical axis they are misaligned in respect of the midline. The upper and lower apexes fall to the left of the figure axis and the centre apex to the right of it.

The proposed explanation is that there is a compromise in perception between the cue to alignment in the alignment axis and that of misalignment in the midline or figure axis. The compromise takes the form of an apparent shift away from alignment in the vertical in the direction of misalignment in the inflected figure axis.

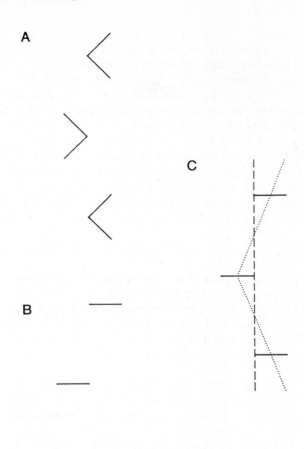

Figure 1. The Morinaga illusion. A: The three apexes are vertically aligned but appear to be misaligned. B: The three line ends are vertically aligned but appear to be misaligned. C: The line ends are aligned in the vertical axis (dashed) but misaligned in respect of the figure axis (dotted). The illusion is held to be a compromise between these two states - alignment in one axis and misalignment in the other.

Can we apply this argument to the Poggendorff effect? The standard figure consists of two aligned transversals in an oblique axis separated by two parallels in the vertical axis as shown in Figure 2A. The transversals are aligned in the oblique axis but misaligned in respect of the vertical axis of the parallels (Figure 2B). The apparent misalignment of the transversals which characterizes this classical figure is a shift away from alignment in the oblique axis in the direction of misalignment in the vertical axis. The shift is held to be due to a compromise between the two cues.

As stated earlier, a few years ago we came across an apparent misalignment effect in an arc figure quite by chance. As can be seen in Figure 3A, the centre of the lower arc and the ends of the upper arc appear to be misaligned. They are in fact exactly aligned horizontally. The same effect occurs, but less strongly, in a chevron figure. We have carried out a series of experiments on both figures (Day, Jee & Duffy, in press). The same explanation can be applied: whereas the three points are aligned in the horizontal they are misaligned in respect to the midline of the figure as shown in Figure 3B. It is suggested that this illusion is also the outcome of a compromise between alignment in one axis - the horizontal - and misalignment in the other - the midline or "figure axis". As can be seen, the shift is in the same direction as in the other figures.

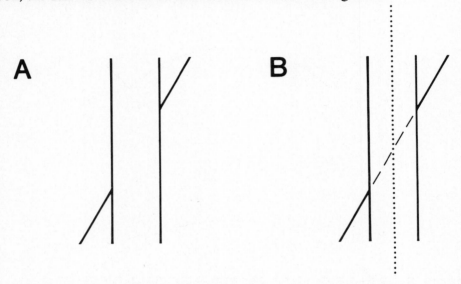

Figure 2. The Poggendorff figure. A: The two oblique lines are exactly collinear but appear not to be so. B: The obliques are aligned in the oblique axis (dashed) but misaligned in respect of the vertical axis of the parallels (dotted). The illusion is held to be a compromise between these two states - alignment in one axis and misalignment in the other.

Recently we showed that Tolanky's "misbisection" version of the Poggendorff illusion occurs as strongly with dots on oblique parallels as with vertical lines that intersect them (Day & Kaspercyzk, 1985a). The effect is shown in Figure 4A and 4B. While this has been questioned we have confirmed it and we are now convinced it is a reliable finding. Essentially the same argument in terms of a compromise between, in this case, bisection in the vertical axis and misbisection in respect of the oblique axis of the figure can be invoked to explain this effect (see Day & Kasperczyk, 1985b).

In summary, it is proposed that the various illusions of misalignment to which I have drawn attention can be explained in essentially the same terms. There are cues for alignment (or bisection) in respect of one spatial reference and misalignment in respect of another reference delineated by the figure itself. The outcome in each case is a perceptual compromise between these two states of affairs.

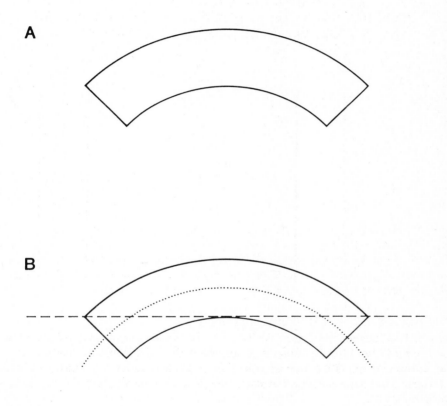

Figure 3. A: Apparent misalignment of three features in an arc figure. The ends of the upper arc are aligned with the centre of the lower arc but the latter appears to be too low for alignment with the former. B: The features are aligned in the horizontal axis (dashed) but misaligned in respect of the figure midline (dotted). The illusion is held to be a compromise between these states: alignment and misalignment relative to the horizontal and the figure midline respectively.

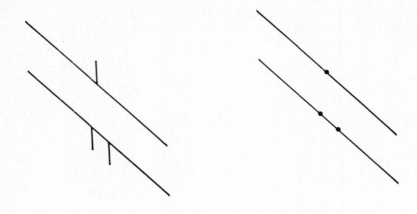

Figure 4. Left: Tolansky's version of the Poggendorff figure in which the upper vertical line which if extended downward would exactly bisect the space between the two lower vertical lines but does not appear as if it would do so. Right: The same effect is evident for dots on the parallels; if the upper dot were moved vertically downward it would bisect the space between the lower dots.

1.4 Illusions of Size and Perceptual Compromise

The argument can be extended to Müller-Lyer's well known illusion of extent shown in Figure 5A. In the Müller-Lyer figure the two horizontal extents between the apexes are the same length whereas the overall extents of the figures themselves are different. The figure with outward-directed angles is greater than that with inward-directed angles. In addition, the parallel flanking distances are greater than the distance between the apexes in one figure and less than it in the other. In *essentially* the same way as for apparent misalignment the illusion of size in each of the two figures can be reasonably attributed to a compromise between different cues for size. The distance between the apexes is one, that of the whole figure another, and those between the angles on either side of the interapical extent a third. In consequence, the apparent extent

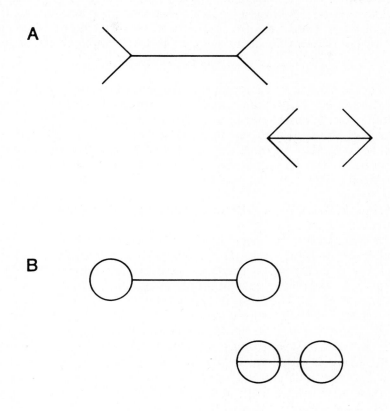

Figure 5. Two versions of the Müller-Lyer figure. A: The original figure. B: The "dumbell" version. In both figures the two horizontal lines are equal in length but appear not to be so; the line on the left appears to be longer than that on the right. In both figures the apparently shorter line is associated with the shorter figure and the apparently longer line with the longer figure.

between the apexes in the upper figure of Figure 5A appears greater and in the lower figure smaller. There is, in brief, a compromise between the interapical extent and extents greater than it in one figure and less than it in another.

If this argument is valid it can be expected that the Müller-Lyer effect will be evident in figures different from the conventional and frequently reproduced ones with the angles but in which the same conditions obtain. That this expectation is realized can be seen in the so-called "dumbell" version of the figure in Figure 5B. It is also to be expected that the effect will occur in the haptic mode. It does, as Rèvèsz (1934) showed a long time ago. His observations have long since been confirmed (see Rudel & Teuber, 1963; Over, 1967). Recently we informally confirmed the occurrence of the Müller-Lyer effect in haptic space.

The occurrence of geometrical illusions in haptic space is by now well documented but often ignored. An explanation in terms of perceptual compromise between two or more cues (or references) accounts for haptic effects as well as it does for visual effects. The explanation can also account for the transfer of a practice effect in the visual mode to the haptic mode and vice versa as shown by Rudel & Teuber, 1963.

1.5 Perceptual Compromise between Natural and Artificial Cues

A distinction has been drawn (see above) between natural and artificial cues; natural cues arise from features actually present in the physical world and artificial cues are contrived to occur in the absence of those features. Depth is a case in point. A picture of a landscape relies on numerous contrived cues for its appearance of depth. These include overlay, linear perspective, elevation in the field, and aerial perspective. However, whereas when we look at a picture like Canaletto's "Piazza San Marco" we have a strong impression of depth, that impression is by no means as strong as when we look across the piazza itself. The difference between the pictured and the real can be presumed to derive from a compromise between the natural cues for flatness in the picture, cues such as retinal disparity, motion parallel, and possibly surface texture, and the various contrived cues for depth such as perspective, overlay, and elevation. What is to me of primary interest about a picture is that flatness and depth are not in rivalry, as, for example, with ambiguous figures. Rather, the cues conveying information for the two states, depth and no depth, achieve a compromise such that apparent depth is less than in the real scene and less convincing as a perceptual experience. This is also the case with stereograms viewed in a stereoscope, an aspect of the contrived retinal disparity cue which is usually overlooked. Depth using a stereoscope appears not only less than in the real scene but curiously static, presumably because of the absence of motion parallel when the head is moved relative to the depicted scene.

The same argument applies to illusory contours. While there is a distinct appearance of an illusory edge it is weaker and more "ephemeral" than a real edge. This can reasonably be attributed to the presence in the figure not only of contrived cues for edge such as a step-function difference in colour, line ends, and overlay, but a cue or cues for a continuous surface. What these latter cues might be is unclear simply because they have not so far been investigated.

1.6 Intermodal Perceptual Compromise

In the 1960s, Singer and I undertook a series of experiments on the problem of the relationship between the visual and kinesthetic systems (see Day & Singer, 1967). Our research was focused on the effect of optical distortion of a visually perceived feature on kinesthetic perception of the same feature. Optical distortion was achieved by placing a wedge prism between the viewed object and the eye. The most common outcome was that visual distortion resulted in kinesthetic distortion, an effect that came to be referred to as "visual capture". For example, a horizontal edge which *appeared* to be tilted when viewed through an optical system also felt tilted when the hand was moved over it.

This intermodal effect can be construed as another instance of perceptual compromise, in this case between visual and kinesthetic cues for orientation. The visual cue is presumably the tilted retinal image with the head upright and the kinesthetic cue the horizontal movement of the hand with body upright. The compromise is the kinesthetic impression of a tilted bar when it is physically horizontal.

1.7 The Moon Illusion and Perceptual Compromise

Recently we prepared a commentary for a forthcoming book on the moon illusion (Day & Parks, in press). In the last section we argued that it is possible that perceived *size* is also determined by multiple cues. Distance, itself determined by cues, might serve as *one* cue to size and, similarly, size might serve as *one* cue to distance. Therefore, depending on the conditions of viewing, other cues for both these features might well come into play. Thus, the apparent size of the moon at horizon and zenith might include its apparent distance *along with other cues*. Likewise, the apparent distance of the moon in the two locations might serve as a cue to its apparent size, along with other cues.

This tentative interpretation of the still enigmatic moon illusion in terms of cues additional to those for distance gets round two major problems in explaining the illusion. First, the horizon moon not only looks bigger, it looks *nearer*, and that is contrary to the size-distance invariance notion. Second, the experiments of Baird and Wagner (1982) a few years ago seem to have ruled out apparent distance *alone* as the basis of the moon illusion. What we have suggested in our reinterpretation of the illusion avoids the problems inherent in the still widely held size-distance explanation.

Incidentally, if there is any doubt that there are cues *other* than those for distance involved in the perception of size it is only necessary to contemplate a scene from one of the author's favourite movies - "Brats", made in 1932 with Stan Laurel and Oliver Hardy. The scene is shown in Figure 6. The actors appear small, not only because they are dressed as children but because they are presented in a large armchair - a trick ably and effectively exploited by P.T. Barnum in his exhibition of Tom Thumb.

Figure 6. Laurel and Hardy appear relatively small. The chair in which they sit is much larger than normal. (From "Brats", 1932).

What is urgently needed is a systematic investigation of cues to size. Cues to distance have a long history; those for size no history at all.

1.8 Cue Salience

There is good evidence to show that the salience of particular feature cues can vary. By salience is meant the degree to which that cue is weighted in the process of perceptual compromise. Salience can vary in three ways, by rendering it more prominent or striking in the stimulus array, by deliberate reinforcement of its use during repeated exposure (as in the "practice experiment" with illusory figures), or by informal reinforcement in the normal course of stimulation. All three ways of varying salience can be demonstrated by reference yet again to the Müller-Lyer figure. It can be noted that when spots are introduced at the apexes of the angles the illusion of length is markedly reduced (see Figure 7). By introducing these spots and thereby making the interapical extents more prominent the tendency to compromise with the extents of the figures seems to be reduced.

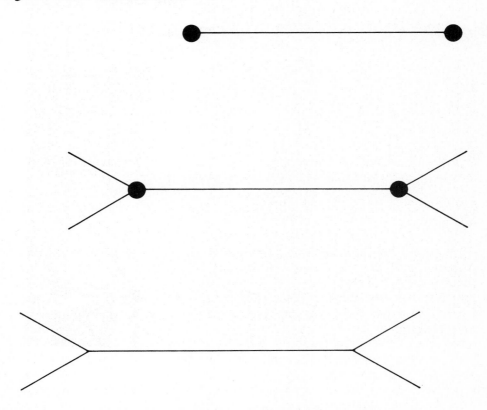

Figure 7. The Müller-Lyer illusion of extent is markedly reduced by the addition of prominent spots at the intersection of the apexes and the horizontal line.

We have shown in two separate series of experiments involving the Poggendorff and Morinaga figures (Day & Kasperczyk, 1985a; Day, 1988) that the illusions can be considerably reduced or eliminated altogether by the simple device of enhancing the axis of alignment of the apparently misaligned features. This can be seen in Figure 8 in which short end-lines are added to the misaligned features in the Morinaga figure.

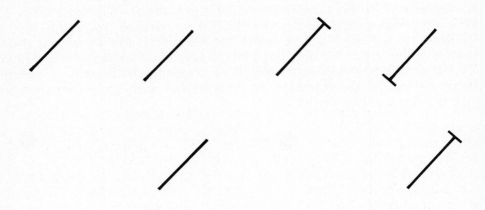

Figure 8. The addition of short orthogonal lines at the ends of the parallel lines (right) markedly reduces the magnitude of the Morinaga misalignment effect (left).

1.9 Perceptual Illusions as a Function of Practice, Developmental Stage, and Culture

Geometrical illusions vary in size with repeated presentation and judgments of the figure, age of the observers, and the culture in which they live. A general theory of perception can reasonably be expected to account for the effects of these often overlooked determinants. The cue-based theory I have presented can do so without making any extra assumptions.

Since Judd's (1902) early observations it has been known that the size of illusions such as the Müller-Lyer and the Poggendorff progressively declines with repeated judgments. Our early experiments on this effect (Day, 1962), followed soon after by those of Parker and Newbigging (1963), showed that the decline is probably due to a learning process. But what is learned? We pointed out that in the geometrical arrangements in which spatial illusions occur there are two or more cues for a particular feature. Depending on the conditions of reinforcement and the feedback to subjects - what used to be called "knowledge of results" - it can be expected that one cue rather than another will come to be favoured. In this way the balance of compromise between cues undergoes change. There is, as straightaway will be noted, a whiff of

Brunswik's "probabilistic functionalism" (Hammond, 1966) and Helson's (1964) adaptation-level theory in this interpretation. But what is most interesting about the idea in the context of illusions and perceptual compromise is that by reinforcing a particular cue the illusion could presumably be made to *increase*. That is to say, when there are numerous cues for, let us say, length - or alignment, orientation, size - and a compromise between them determines how things look, then reinforcement could presumably lead either to veridicality or illusion; to the world appearing as it is physically *or* as it is not physically. This idea has not yet been tried out but is certainly worth vigourous pursuit.

It is suggested that what goes on with illusions under the tightly controlled conditions of the laboratory also goes on in a more uncontrolled way during development and in different cultures (see McKenzie & Day, 1987; Segall, Campbell & Herskovits, 1966). Cues for different states of affairs in the real world - for distance, for orientation, for edges, for form, and for movement - are variously available in different situations. Therefore, depending on whether the *particular* cues for these features *are* available and the extent to which one has been more successful than another, so the compromise between them will vary. Again, Brunswik's views will be apparent. It can also be suggested that the considerable variation in the trends for perceptual illusions as a function of age and culture, which has emerged clearly in Robinson's (1972) review, derives in large part from the different availability of cues and, most critically, the learning histories of the individuals concerned. It seems that a closer understanding of perceptual development and cross-cultural differences in perception will come, not from studying individuals *in situ*, so to speak, but from careful laboratory investigations of the effects of feedback or reinforcement on "cue favouring" and its effect on perceptual compromise.

1.10 The Tilted Room

The favouring of one cue over another in the process of perceptual compromise emerges with exceptional clarity in the case of the tilted-room effect described in a series of papers by Asch and Witkin in the 1940s (see Asch & Witkin, 1948; Witkin & Asch, 1948). Asch and Witkin showed that for a rod to appear vertical or horizontal in a room tilted at about 22 degrees from the true vertical it had to be tilted in the same direction as the room. Thus the orientation of the space in which the rod was located was one cue for its orientation. But so was the orientation of the subject. When the subject was tilted in the same direction as the room the tilted-room effect was greater and, in the opposite direction, less. Thus it can be presumed that there are also gravitational and kinesthetic cues for the orientation of the rod.

In this intermodal-cue situation for object orientation it can be presumed that the room cue for rod orientation resulted in an illusory effect and the self orientation cue (when the subject was upright) to a more or less veridical effect. The outcome was a compromise. But what was particularly interesting about this early and, largely neglected experiment was the range of settings of the bar for apparent horizontality and verticality. The settings for the 76 subjects ranged from 2 to 22 degrees from the true vertical. This can be taken to mean that the extent to which visual and non-visual cues are favoured in determining the apparent cardinal axes of space varied widely across subjects. For some, greater reliance is placed on the cue provided by room or frame orientation and, for others, on gravitational, kinesthetic and conceivably other cues. Thus what came in due course to be called "field-dependent" and "field- independent" subjects refers to subjects differentially favouring visual and vestibular-kinesthetic cues in the process of perceptual compromise, presumably as a function of their perceptual histories and learning.

1.11 Illusory Perception and Veridical Perception

What has all this talk about illusory effects in line figures and tilted rooms and frames got to do with normal, veridical perception - the everyday business of perceiving the world? There are two answers to this question. The first is simply that by contriving cues and thereby producing the appearance of a feature where none exists physically, we clearly identify the cues that operate in normal perception. Wheatstone's (1838) demonstration is the classic example; by contriving binocular disparity he demonstrated its role in depth perception.

The second answer bears on the notion of perceptual compromise. The pivotal point of the proposal set out here is that in perception a compromise occurs between cues for disparate states of affairs. This compromise, mainly in stimulus arrays of our own ingenious contrivance, is the basis of perceptual illusions. In addition, more than one cue is associated with particular features of situations and events. The multiple cues for visual depth and edge are cases in point. *It must be presumed, of course, that these cues are somehow integrated in the process of achieving a veridical representation of the world and one's activities in it.*

The point is this: the process *normally* involved in the integration of multiple cues for a particular feature is also invoked when artificial cues as well as natural cues are present in the stimulus array. Thus essentially what we do in the laboratory is to demonstrate the *normal* process of integration of natural cues by "planting" artificial cues in the array. The same process of combining the cues takes place but the representation of the feature which emerges is non-veridical.

There has been much talk about perception being a "hypothesis-based" intelligent process. The evidence is hardly in favour of this view. Give the sensory system artificial cues mixed in with the natural cues and it seems blithely to mix them together to generate an illusion - a representation that is consistently at variance with the real-world state of affairs.

CONCLUSION

With respect to the predictive power of the theory, O'Neil (1969), referred to previously, stated that theories anticipate facts and so provide leads to the observation of further facts. It has been argued here that once a cue to a particular feature is isolated and identified, and then contrived in the absence of the feature, an illusion will occur. Therefore, if a cue for a particular event is successfully identified and then contrived in the absence of that event, it can be expected that the latter will be perceived. Likewise, if that contrived cue is combined with a natural cue (or cues), a compromise in perception can be expected.

If this conceptualization of perception is valid, it should be capable of explaining an adventitiously observed visual illusion. Figure 9A shows a view through the kitchen window of the author's house. It has been observed most mornings for well over twenty years! The corner of the railing at the top-left appears to be higher than that at the bottom-right. In fact the two corners are nearly in the same horizontal axis. The reason for this apparent difference is that, relative to the oblique axis of the structure itself, the top-left corner lies above it and the bottom-right corner below it as shown in Figure 9B. There is a compromise in perception between these two cues to position - horizontal-axis relative and structure-axis relative - and the outcome is a shift in perception away from the former in the direction of the latter.

The argument presented here provides a conceptual scheme for the interpretation of a wide range of illusory effects that previously appeared to be unrelated. It also helps to tie together illusory and veridical perception - to see better how they are interconnected. The argument in many places is loose but at least it is testable. The main task now is to test and to quantify it.

A

B

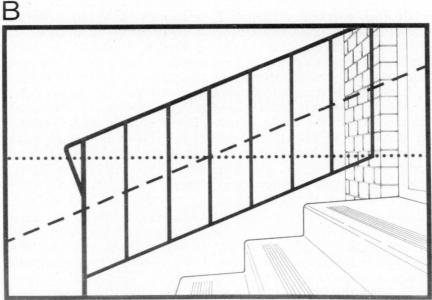

Figure 9. A: The upper-left and the lower-right corners of the railing are on the same horizontal axis but the former seems higher than the latter. B: The corners fall nearly on the horizontal axis (dotted) but fall above and below the axis of the railing (dashed). The illusion is held to be a compromise in perception between the positions relative to the horizontal and railing axes.

CORRESPONDENCE

Correspondence concerning this paper should be sent to Professor R. H. Day,Department of Psychology, Monash University, Clayton, Victoria, 3168,

REFERENCES

Asch, S. E., & Witkin, H. A. (1948). Studies in space orientation.II. Perception of the upright with displaced visual fields and with body tilted. Journal of Experimental Psychology, 38, 455-477.

Baird, J. C. & Wagner, M. (1982). The moon illusion: I. How high is the sky? Journal of Experimental Psychology, 111, 296-303.

Day, R. H. (1962). The effects of repeated trials and prolonged fixation on error in the Müller-Lyer figure. Psychological Monographs, 76, (14, Serial No. 533).

Day, R. H. (1986). Enhancement of edges by contrast, depth and figure: the origins of illusory contours. In J. D. Pettigrew, K.J.Sanderson and W. R. Levick (Eds.), Visual Neuroscience, (pp.352-364). Cambridge, Cambridge University Press.

Day, R. H. (1987). Cues for edge and the origin of illusory contours: An alternative approach. In S. Petry & G. E. Meyer (Eds.), The Perception of Illusory Contours, (Pp. 53-61). New York, Springer-Verlag.

Day, R. H. (1988). Reduction and elimination of the Poggendorff misalignment effect by minor changes at intersections: implications for the perceptual compromise explanation. Psychological Research, 50, 7-11.

Day, R. H., Bellamy, S., & Norman, A. (1983). On the Morinaga misalignment illusion. Journal of Experimental Psychology: Human Perception & Performance, 9, 113-125.

Day, R. H., & Duffy, F. M. (1988). Illusions of time and extent when the Müller-Lyer figure moves in an aperture. Perception & Psychophysics, 44, 205-210.

Day, R. H., Jee, F. M., & Duffy, F. M. (in press). Visual misalignment in arc and chevron figures. Journal of Experimental Psychology: Human Perception and Performance

Day, R. H., & Jory, M. K. (1978). Subjective contours, visual acuity and line contrast. In J. C. Armington, J. E. Krauskopf, & B. Wooten (Eds.), Visual Psychophysics and Physiology (pp. 331-340). New York, Academic Press.

Day, R. H., & Kasperczyk, R. T. (1985a). The Morinaga misalignment effect: reduction and reversal by modification of figural extremities. Psychological Research, 47, 95-101.

Day, R. H., & Kasperczyk, R. T. (1985b). Apparent displacement of lines and dots in a parallel-line figure: A clue to the basis of the Poggendorff effect. Perception and Psychophysics, 38, 74-80.

Day, R. H., & Parks, T.E. (in press). To exorcize a ghost from the perceptual machine. In M. Hershenson (Ed.), The Moon Illusion. Hillsdale, N.J., Lawrence Erlbaum Associates.

Day, R. H., & Singer, G. (1967). Sensory adaptation and behavioural compensation with spatially transformed vision and hearing. Psychological Bulletin, 67, 307-322.

Gibson, J. J. (1959). Perception as a function of stimulation. In S.Koch (Ed.), Psychology: A Study of a Science. Study I. Conceptual and Systematic. Volume 1 Sensory, Perceptual and Physiological Formulations. New York, McGraw-Hill.

Gibson, J. J. (1962). The survival value of sensory perception. In E.E.Bernard, & M. R. Kare (Eds.), Biological Prototypes and Synthetic Systems (Pp. 230-232). New York, Plenum Press.

Haber, R. N. (1980). How we perceive depth from flat pictures.American Scientist, 68, 370-380.

Hammond, K. R. (Ed.) (1966). The Psychology of Egon Brunswick. New York, Holt, Rinehart and Winston.

Helson, H. (1964). Adaptation-Level Theory An Experimental and Systematic Approach to Behaviour. New York, Harper & Row.

Judd, C. H. (1902). Practice and its effects on the perception of illusions. Psychological Review, 9, 27-39.

Julesz, B. (1960). Binocular depth perception of computer generated patterns. Bell System Technical Journal, 39, 1125-1162.

Julesz, B. (1971). Foundations of Cyclopean Perception. Chicago, University of Chicago Press.

Koffka, K. (1935). Principles of Gestalt Psychology. London, Routledge & Kegan Paul.

McKenzie, B. E., & Day, R. H. (1987). Perceptual Development in Early Infancy: Problems and Issues. Hillsdale, N.J., Lawrence Erlbaum Associates.

Metelli, F. (1974). The perception of transparency. Scientific American, 230, 90-98.

O'Neil, W. M. (1969). Fact and Theory. An Aspect of the Philosophy of Science. Sydney, Sydney University Press.

Over, R. (1967). Intermanual transfer of practice effects with a haptic illusion. The Quarterly Journal of Experimental Psychology, 19, 215-218.

Parker, N. I., & Newbigging, P. L. (1965). Decrement of the Müller-Lyer illusion as a function of psychophysical procedure. The American Journal of Psychology, 78, 603-608.

Rèvèsz, G. (1934). System der optischen und haptischen Raumtäuschungen. Zeitschrift fuer Psychologie, 131, 296-375.

Robinson, J. 0. (1972). The Psychology of Visual Illusion. London, Hutchinson.

Rudel, R. G., & Teuber, H. L. (1963). Decrement of visual and haptic Mueller-Lyer illusion on repeated trials: A study of crossmodal transfer. Quarterly Journal of Experimental Psychology, 15, 125-131.

Segall, M. H., Campbell, D. T., & Herskovits, M. J. (1966). The Influence of Culture on Visual Perception. Indianapolis, Bobbs-Merrill Company Inc.

Wheatstone, C. (1838). Some remarkable phenomena of binocular vision. Philosophical Transactions, Royal Society of London, 128, 371-394.

Witkin, H. A., & Asch, S. E. (1948). Studies in space orientation.IV. Further experiments on perception of the upright with displaced visual fields. Journal of Experimental Psychology, 38, 762-782.

Human Information Processing: Measures,
Mechanisms, and Models, D. Vickers and P.L. Smith (eds.)
© *Elsevier Science Publishers B.V. (North-Holland), 1989*

ANALYSIS OF THE SPATIAL NATURE OF GEOMETRIC ANALOGIES

M.J. GONZALEZ LABRA

Universidad Nacional de Educación a Distancia

The present study was designed to address two main issues in analogical performance: (1) the notion of feature changes, and (2) the influence of item difficulty on the nature of the task. Geometric analogies were systematically generated in terms of number and type of figures and transformations. The results indicated that analogical performance is a function of the quantitative (number of figures) and qualitative (type of transformations) features contained in the problems. The interaction between both factors attenuated the transformational complexity effects as the number of figures increases, even if no transformation is applied to some of the figures. Working memory load exerts a critical influence on performance as problems increase in difficulty. The high correlations encountered in previous studies between item difficulty and performance on reasoning tests could be tapping the control strategies used to manage working memory load.

1. INTRODUCTION

Three major studies (Evans, 1968; Mulholland, Pellegrino & Glaser, 1980; Sternberg, 1977) have examined geometric analogy performance, focusing primarily on data for item or item types. The experimental task format most commonly used for the presentation of analogical problems is "A:B :: C:D" (A is to B as C is to D). This proportional format expresses the correspondence between the relations of the first and second pairs of terms. But regardless of this fundamental relational structure, previous research has focused mainly on the amount of the information contained in the relations, and less on the type of content.

Geometric analogy problems are generally defined by the notion of feature changes, either in terms of subjective distance ratings between terms (Sternberg, 1977) or as a function of objective characteristics of the stimuli (Gardner, 1982; Mulholland et al., 1980). In the case of subjects' ratings of distances between analogical terms, a larger distance rating is assumed to reflect a larger number of feature changes. Likewise, the objective manipulation of item difficulty is determined as a function of the number of figures or elements, and the number of transformations applied to these elements. Consequently, the processing models proposed account for the differential difficulty encountered in analogical performance in terms of the amount of information that must be processed. Moreover, variations in the amount of information are assumed to be directly related to the number of executions of a particular operation. Therefore, execution time for each operation depends on item complexity, so that as the amount of information increases there is also a direct increase in the number of times a given operation has to be performed.

However, further research on the task variables used in the manipulation of item difficulty has shown that the different types of transformations generated in geometric analogies should be considered as an additional source of item complexity (Whitely & Schneider, 1981; Bethell-Fox, Lohman, & Snow, 1984). The results obtained in these studies indicated that problems with the same number of transformations did not present the same difficulty graduation when the data were analyzed in terms of transformational content. Furthermore, analogies with two and three transformations produced solution times that were closer to the dimensional change which showed the highest difficulty level in problems with a single transformation (González Labra, 1987). These findings suggest that averaging solution times as a function of the number of transformations cancels the significant effects of content type on item difficulty. As a result of these studies, it does not seem permissible to equate amount of information and number of component executions.

While the nature of the analogical transformations is recognized as the major determinant of performance, the other task variable is still controversial. In general, the elements of the analogical terms are conceived as easily perceived geometric figures. Thus, provided the elements of the analogical terms are sufficiently simple, their particular form does not contribute to the differential difficulty patterns encountered in task variance. However, number of elements emerges as a more important factor than number of transformations in the study by Bethell-Fox et al. (1984), whereas Mulholland et al., (1980) obtained the reverse, and Whitely et al., (1981) found a nonsignificant effect for number of elements.

Previous research has indicated that the processing components involved in detecting feature transformations bear no significant relation to perceptual speed ability (Gardner, 1982; Sternberg, 1977; Sternberg & Gardner, 1983). The correlation between these components and performance on reasoning tests becomes stronger as analogical problems increase in complexity. It seems that item difficulty can influence the nature of the task, and, as Carpenter and Just (1986) have pointed out, more difficult problems might require a higher level of information elaboration that could obscure the spatial nature of the task.

The present study is designed to address two main issues related to geometric analogy performance: (1) the analysis of the main task variables used in item generation, and (2) the specification of item difficulty in terms of perceptual and/or logical relations. Taking into consideration that both transformations and elements constitute the information structure of geometric analogies, the first objective seeks to determine the stimulus characteristics governing item difficulty. In order to achieve this goal, the experimental tasks were designed so as to systematically examine the effects of these variables: number and type of transformations and elements. The second objective was to determine whether intermediate and high difficulty problems can actually overshadow the perceptual relational nature that characterizes these problems.

2.METHOD

2.1 Subjects

Twenty undergraduates from the Complutense University of Madrid participated in the experiment. Their cooperation was completely voluntary.

2.2 Procedure

In order to generate the geometric analogies, the basic components were kept constant and item complexity was varied by increasing the number of transformations and figures. The problems were systematically generated from four types of figures (triangle, square, pentagon, and hexagon), and seven types of transformations (size, rotation, colour size x rotation, rotation x colour, size x colour, and size x rotation x colour). The problems required that each of the seven transformations be performed on one, two, and three figure terms. Therefore, one figure problems underwent each of the seven transformations. Problems with two figures required one transformation on one of the two figures in the one transformation condition, one transformation on each figure in the two transformations condition, and two transformations on the same figure and one transformation on the other figure in the three transformations condition. The same strategy was followed in problems with three figures, and in this case no figure underwent more than one transformation.

There were 21 problem types and 10 observations for each type. The geometric figures were randomly assigned to the first and second pair of terms. The transformations applied to these figures were counterbalanced across problem types so that no figure could be associated with any particular transformation.

Analogies were also presented in a true/false format, and the complete experimental task included 210 true and 210 false problems. Number of figures was kept constant across different problem types, and false items were obtained either by replacing an incorrect transformation in the one transformation condition or by not applying one of the correct transformations in the remaining cases.

The individual experimental sessions were approximately three hours long. Problems were presented on a one field tachistoscope that incorporated a self-presentation key device and a vocal response key.

In order to counterbalance possible fatigue and practice effects, the problems were also assigned to two homogeneous blocks. Each block was crossed with true/false versions and problem types. Ordering within blocks was random and the blocks were presented in two alternative orders.

3. RESULTS

True and false problems were analyzed separately using a two way repeated measures analysis of variance: Number of figures (3) x Type of transformation (7). The main effects of these task variables were significant for both true and false problems: significant solution time differences were obtained for both true and false problems that varied in number of figures $F(2, 38) = 31.60$, $p < .001$, and $F(2, 38) = 33.27$, $p < .001$, respectively; type of transformations in true problems $F(6, 114) = 11.35$, $p < .001$, and false problems $F(6, 114) = 6.11$, $p < .001$; and the interaction between these factors was also significant in true and false problems, $F(12, 228) = 5.57$, $p < .001$, and $F(12, 228) = 4.63$, $p < .001$, respectively.

The results of a Newman-Keuls comparison of means ($p < .01$) showed that the differences between true problems containing the same number of figures under different transformations (1 figure x size compared to 1 figure x rotation, ...)were significant in 22.22% of the cases, whereas 38.09% of the differences between problems with same transformation and different number of figures (1 figure x size compared to 2 figures x size, ...) reached significance. In the case of false problems, 11.11% of the comparisons were significant when number of figures was held constant and type of transformation was varied, and 33.33% in problems with same transformation and different number of figures.

These results indicate that, overall, analogical performance is a function of both the quantitative and qualitative aspects of the information structure of the problems. As can be seen in figures 1 and 2, the effects of these two variables are interactive.

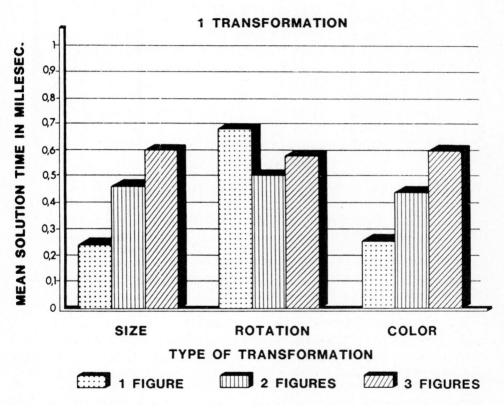

Figure 1.- Mean solution times (milliseconds) for true analogies under the transformations of size, rotation, colour, and number of figures (one, two, and three).

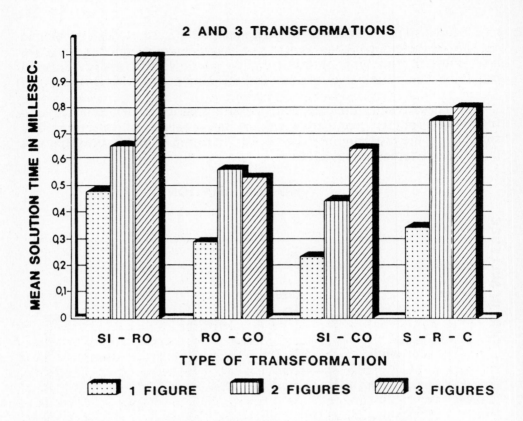

Figure 2.- Mean solution times (milliseconds) for true analogies under the transformations of size-rotation, rotation-colour, size-colour, and size-rotation-colour and number of figures (one, two, and three).

In general, solution times systematically increase with the number of figures, whereas number of transformations does not exhibit this relationship. This can be clearly appreciated, for example, by considering problems with one transformation (size, rotation, or colour): if the transformation is held constant, the differences between problems with different number of figures is significant, but if the comparison is inverted (different transformations and same number of figures), the differences did not reach significance. In line with the Bethell-Fox et al. (1984) study, number of figures seems to be a more important determinant of performance than number of transformations. Furthermore, the dimensional effects obtained in previous experiments and replicated here in the one figure term problems, were overshadowed by this quantitative variable. Although the nature of the transformation influences solution times, the interaction between both factors attenuate the transformational complexity effects as the number of figures increases, even when no transformation is applied to some of the figures.

As Mulholland et al. (1980) have suggested, working memory capacity is a critical determinant of analogical performance as problems increase in difficulty. It seems as though information in terms of number of figures is harder to retain. However, the major determinant of performance is neither transformation complexity, nor number of elements, but rather the combined contribution of both variables. Thus, the high correlations encountered between item difficulty and performance on reasoning tests could be tapping the control strategies used to manage working memory load.

4. DISCUSSION

In order to determine what stimulus characteristics govern item complexity in geometric analogies, the current study examined analogical performance as a function of systematic variations in the information structure of analogical terms. The results obtained point toward two distinctive factors that influence solution times.

One of the major determinants of performance involves the transformational complexity of the rules to be inferred. The relevance of the relational content in the difficulty pattern across items has also been supported by the research done on other inductive tasks (Holzman, Pellegrino, & Glaser, 1983; Kotovsky & Simon, 1973; LeFevre & Bisanz, 1986). The influence of the dimensional properties of geometric analogies is a function of the dimensional changes between terms, with solution times being increased, not by the number of dimensional value changes, but by the type of content.

However, when assessing the effects of item complexity it is also necessary to consider the number of geometric figures that constitute the analogical terms. Thus, as the number of figures increases, whether the figures are transformed or not, the dimensional effects are overshadowed by the interaction between both variables.

With regard to the possible levels of abstraction associated with item complexity, the conclusion of this study considers geometric analogies as reflecting logical relations in terms of spatial information. Thus, geometric analogy solution might be accomplished by an intermediate stage of abstraction, which could be obtained by the reduction of irrelevant information from a detailed dimensional description of the terms. As Gick & Holyoak (1980) have indicated, the optimal level of abstraction in analogical performance is that at which similarities are maximized and differences are minimized. Therefore, the spatial nature of the task, which is critical for rule induction, is overshadowed not by a higher level of information elaboration, but by memory loading restrictions. Performance on difficult items requires subjects to create a complex relational structure in working memory to manage number of figures, as well as type of dimensional changes applied to them. The item difficulty manipulation in geometric analogies may therefore be seen as tapping time for information management in working memory.

CORRESPONDENCE

Correspondence concerning this paper should be addressed to M.J.GONZALEZ LABRA, Departamento de Piscología Básica, Universidad Nacional de Educación a Distancia, P.Box 50487, Madrid, Spain

REFERENCES

Bethell-Fox, S.E., Lohman, D.F. & Snow, R. (1984). Adaptive reasoning: Componential and eye movement analysis of geometric analogy performance. Intelligence, 8, 205-238.

Carpenter, P.A. & Just, M.A. (1986). Spatial ability: An information processing approach to psychometrics. In R.J. Sternberg (Ed.): Advances in the psychology of human intelligence. (pp. 221-253) Hillsdale, N.J., Lawrence Erlbaum Associates.

Evans, T.G. (1968). A program for the solution of geometric analogy intelligence test questions. In M. Minsky (Ed.): Semantic information processing. (pp. 271-353) Cambridge, MIT Press.

Gardner, M.K. (1982). Some remaining puzzles concerning analogical reasoning and human abilities. Ph. D., Yale University.

Gick, M.L. & Holyoak, K. (1980). Analogical problem solving. Cognitive Psychology, 12, 306-355.

González Labra, M.J. (1987): Analogías Geométricas: Un estudio de los efectos de las dimensiones estimulares y de algunas de las alternativas metodológicas. Ph. D., Universidad Nacional de Educación a Distancia (Madrid).

Holzman, T.G., Pellegrino, J.W., & Glaser, R. (1983) Cognitive variables in series completion. Journal of Educational Psychology, 75, 605-618.

Kotovsky, K. & Simon, H.A. (1973). Empirical tests of a theory of human acquisition of concepts for sequential pattern. Cognitive Psychology, 4, 399-424.

LeFevre, J. & Bisanz, J. (1986). A cognitive analysis of number series problems: Sources of individual differences in performance. Memory and Cognition, 14 (4), 287-298.

Mulholland, T.M., Pellegrino, J.M. & Glaser, R. (1980). Components of geometric analogy solution. Cognitive Psychology, 12, 252-284.

Sternberg, R.J. (1977). Intelligence, information processing and analogical reasoning: The componential analysis of human abilities. Hillsdale, N.J., Lawrence Erlbaum Associates.

Sternberg, R.J. & Gardner, M.K. (1983). Unities in inductive reasoning. Journal of Experimental Psychology: General, 112 (1), 80-116.

Whitely, S.E. & Schneider, L.M. (1981). Information structure for geometric analogies: A test theory approach. Applied Psychological Measurement, 5 (3), 383-397.

SECTION 3

CONTROL OF MOVEMENT

PERCEPTION-ACTION COUPLING IN A SIMPLE COINCIDENCE-TIMING TASK

Bruce Abernethy

University of Queensland

Boris Crassini

Deakin University

Lee's (1976) notion that actions are timed in relation to environmental events through the use of a unitary, directly perceivable variable τ (specified as the inverse of the relative rate of retinal expansion of approaching objects) was examined. Seventeen subjects viewed an apparently-approaching light source from a front-on position and were required to coincide a simple manual response with the arrival of the light source at a target point 57cm in front of them. The approaching motion was viewed either monocularly or binocularly in order to test the τ-based assumption that information about time-to-contact (t_c) is equally accessible to one eye as to two. It was found, in support of the τ-based assumption, and an earlier study by McLeod (1985), that overall timing accuracy and consistency were similar regardless of whether the approaching motion was viewed monocularly or binocularly. However, systematic biases in the direction of late responding under monocular viewing were observed, suggesting that information in addition to τ is incorporated into the judgment of t_c. Approach velocity was also found, unexpectedly, to exert a significant influence on all aspects of coincidence-timing performance, with the most pronounced effect being a systematic over-estimation of actual tc with increased approach velocity. This suggested that if τ is indeed utilised to predict t_c then this prediction involves a velocity-proportionate error.

1. INTRODUCTION

The performance of many human activities is dependent upon the availability of visual information about the time-to-contact (t_c) of approaching objects or surfaces (Dietz & Noth, 1978; Lee, Lishman, &

Thomson, 1982; Lee & Young, 1985). For example, consider a child attempting to determine whether it is safe to cross a busy road, a tennis player attempting to precisely'time' a forehand stroke, or a shopper seeking to step from a moving escalator on to a stationary walkway; in all cases, reliable perceptual information about t_c as a basis for initiating and controlling these actions is needed. In this paper we examine the question of how such visual information about t_c may be obtained by comparing two contrasting perspectives about the visual bases of the perception of t_c. Such an examination is seen as an important starting point for the more general question of how the processes of perception and action become linked in the performance of skilled movements.

One possible means of determining t_c is to compute the ratio of the velocity of the approaching object (expressed relative to the observer) and the observer-object distance. Within this computational approach, distance and velocity information is assumed to be more elementary and easier to obtain than direct temporal information, and the accuracy of t_c judgments is considered to be limited both by the individual observer's sensitivity to distance and velocity information and by the time taken to perform the computations required to derive t_c. The alternative viewpoint is that t_c information does not need to be computed in the visual cortex from more fundamental cues but rather is specified directly by the pattern of light which reaches the retina. Using the Gibsonian notion of ecological optics (Gibson, 1961, 1979), Lee (1976, 1978) has demonstrated that the potential exists for t_c to be picked up directly from the optic flow field on the basis of a single optical parameter. This parameter, τ, given mathematically as the inverse of the relative rate of expansion of the retinal image of the approaching object, precisely specifies t_c (to the plane of the eyes) under those conditions where the object approaches the observer directly at constant velocity, and where the size of the object is known in advance by the observer.

McLeod et al. (1985) attempted to determine which of these two means of extracting t_c information was used by giving subjects a task in which vertically-dropping squash balls had to be struck horizontally towards a small target area. Subjects performed this task either binocularly or monocularly, and performance was expressed in terms of the percentage of successful hits made. The logic of the monocular-binocular manipulation was a simple one. If the time to contact the falling ball is determined directly from the relative rate of retinal expansion (or "looming") then this information should be as accessible to one eye as to two, and hitting performance under monocular and binocular viewing should be equivalent. On the other hand, if t_c is computed from the velocity/distance ratio then one might expect superior performance under the binocular viewing conditions simply because distance judgments, inside a few metres, are performed better when stereoscopic vision is available (Leibowitz, Shiina, & Hennessy, 1972).

McLeod et al. (1985) found that subjects performed slightly better, (but importantly, not significantly better), under binocular viewing conditions, than monocular viewing conditions and this was taken as evidence in favour of Lee's (1976) proposition that timing judgments are made on the basis of the monocularly available τ. However, a second experiment, in which the approaching object varied in its directional characteristics in addition to its time of arrival, did reveal a significant advantage for binocular viewing. Collectively, these two experiments were taken to support the conclusion that monocular information (presumably from τ) is all that is needed to determine the time of arrival of an approaching object, while binocular vision appears to be of use in determining the direction of an approaching object.

Three limitations in the McLeod et al. (1985) study however, suggest that some caution is needed before accepting this conclusion unequivocally. Firstly, since the initial experiment contained not only temporal uncertainty but also some directional uncertainty, one cannot be entirely certain whether the observed (but non-significant) trend in the direction of better performance under binocular viewing was due to chance, due to the known binocular superiority for directional judgments, or due perhaps to a binocular advantage for timing judgments. Secondly, the design of the experiment was such that support of the τ notion was contingent upon the support of the null hypothesis (a statistically probable outcome) and this provides an interpretative problem. Thirdly, the measure of performance used was a relatively insensitive one and was not well suited to providing information on how the task was performed under the different viewing constraints. In particular, the measure used did not shed light on the type of timing errors made by the subjects under the different viewing conditions (i.e., whether responses were early or late). A response analysis of this type may be an important indicator of the type and quality of information available monocularly and binocularly. Previous attempts to examine the relationship between estimates of t_c and actual t_c (e.g., McLeod & Ross, 1983; Schiff & Detwiler, 1979) suggest that examination of this aspect of errors in t_c may indeed be critical to understanding timing.

In this study the monocular-binocular paradigm of McLeod et al. (1985) was replicated, but within a coincidence-timing task which presented no directional uncertainty to the subjects, and within a task in which the performance measures revealed information about the extent of under-estimation and over-estimation of t_c. Subjects viewed the apparent motion of a light source moving directly towards them along a linear runway and their task was to make a simple button-press response such that the occurrence of this response coincided exactly with the arrival of the light at the end of the runway. The basic hypothesis being tested, as in the original McLeod et al. (1985) study, was that timing accuracy should be equivalent under monocular and binocular viewing conditions if the t_c information is derived from τ . If t_c is computed from the velocity/distance ratio, timing performance under binocular viewing should be superior to performance under monocular viewing.

As an additional test of the τ notion, the velocity of the approaching 'object' was also manipulated in the current study. It was hypothesized that, if t_c information is derived from τ coincidence-timing, performance should be as accurate under fast approach velocities as under slow approach velocities. (The mathematics of τ is such that, providing the approaching object moves at constant velocity, τ should specify t_c exactly regardless of the speed of the object). If, on the other hand, stereoptic cues are essential for precise determination of t_c, and computational processes are involved, then timing performance might be expected to be somewhat less accurate when approach velocity is high and the time available for computation is correspondingly reduced (McLeod & Ross, 1983).

2.   METHOD

2.1 Subjects

Nine male and eight female university undergraduate students, ranging in age from 17 to 43 years participated voluntarily in this experiment. The near and far static visual acuity of all subjects was pre-tested under binocular, left monocular, and right monocular viewing conditions to ensure that none of the subjects carried uncorrected visual defects into the experiment. These tests were administered using the checkerboard test cards of the Bausch and Lomb Professional Vision Tester (model #71-22-41). All subjects had acuities in each eye in excess of the level of 20/25 Snellen acuity.

2.2 Apparatus

A Bassin Coincidence-Timer (Lafayette model #50575) with a runway length of 4.3m was used to present the apparent motion stimuli to the subjects. The proximal end of the runway was positioned directly at eye level of the seated subject and was viewed by the subject through a 9cm x 4cm opening in an eyepiece used to restrain head movements. The eyepiece, set within a wooden frame, was positioned at a distance of 57cm from the proximal (target) end of the runway. Monocular viewing conditions were produced by placing an opaque plate in the eyepiece immediately in front of either the left or right eye. The distal end of the runway was raised 56.5cm higher than the proximal end so as to provide the subjects with a clear view of the approaching light source over the full length of the runway.

2.3 Procedure

Subjects were administered in total 450 coincidence-timing trials with each trial involving the following sequence of events. At the commencement of each trial an amber warning light was presented at the distal end of the runway and then this was followed, 1.5 sec. later, by the onset of apparent motion of a red light directly towards the subject. The subject's task was to depress a hand-held response key with his/her thumb such that the completion of this simple action coincided precisely with the arrival of the moving light at the proximal end of the runway. Subjects were given verbal feedback at the completion of each trial regarding whether their response was early or late, and regarding the magnitude of any error made (in ms).

2.4 Experimental Design

The two independent variables of Viewing Condition (binocular, left monocular, or right monocular) and Approach Velocity (2.24, 4.47, 8.94 m/sec) were presented to the subjects using a fully repeated-measures design. Fifty trials were presented to the subjects in each of the nine Viewing Condition by Approach Velocity combinations, and the order of presentation of each of these combinations was randomised using a modified Latin Square design. The approach velocities of 2.24, 4.47, and 8.94m/sec gave total viewing times of 1.920, 960, and 480ms respectively.

2.5 Analysis of Data

Three dependent measures of the subject's coincidence-timing accuracy were derived; absolute error (AE), variable error (VE), and the percentage of early responses. AE is the mean error in timing expressed without regard to the direction (or sign) of the errors made (Schmidt, 1982). It provides an overall indicator of timing performance although its magnitude is influenced somewhat by the variability in the subject's responses (Schutz & Roy, 1973). VE provides an indicator of response consistency without regard to overall accuracy and is simply defined as the standard deviation of the subject's scores. The percentage of early responses made by the subjects under each condition was calculated in order to determine any possible response biases in terms of either under- or over-estimating t_c: The former bias would be manifest in a relative frequency of early responses greater than 50%, the latter in fewer than 50% of early responses.

All three measures were calculated for each subject under each of the nine Viewing Condition by Approach Velocity conditions, and then these mean subject scores were subjected to two-way analyses of variance using an alpha level of 0.05 and the Scheffe method to isolate, post hoc, the source of any significant main or interactive effects.

RESULTS

3.1 Absolute Error

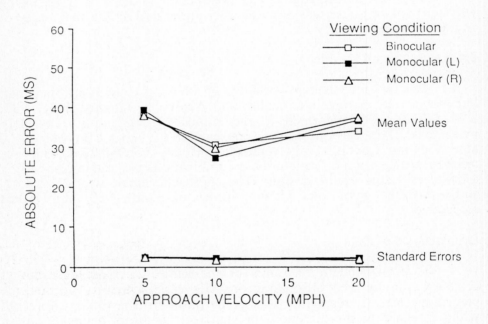

Figure 1. AE as a function of approach velocity and viewing conditions.

Figure 1 shows AE as a function of the velocity of the approaching 'object' and of the monocular and binocular viewing conditions. Approach velocity was found to exert a significant influence upon AE (F (2,32) = 17.31; p < .05) and this was due to significantly lower AE under the 4.47 m/sec conditions. However, AE did not differ significantly between the binocular and monocular viewing conditions (F (2,32) = 0.26; p >.05) nor was there any evidence of a Viewing Condition by Approach Velocity interaction (F (4,64) = 1.90; p >.05).

3.2 Variable Error

As was the case with AE, VE was influenced significantly by Approach Velocity (F (2,32 = 17.86; p <.05) but again in the absence of any Viewing Condition main effect (F (2,32) = 0.64; p >.05) or interaction (F (4,64) = 1.24; p >.05) (see Figure 2). Subjects' timing responses were more consistent when the approach velocity was 4.47 m/sec than when it was either slower (2.24 m/sec) or faster (8.94 m/sec).

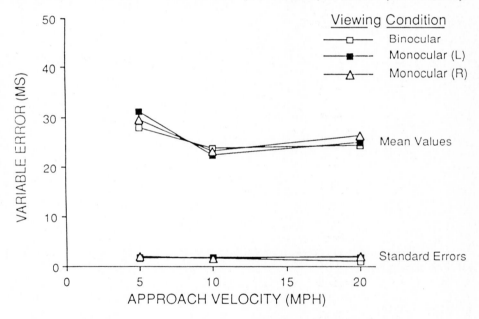

Figure 2. VE as a function of approach velocity and viewing conditions.

3.3 Percentage of Early Responses

Figure 3 shows that subjects made fewer earlier responses, progressively over-estimating actual t_c, as the approach velocity of the object increased. This effect of approach velocity was a significant one (F (2,32) = 14.43; p <.05) and was attributable to significant reductions in the percentage of early responses as Approach Velocity was increased both from 2.24 ms to 4.47 m/sec and from 4.47 m/sec to 8.94 m/sec. Moreover, the percentage of early responses was also significantly influenced by the Viewing Condition manipulation (F (2,32) = 6.21; p <.05), there being a higher percentage of early responses under binocular viewing compared to either left or right monocular viewing. This effect held systematically across all approach velocities with no significant Viewing Condition by Approach Velocity interaction (F (4,64) = 0.248; p >.05). Both monocular viewing conditions, unlike their binocular counterpart, produced mean percentages of early responses which differed significantly from 50% suggesting that monocular viewing caused subjects to over-estimate t_c slightly yet systematically.

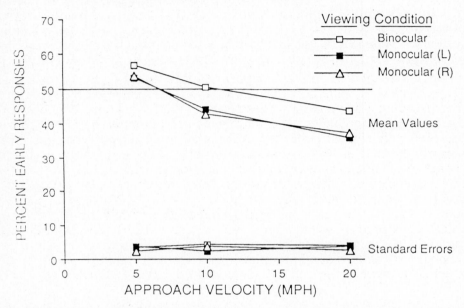

Figure 3. The percentage of early responses at each approach velocity under each of the viewing conditions.

4. DISCUSSION

Both the analyses of overall timing accuracy (AE) and variability (VE) were consistent with the conclusion that coincidence-timing performance was influenced only by the approach velocity of the 'object' and not, more importantly, by the monocular-binocular viewing manipulation. This equality of timing accuracy and consistency across both the monocular and binocular viewing conditions supports the conclusion of McLeod et al. (1985) that the visual information needed to determine when an object will arrive at the point of observation is equally accessible whether viewing with one eye or two. The almost identical mean binocular and monocular scores attained on this task from which all directional uncertainty has been removed suggests that the small, but non-significant differences obtained in the McLeod et al. (1985) study were possibly due to the slight directional uncertainty contained within their task. The absence of any binocular superiority for AE and VE in the current task argues against the importance of stereoptic depth cues in t_c judgments and therefore, by implication, argues against a computational basis for deriving t_c information, and in favour of a τ-based explanation.

On the other hand, analysis of the type of timing errors made by the subjects under the different viewing conditions (Figure 3), argues against the solitary utilisation of τ as a basis for determining t_c. When subjects view the approaching 'object' monocularly they respond later than they do when they view the 'object' binocularly; this occurs in a systematic way across all velocity conditions. This suggests that the monocularly-viewed 'object' appears further away than does the same 'object' viewed with both eyes, and t_c is consequently over-estimated during monocular viewing. These differences in response bias under the different viewing conditions cannot be explained on the basis of subjects' use of τ and suggest rather the differential utilisation of some additional parameters used in the determination of t_c. One possibility is that the monocular-binocular manipulation may cause differences in vergence angle of the eyes which in turn may cause differences in the perception of the relative distance of the approaching 'object'. Vergence angle is known to be important in the determination of both the absolute and relative distance of static objects (von Hofsten, 1976). If vergence angle can indeed be shown to be involved in t_c judgment then this argues against the simple determination of t_c from τ and in favour of a mechanism which also actively incorporates distance information.

A more substantial challenge to the adequacy of the τ-based explanation of t_c judgments comes from the observation that the velocity of the approaching 'object' exerts a significant effect upon the overall accuracy (Figure 1), consistency (Figure 2), and response bias (Figure 3) of coincidence-timing. The a priori expectation was that, given conditions of constant (non-accelerating) approach velocity, τ would provide equally accurate t_c information across all approach velocities. However, the AE and VE data show that timing performance is both more accurate and more consistent at the intermediate approach velocity of 4.47 m/sec than at either the faster 8.74 m/sec or slower 2.24 m/sec velocities. It should be noted, however, that these velocity effects are also inconsistent with a velocity/distance computational model for t_c. A computational model would predict timing performance to be systematically poorer with increasing velocity as both the time to perform computations is reduced at the faster velocities (McLeod & Ross, 1983), and velocity sensitivity is poorer (Shea & Northam, 1982).

A clearer insight into the cause of the approach velocity effects upon AE can be gained from examining the data on the percentage of early responses. Figure 3 reveals that subjects, regardless of whether they view the approaching 'object' binocularly or monocularly, respond increasingly later as the approach velocity increases, and this results in a shift in response bias from a predominance of early responses at the slowest velocity condition to a predominance of late responses at the fastest velocity condition. This linear decrease in early responses with increasing approach velocity (indicative of an increasing over-estimation of actual t_c) is consistent with observations made in some earlier studies (e.g., McLeod & Ross, 1983; Schiff & Detwiler, 1979) where subjects were required to estimate t_c throughout a period of stimulus occlusion. The lower AE observed under the 4.47 m/sec condition is therefore probably not a consequence of this speed being the optimal one for t_c judgments but is rather, more coincidentally, a consequence of this velocity being the one at which response bias is minimal and the subjects' t_c judgments are best calibrated to actual t_c.

The important question which begs solution is therefore why subjects should respond later at faster velocities. The observation cannot be simply a range effect (due to subjects being caught unprepared by the faster approach velocities) as the timing trials were presented to the subjects in blocks of common velocity. Two explanations for the systematic response bias in estimating t_c seem possible. The response bias effects may be a consequence of subjects' attempts to compensate for the 57cm difference between the target position (the proximal end of the runway) and the frontal plane of the eyes to which τ information is referenced. Alternatively, the response bias may reflect the presence of some proportional error within the estimate of t_c provided by τ. Ongoing research in our laboratory is directed at isolating the cause of these response bias effects evident in t_c judgments in an attempt to reconcile their occurrence with the use of either a computational or direct perception method of visually determining t_c.

In sum, the results of this study provide some support for Lee's (1976, 1978) direct perception notion of τ in that the information needed for accurate and consistent visual judgment of t_c appears to be equally accessible to one eye as two. It appears, however, that information in addition to τ plays a role in t_c judgment, as revealed by (i) the different monocular-binocular biases for early and late responding and (ii) the presence of velocity-dependent biases in responding. The isolation of the supplementary visual cues providing the additional information which influences t_c judgments, and the resolution of how this information is combined with information available from τ, represents an important hurdle to our understanding of how the processes of perception and action become linked in the timing of motor responses.

CORRESPONDENCE

Correspondence to be addressed to Bruce Abernethy, Department of Human Movement Studies, University of Queensland, St. Lucia, Queensland, 4067, Australia.

REFERENCES

Dietz, V., & Noth, J. (1978). Preinnervation and stretch responses of tricepts brachii in man falling with and without visual control. Brain Research, 142, 576-579.

Gibson, J.J. (1966). The senses considered as perceptual systems. Boston: Houghton-Mifflin.

Gibson, J.J. (1979). The ecological approach to visual perception. Boston: Houghton-Mifflin.

Hofsten, C. von (1976). The role of convergence in space perception. Vision Research, 16, 193-198.

Lee, D.N. (1976). A theory of visual control of braking based on information about time-to-collision. Perception, 5, 437-459.

Lee, D.N. (1978). The functions of vision. In H.L. Pick, & E. Saltzman (Eds.), Modes of perceiving and processing information. Hillsdale, NJ: Lawrence Erlbaum. (pp.159-170).

Lee, D.N., Lishman, J.R., & Thomson, J.A. (1982). Regulation of gait in long jumping. Journal of Experimental Psychology: Human Perception and Performance, 8, 448-459.

Lee, D.N., & Young, D.S. (1985). Visual timing of interceptive action. In D. Ingle, M. Jeannerod, & D.N. Lee (Eds.), Brain mechanisms and spatial vision. Dordrecht: Martinus Nijhoff (pp.1-30).

Leibowitz, H.W., Shiina, KJ., & Hennessy, R.T. (1972). Oculomotor adjustments and size constancy. Perception & Psychophysics, 12, 497-500.

McLeod, P., McLaughlin, C., & Nimmo-Smith, I. (1985). Information encapsulation and automaticity: Evidence from the visual control of finely timed actions. In M.I. Posner, & O. Marin (Eds.), Attention and Performance XI. Hillsdale, NJ: Lawrence Erlbaum (pp.391-406).

McLeod, R.W., & Ross, H.E. (1983). Optic-flow and cognitive factors in time-to-collision estimates. Perception, 12, 417-423.

Schiff, W., & Detwiler, M.L. (1979). Information used in judging impending collision. Perception, 8, 647-658.

Schmidt, R.A. (1982). Motor learning and control: A behavioural emphasis. Champaign, IL: Human Kinetics.

Schutz, R.W., & Roy, E.A. (1973). Absolute error: The devil in disguise. Journal of Motor Behaviour, 5, 141-153.

Shea, C.H., & Northam, C. (1982). Discrimination of visual linear velocities. Research Quarterly for Exercise and Sport, 53, 222-225.

Human Information Processing: Measures,
Mechanisms, and Models, D. Vickers and P.L. Smith (eds.)
©Elsevier Science Publishers B.V. (North-Holland), 1989

TEMPORAL CONSTRAINTS IN THE PERFORMANCE OF BIMANUAL TASKS

Jeffery J. Summers

University of Melbourne

A general finding that has emerged from studies of bimanual coordination is that there are strong temporal constraints on the performance of simultaneous motor actions. In particular, subjects experience great difficulty in producing different timing specifications for the two hands when the time periods are not harmonically related, as is the case in polyrhythms. Highly skilled pianists, however, seem able to maintain independent rhythmic specifications for the two hands. In this paper a review is presented of a series of experiments examining the ability of skilled (musically trained) and unskilled subjects to perform various bimanual tapping tasks. The results are consistent with the view that in tasks requiring the precise phasing of the hands central control can be exerted over low-level oscillatory mechanisms.

1. INTRODUCTION

The majority of skilled actions we perform involve the coordination of different limbs into a smooth pattern. A general finding that has emerged from studies of inter-limb coordination is that there are strong temporal constraints on the performance of simultaneous motor actions. For example, Kelso, Southard and Goodman (1979) examined the ability of subjects to make two- handed movements to separate targets that differed in size and in distance from the resting position. Under these conditions, the hands appeared to move in synchrony, so that they arrived at their respective targets at the same time. Thus, even though the spatial demands for the two limbs were quite different, the timing relations between the two limbs remained constant.

Studies using bimanual tapping tasks have shown a similar disposition toward simple timing relations in the coordination of the two hands (Deutsch, 1983; Klapp, 1979). Subjects have little difficulty in producing two isochronous sequences in parallel, one with each hand, when the sequences have identical or harmonically related time intervals (e.g., 2:1, 3:1, 4:1, etc). However, great difficulty is experienced in the concurrent performance of nonharmonically related motor sequences such as polyrhythms (e.g., 3:2, 4:3, 5:4, etc). In such sequences both left and right hand responses usually exhibit interference.

2. MECHANISMS CONTROLLING BIMANUAL COORDINATION

2.1 The central timer model

The temporal constraints evident in bimanual performance have been interpreted as indicating the existence of a single central timing mechanism or clock controlling the right and left hand motor subsystems (e.g., Deutsch, 1983; Klapp, 1979; Peters, 1985a). It is assumed that the central mechanism is limited in the extent to which it can simultaneously generate two different timing specifications for the two hands. Peters (1985a) has argued that the central mechanism can cope with this situation only by assigning priorities, through the allocation of attention, so that one limb drives the other and the two hands become synchronized. It is also proposed that in the guidance of concurrent tasks there is a preferential allocation of attention to the preferred hand. Support for this view has come from performance asymmetries frequently observed in the performance of bimanual tasks (e.g., Ibbotson & Morton, 1981; Peters, 1985a, 1985b). For example, when subjects are required to perform rubato (the gradual speeding or slowing of one hand with respect to the other), performance is better when the preferred hand takes the rubato (Peters, 1985b).

The central timer model, therefore, assumes that the interaction between the two hands observed in the performance of nonharmonically related time periods is due predominantly to limitations in a central timing system, rather than the result of cross-talk between the motor subsystems controlling the right and left hands. Recently, it has been suggested that not only do different effectors share a common timekeeper but that the same mechanism underlies both perceptual timing (perception of auditory events) and motor timing (Keele & Ivry, 1987; Keele, Pokorny, Corcos & Ivry, 1985).

2.2 The oscillator model

A radically different account of the temporal constraints evident in bimanual performance has been offered by proponents of the ecological or action system approach to the study of motor behaviour. This approach rejects the view that constraints on coordination arise from limitations in some central timing system and argues that time per se is not directly controlled in movement. Rather, timing is seen as an emergent property of the dynamic behaviour of the neuromotor system itself (Kelso, 1981). Proponents of the ecological approach have focussed on the periodicities evident in cyclic repetitive movements and suggest that such periodicities indicate some underlying oscillatory process. Specifically, it is assumed that the motor system contains ensembles of coupled and mutually entrained nonlinear neural oscillators and that motor timing is a consequence of this fact. The timing constraints evident in the performance of concurrent movements by the two hands, therefore, depend upon the entrainment properties of neural oscillators.

Evidence of entrainment-like phenomena in voluntary human actions has come from studies of cyclic finger or hand movements. Kelso, Holt, Rubin and Kugler (1981), for example, asked subjects to move the index fingers of one or both hands in a cyclical (flexion-extension) manner. In one experiment the preferred frequency of each limb in isolation was first determined and then possible interactions between the limbs when the actions were performed together were examined. When the two hands moved together mutual entrainment effects were observed. In right-handed subjects the left hand was "attracted" to the right hand. Furthermore, when subjects were asked to move one finger at their preferred frequency and to move the other finger at a different frequency, nearly all subjects employed low integer subharmonics such as 2 to 1 and 3 to 1.

Yamanishi, Kawato and Suzuki (1980) also obtained results consistent with the view that the temporal constraints evident in bimanual movements are a consequence of entrainment between neural oscillators. They asked subjects to tap each hand at a constant rate of one tap every 1000 ms. The time difference between left and right responses was varied from 0 (synchronous tapping) to 900 ms., in 100 ms. intervals. For both skilled (musically trained) and unskilled subjects accurate and stable performance was obtained when the two hands tapped in synchrony or alternated, that is were 180 degrees out of phase. Furthermore, intermediate phases produced unstable performance and a tendency to entrain to the nearest stable phase - synchrony or alternation. The authors concluded that in-phase and anti-phase motion are stable modes of coupling the hands. Tuller and Kelso (cited in Haken, Kelso & Bunz, 1985) obtained similar results with patients with surgical section of the corpus callosum suggesting that the coupling between the hypothesized oscillators is sub-cortical.

In summary, two very different explanations of the temporal constraints in bimanual performance have been offered. One emphasises the central control of timing and the limitations of a central mechanism, the other stresses biomechanical constraints operating at a fuctionally low level in the motor system.

3. TIMING IN BIMANUAL RHYTHMIC PERFORMANCE

Recently we have conducted a series of experiments in an attempt to gain further understanding of the mechanisms underlying bimanual coordination. In two of the experiments we investigated the production of polyrhythms. Polyrhythms require the simultaneous production of two (or more) conflicting but isochronous motor sequences. Although polyrhythms are extremely difficult to perform, people, such as highly skilled musicians, can accurately perform complex polyrhythms following extensive training.

The ability of skilled musicians to produce two differently timed motor sequences in parallel may depend on the development of an internal representation of the patterns as an intergrated whole (Deutsch, 1983). Alternatively, with practice, there may be a reduction in the influence of the superordinate controlling mechanism and the learner may develop the ability to utilize independent timing mechanisms for the two hands.

The oscillator model of bimanual coordination would also suggest that successful performance of polyrhythms is the result of achieving independence between the two hands. According to this view, however, the independence may reflect the weakening of the interaction between coupled neural oscillators, perhaps through the increasing influence of some higher-level control process (Summers, 1986; Yaminishi et al., 1980).

3.1 The production of polyrhythms

In the first study (Summers, Burns & Gazis, 1989) we compared the ability of skilled (musically trained) and unskilled subjects to produce the five polyrhythms shown in Figure 1. Of particular interest was the degree to which subjects could reproduce the phase relationships between the two hands demanded by the various polyrhythms. It was hypothesized that if in the early stages of learning polyrhythms the phasing of the hands is largely determined by the action of endogenous oscillatory mechanisms, then unskilled subjects should exhibit strong interference between the hands and a tendency toward synchrony or alternation of the two hands.

The polyrhythms were presented to subjects as two parallel tone sequences through headphones, one to each ear. For each polyrhythm subjects were first given a series of trials in which they were asked to tap the right hand in synchrony with the tones presented to the right ear and the left hand in synchrony with the tones delivered to the left ear. Subjects were also shown a diagram of the required phasing of the two hands. Following the synchronization trials subjects were tested on their ability to reproduce the polyrhythm from memory. During the test trials, after an initial period of synchronization the pacing tones were terminated and subjects continued tapping the polyrhythm from memory for a further twenty repetitions. Subjects were tested over five sessions and performed each polyrhythm with the right hand taking the faster beat and the left hand the slower beat and vice versa. There were, however, no performance asymmetries with respect to hand arrangement. Subjects also performed each polyrhythm at either a slow rate (total period 2250 ms.) or a fast rate (total period 1500 ms.).

The results showed that skilled and unskilled subjects were able to accurately reproduce the 3 against 2 and 5 against 2 polyrhythms. There was no effect of execution speed. Accurate reproduction of these two polyrhythms is consistent with an oscillator model of timing, as the second tap with the slow hand bisects the interval between two taps with the fast hand, thus necessitating a simple alternation of the hands. Furthermore, unskilled subjects showed a strong tendency toward alternation of the two hands in the reproduction of the other three polyrhythms (4:3, 5:3, 5:4). This tendency was stronger at the faster rate of execution and is illustrated in Figure 1.

There were a number of other features of the data, however, that were not consistent with an oscillatory type of process operating in the phasing of the two hands (see Summers, Burns & Gazis, 1989, for details). Of particular importance was the finding (see Figure 1) that subjects reproduced the intervals for the fast hand with a high degree of accuracy across all the polyrhythms tested. In fact, the main difference between the performance of skilled and unskilled subjects was in the accuracy of the intervals produced by the slow hand. If bimanual coordination is controlled by coupled neural networks, one for each hand (Yaminishi et al. 1980), then both hands would be expected to exhibit interference. The response profiles, however, are more consistent with the view that subjects adopted the strategy of allocating attention to the fast hand and then trying to interlace the movements of the slow hand into the movements of the fast hand - for unskilled subjects the simplest solution being to place the slow hand tap roughly midway between two taps with the fast hand. Peters and Schwartz (1988) have reported a similar strategy in the performance of a 3 against 2 polyrhythm.

Our results suggest that the tendency toward alternation of the two hands in the reproduction of the polyrhythms was not a consequence of

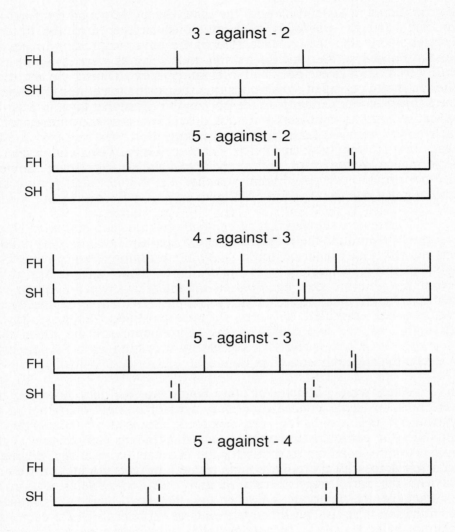

Figure 1. Schematic of the temporal relationships between the two hands required in the performance of the polyrhythms used in Experiment 1 (one cycle of each repeating pattern is shown). Each solid vertical line represents a tap with either the hand taking the faster beat (FH) or the hand taking the slower beat (SH). Each cycle of a polyrhythm was initiated by a simultaneous right and left hand response. Dashed vertical lines indicate the distortions of intervals in the reproductions of unskilled subjects at the fast rate.

motor interactions operating at a functionally low level in the motor system. We do not wish to deny, however, the influence of motor interactions in the performance of bimanual tasks. Rather it appears that in tasks requiring the precise phasing of the hands some central control can be exerted over low level oscillatory mechanisms. Much of the evidence for coupled oscillatory mechanisms operating in bimanual performance has come from tasks involving simple cyclic repetitive actions, such as self-paced flexion and extension movements of the fingers or hands. In such tasks the precise timing of movements is not an explicit part of the task and the timing observed may be a consequence of the inherent dynamics of the motor system. In our experiment, however, a great deal of effort was taken to ensure that subjects clearly understood the sequencing and timing requirements of each polyrhythm prior to testing (see Summers, Burns & Gazis, 1989 for details).

Some support for this view was obtained in a second study of polyrhythm performance. In this study we were interested in the effect of different types of training on the performance of a 5 against 3, repeating rhythmic pattern, with the right hand taking the faster beat. In one training condition six skilled and six unskilled subjects received extensive training at producing the rhythm for the right hand (one tap every 300 ms.) and left hand (one tap every 500 ms.) separately before attempting to perform the two rhythms concurrently to produce the 5 against 3 polyrhythm. By the end of training both groups of subjects were able to produce the rhythm for each hand alone with high accuracy. Following the training phase, and in preparation for the dual-task trials, subjects were given a series of trials in which a simultaneous left and right hand tap was introduced at the beginning of each cycle of a single-hand rhythm. Subjects then performed a series of test trials in which they were asked to perform the two rhythms concurrently. No specific information was given to subjects regarding the phasing of the two hands, other than to produce the rhythms they had practised.

None of the unskilled subjects was able to perform the two rhythms concurrently. The majority of these subjects tended either to tap the two hands in synchrony (i.e., 5 against 5) or produce five taps with one hand followed by three taps with the other. Four of the skilled subjects produced the polyrhythm with a strong tendency towards alternation of the two hands. However, as in the previous experiment, this was mainly due to changes in the intervals produced by the left (slow) hand (see Figure 2a). Of the two remaining skilled subjects, one accurately produced the slow hand intervals but made six taps with the fast hand so that every third response involved a simultaneous right and left hand tap (see Figure 2b). The other subject produced a 5 against 3 pattern but showed a strong tendency to synchronize the movements of the slow hand with movements of the fast hand (see Figure 2c).

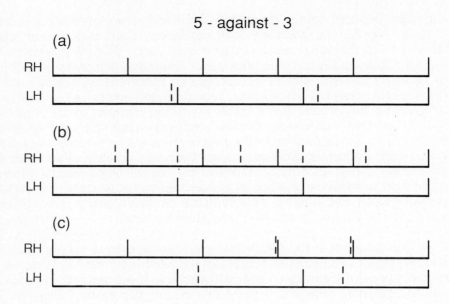

Figure 2. Schematic of the temporal relationships between the two hands required in the performance of the 5 against 3 polyrhythm used in Experiment 2 (one cycle of each repeating pattern is shown). Each solid vertical line represents a tap with either the right (RH) or left hand (LH). Dashed vertical lines indicate distortions of intervals in the reproductions of skilled subjects. Figure 2a shows the pattern produced by four subjects. Figures 2b and 2c the patterns produced by the two remaining subjects in the skilled group.

The results of this experiment clearly show that the constraints on bimanual performance cannot be reduced by extensive practice on the rhythm for each hand separately. In fact, in their attempts to perform the dual-task, most subjects showed a strong tendency towards synchronization of the two hands. This result is consistent with recent research by proponents of the oscillator model of bimanual coordination showing that in-phase motion is a more stable or attractive mode of coupling the hands than anti-phase motion (Kelso, 1981, 1984).

In our previous study, however, even unskilled subjects were able to produce a 5 against 3 pattern, although exhibiting a tendency to alternate the hands. We believe that the different response tendencies evident in the two studies reflect differences in the level at which timing was controlled. In the first study, providing subjects with explicit information regarding the required phasing of the two hands and practice at synchronizing their responses with pacing tones allowed central control of timing to be exerted. On the other hand, when no explicit information about the bimanual requirements was given (Experiment 2) subjects reverted to a lower level of control, and performance was dominated by motor interactions.

The results of a study we have recently completed are consistent with the view that motor interactions are not a necessary consequence of bimanual performance (Summers, Bell & Burns, 1988). The basic task was similar to that used by Yamanishi et al. (1980), requiring subjects to maintain various phase relationships between the two hands. A constant interval of 1200 ms was used for both hands, but the phase of one hand lagged the other by a constant amount (Figure 3). Six two-interval sequences were obtained by dividing the 1200 ms base interval into 100 ms steps. Thus, the sequences comprised intervals of 100-1100, 200-1000, 300-900, 400-800, 500-700 and 600-600 ms. In addition to the two-hand condition described above, subjects were also required to tap out the sequences using one hand only. For each sequence subjects first synchronized their key taps with auditory pacing signals. The pacing tones were then terminated and subjects continued tapping until they had reproduced the sequence 20 times.

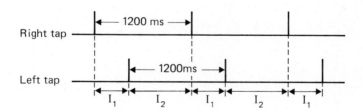

Figure 3. Schematic of an experimental trial in the two-hand condition (two cycles of the repeating pattern for each hand are shown). Each vertical line represents a tap with either the right hand or left hand. The two intervals to be produced are denoted by I_1 and I_2.

Figure 4 shows the accuracy of reproduction of the component intervals (t_1 - t_2) for the six sequences, in terms of the signed deviation from the presented intervals. The deviation scores for the two response conditions are presented separately. As can be seen, very similar trends were observed in the one-hand (where motor interactions are not involved) and two-hand conditions. The pattern with intervals relating as 1:1 (600-600 ms) was accurately reproduced. Imitation of the other patterns showed a general tendency towards an interval relation of 1:2.

These results are not consistent with the predictions of the oscillator model of two-handed tapping. In particular, such a model would predict a strong tendency towards synchrony of the hands in the reproduction of Sequence 1 (100-1100 ms) and a tendency towards alternation of the hands in the imitation of Sequence 5 (500-700 ms). Neither of these tendencies was evident, however, in the two-hand condition. In fact, in the reproduction of Sequence 5, subjects exhibited a strong tendency towards an interval relation of 1:2 rather than 1:1. The response tendencies observed in this experiment are consistent with those reported in previous studies of single finger tapping (e.g., Essens & Povel, 1985; Summers, Hawkins & Mayers, 1986). Similar performance for one-hand tapping and two-hand tapping has been found also by Klapp, Hill, Tyler,

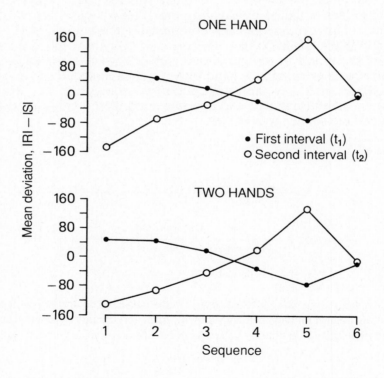

Figure 4. Mean deviation scores for the two intervals in each sequence for the two response conditions. Deviation scores represent the signed difference between the interval in the reproduced pattern (interresponse interval, IRI) and the presented pattern (interstimulus interval, ISI).

Martin, Jagacinski, and Jones (1985). Subjects were required to tap with one hand or two hands in synchrony with tone and light stimulus sequences that contained compatible (harmonic time ratio) or incompatible (polyrhythm) temporal structures (Experiment 2). The effect of temporal compatibility was similar for the two response conditions, indicating that the difficulty in responding to incompatible rhythms is not due to interference between the hands.

4. CONCLUSIONS

In summary, the experiments reviewed in this paper suggest that in tasks requiring the precise phasing of the two hands central control can be exerted over low-level oscillatory mechanisms. The general model of bimanual performance that emerges from these studies is depicted in Figure 5. The model suggests that timing in dual-task movements may be a secondary consequence of the entrainment between low-level oscillatory mechanisms, or it may reflect some higher-level control process. The interaction between oscillator mechanisms is responsible for the preferred relationships (i.e., synchrony and alternation) observed between the limbs in voluntary activity. Higher-order processes that can influence the low-

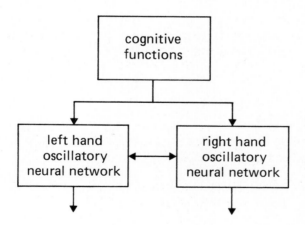

Figure 5. General model for the timing of two-handed movements.

level systems produce the adaptability and flexibility characteristic of skilled motor performance. The particular level at which timing is controlled is determined by such factors as the task demands and stage of learning.

There is increasing evidence that most motor activities are cognitively penetrable. Even actions that have previously been considered as low-level automatisms, such as the maintenance of posture, locomotion and reflexive responses to unexpected perturbations of movement have been shown to be influenced by specific cognitive states such as expectations, goals or knowledge (see Hughes & Stelmach, 1986). Furthermore, differences in timing performance obtained across different pattern structures (e.g., Essens & Povel, 1985), tasks (e.g., Summers, Hawkins, & Mayers, 1986), and modalities (e.g., Kolers, & Brewster, 1985) support the view that different strategies may be employed in the timing of movements (see Summers & Burns, in press, for review). Understanding the interface between cognitive processes and low-level neurological mechanisms is clearly an important issue for future research in bimanual coordination.

ACKNOWLEDGEMENTS

Preparation of this paper was supported by the Australian Research Grants Scheme, Project No. A28115899

CORRESPONDENCE

Correspondence concerning this paper should be addressed to Jeffery J. Summers, Department of Psychology, University of Melbourne, Parkville, Victoria, Australia, 3052.

REFERENCES

Deutsch, D. (1983). The generation of two isochronous sequences in parallel. Perception & Psychophysics, 34, 331-337.

Essens, P.J. & Povel, D.J. (1985). Metrical and nonmetrical representations of temporal patterns. Perception & Psychophysics, 37, 1-7.

Haken, H., Kelso, J. A. S., & Bunz, H. (1985). A theoretical model of phase transitions in human hand movements. Biological Cybernetics, 51, 347-356.

Hughes, B.G., & Stelmach, G.E. (1986). On Bernstein as a contributor to cognitive theories of motor behaviour. Human Movement Science, 5, 35-45.

Ibbotson, N.R. & Morton J. (1981). Rhythm and dominance. Cognition, 9, 125-138.

Keele, S.W. (1987). Sequencing and timing in skilled perception and action: An overview. In A. Allport, D. MacKay, W. Prinz, & E. Scheerer (Eds.), Language Perception and Production (pp. 463-487). New York: Academic Press.

Keele, S.W., & Ivry, R.I. (1987) Modular analysis of timing in motor skill. In G. Bowers (Ed.), The psychology of learning and motivation, Vol. 21 (pp. 183-228). New York: Academic Press.

Keele, S.W., Pokorny, R.A., Corcos, D.M., & Ivry, R. (1985). Do perception and motor production share common timing mechanisms: A correlational analysis. Acta Psychologica, 60, 173-191.

Kelso, J. A. S. (1981). Contrasting perspectives on order and regulation in movement. In J. Long & A. Baddeley (Eds.), Attention and performance IX, (pp. 437-457). Hillsdale, NJ: Erlbaum.

Kelso, J. A. S. (1984). Phase transitions and critical behaviour in human bimanual coordination. American Journal of Physiology: Regulatory, Integrative and Comparative, 246, R1000-R1004.

Kelso, J. A. S., Holt, K. G., Rubin, P., & Kugler, P.N. (1981). Patterns of human inter-limb coordination emerge from the properties of non-linear, limit cycle oscillatory processes: Theory and data. Journal of Motor behaviour, 13, 226-261.

Kelso, J. A. S., Southard, D. L., & Goodman, D. (1979). On the coordination of two-handed movements. Journal of Experimental Psychology: Human Perception and Performance, 5, 229-238.

Klapp, S. T. (1979). Doing two things at once: The role of temporal compatibility. Memory & Cognition, 7, 375-381.

Klapp, S. T., Hill, M. D., Tyler, J. G., Martin, Z. E., Jagacinski, R. J., & Jones, M. R. (1985). On marching to two different drummers: Perceptual aspects of the difficulties. Journal of Experimental Psychology: Human Perception and Performance, 11, 814-827.

Kolers, P. A., & Brewster, J. M. (1985). Rhythms and responses. Journal of Experimental Psychology: Human Perception and Performance, 11, 150-167.

Peters, M. (1985a). Constraints in the coordination of bimanual movements and their expression in skilled and unskilled subjects. Quarterly Journal of Experimental Psychology, 37A, 171-196.

Peters, M. (1985b). Performance of a rubato-like task: When two things cannot be done at the same time. Music Perception, 2, 471-482.

Peters, M., & Schwartz, S. (1988). Coordination of the two hands in rhythm production. Manuscript submitted for publication.

Summers, J. J. (1986, July). Timing of human movement. In H. T. A. Whiting (Chair), Acquisition of Skill. Symposium conducted at the 21st International Congress of Applied Psychology, Jerusalem.

Summers, J. J., & Burns, B. D. (in press). Timing in human movement sequences. In R. A. Block (Ed.), Cognitive models of psychological time. Hillsdale, N.J.: Erlbaum.

Summers, J. J., Bell, R., & Burns, B. D. (in press). Perceptual and motor factors in the imitation of simple temporal patterns. Psychological Research.

Summers, J. J., Burns, B. D., & Gazis, J. (1989). The production of polyrhythms. Manuscript submitted for publication.

Summers, J. J., Hawkins, S. R., & Mayers, H. (1986). Imitation and production of interval ratios. Perception & Psychophysics, 39, 437-444.

Yamanishi, J., Kawato, M., & Suzuki, R. (1980). Two coupled oscillators as a model for the coordinated finger tapping by both hands. Biological Cybernetics, 37, 219-225.

Human Information Processing: Measures,
Mechanisms, and Models, D. Vickers and P.L. Smith (eds.)
© Elsevier Science Publishers B.V. (North-Holland), 1989

THE NATURE OF CONTROL MECHANISMS IN REACHING BY YOUNG INFANTS

Anne Mathew and Michael Cook

Australian National University

Samples of reaches were obtained from groups of infants aged 4.5, 6 and 7.5 months of age. Split-screen video recordings were transcribed as sequences of (x,y,z) hand coordinates and the hand path was examined for evidence of initial aiming and subsequent correction of the movement path. At all ages, the initial direction of the movement was correlated with target direction, providing evidence that the hand was aimed towards the target. Additionally, changes in movement direction made after the commencement of the movement tended to adjust the hand path towards the target, providing evidence of error correction. Local minima of hand speed evident within segments of continuous motion were associated with turn towards the target. However, the movement path was also corrected within the movement elements bounded by these minima. This finding was seen as evidence of 'continuous' correction of movement errors and as contrary to the suggestion that infant movements are concatenations of ballistic movement units whose boundaries are marked by troughs in the velocity profile.

1. INTRODUCTION

When an adult reaches towards a viewed object, he or she reliably contacts the target, the hand path is smooth and direct, and the movement is characterised by a continuous, single peaked velocity curve. The first clearly identifiable reaching movements made by infants occur in the fourth month. These early reaching movements are inaccurate and tortuous and the velocity profile is marked by multiple peaks with intermittent pauses of the hand. During the subsequent months there is a rapid improvement in reaching competence, and by the end of the first year, the child shows the main features of adult reaching performance.

There has been some discussion about the nature of the control mechanisms directing the hand in early reaching. The very earliest movements are usually seen as "ballistic" in nature, in the sense that they are composed of preplanned movement units. For example, the well known study by von Hofsten, of infants reaching to moving targets was based on this assumption (von Hofsten, 1980). In order to make his analysis of the hand path, von Hofsten examined the velocity profile of the movement. He assumed that each trough in the record marked the boundary between two ballistic movement units and that corrections to the hand path were confined to element boundaries. According to this view, the whole movement sequence is under visual control, in the sense that each unsuccessful movement unit is immediately followed by another, which changes the course of the hand towards the target on the basis of visual information about target location.

In fact, in another publication concerning the same study, von Hofsten and Lindhagen (1979) appear to contradict this assumption. They state that the infants were "undoubtedly correcting their movements". It is not clear what they meant by this comment. However, it seems that they wished to indicate that the supposed pre-planned, aimed, movement units are concatenated until successful contact with the target is achieved. That is, the units themselves are not corrected, and feedback about the relative position of hand and target is not involved in the process of "correction".

Parenthetically, we point out that the question of whether correction was occurring within the movement units is of particular importance to the von Hofsten study. He concluded that his infants were preadjusting the direction of each unit to allow for the motion of the target - that is, they were aiming ahead of the target with the contralateral hand, at least. This carries strong implications of a sophisticated motor intelligence on the part of young infants, and it has been widely cited. However, if movement units were in fact corrected during their execution, this conclusion might be false. Von Hofsten's data could instead have been generated by a process which simply aimed the hand at the current target position and adjusted the path so as to "chase" the target during the execution of the movement.

The study to be described here analysed reaching movements in infants between 4.5 and 7.5 months. It addressed the question of whether the infant reach can simply be regarded as a concatenation of ballistic movement units. The methodology used was based on that of von Hofsten. However, it was extended to analyse the course of the hand within as well as between movement units, and interest in this study was confined to stationary targets. Samples of naturally occurring reaches by infants of various ages were recorded and analysed in terms of various indices of target-directedness, with the intention of identifying the contributions of aiming and correction in the execution of the movement.

2. METHOD

The strategy employed in the study was to elicit reaches to a range of target positions, from a variety of starting positions, so as to generate a heterogeneous set of movements. We then measured covariation across reaches between target direction and various measures of the hand movement. The variation of target position was manipulated experimentally, while variability of initial hand position occurred naturally.

The subjects were 4.5-month, 6-month and 7.5-month old infants, with 10 subjects in each group. In addition, a sample of reaches were obtained from two adult subjects. The adult data was intended, firstly, to provide a standard against which the infant performance could be judged, and, secondly, to provide an indication of the precision of our methodology.

The subjects were seated in front of a strip curtain and the stimuli were presented one at a time from behind the curtain. Four stimulus positions were used. Three of these lay in a frontoparallel plane at shoulder level. Distance was adjusted so that all stimuli could be reached with the arm partially extended (about 24 cm). The fourth stimulus position lay in the mid-line at about eye level. The stimuli were brightly coloured discs, 6 cm in diameter.

Arm movements were analysed in terms of an xyz coordinate system (x=lateral position, y=height, z=distance). The experimental session was videorecorded using 2 cameras. A top camera looked along the y axis into the x-z plane and a side camera looked along the x axis into the z-y plane. Mirrors were used to increase the viewing distance for each camera. The views from the two cameras, together with a timer output were recorded as a split-screen image.

An attempt was made to obtain at least 3 reaches to each target position for each subject. This was not possible for some of the younger infants within the time limits set for the procedure.

Data transcription entailed, firstly, identifying on the video tape the boundaries of the movements which were to be analysed and, secondly, computing the course of the hand during these movements as a sequence of (x,y,z) coordinates specifying position in three-dimensional space. Two types of movements were transcribed. Where possible, at least three Contacts were analysed for each target position. Contacts were defined as extensions of the arm, accompanied by fixation of the stimulus, which ended in a touch/grasp. An Approach was defined as an arm extension accompanied by fixation which approached within 10 cm of the target. If three Contacts were not available for analysis at each target, then Approaches were included in the analysis to make up the required sample. In the case of the bimanual reaches, analysis was confined to the hand which first contacted the target or (for Approaches), the hand which most closely approached the target.

In transcribing the hand trajectory, the recording was viewed frame by frame and the positions of the hand in the top and side view video-images were measured by manually positioning electronically generated cursors at the base of the index finger. These measurements were then passed to the laboratory computer for calculation of (x,y,z) coordinate values.

Data analysis was carried out interactively. Top views ((x,z) coordinates) and side views (y,z) were plotted on a graphics screen together with a velocity-time plot and a distance-time plot. The analysis program enabled the user to select a point in the data record and to move between points, the current point being marked by a cursor in each plot in the display. Figure 1 shows an example of these plots for a reach by a six-month infant.

Analysis involved selecting sections of the trajectory and computing various functions of the movement record for that section, describing the position of the hand relative to the target, its movement direction and its velocity. Following von Hofsten (1979), segmentation of the hand path was based upon inspection of the velocity-time curve. Tangential hand velocity at each point in the record was calculated as (distance travelled/time elapsed) across a window of five points spanning that point.

2.1 DIRECTIONAL ANALYSIS OF THE ARM MOVEMENT

The path analysis program provided various indices of accuracy of aiming and correction of the movement. All of these were based upon measures of movement direction. The constructions used in the analysis are shown schematically in Figs. 2 and 3.

Fig. 2 shows a movement path. This path has an Initial Direction of movement (obtained by fitting a line to the first 5 cm of the movement), and a Final Direction of movement (obtained by drawing a line between the initial and final positions of the hand). The Target Direction is defined at the beginning of the movement by joining the initial hand position to the target position. Each of these lines of direction can be specified in terms of two angles, its azimuth and its elevation, taken relative to the straight ahead direction.

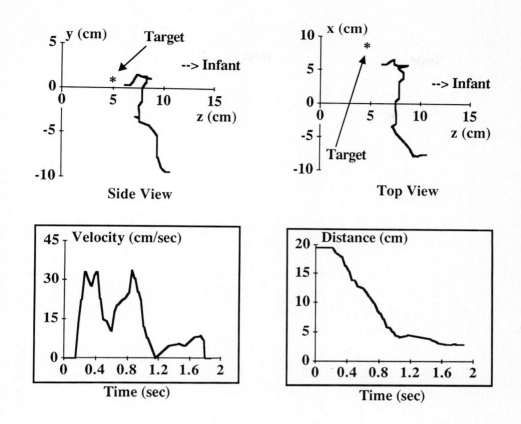

Fig. 1 Sample reaching movement by a six-month infant.

Accuracy of aiming was analysed by comparing the Initial Direction of the movement with the Target Direction. This was done, in the first place, by measuring the Initial Error of the movement (defined as the unsigned angle subtended at the starting position between the Initial Direction and the Target Direction). Secondly, an examination was made of how well Initial Direction was adjusted to changes in Target Direction. This was done by correlating Initial Direction with Target Direction over a sample of movements. This was done separately for the azimuthal and elevational components of direction.

Error correction was analysed in two ways. In the first place the overall Veer of the movement was estimated. This was defined as the angle separating the Initial and Final Directions. If correction occurs during a movement, the magnitude of its Veer should be related to the magnitude of its Initial Error. This question was examined by correlating Veer with Initial Error over a sample of movements. Evidence as to whether any veer which occurred during the movement was indeed made in the correct direction was provided by comparing the magnitudes of the Initial and Final Errors.

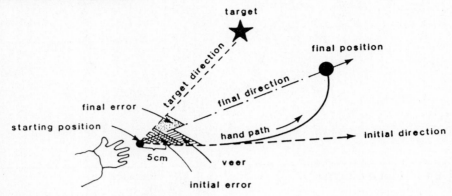

Fig. 2 Analysis of a movement path

Finally, changes in direction occurring at a particular point on the hand path were assessed calculating the Turn at that point. This measure is illustrated in Fig. 3.

The Turn at the point concerned was equal to the (unsigned) angle between the direction of exit (Exit Direction) from that point and the direction of approach to the point (Entry Direction). The Entry Direction was obtained by drawing a line to the point from its closest predecessor in the record lying at a distance of more than 2 cm away, and extending it ahead. The Exit Direction was the line joining the point to the nearest successor in the record lying at a distance of more that 2 cm. In addition, the Target Direction was the line joining the point to the target. We then defined the Entry Error as the (unsigned) angle between Entry Direction and the Target Direction. Similarly, the Exit Error was the angle between the Exit Direction and the Target Direction. The Turn index provided a measure of curvature at the point, while comparison of Entry and Exit Errors enabled us to assess the appropriateness of the direction change.

3. RESULTS

A total of 310 reaches were analysed over the three infant age-groups and the two adults.

Our concern was the nature of the control processes which were directing these movements and, in particular, the roles of aiming and correction in the execution of these movements. The strategy employed to examine these processes was to measure how well the initial

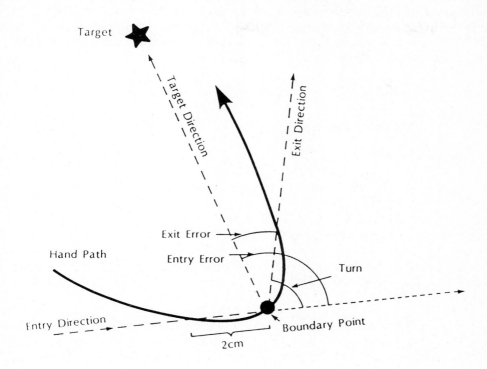

Fig. 3. Analysis of turn in a movement path

components of the movement were adjusted to the position of the target, and to examine subsequent parts of the movement for evidence of error correction.

Three units of analysis of the movement were considered. These were: (i) the movement considered as a whole (a movement); (ii) a period of continuous motion occurring within the movement and bounded by pauses of the hand (a segment); and (iii) a period of continuous motion bounded by local minima in the velocity curve (an element). This analysis is illustrated in Fig. 4 for the reach shown in Fig. 1.

In applying this analysis, the problem arose that small 'elements' might be generated by measurement error. This problem is often handled by filtering out small peaks mathematically. We have not smoothed our curves apart from the use of the moving window employed in computing velocity. Instead we have simply excluded small peaks from the analysis.

A velocity trough was considered to be an element boundary only if it was less that 70% of the smaller of the two flanking peaks and if it was separated from both adjoining peaks by more that two data points. On this basis, the illustrated sample comprises one movement, 2 segments and 3 elements.

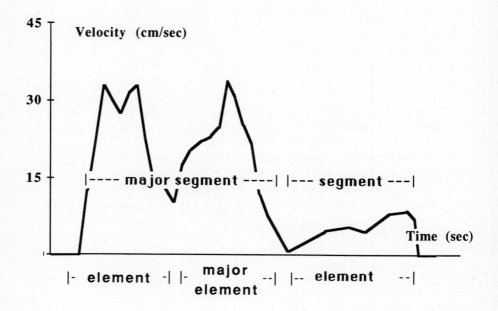

Fig. 4. Segmentation of the velocity profile

With increasing age, there was a progressive convergence between the three levels of analysis as numbers of segments within movements, and numbers of elements within segments reduced. At the adult level the three levels of analysis were identical, since the adult movements all comprised only one segment and one element.

3.1 ANALYSIS OF THE WHOLE MOVEMENT

Table 1 shows the mean frequency of contacts for subjects of different ages. Note the expected increase in contact rate with age. Note also, that reasonably high contact rate was evident even at the youngest age while even the oldest infants occasionally missed the target.

Table 1

Distribution of reaches for subjects of various ages

GROUP

	4.5 m	6.0 m	7.5 m	Adult
Total number	79	113	108	10
% Right hand	57	65	66	40
% Contacts	71	81	95	100

The data in Table 2 summarise means of various measures of performance for whole movements made by subjects of different ages.

Approach movements were analysed only as far as their closest approach to the target and, as a consequence, some of the measures shown in the table might have been inflated artefactually for movements of this type. Therefore, the table presents data for Contact movements only.

It is evident from Table 2 that successful reaches were executed more efficiently with increasing age. For example, movement time reduced with age. There was also a progressive smoothing of the velocity profile, as evidenced by the decreasing number of velocity peaks and segments. However, the 7.5 m infants still showed an average of more than three peaks per movement.

The Mean Effective Velocity was defined as the ratio of the mean initial target distance to the movement time. This index, which rises substantially with age, provides a useful global indicator of temporal efficiency. The change in its value across the infant groups is not due to increased hand speed, which does not differ for the three infant groups. The improved efficiency is partly due to the progressive simplification of the velocity profile. It also reflects increasing directness of the hand path. Thus, the total distance travelled decreased with age, even though target distance increased. The directness of the hand path is summarised by the linearity index (defined as the ratio of initial target distance to total distance travelled). There is a marked increase in linearity with age.

In spite of the non-linearity of their arm trajectories, the infants generally maintained a progressive approach towards the target during the course of the reach. The table shows the mean number of distance reversals at each age — a Distance Reversal was defined as a retreat from

Table 2.

General characteristics of whole Contact movements of subjects of various ages (mean distance in cm, time in sec, velocity in cm/sec). Standard deviations are in parentheses.

GROUP

	4.5 m (n=56)	6.0 m (n=92)	7.5 m (n=103)	Adult (n=10)
target distance	16.2 (4.3)	20.2 (5.7)	21.9 (4.2)	28.6 (7.8)
movement time	1.59(0.23)	1.54(0.40)	1.27(0.25)	0.67(0.03)
distance travelled	42.3 (17.5)	42.9 (17.2)	35.2 (12.2)	32.0 (5.0)
n(velocity peaks)	5.6 (1.1)	5.0 (1.8)	3.1 (1.1)	1 (0)
n(segments)	2.9 (1.2)	3.1 (1.5)	2.0 (0.7)	1 (0)
maximum velocity	82.9 (36.4)	89.2 (35.8)	81.3 (28.1)	108.1 (18.3)
mean effective vel.	10.2	13.1	17.3	42.7
linearity	0.38(0.12)	0.48(0.09)	0.64(0.09)	0.86(0.11)
n(dist. reversals)	1.6 (0.7)	1.6 (0.5)	0.4 (0.2)	1 (0)

the target following an approach. There was a significant reduction in number of reversals between the sixth and eighth month, so that by 7.5 m the control of the arm movement was good enough to ensure a progressive approach to the target on the majority of occasions. However, it is impressive that there were, on average, less than two reversals per movement, even for the youngest infants. This indicates that, in spite of the non-linearity of the movement paths of these infants, they tended to show a general progression towards the target.

These data show that infants of all ages were reasonably successful in contacting the target and that success rate and efficiency improved with age. We were interested in how this success was achieved. One attribute which would be expected to influence both the likelihood of success and efficiency is the accuracy of the initial direction of the reach. The accuracy of aiming of the total movement was investigated by examining the relationship between the Initial Direction of movement (Fig. 2) and the Target Direction at the beginning of the movement. Table 3 shows the analysis of aiming of the hand using these constructions.

Table 3.

Analysis of total reaching movements of subjects of various ages.

(a) Means (and standard deviations) of initial error (in deg).

GROUP

4.5 m	6.0 m	7.5 m	Adult
7.5 (7.1)	38.0 (9.2)	29.9 (9.8)	15.9 (6.4)

(b) Correlations between target direction and initial direction of movement

Age	n	Azimuth	Elevation
4.5m	79	.300 **	.520 **
6.0m	113	.310 **	.400 **
7.5m	108	.030 [NS]	.680 **
Adult	10	.810 [NS]	.610 [NS]

Table 3(a) shows the distributions (means and standard deviations) of the Initial Errors for each group.

There was a reduction in mean Initial Error between 6 and 7.5 months. However, this was not significant, suggesting that improvement in the accuracy of the initial bearing of the reach did not occur until some time after the eighth month. However, Table 3(b) provides evidence that infants of all ages were initially aiming the movement towards the Target. Thus at all ages there were significant correlations between Target Direction and Initial Direction of movement for either azimuth or elevation or both. (The correlations shown here and elsewhere were obtained by calculating correlations individually for each infant across reaches and pooling values across the group by Fisher's z' method.)

Nevertheless, initial errors of direction were often substantial, as indicated by the mean errors presented in Table 3(a). The fact that infants of all ages usually contacted the target in spite of these errors, might imply that error correction was occurring during the course of the movement at all ages. However, it is not incompatible with the suggestion that the reaches were simply sequences of aimed sub-units (which eventually contacted the target). Most of the movements made by

Table 4.

Analysis of major segments of reaching movements by subjects of various ages.

(a) Means (and standard deviations) of errors of direction (figures enclosed by [ ]
exclude segments which contacted the target).

GROUP

	4.5m	6.0m	7.5m	Adult
Mean initial error	40.5(11.8) [42.4(12.1)]	36.5(8.6) [37.7(11.7)]	29.8(10.1) [33.1(16.9)]	15.9(6.4) [0]
Mean final error	22.9(10.2) [27.1(10.2)]	16.0(5.7) [20.0(7.7)]	9.0(3.7) [12.3(6.6)]	8.2(3.5) [0]

(b) Correlations between target direction and initial direction of movement.

Age	n	Azimuth	Elevation
4.5m	79	.370 **	.660 **
6.0m	113	.350 **	.560 **
7.5m	108	.330 **	.700 **
Adult	10	.810	.610

(c) Correlations between initial error and veer.

Age	n	Correlation
4.5m	79	.770 **
6.0m	113	.760 **
7.5m	108	.920 **
Adult	10	.760

* p<.05   ** p<.01

the infant subjects consisted of several discrete episodes of continuous movement (segments), and 'corrective' intervention might have been confined to re-aiming the hand at the commencement of each segment of the movement. In order to examine this question, an examination was made of the internal structure of the reaching movements. In the first place, the properties of individual segments of continuous movement were examined.

3.2 ANALYSIS OF MOVEMENT SEGMENTS

Only the major segment within each movement record was included in this analysis. This was the segment in which the hand travelled the greatest cumulative distance. At all ages, the distance covered within the major segment was approximately 30 cm and the segment lasted about 1 sec.

The analysis of the major segments is summarised in Table 4. The accuracy of aiming of the major segment was assessed, as for the movement as a whole, in terms of the initial line of direction (now taken relative to the starting point for this particular segment). Table 4(a) shows mean initial errors for each age group and Table 4(b) shows correlations between initial azimuth and elevation and the corresponding components of the target direction. In contrast to the whole-movement analysis there was a significant reduction of mean initial error with age. More importantly, there were significant correlations between the initial azimuth and elevation of the target and the corresponding components of the target direction. This implies that the major segments were aimed towards the target for all age groups. The reduction in mean error, and the improvement of the initial direction-target direction correlations (which occurred in spite of the reductions in mean error) imply that accuracy of aiming improved with age.

The important question was whether error correction occurred within the major segment. The correlations shown in Table 4(c) suggest that correction was occurring within the segment. There was a significant correlation between the Veer of the segment and its Initial Error for all age groups, so that more erroneous movement showed greater shifts in bearing. Evidence that these shifts were in the correct direction is provided in Table 4(a). The mean Final Error of the major segment was significantly less than the mean Initial Error for subjects of all ages.

These data suggest strongly that infants of all ages were correcting the direction of movement. Since these corrections were taking place within an episode of continuous movement, these results mean that error correction, even in the youngest sample was not confined to the pauses between the movement segments.

This evidence establishes a continuous process of error correction, to the extent that infants of all ages were able to adjust the bearing of the hand without stopping the movement. However, for the infant samples, most of the major segments analysed were composed of multiple elements, marked by peaks and troughs in the velocity curve. It was seen earlier, that von Hofsten's analysis of reaching movements was based on the assumption that such a structure reflects a division of the continuous movement into 'ballistic' control elements. If this is true, then the error correction seen within the major segment must have been the result of directional changes at element boundaries. Corrective activity would not have occurred within movement elements. In order to examine this possibility, an analysis was made of the internal structure of the major segments of the reaching movements. The adult subjects were omitted from this analysis, since their single-peaked velocity curves could not be divided into elements.

Table 5.

Analysis of major segment: mean direction changes at element boundaries.

Age	N	Relative Turn *	Entry Error	Exit Error
4.5 m	141	35.1(16.8) **	70.3(11.9)	55.7(11.7) ++
6.0 m	111	44.7(19.5) **	67.3(19.2)	48.2(9.2) ++
7.5 m	73	32.1(17.9) **	49.5(14.0)	40.5(15.9) ++

*   Relative Turn = (Turn at boundary - mean of Turn at the flanking velocity peaks)

**   differs from zero at .01 level of significance

++   difference between Entry and Exit errors is significant at .01 level of significance

First, we asked whether element boundaries were structurally significant. We measured the Relative Turn at each element boundary within the major segment by determining the difference between the Turn at that point (Turn was defined in Fig.3) and the average of the Turn measures at the two adjoining velocity peaks. Table 5 shows mean Relative Turn measures for each of the three groups of infants.

The mean Relative Turn measure was significantly greater than zero for each group, indicating that element boundaries were, in fact, associated with relatively large changes in hand direction. The table also shows that mean Exit Errors were significantly less than mean Entry Errors at all ages. Therefore, these changes were turns towards the target.

These data are consistent with the notion that the veer towards the target which occurred over the whole movement segment was a consequence of intermittent error correction, and that multi-element movement segments were sequences of ballistic units, as assumed by von Hofsten (1979). Of course, the fact that the hand is not stationary at the commencement of most elements would complicate such an account. It would imply either a sophisticated planning process which allows for the current hand motion, or, which is more likely in young infants, an approximation designed simply to turn the trajectory in the correct direction.

If multi-element movements are really sequences of ballistic submovements then error correction should be confined to the boundaries between movement elements. They should not occur within elements. We examined this question by analysing the internal structure of individual elements. For this purpose only the major element of each major segment was considered.

3.3 ANALYSIS OF MOVEMENT ELEMENTS

The analysis corresponded to that carried out on the major segment of each movement (Table 4), but the various directions involved in the analysis were computed relative to the beginning and end of the element. The average distance covered by the major element was about 20 cm and the movement time was about 0.5 second for all age groups. The results of this analysis are shown in Table 6.

The picture of control presented by this Table for a single movement element is very similar to that presented earlier (Table 4) for a movement segment. In the first place, the Initial Direction of the element was positively correlated with the position of the target, at all ages, confirming that individual elements were initially aimed towards the target. This is consistent with the evidence presented in the previous table that error correction was concentrated at element boundaries.

In the second place, there were significant correlations between Initial Error and Veer for all age groups (Table 5(c)) and Final Error was significantly less than initial error in each case (Table 5(a)). As for the earlier segment analysis, these results indicate that errors of aiming were corrected during the course of this particular section of the movement. The importance of the present data is that these corrections were occurring within a single movement element. The table also shows that the amount of error correction increased with age. Thus the 7 deg shift

Table 6.

Analysis of major elements of reaching movements by subjects of various ages.

(a) Means (and standard deviations) of errors of direction. Figures enclosed by [ ] exclude elements which contacted the target.

	GROUP			
	4.5 m	6.0m	7.5 m	Adult
Initial error	33.6(4.8)	31.6(4.8)	28.1(8.5)	15.9(6.4)
	[34.9(5.4)]	[32.2(5.2)]	[30.4(9.5)]	[0]
Final error	26.4(9.5)	22.9(4.2)	14.6(4.7)	8.2(3.5)
	[30.3(5.6)]	[24.9(5.7)]	[16.3(6.0)]	[0]

(b) Correlations betwen target direction and initial direction of movement.

Age	n	Azimuth	Elevation
4.5m	79	.510 **	.770 **
6.0m	113	.520 **	.710 **
7.5m	108	.470 **	.700 **
Adult	10	.810 [NS]	.610 [NS]

(c) Correlations between initial error and veer.

Age	n	Correlation
4.5 m	79	.480 **
6.0 m	113	.540 **
7.5 m	108	.750 **
Adult	10	.760 [NS]

** $p<.01$

for the youngest infants was only 21% of the Initial Error. By the eighth month, the veer during the major element reduced the Initial Error by 14 deg, constituting 50% of the Initial Error.

4. CONCLUSIONS

The evidence that we have presented here shows that movement units at all levels of analysis were aimed towards the target, for infants of all ages. We have also shown that the velocity troughs which are seen within an episode of continuous movement are associated with adjustments of the movement towards the target. Nevertheless, our evidence also indicates the presence of error correction within the movement units which are supposedly bounded by these troughs.

We conclude that infant movements should not simply be regarded as concatenations of ballistic elements whose boundaries are marked by troughs in the velocity profile. As foreshadowed in our Introduction, this conclusion leads us to query the basis of von Hofsten's claim that his infants were aiming ahead of the target in reaching to moving objects.

It is important to note that, while these results offer evidence of error correction by all age groups, they do not establish that this correction was necessarily visually based. Thus, adjustments to the hand path might have been based upon somatic rather than visual information about hand position. However, evidence that infants in the two older age groups, at least, were capable of using visual information is provided by Lasky's (1977) finding that reaching performance in enhanced by vision of the hand from 5.5 m. Similarly, the observations by McDonnell (1975) and von Hofsten (1977) of accurate reaching to targets displaced by prisms implies sensitivity to visual information from the fourth month. In principle, evidence clarifying the issue could be provided by a detailed kinematic analysis of movements subjected to visual perturbations, such as unpredictable target shifts, prism displacement or interrupted view of the target. We are currently engaged in such a study.

CORRESPONDENCE

Correspondence concerning this paper should be addressed to Dr. M.L. Cook, Department of Psychology, Australian National University, G.P.O. Box 4, Canberra, ACT 2601 Australia.

REFERENCES

von Hofsten, C. (1979) Development of visually directed reaching: the approach phase. Journal of Human Movement Studies, 5, 160-178.

von Hofsten, C. & Lindhagen, K. (1979) Observations on the development of reaching for moving objects. Journal of Experimental Child Psychology, 28, 158-173.

von Hofsten, C. (1980) Predictive reaching for moving objects by human infants. Journal of Experimental Psychology, 30, 369-382.

Lasky, R.E. (1977) The effect of visual feedback of the hand on the reaching and retrieval behavior of young infants. Child Development, 48, 112-117.

McDonnell, P.M. (1975) The development of visually guided reaching. Perception & Psychophysics, 18, 181-185.

Human Information Processing: Measures,
Mechanisms, and Models, D. Vickers and P.L. Smith (eds.)
©Elsevier Science Publishers B.V. (North-Holland), 1989

ACCOUNTING FOR NOVEL RESPONSE TRANSFER: CURRENT EFFORTS AND FUTURE NEEDS

Richard A. Magill

Louisiana State University

A characteristic of motor skill performance that continues to elude satisfactory explanation is that people can successfully perform variations of an action that have not previously been practised. It was not until Schmidt's 'schema theory' in 1975 that a formal theoretical accounting of novel response success was presented. According to this view, novel response performance is accounted for by the strength of a schema representation of motor program parameter values. The strength of the schema, and hence the likelihood of novel response success, is said to be a function of the amount of and variability of practice of responses within a class of movements under the control of a common motor program. Two levels of concern are raised in this presentation regarding the adequacy of schema theory to satisfactorily account for novel response performance. First, empirical evidence is presented from contextual interference and spacing of repetitions research that demonstrates that novel response success cannot be exclusively attributed to prior practice variability. Second, theoretical issue is taken with the underlying assumption of schema theory that only a schema form of representation can account for novel response generation. Current exemplar models of representation can also account for such performance. Some recent results of tests of these models are presented. The concerns raised here regarding the current status of how we account for novel response success indicate the need for future efforts directed to answering this question.

1. INTRODUCTION

An important characteristic of motor skill performance that has eluded satisfactory explanation is that people can successfully perform variations of a motor action that previously have not been experienced. For example, each time that a tennis ball is hit during a rally, it is virtually certain that the exact motor action required to successfully hit the ball will not have been experienced prior to that shot. There are certain features related to the action of the ball, the action of the other player, and your own action, as well as features about competitive and emotional situations that cause unique characteristics to occur. When these unique features combine with previously experienced features, the result is that a response is required that has not been practised. Yet, we all know that the skilled tennis player can be very successful in these situations. Otherwise, the player would be unable to play the game with any success.

While there are several important theoretical and practical issues related to this novel response situation, I will consider only two. I see these two as critical to developing an adequate understanding of the learning and control processes involved in successful performance in these situations. First, at a basic level of understanding, it is important to determine the nature of the memory representation of skilled action that enables the performer to achieve novel response success. Given that we represent motor actions in memory, we must establish how the memorial representation of this action is characterized. Second, from the point of view of learning and instruction, it is important to determine the type of types of practice conditions that will lead to the greatest probability of achieving success in these novel response performance situations.

Before addressing these two issues, I want to briefly consider the current status of theory regarding these two issues. As we look through the motor skills literature, it is interesting to note that at the theory level, only Schmidt's schema theory (Schmidt, 1975) directly addresses this novel performance situation. While other theoretical accounts have been proposed to explain human motor learning and control, none has specifically included the novel performance situation.

Schmidt (1975) proposed that the representation of an action is in a schema form in both a generalized motor program and its ancillary motor response schema. That is, when a motor response situation is encountered and a performance is carried out, certain information related to this episode is stored in memory while other information is not stored. Additional experiences of this action lead to a synthesis of the abstracted information of each experience and a schema is formed to establish specific rules to control future performance situations involving this action. Thus, rather than storing every episode or every feature of each performance situation, specific information is abstracted from each episode and is used to update the abstract schematic representation.

With regard to the practice issue related to the novel performance situation, Schmidt's (1975) hypothesis was rather simple and straightforward. That is, he proposed that the probability of successful novel response performance will increase as a function of the amount and/or variability of practice of skills involved in the same movement class.   A movement class is defined by the invariant features characterizing several related actions. When the critical features are the same across varying exemplars of a skill, then it can be said that these responses are part of the same movement class.   While these critical features have not been empirically identified, Schmidt has argued that they involve such characteristics of movement as relative timing of the component parts of the skill, relative force of the component parts, the sequence of events required by the skill, and so on. Thus, it could be argued that an overarm throw is a movement class and could include throws of different speeds, using different objects, or either arm. These latter features are what Schmidt called parameters. It is the variable practice of these parameter features that is especially critical for increasing future performance success.

It is interesting to note with regard to these two tenets of Schmidt's Schema theory, that only the variable practice hypothesis has received any degree of attention by researchers. Reviews of this work can be found in works by Shapiro and Schmidt (1982) and by Lee, Magill, and Weeks (1985). The conclusion of each of these reviews was that the variable practice hypothesis has equivocal empirical support. Only two experiments have been reported that have addressed the question of the nature of the memory representation, one by Solso and Raynis (1979) and one by Lee (1985), and these were based on the recognition of movement patterns rather than on the active production of movement. Thus, it is evident that much work remains to be done before we can feel confident in answering either of the two novel performance issues we are considering.

Given this background then, I want to discuss two experiments that are examples of research going on in our laboratory that specifically address these two novel response performance issues.   The first experiment relates to addressing the nature of the memory representation while the second concerns the structure of practice issue.

2. THE SCHEMA FORM OF REPRESENTATION ISSUE

The assumption by Schmidt (1975) in his schema theory presentation was that if a novel response within a movement class can be successfully performed, then the memory representation underlying this action must be in a schema, or prototypic, form. Apparently, Schmidt was not aware of alternative views of representation form that could also predict novel response success. These alternative views, which I will group together with the label of exemplar views, were, however, popular only in the verbal skills literature, and have not influenced investigators concerned with motor skill memory. In fact, Adams' closed-loop theory

(1972), which was the predecessor of Schmidt's schema theory, also proposed a prototypic form of representation by proposing that both the memory and perceptual traces are actually prototypes of all the traces that have been experienced. However, it has become evident that memory theorists clearly do not assume that novel response success means a schema or prototypic form of memory representation (e.g., Brooks, 1978; Estes, 1986).

To test the schema vs. exemplar form of representation viewpoints, Craig Chamberlin (1988) conducted two experiments in our laboratory, one of which was designed to address the novel response performance issue, and which I will present here. According to the schema form of memory representation view, if a generalized motor program and recall schema have been well established for a class of movement, then performance on novel variations within that class should be performed well. Further, and more importantly for our purpose, the relationship between the novel responses and the responses that were practised should not influence performance of the novel responses. On the other hand, an exemplar model of memory representation predicts that the relationship between previously experienced responses and the novel responses will influence novel response performance. This influence will be seen by novel response performance error being a function of the degree of similarity between novel response features and previously experienced features. That is, the more features that are in common, the less error will occur in novel response performance.

To investigate these different predictions for schema and exemplar forms of memory representation, we had subjects practise three exemplars of one movement class, where the only movement feature varied was movement distance. Following practice with these exemplars, subjects performed novel variations of the practised exemplars that varied according to the distance moved. Thus, the predictions could be tested in this experiment by comparing novel exemplar performance as a function of the degree of closeness of the novel exemplars to the practised exemplars.

For all exemplars, subjects were required to move their preferred arm through a three-segment movement on a response panel located on a table top in front of the subjects. The goal for each exemplar was to perform the total movement in a criterion time of 1200 msec. Each of the three segments of the movement pattern was a unique distance, although all exemplars had a 2:3:1 ratio of movement distance for the segments. Thus the three practice exemplars consisted of segment distances of 5, 7.5, and 2.5 cm. for the short distance exemplar (for a total distance of 15 cm.), 15, 22.5, and 7.5 cm. for the medium distance exemplar (for a total distance of 45 cm), and 45, 67.5, and 22.5 cm. for the long distance exemplar (for a total distance of 135 cm.). Practice on these exemplars consisted of four days of 100 trials of practice for each exemplar each day. Organization of exemplar practice on each day and practice with and without knowledge of results varied so that on the last day, practice of the three exemplars was random and with knowledge of results (KR) on only every tenth trial.

On the fifth day, following 20 additional no-KR practice trials on each of the three exemplars, subjects performed 10 trials on each of four novel exemplars. Two of these novel exemplars were considered more similar to the practised exemplars than were the other two. That is, two exemplars were closer in total distance to the practised exemplars (22.5 and 112.5 cm) than were the other two novel exemplars (30 and 90 cm). The average distance differences between the two similar exemplars and the closest practised exemplars was 15 cm. For the less similar novel exemplars, this average distance differences was 30 cm. For all of the novel exemplars, the segment ratios were the same 2:3:1 ratio as for the practised exemplars.

The predicted performance on these novel transfer responses for the schema form of representation view is that there should be no difference in amount of error among the four novel exemplars. However, the exemplar view would expect less performance error on the two more similar novel exemplars than on the two less similar exemplars. Before looking specifically at the test of these predictions, it is important to note that subjects were able to perform the three practice exemplars with reasonable accuracy and consistency as absolute error was consistently below 50 msec for the last two days of practice. Also, there were no differences among the three exemplars by the end of the practice period. With regard to the important transfer performance, results showed that while error differed for the four novel exemplars, the difference was not statistically significant, nor did the amount of error follow a pattern related to the similarity of the novel and practised exemplars. In fact, the average absolute error for the two similar novel exemplars was 77.3 msec. and 75.9 msec. for the two less similar novel exemplars, a difference of only 1.4 msec.

These results provide strong evidence in support of a schema form of memory representation for the class of movement learned in this experiment. As such, they are in line with results reported by Solso and Raynis (1979) and Lee (1985) that were based on the recognition of similarity of novel and practised movement patterns. Thus, a schema form of memory representation has been supported for both movement pattern recognition and for active movement production. What is especially interesting about these results is that according to mixed schema-exemplar models, the typical expectation is that with few exemplars to be learned, an exemplar model is appropriate, whereas the schema form of representation comes into play for large numbers of exemplars within the category, or class. In the present experiment, evidence for a schema form of representation was found for only three practised exemplars.

3. THE STRUCTURE OF PRACTICE ISSUE

The second issue concerning understanding novel response performance success concerns the issue of the type of practice that will best prepare the performer to be successful when confronted with a novel response situation. According to Schmidt's schema theory, the key practice characteristic is practice variability. Schmidt hypothesized that as practice variability increases, the probability of successful performance on a novel response also increases. However, a review of the empirical literature investigating this hypothesis shows equivocal results. In our view of this literature (Lee, Magill, & Weeks, 1985), we proposed that one possible reason for this equivocality was that in experiments, in which support for the variability hypothesis was found, the variable experiences were arranged in random practice schedules. On the other hand, when support for the hypothesis was not found, the variable experience was typically arranged in a blocked practice order, where each variable experience was practised in a block of trials. In two experiments, we provided empirical support for this proposal. Thus, the organization of the variable practice session is also an important practice characteristic related to predicting novel responses success.

This random schedule of practice organization benefit supports previous research on what is known as the contextual interference effect (e.g., Lee & Magill, 198; Shea & Morgan, 1979). This effect occurs when variable exemplars must be learned together in the same practice session. A more contextually interfering arrangement of practice, such as occurs when the exemplars are scheduled in a random way throughout practice, leads to better retention and transfer than when exemplars are scheduled in blocks or units of practice trials. One possible explanation for this effect follows a view of why the classic spacing of repetitions effect occurs in learning verbal skills, such as espoused by Jacoby (1978; Cuddy & Jacoby, 1982). The benefit is that random practice induces a type of spacing between trials of the same exemplar. The effect of this spacing is to cause interference and thus some forgetting of the encoded information from the previous trial. On a subsequent trial of the same exemplar, more effortful action plan generation is required by the subject. As practice continues, the result of this increased effortful processing is a stronger memory presentation. Additionally, when transfer to a novel exemplar is required, superior performance occurs due to the greater similarity of processing requirements between the spaced practice and novel transfer situations than between the non-spaced practice and novel transfer situations, since the novel transfer case requires the effortful generation of an appropriate action plan. In spaced practice, subjects are regularly engaged in the effortful generation of relatively new action plans on subsequent practice trials for even the same exemplar, since much of the information from the plan used on the previous trial for this exemplar has been forgotten.

To test this notion of forgetting and the spacing of repetitions for novel transfer success, we conducted two related experiments that are included in a manuscript currently in preparation (Magill, Meeuwsen, Lee, & Mathews, 1988). I will briefly describe one of these experiments to illustrate how non-variable practice can lead to novel transfer success that is similar to variable practice.

Subjects practised a two-segment timing task where they were required to move their preferred arm from one microswitch to a second switch in a criterion time of 500 msec., and then to a third switch in 800 msec. All subjects practised this task for 35 trials with knowledge of results provided on each trial. The independent variable in this experiment was what characterized the interval between practice trials of this criterion exemplar. In the Non-spaced practice condition, subjects performed each trial within a few seconds of receiving KR for the previous trial. There were four Spaced practice conditions in which subjects experienced a 20 sec. interval between receiving KR and beginning the next trial. In the Empty Interval Spaced condition, subjects sat quietly during the interval before attempting the next trial. In the Non-Related Motor Activity Spaced condition, subjects performed a mirror tracing task during this interval. In the Related Motor Activity Spaced condition, subjects performed two additional timing tasks, similar to the one previously practised, during the interval. Finally, in the Verbal Activity Spaced condition, subjects guessed a three-digit number by saying three numbers and being told if each was too high, too low, or correct, until they guessed the number or the interval ended. Thus, if variable practice is the single key to predicting novel response success, then subjects in the Related Motor Activity Spaced practice condition should perform better than all other groups.

Results showed that all practice groups eventually performed the criterion exemplar similarly by the end of the practice trials. However, for the novel transfer response, the four spaced practice groups performed similarly, and, they all performed better than the non-spaced group or a control group that had no previous experience and practised only the transfer task. An interesting point to note is that while not statistically significant, the no previous practice control group performed the transfer task with less error than did the Non-spaced practice group. One view of this result is that the lack of between-trial spacing so proceduralized the learning of the skill that subjects had difficulty performing even a similar transfer task.

We view these results as not only supporting a "forgetting" hypothesis for the spacing of repetitions effect, but also as providing evidence that variable practice experiences are not the sole practice characteristic to increase novel response transfer success. The variable practice group was no better than the other spaced groups in novel response success. What these results suggest is that *disruption* of the practice routine is also an important practice characteristic. In our experiment, subjects who had their practice of the criterion task disrupted by being required to wait for a period of time, or to do other tasks between trials, developed a stronger capability of more accurately performing a novel response than subjects who were able to repetitiously practise. In effect, these results support a view of practice espoused by Bernstein (1967) who indicated that the best form of practice was "repetition without repetition." In terms of this experiment, subjects were engaged in repetition of the task, as they all practised the task for 35 trials, but without repetition, as these trials were consistently disrupted.

4. CONCLUSION

From the results of the experiments I have discussed in this paper, two points can be made about the novel response performance issues that have been considered. First, research evidence clearly supports the view that motor skills are represented in memory in a schema or prototypic form rather than in some exemplar-type form. Second, variability of practice cannot be considered to be the sole practice characteristic that increases the probability of success for novel response performance. Disruption of the practice routine will similarly increase the probability of success. While these two conclusions point out the present status of these two issues, there remains a great deal to be known about the novel response performance situation. An important future direction for motor skills researchers is to investigate the many issues related to this situation and to develop a viable theory accounting for this intriguing phenomenon of human behaviour.

CORRESPONDENCE

Correspondence concerning this paper should be addressed to Richard A. Magill, Louisiana State University, Baton Rouge, Louisiana, USA.

REFERENCES

Bernstein, N. (1967). The co-ordination and regulation of movements. Oxford: Pergamon.

Brooks, L. (1978). Nonanalytic concept formation and memory for instances. In E. Rosch & B.B. Lloyd (Eds.), Cognition and categorization (pp. 169-211). Hillsdale, N.J: Erlbaum.

Chamberlin, C.J. (1988). The memory representation of motor skills: A test of schema theory. Unpublished doctoral dissertation, Louisiana State University, Baton Rouge, Louisiana.

Cuddy, L.J. & Jacoby, L.L. 91982). When forgetting helps memory: ,An analysis of repetitive effects. Journal of Verbal Learning and Verbal Behaviour, 21, 451-467.

Estes, W.K. (1986). Array models for category learning. Cognitive Psychology, 18, 500-549.

Jacoby, L.L. (1978). On interpreting the effects of repetition: Solving a problem versus remembering a solution. Journal of Verbal Learning and Verbal Behaviour, 17, 649-667.

Lee, T.D. (1985). Effects of presentation schedule on retention and prototype formation for kinesthetically presented figures. Perceptual and Motor Skills, 60, 639-643.

Lee, T.D., & Magill, R.A. (1983). The locus of contextual interference in motor-skill acquisition. Journal of Experimental Psychology: Learning, memory, and Cognition, 9, 730-746.

Lee, T.D., Magill, R.A., & Weeks, D.J. 91985). Influence of practice schedule on testing schema theory predictions in adults. Journal of Motor Behaviour, 17, 283-299.

Magill, R.A., Meeuwsen, H.J., Lee, T.D., & Mathews, R.C. (1988). The effects of spacing of repetitions on the retention and transfer of motor skills. (Manuscript in preparation).

Schmidt, R.A. (1975). A schema theory of discrete motor skill learning. Psychological Review, 82, 255-260.

Shapiro, D.C., & Schmidt, R.A. (1982). The schema theory: Recent evidence and developmental implications. In J.A.S. Kelso & J. E. Clark (Eds.), The development of movement control and coordination (pp. 113-150). New York: Wiley.

Shea, J.B. & Morgan, R.L. (1979). Contextual interference effects on the acquisition, retention, and transfer of a motor skill. Journal of Experimental Psychology: Human Learning and Memory, 5, 179-187.

Solso, R.L., & Raynis, S.A. (1979). Prototype formation from imagined kinesthetically and visually presented geometric figures. Journal of Experimental Psychology: Human Leaning and Memory, 5, 701-712.

SECTION 4

PSYCHOPHYSICAL PROCESSES

Human Information Processing: Measures,
Mechanisms, and Models, D. Vickers and P.L. Smith (eds.)
© *Elsevier Science Publishers B.V. (North-Holland), 1989*

METRIC AND PERCEIVED STRUCTURES OF LINES VARYING IN INCLINATION AND LENGTH

Soledad Ballesteros

Universidad Nacional de Educación a Distancia

Two experiments were performed in order to investigate the characteristics of subjects' two-dimensional representations. Sixteen stimuli constructed from the orthogonal combination of four levels of inclination and four levels of length of straight lines were generated. In Experiment 1, subjects had to rate the dissimilarity of pairs of lines differing in inclination, in length, or in both. PRO ALSCAL multi-dimensional scaling showed that the best fitting configuration was not totally orthogonal. Parametric tests conducted on uni-dimensional and bi-dimensional variations showed that inclination and length were not psychologically independent. Length judgments were independent of inclination but inclination judgments were not independent of length. In Experiment 2, a restricted classification task using triads of stimuli from the same stimulus matrix indicated that the number of dimensional classifications given to triads that shared a level on length was significantly higher than the number given to triads that shared a level on inclination. The opposite occurred with the number of similarity classifications. The results of both experiments were discussed in terms of the integral-separable model of information processing.

1. INTRODUCTION

In the last few years, much research related to the study of mental representation of perceptual stimuli has been done (Garner 1974; Palmer, 1977, 1978; Shepard & Cooper, 1982; Shepp, 1983; Cooper, 1989). Recent research using multidimensional stimuli has shown that the decomposition of stimuli into their component dimensions is only possible for some multi-dimensional stimuli. There are some stimuli that can be easily analyzed or separated into their component dimensions, whereas others are very difficult if not impossible to analyze. Evidence from a number of information processing tasks supports the distinction between integral and separable dimensions Lockhead, 1966; Garner, 1974, 1976). Stimuli varying on integral dimensions are processed holistically whereas stimuli varying in separable dimensions are processed analytically.

Some kinds of stimuli, like those generated by the combination of saturation and brightness, cannot be easily analyzed into their component dimensions; they produce interference when the subject must selectively attend to one relevant dimension and ignore the other, irrelevant dimension, (Garner & Felfoldy, 1970; Burns & Shepp, 1988; Ballesteros, 1989), but yield an improvement in processing speed when both dimensions are correlated and perceptual integration is required, or when the two dimensions must be attended at once. In this case, selective attention to a dimension is not possible, and perception is dominated by the overall similarity structure. Furthermore, when subjects have to judge the similarity between stimuli, the results fit better into the Euclidean metric.

In contrast, other stimuli like those generated by the orthogonal combination of colour and form, or schematic faces varying in shape of the face, type of mouth, and empty or filled eyes, are easily analyzed into constituent dimensions. Variation in the irrelevant dimension does not interfere with the processing of the relevant dimension, and there is no loss in processing speed when the stimuli vary orthogonally, but neither is there gain with dimensional redundancy. Furthermore, the data from similarity judgements fit better into the city-block metric.

A more formal approach to the study of dimensional structure is given by the *Additive Difference Model* of dimensional organization (Beals, Krantz & Tversky, 1968; Tversky & Krantz, 1970). This model specifies the formal properties of psychological dimensions: inter-dimensional additivity and intra-dimensional subtractivity. Since then, other researchers have made use of one of the axioms of the model, called interdimensional additivity, to prove the psychological independence of several physical dimensions (Burns, Shepp, McDonough & Wiener-Ehrlich, 1978; Wiener-Ehrlich, 1978; Dunn, 1983; Burns & Shepp, 1988; Ballesteros & Gonzalez Labra, 1987).

The *inter-dimensional additivity axiom* states that the perceived dissimilarity between a pair of stimuli is an additive function of their difference along their component dimensions. The *equality prediction* that follows from this principle states that equal physical differences along one dimension should lead to equivalent amounts of perceived dissimilarity, independently of the fixed level of the stimuli on the other dimension.

Therefore, any pair of stimuli designated by the same interval notation should have equal dissimilarity ratings. Pairs occupying the same cell in Table 1 should have equal dissimilarity ratings. The second prediction from the axiom is the *ordering prediction*. This states that a given dissimilarity ordering of intervals along one dimension should be preserved when adding any interval from the second dimension to each of them. Several studies have shown that the equality prediction holds for separable dimensions, but is strongly violated by integral ones. Confirmation of the equality prediction would be consistent with the principle of inter-dimensional additivity, and psychologically independent dimensions.

The other basic principle of subjective dimensions is *intra-dimensional subtractivity*, which assumes that the contribution of any single dimension to overall dissimilarity depends on the absolute difference of the stimuli on that dimension. For example, a pair of stimuli that is three times as dissimilar on both dimensions as another pair would be expected to produce a mean dissimilarity rating that is larger than the latter pair.

The purpose of the present experiments was to examine systematically the relation between the metric and perceived structures of straight lines generated by the orthogonal combination of length and inclination. In order to achieve this, two experiments were conducted. In Experiment 1, subjects judged the dissimilarity between all pairs of lines differing in length and inclination. The judgments were examined for inter-dimensional additivity in order to determine if these dimensions were subjectively independent. The best fitting solution was then examined using Multi-dimensional Scaling techniques. Experiment 2 required subjects to perform a restricted classification task of triads generated from the same stimulus matrix. The dimensions used in this work have not been studied in depth, but there is some indication of support for the claim that line location and orientation are perceived in an integral manner (Redding & Tharp, 1981; Dunn, 1983), or at least produce some intermediate results (Smith & Kilroy, 1979; Smith, 1980).

At the same time, previous studies of line orientation have shown that subjects have greater difficulty in processing stimuli that are obliquely aligned than in processing vertical or horizontal stimuli. This phenomenon is known as "oblique effect" (Appelle, 1972; Essock, 1980; Lasaga & Garner, 1983), and does not seem to be due to any single factor. Many efforts have been directed to discover the neurophysiological mechanisms involved in this effect (Campbell & Maffei, 1970; Maffei & Campbell, 1970). Studies such as those of Campbell & Maffei focus on the neural sensitivity of the visual system to stimuli of varying orientation. Other researchers are interested in higher levels of cognitive processing. They think that the effect depends on the frame of reference used by the subject rather than on neuro-physiological biases, given that the stimuli are supra-threshold, and the frame of reference can be manipulated by instructions (Attneave & Olson, 1967; Rock, 1973). Lasaga & Garner (1983) examined the basis for the oblique effect in several information processing tasks using the horizontal, the vertical and the two diagonal lines. They concluded that two factors are responsible for the effect: greater confusability between the two diagonals and more favourable stimulus-specific properties for vertical and horizontal stimuli.

2. EXPERIMENT 1

2.1 Method

2.1.1 Subjects

Twelve undergraduate psychology students at the Universidad Nacional de Educación a Distancia participated in this experiment, 8 females and 4 males. All had normal or corrected to normal vision.

2.1.2 Stimuli

The stimulus matrix was generated by the orthogonal combination of two dimensions and four levels on each dimension. Thus, as shown in Figure 1, the stimulus set is represented as a 4 x 4 structure of lines that differed in length and inclination. The values of length were 0.62, 0.81, 1.05, and 1.37 cm. The values of inclination were 45, 90, 135, and 180 degrees, starting from the horizontal position. A total of 120 stimulus pairs were generated to form a complete factorial design, where the factors were the interval distance on each dimension. Table 1 shows the seven interval distances.

An interval distance defined as "zero step" means that the pair of stimuli shared a level in one dimension, so the pairs (1,2), (5,6), (9,10), and (13,14) shared a level on dimension Y, and differed by a level on dimension X. There are three one step variations in each dimension (X_1, X_2, X_3), two "two step" variations (X_{12}), (X_{23}), and one "three step" variation (X_{123}).

2.1.3 Procedure

In the dissimilarity judgment task, subjects were presented with a sequence of 120 pairs of stimuli during one experimental session and were instructed to rate the dissimilarity of each pair on a 10-point scale. A single random order of the pairs was prepared, but this order was counterbalanced across subjects, so half of the participants received the 1-to-120 order, and the other half the 120-to-1 order. Words like "similarity" or "difference" were avoided, and no mention was made of any property of the stimuli. In the similarity judgment task, subjects are required to combine differences on a number of dimensions in order to yield a single estimate of the overall dissimilarity between the two stimuli. These ratings are commonly used to represent these objects as points in a metric space (Tversky & Gati, 1982).

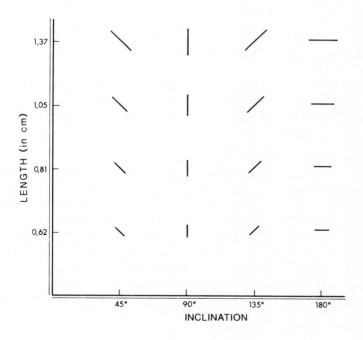

FIGURE 1. The sixteen lines used in these experiments, generated by the orthogonal combination of four levels of length and four levels of inclination.

TABLE 1

The 120 experimental pairs arranged in an X interval by Y interval matrix

	0_x	X_1	X_2	X_3	X_{12}	X_{23}	X_{123}
0_y		1,2 5,6 9,10 13,14	2,3 6,7 10,11 14,15	3,4 7,8 11,12 15,16	1,3 5,7 9,11 13,15	2,4 6,8 10,12 14,16	1,4 5,8 9,12 13,16
Y_1	1,5 2,6 3,7 4,8	1,6 2,5	2,7 3,6	3,8 4,7	1,7 5,3	2,8 6,4	1,8 4,5
Y_2	5,9 6,10 7,11 8,12	5,10 6,9	6,11 7,10	7,12 11,8	5,11 7,9	6,12 8,10	5,12 8,9
Y_3	9,13 10,14 11,15 12,16	9,14 10,13	10,15 11,14	11,16 12,15	9,15 11,13	10,16 14,12	9,16 12,13
Y_{12}	1,9 2,10 3,11 4,12	1,10 2,9	2,11 3,10	3,12 4,11	1,11 3,9	2,12 4,10	1,12 4,9
Y_{23}	5,13 6,14 7,15 8,16	5,14 6,13	6,15 7,14	7,16 8,15	5,15 7,13	6,16 8,14	5,16 8,13
Y_{123}	1,13 2,14 3,15 4,16	1,14 2,13	2,15 3,14	3,16 4,15	1,15 3,13	2,16 4,14	1,16 4,13

3. RESULTS AND DISCUSSION

3.1 Parametric techniques

Figure 2 shows the mean dissimilarity ratings of stimulus pairs as a function of difference in length, with inclination held constant (left panel). The right hand panel presents the mean dissimilarity ratings of stimulus pairs as a function of difference in inclination, with length held constant. Note that the length function is approximately linear; the dissimilarity ratings increase as a function of length intervals, and the intervals that are at the same step in length have almost the same dissimilarity ratings. This is not the case with the inclination function. The function is flat and there is no increase in the ratings with increases in the number of steps.

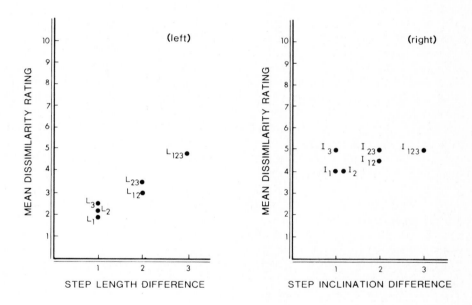

FIGURE 2. Psychological difference between lines as a function of difference in length, with inclination held constant (left panel), and as a function of difference in inclination, with difference in length held constant at six values (bottom panel).

Parametric techniques were applied to uni-dimensional and bi-dimensional variations separately for each of the 24 stimulus pairs exhibiting uni-dimensional variation and the stimulus pairs exhibiting bi-dimensional variation. The predictions for separable dimensions were: (a) uni-dimensional and bi-dimensional stimulus pairs should yield a non-significant stimulus pair effect; and (b) bi-dimensional stimulus pairs should yield a non-significant interaction effect when analyzed in terms of their dissimilarity ratings.

The two univariate analyses of variance included the level of unidimensional difference (6 levels) and the levels of the opposite, constant dimension (4 levels) as within subject factors. A significant effect of the opposite dimension means a violation of the equality prediction, whereas a significant interaction effect was taken as a violation of the ordering prediction.

The diagonal was analyzed in a separate within-subjects design, having 6 levels of length by 6 levels of inclination by 2 pairs of stimuli per cell.

The results can be summarized as follows: with intervals of length held constant, $F(3,33) = 7.45$, $p < .01$, increases in inclination did not produced a reliable effect, $F(5,55) = 1.47$, $p > .05$. No other effect was significant. With intervals of inclination held constant, $F(3,33) = .72$, $p > .05$, increases of length produced a reliable effect, $F(5,55) = 27.52$, $p < .01$, but there was an interaction between length and inclination, $F(15,165) = 2.38$, $p < .01$. A non-reliable effect of the dimension held constant for length supports the equality prediction, but a reliable effect for inclination failed to support the prediction for this dimension. The interaction term assesses the degree to which the rating of a constant interval on one dimension changes as the interval of the second dimension varies. A reliable interaction effect between both dimensions does not support the ordering prediction.

The ANOVA of the bi-dimensional variation pairs showed that the effect of levels of length was significant, $F(5,55) = 57.65$, $p < .01$, but not levels of inclination, $F(5,55) = .71$. A non-significant interaction between levels of length and levels of inclination, $F(25,275) = 1.15$, $p > .05$, supports the ordering prediction, whereas a significant stimulus pair effect, $F(1,11) = 69.86$, $p < .01$, does not confirm the equality prediction. This implies that fixed intervals on one dimension did not contribute the same amount of dissimilarity, irrespective of the level of the orthogonal dimension. Figure 3 presents the mean dissimilarity ratings corresponding to the bi-dimensional variation stimulus pairs. Each set of curves shows the effect of varying differences in one dimension, with difference in the other held constant at the same value. The top panel represents the mean dissimilarity ratings of length intervals with inclination intervals held constant while the bottom panel represents the mean dissimilarity ratings of inclination intervals with length held constant.

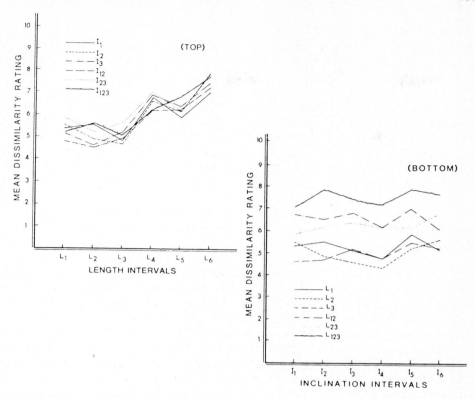

FIGURE 3. Psychological difference between lines as a function of difference in length, with difference in inclination held constant at six values (top panel), and as a function of difference in inclination, with difference in length held constant at six values (bottom panel).

3.2 Multi-dimensional scaling

A representation of the straight lines in a two-dimensional space was obtained by applying the PRO ASCAL Multi-dimensional Scaling Program to the dissimilarity ratings of the 120 stimulus pairs by the 12 subjects. The best fitting configuration is shown in Figure 4. Inspection of Figure 4 shows that length and inclination are not orthogonal dimensions. The configuration obtained is composed of lines which are not totally parallel. The perceived distance between lines tilted 135 degrees (right 9 diagonal) and the horizontal lines, tilted 180 degrees, is much smaller than the other distances. The results of this study seem to disconfirm the hypothesis that length and inclination contribute independently to the perception of straight lines.

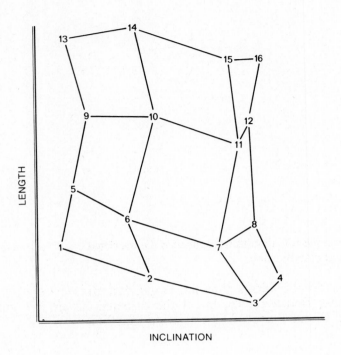

FIGURE 4. Best fitting configuration of length and inclination obtained from PROC ASCAL; two dimensional space; Euclidean metric; Stress = .12.

4. EXPERIMENT 2

In this experiment, a restricted classification task was used. Subjects had to put together two out of the three stimuli that appeared in the card, according to which "go best together". This classification task assesses more directly the dimensional organization of stimuli (Garner, 1974; Burns et al., 1978).

Figure 5 shows the dimensional relations of the three stimuli in a triad. The task allows three types of classification: (a) The dimensional classification, stimuli A and B are put together. The perceiver discovers the dimensional relation between the two stimuli; (b) Similarity classification, stimuli B and C are put together. The perceiver only takes into account the overall distance between stimuli; and (c) The haphazard classification. The perceiver puts A and C together; these two stimuli are not similar overall, nor do they share a value in one dimension.

TYPE OF CLASSIFICATIONS

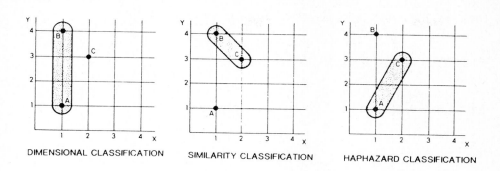

FIGURE 5. Examples of stimulus triads used in the restricted classification task showing the three types of classification.

For stimulus combinations that are organized dimensionally, A and B should be classified together, but if the dimensions are not subjectively independent, B and C should be classified together.

4.1 METHOD

4.1.1 Subjects

The subjects were 12 undergraduate students, six females and six males, none of whom had taken part in the first experiment.

4.1.2 Stimuli and task

From the stimulus matrix shown in Figure 1, twelve different triads were constructed. Half of them shared a value in length, and the other half shared a level in inclination. From each of these triads, 6 were generated by varying the spatial position of the three stimuli in the card. The total experimental task consisted of 72 trials. For a more complete description of the task and procedure see Ballesteros (1989).

The card presentation was made using a three field tachistoscope fitted with an automatic card changer; this procedure allowed the illumination to be precisely controlled at 1.5 lux. The exposure time was up to 3 seconds, but the stimulus disappeared as soon as the subject pressed one of the two buttons situated in the response panel. Subjects' reaction times to each triad were recorded, as well as the type of classification. Half way through the experiment, subjects were permitted to rest for 5 minutes and to change hand. Half of the subjects started with the right hand and the other half with the left hand.

5. RESULTS AND DISCUSSION.

Figure 6 shows the mean number of dimensional, similarity and haphazard classifications obtained in this task.

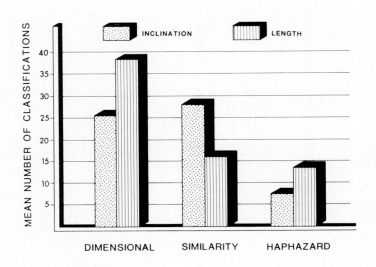

FIGURE 6. Mean number of dimensional, similarity, and haphazard classifications when the shared dimension in the triad was length, and when it was inclination.

A within-subjects analysis of variance was conducted on the number of dimensional, similarity, and haphazard classifications, separately, having shared dimension as a factor. The number of dimensional classifications was larger when the shared dimension was length than when it was inclination, $F(1, 23) = 10.35$, $p < .01$. Just the opposite result was found with respect to the number of similarity classifications. The number was larger when the shared dimension was inclination than when it was length, $F(1,23) = 23.73$, $p < .01$. The difference between the number of haphazard classifications did not differ significantly. The difference between reaction times corresponding to dimensional classification of triads that shared a level in length was not significantly different from the reaction times corresponding to the triads that shared a level in inclination, as it can be seen in Figure 7.

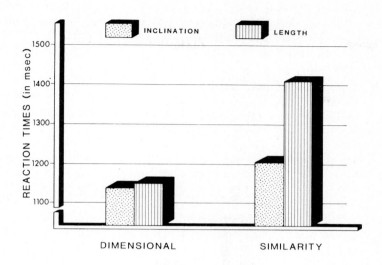

FIGURE 7. Mean reaction times (in msec) corresponding to dimensional and similarity classifications when the shared dimension was length, and when it was inclination.

Reaction times of similarity classifications corresponding to triads that shared a level on inclination were significantly faster than those corresponding to triads that shared a level on length, $F(1, 23) = 14.16$, p < .01.

GENERAL DISCUSSION

The results obtained in these experiments clearly show that multidimensional stimuli generated from the orthogonal combination of length and inclination interact in an asymmetric way, i.e. they are not psychologically independent. Even though these stimuli could be embedded in a two-dimensional Euclidean space, the best fitting solution to the proximity data was a configuration of interacting dimensions (spatial arrangements of non-parallel lines). Subjects judged stimuli in an additive manner when inclination was held constant, but failed to do so when length was the dimension held constant, and they were required to judge the dissimilarity between pairs of lines differing in inclination.

This result was corroborated by performance in the restricted classification task. The results of the second experiment showed that the number of dimensional classifications was significantly larger when the triads shared a level in length than when they shared a level in inclination.

The opposite occurred with the number of similarity classifications. Subjects could attend selectively to the length dimension and classify according to the shared dimensional value, whereas, when the shared dimension, was inclination, they classified stimuli according to overall similarity relations.

Other experiments, (Ballesteros, 1989) have been designed to test whether experimental manipulations, such as instructing the subjects to respond on the basis of their first impression, or to be very careful in the classification, could modify the type of triad classification. These experiments showed that the "careful" group produced more dimensional classifications than the "first impression" group in the case of triads that shared a level in length. There were no differences in the case of triads that shared a level in inclination. The results also showed that the type of instruction had a significant effect on performance, with stimuli generated from separable dimensions such as form and length. It therefore appears that it is easier to analyze certain perceptual dimensions than others. Selective attention to length of lines is possible, whereas it is more difficult to attend to line inclination.

In summary, this study has been concerned with the usefulness of the additive difference model to distinguish between features of subjectively independent dimensions. As Burns et al. (1978), Burns & Shepp (1988) have shown, this model provides an excellent basis for discovering different types of dimensional interactions. Some dimensional combinations (separable dimensions) satisfy the axioms of the model, whereas others (integral dimensions) do not. Inclination and length were not psychologically independent dimensions, interacting in an asymmetric way.

ACKNOWLEDGMENTS

This paper was supported in part from the CAICYT and the Spanish-North American Joint Committee. I am indebted to Brown University for its computer facilities and to Bryan E. Shepp for his help.

Correspondence should be sent to S. Ballesteros, Dept. Psicología Básica, UNED. P.B. 50.487, Madrid, Spain.

REFERENCES

Apelle, S. (1972). Perception and discrimination as a function of stimulus orientation: The "oblique effect" in man and animals. Psychological Bulletin, 78, 266-278.

Attneave, F., & Olson, R. K. (1967). Discriminability of stimuli varying in physical and retinal orientation. Journal of Experimental Psychology, 74, 149-157.

Ballesteros, S. (1989). Some determinants of perceived structure: Effects of stimulus and tasks. In B. E. Shepp & S. Ballesteros (Eds.), Object perception : Structure and process, (pp. 235-266). Hillsdale, N.J.: Lawrence Erlbaum Associates.

Ballesteros, S., & Gonzalez Labra, M.J. (1987, November). The perceived structure of form and size dimensions. Paper presented at the Twenty-Eighth Annual Meeting of the Psychonomic Society, November 6-8, 1987, Seattle, WA.

Beals, R., Krantz, D. H.,& Tversly, A. (1968). Foundations of multidimensional scaling. Psychological Review, 75, 127-142.

Burns, B., & Shepp, B. E. (1988). Dimensional interactions and the structure of the psychological space: Are hue, saturation and brightness uniformly represented as integral dimensions? Perception & Psychophysics, 43, 494-507.

Burns, B., Shepp, B. E., McDonough, D., & Weiner-Ehrlich, W. K. (1978). The relation between stimulus analizability and perceived structure. In G. H. Bower (Ed), The psychology of learning and motivation (Vol. 12, pp. 77-115). Academic Press.

Campbell, F. W., & Maffei, L. (1970). Electrophysiological evidence for the existence of orientation and size detectors in the human visual system. Journal of Physiology, 207, 635-652.

Cooper, L. A. (1989). Mental models of the structure of Visual objects. In B. E. Shepp & S. Ballesteros (Eds), Object perception: Structure and process, (pp. 91- 119).. Hillsdale, N.J: Lawrence Erlbaum Associates.

Dunn, J. C. (1983). Spatial metrics of integral and separable dimensions. Journal of Experimental Psychology: Human Perception and Performance, 9, 2, 242-257.

Essock, E. A. (1980). The oblique effect of stimulus identification considered with respect to two classes of oblique effects. Perception, 9, 37-46.

Garner, W. R. (1974), The processing of information and structure. Potomac, M.D. Lawrence Erlbaum Associates.

Garner, W. R.(1976). Interactions of stimulus dimensions in concept and choices processes. Cognitive Psychology, 8, 98-123.

Garner, W. R., & Felfoldy, G. L. (1970). Integrality of stimulus dimensions in various types of information processing. Cognitive Psychology, 1, 225-241.

Lasaga, M., & Garner, W. R. (1983). Effect of line orientation on various information-processing tasks. Journal of Experimental Psychology: Human Perception and Performance, 9, 2, 215-225.

Lockhead, G. R. (1966). Effects of dimensional redundancy on visual discrimination. Journal of Experimental Psychology, 72, 95-104.

Maffei, L., & Campbell, F.W. (1970). Neurophysiological localization of the visual and the horizontal visual coordinates in man, Science, 167, 386-387.

Palmer, S. E. (1977). Hierarchical structure in perceptual representation. Cognitive Psychology, 9, 441-474.

Palmer, S. E. (1978). Fundamental aspects of cognitive representation. In E. Rosch & B. Lloyd (Eds), Cognition and Categorization, (pp. 264-304). Hillsdale, N.J. Lawrence Erlbaum Associates

Redding, G. M., & Tharp, D. A. (1981). Processing line location and orientation. Journal of Experimental Psychology: Human Perception and Performance, 7, 1, 115-129.

Rock, I. (1973). Orientation and form. New York: Academic Press.

Shepard, R. & Cooper, L. A. (1982). Mental images and their transformations. Cambridge: The MIT Press.

Shepp, B. E. (1983). The analyzability of multidimensional objects: Some constraints on perceived structure, the development of perceived structure and attention. In T. Tighe & B. E. Shepp (Eds). Perception, cognition and development: An interactional analysis (pp. 39-75). Hillsdale, N.J.: Lawrence Erlbaum Associates.

Smith, L. B. (1980). Development and the continuum of dimensional separability. Perception & Psychophysics, 28, 164-172.

Smith, L. B., & Kilroy, M. C. (1979). A continuum of dimensional separability. Perception & Psychophysics, 25, 285-291.

Tversky, A., & Gati, (1982). Similarity, separability and triangle inequality. Psychological Review, 89, 2, 123-154.

Tversky, A., & Krantz, D. H. (1970). The dimensional representation and the metric structure of similarity data. Journal of Mathematical Psychology, 7, 572-596.

Wiener-Ehrlich, W. K. (1978). Dimensional and metric structures in multidimensional stimuli. Perception & Psychophysics, 24, 5, 399-414.

Human Information Processing: Measures,
Mechanisms, and Models, D. Vickers and P.L. Smith (eds.)
© *Elsevier Science Publishers B.V. (North-Holland), 1989*

DISCRIMINATION OPTIMIZATION: A GOVERNING PRINCIPLE FOR PSYCHOPHYSICS

Åke Hellström

University of Stockholm

Perception is specialized for monitoring information-carrying changes in stimulus levels and relations. Such changes are perceptually highlighted, even at the expense of veridicality. Subjects' comparison of two successive stimuli is adequately described as forming the difference between two compounds, each a weighted sum of the sensory magnitudes of one stimulus and of the momentary adaptation level. This strategy can greatly enhance the signal-to-noise ratio (S/N) of a change in the stimulus difference, but one side-effect is the time-order error. The optimal weight for a stimulus decreases monotonically with its subjective variability. S/N will therefore be maximized also for changes in stimulus ratios if the relative subjective variability is constant (Ekman's law). Over modalities, this implies an inverse relation (Teghtsoonian's second law) between Weber fractions and power-function exponents.

1. INTRODUCTION

Through our senses, we continuously receive information about objects and events in our environment. This information is carried by changes over space and time, not only in the magnitude levels of stimuli but also in their patterns, gradients, and other relations. Our perception is specialized to detect, monitor and interpret these changes - sometimes at the expense of strict veridicality.

2. The time-order error

Suppose that two stimuli are presented with a short time interval in between, and that I am to compare them as to, say, their brightness. Even if the stimuli are physically identical, I am then likely to systematically judge one as greater than the other. This phenomenon is called the time-order error (TOE) (Fechner, 1860). The nature of the TOE has been hard to understand, largely due to the fact that it is not adequately studied by the standard experimental designs of classical psychophysics (Hellström, 1977).

2.1 TOEs for loudness: A factorial experiment

In order to investigate the TOE for loudness (Hellström, 1979) I constructed 16 tone pairs by factorially combining four dB differences and four mean dB levels. I also used 16 combinations of interstimulus interval (ISI) and tone duration. For each combination, a separate group of 12 subjects answered the question, "Which tone was louder - First, Second, or Equal?" By a Thurstonian method, for each stimulus pair the distribution of judgments over these categories in the group data was used to scale the mean experienced loudness difference, D, between the first and the second tone in units of the half-width, T, of the Equal category. The TOE was defined as the value of D/T for two physically equal stimuli. As Figure 1 shows, the stimulus level had strong effects on the TOE, with the direction and slope of these effects depending on the ISI and tone duration (cf. Needham, 1935).

2.2 A quantitative model of comparison

The following model, which is a generalized version of the model of Michels and Helson (1954), explained 95% of the total variation in D/T:

$$D/T = [s_1 \psi_1 + (1 - s_1) \psi_{a1}] - [s_2 \psi_2 + (1 - s_2) \psi_{a2}] \qquad (1)$$

where ψ_1 and ψ_2 are the sensation magnitudes of the compared stimuli, ψ_{a1} and ψ_{a2} are the sensation magnitudes that correspond to the adaptation level (AL) at the respective moments of presentation of the two stimuli. The experienced stimulus difference, D/T, is the difference between two weighted compounds, one for each stimulus. The weights s_1 and s_2 indicate the relative contributions of the stimulus magnitudes to the compounds. In Figure 2 the fitted s values are plotted against the ISI for each tone duration.

2.3 The origin of the TOE

Setting $\psi_1 = \psi_2 = \psi$ and $\psi_{a1} = \psi_{a2} = \psi_a$ yields

$$TOE = (s_1 - s_2) (\psi - \psi_a) \qquad (2)$$

From this we see that TOEs occur when the stimuli differ from the AL and at the same time $s_1 \neq s_2$ (cf. Hellström, 1979, 1985).

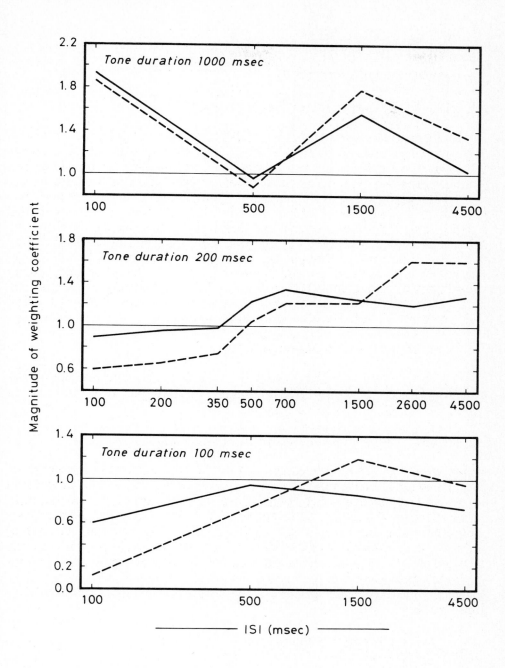

Figure 1. Mean estimated loudness difference D in units of subjective "Equal" category half-width T of pairs with SPL difference ± 0.5 dB vs. mean SPL for each condition (group). Group number indicated at both ends of each curve, ISI to the right of panel. Some of the lines are dashed for clarity.1

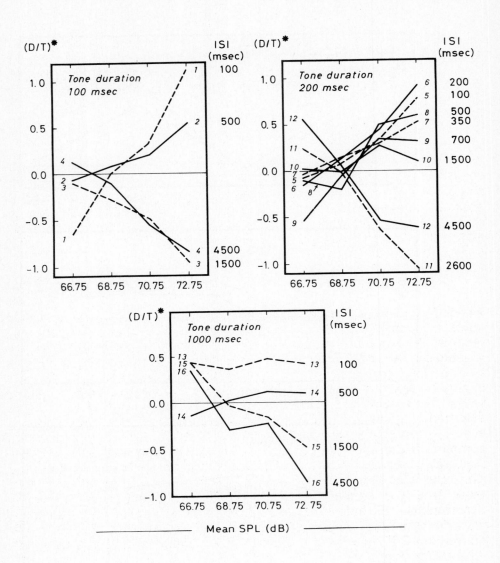

Figure 2. Stimulus weights s_1 (continuous lines) and s_2 (dashed lines) vs. ISI for each tone duration.[1]

3. DISCRIMINATION OPTIMIZATION

3.1 Combining information in comparing

As Figure 2 shows, the s values may not only fall below 1, which indicates compromise, or assimilation, between the stimulus and AL, but may in favorable perceptual conditions - long durations and short ISIs - also exceed 1, indicating contrast. The results reflect a flexible combining of magnitude information from the stimulus, with weight s, and from the AL, with weight (1-s) (cf. Hellström, 1985). What principle could it be that determines the value of s?

3.2 Maximizing the signal-to-noise ratio

Perception should maximize the detectability of a non-random change in the physical stimulus difference. This requires that the resulting change in the momentary experienced difference, d, becomes as large as possible, relative to the noise. This signal-to-noise ratio (S/N) can be defined as Dd / sd , where Dd is the change in d (the signal magnitude), and sd its standard deviation (the noise magnitude). The occurrence of Dd must be due to a change in y1 and/or in y2. We thus get

$$S/N = [\Delta \psi_1 (\partial d / \partial \psi_1) + \Delta \psi_2 (\partial d / \partial \psi_2)] / \sigma_d \qquad (3)$$

where $\Delta\psi_1$ and $\Delta\psi_2$ are the changes in ψ_1 and ψ_2. Taking the expected absolute ψ change as our unit (given that such a change occurs, and ignoring the possibility of simultaneous changes in ψ_1 and ψ_2), we set $\Delta\psi_1$ = 1 and $\Delta\psi_2$ = -1. By Equation 1, this makes the numerator equal to $(s_1 + s_2) / 2$. We may then enter in the denominator the expression for σ_d . Equations can now be derived from which we can calculate the s_1 and s_2 values that maximize S/N (Hellström, 1986a). These optimal s values are determined by the standard deviations, or noise magnitudes, of ψ_1, ψ_2, ψ_{a1}, and ψ_{a2}, and by their intercorrelations. Table 1 gives two series of computer exploration results. Series 1 represents the comparison of two confusable stimuli in a situation that leads to assimilation. Series 2 illustrates what happens when all intercorrelations are zero, which may be more true for stimuli far apart on the continuum (as in scaling experiments - see below). The optimized ratio of s_1 to s_2 varies inversely with the variability ratio of ψ_1 and ψ_2. The gain percentage, G%, is the increase in S/N, in per cent of the S/N that would result by ignoring the ALs and setting $s_1 = s_2 = 1$.

3.3 Perceptual sharpening needed

As the stimulus conditions shift, the noisiness of the compared sensation magnitudes will vary, as well as their correlations with each other and with the ALs. This calls for adjusting the weighting to achieve perceptual sharpening, for instance by reducing the weight for a "noisy" stimulus. The high G% values show that this principle is very powerful. The normally rather slight TOEs that result should not be too high a price to pay. The drastic changes in the s values with the temporal conditions in

Table 1.

Optimal s_1 and s_2 values and signal-to-noise ratio gain per cent (G%) according to the discrimination optimization (DO) model.[2]

$\sigma_{\psi 1}$	Series 1				Series 2			
	opt.	opt.	opt.		opt.	opt.	opt.	
$\sigma_{\psi 2}$	s_1	s_2	s_1/s_2	G%	s_1	s_2	s_1/s_2	G%
0.50	0.75	0.93	0.81	70	0.87	1.13	0.77	4
1.00	0.79	0.79	1.00	124	1.00	1.00	1.00	0
2.00	0.86	0.60	1.44	115	1.32	0.68	1.92	11
3.00	0.91	0.47	1.94	149	1.55	0.45	3.46	34

Assumptions: $\sigma_{\psi a1} = \sigma_{\psi a2} = 1.5$; intercorrelations in Series 1: (ψ_1, ψ_2): 0.9; $(\psi_1, \psi_{a1}),(\psi_2, \psi_{a2})$: -0.5; $(\psi_1,\psi_{a2}), (\psi_2,\psi_{a1})$: -0.3; (ψ_{a1},ψ_{a2}): 0.5; in Series 2: all intercorrelations zero.

the loudness experiment of Hellström (1979) (Figure 2) strongly suggest that a discrimination optimizing mechanism was at work. The low s values in conditions with both short ISIs and short tone durations probably result from stimulus interference, and the crossing over of the curves for longer ISIs, so that s_2 exceeds s_1, from forgetting the first tone (Hellström, 1979, 1985).

4. CLINICAL APPLICATIONS

The intake and processing of stimulus information may also be disturbed by disorders of the brain. By the DO model we may predict that the perceptual system will compensate by changing the weighting when two successive stimuli are compared. Tests built on this task might then be useful in clinical diagnosis, as is also suggested by earlier results (Birch, Belmont, & Karp, 1965; Needham & Black, 1970; Van Allen, Benton, & Gordon, 1966).

Here, I shall briefly mention two clinical studies of mine. In each study, two computerized "TOE" tests were used, one with line lengths as stimuli, and one with tone durations. Due to lack of sufficient data a simplified model was fitted. Its weights W_1 and W_2 are proportional to s_1 and s_2.

4.1 Painters' syndrome.

Hellström, Åslund, and Almkvist (1985) studied solvent-exposed workers with suspected solvent-related brain dysfunction, the "painters' syndrome." Figure 3 shows the main results from the line-length test, in terms of W values. Patients diagnosed (from conventional tests) as dysfunctional had lowered values of W_1 and W_2. Their W_1 values decreased sharply when the ISI increased. This seems to be another instance of the finding that solvent-related brain dysfunction accelerates the forgetting of visuospatial stimuli, in this case the first-presented line.

4.2 Senile dementia.

Hellström, Forssell, & Fernaeus (in press) compared healthy elderly persons with patients with incipient senile dementia of the Alzheimer type (SDAT). Here, the tone duration test gave the clearest indications. For the controls, the second duration was more heavily weighted than the first. This was also true for both groups in the just-mentioned solvent study, and for the healthy subjects of Hellström (1977), and was probably due to forgetting the first duration. But as Figure 4 shows, for the SDAT patients the two durations were weighted about

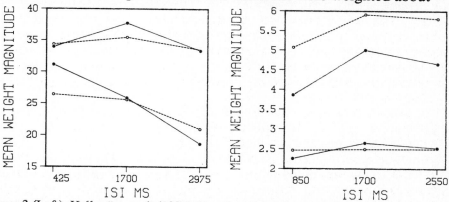

Figure 3 (Left). Hellström et al. (1985), line length: Stimulus weights W_1 (continuous) and W_2 (dashed) vs. ISI for nondysfunctional (upper plots) and dysfunctional (lower plots) solvent-exposed workers. Figure 4 (Right). Hellström et al. (in press), tone duration: Stimulus weights W_1 (continuous) and W_2 (dashed) vs. ISI for healthy controls (upper plots) and patients with Alzheimer-type senile dementia (lower plots).[2]

equally. A likely explanation is that attention capacity was reduced in the SDAT patients, so that listening to the first tone prevented full attention to the second.

The clinical studies, then, are consistent with the DO model, which gives a rationale for the anomalies in the comparing of successive stimuli.

5. SCALING AND THE POWER LAW

5.1 Why the power law?

Present-day psychophysics is much concerned with the scaling of subjective magnitude relations between stimuli where discrimination is no problem. In this situation, one important aim of perception is to detect changes in the physical magnitude ratio of the stimuli. Such changes signal events in the environment, and must therefore be sorted out from general changes in, for instance, illumination, which alter both physical magnitudes proportionally. If the power law (Stevens, 1957) holds between stimulus and sensation magnitudes, then the sensation ratio will change if and only if the physical ratio changes (cf. Yilmas, 1967). The mechanism that maximizes S/N for changes in the interstimulus difference will set the weight for each stimulus to be roughly inversely proportional to the variability of its sensation magnitude (cf. Table 1, Series 2). If this variability is proportional to the mean sensation magnitude, as Ekman's (1956, 1959) law implies, then the weight ratio will become roughly inversely proportional to the ratio of the sensation magnitudes. This in turn implies that the subjective difference d will change if and only if the sensation ratio changes. If the power law holds, d will serve as an indicator of changes in the physical stimulus ratio. This may be one rationale of the power law.

5.2 Sensation variability and the power-law exponent

But what is it that determines the exponent of the power function? Teghtsoonian (1971) formulated two laws, the second of which essentially states that the product of the exponent and the Weber fraction for the same continuum is constant at about 0.03. This implies that the exponents are set to values that give the relative variability of a sensation magnitude this constant value over continua (cf. Hellström, 1986b, 1989), thereby minimizing systematic errors by eliminating the need for an uneven weighting in the comparing of two stimuli whose sensations have equal magnitudes but different qualities.

6. STIMULI, RESPONSES, AND EQUILIBRIA

Finally, a word about responses. Aren't they "evoked" by the percepts? No, it seems that we can better understand psychophysical judgment in terms of matching, that is, the subject's deciding which numbers or other judgments evoke percepts equal in subjective magnitude to those evoked by the stimuli (cf. Ekman, 1964; Goude, 1962; MacKay, 1963). More generally, responses as well as stimuli give rise to sensations, which become subject to adaptation and weighting to yield percepts. The response is selected so as to produce a task-specific equilibrium among the percepts. The generalized DO model then says that the S/N of a non-random deviation from this equilibrium is maximized (Hellström, 1986b). For one thing, this may help us understand the so-called response biases, which should rather be considered perceptual.

FOOTNOTES

1. Figures 1 and 2 are from "Time errors and differential sensation weighting" by Å. Hellström (1979). Copyright 1979 by the American Psychological Association, Inc. Reprinted by permission.

2. Figures 3 and 4, and the data in Table 1, are from "What happens when we compare two stimuli?" by Å. Hellström (1989). In G. Ljunggren & S. Dornic (Eds.), Psychophysics in action. Copyright 1989 by Springer-Verlag Berlin Heidelberg. Reprinted and adapted by permission.

ACKNOWLEDGEMENTS.

This research was supported by the Swedish Council for Research in the Humanities and Social Sciences and by the Åke Wiberg Foundation. Department of Psychology, University of Stockholm, S-106 91 Stockholm, Sweden

Correspondence concerning this paper should be addressed to Åke Hellström, Department of Psychology, University of Stockholm, S-106 91 Stockholm, Sweden.

REFERENCES

Birch, H. G., Belmont, I., & Karp, E. (1965). The prolongation of inhibition in brain-damaged patients. Cortex, 1, 397-409.

Ekman, G. (1956). Discriminal sensitivity on the subjective continuum. Acta Psychologica, 12, 233-243.

Ekman, G. (1959). Weber's law and related functions. Journal of Psychology, 47, 343-352.

Ekman, G. (1964). Is the power law a special case of Fechner's law? Perceptual and Motor Skills, 19, 730.

Fechner, G. T. (1860). Elemente der Psychophysik [Elements of psychophysics]. Leipzig, Germany: Breitkopf & Härtel.

Goude, G. (1962). On fundamental measurement in psychology. Stockholm: Almqvist & Wiksell. Hellström, Å, . (1977). Time errors are perceptual. An experimental investigation of duration and a quantitative successive-comparison model. Psychological Research, 39, 345-388.

Hellström, Å. (1979). Time errors and differential sensation weighting. Journal of Experimental Psychology: Human Perception and Performance, 5, 460-477.

Hellström, Å. (1985). The time-order error and its relatives: Mirrors of cognitive processes in comparing. Psychological Bulletin, 97, 35-61.

Hellström, Å. (1986a). Sensation weighting in comparing: A tool for optimizing discrimination. In B. Berglund, U. Berglund, & R. Teghtsoonian (Eds.), Fechner Day 86 (pp. 89-94). Stockholm: International Society for Psychophysics.

Hellström, Å. (1986b). Sensitivity optimization in psychophysics. In B. Berglund, U. Berglund, & R. Teghtsoonian (Eds.), Fechner Day 86 (pp. 95-100). Stockholm: International Society for Psychophysics.

Hellström, Å. (1989). What happens when we compare two stimuli? In G. Ljunggren & S. Dornic (Eds.), Psychophysics in action. Berlin: Springer.

Hellström, Å, Åslund, U. & Almkvist, O. (1985). Comparing computer-presented successive stimuli: Indications of cognitive malfunctioning in solvent-exposed workers. In: Neurobehavioral methods in occupational and environmental health: Extended abstracts from the second international symposium, Copenhagen, 6-9 August 1985 (Environmental Health, Document 3, pp. 115-119). Copenhagen: WHO.

Hellström, Å., Forssell, L. G., & Fernaeus, S. E. Early stages of late onset Alzheimer's disease. V. Psychometric evaluation of perceptual/cognitive processes. Scandinavian Journal of Neurology (in press).

MacKay, D.M. (1963). Psychophysics of perceived intensity: A theoretical basis for Fechner's and Stevens' laws. Science, 139, 1213-1216.

Michels, W. C., & Helson, H. (1954). A quantitative theory of time-order effects. American Journal of Psychology, 67, 327-334. Needham, J. G. (1935). The effect of the time-interval upon the time-error at different intensive levels. Journal of Experimental Psychology, 18, 530-543.

Needham, E. C., & Black, H. W. (1970). The relative ability of aphasic patients to judge the duration and intensity of pure tones. Journal of Speech and Hearing Research, 13, 725-730.

Stevens, S. S. (1957). On the psychophysical law. Psychological Review, 64, 153-181.

Teghtsoonian, R. (1971). On the exponents in Stevens' law and the constant in Ekman's law. Psychological Review, 78, 327-330.

Van Allen, M. W, Benton, A. L., & Gordon, M. C. (1966). Temporal discrimination in brain-damaged patients. Neuropsychologia, 4, 159-167.

Yilmaz H (1967). Perceptual invariance and the psychophysical law. Perception & Psychophysics, 2, 533-538.

SECTION 5

RESPONSE LATENCY MECHANISMS

Human Information Processing: Measures,
Mechanisms, and Models, D. *Vickers and P.L. Smith (eds.)*
© *Elsevier Science Publishers B.V. (North-Holland), 1989*

CONTEXT, CONTEXT SHIFTS, AND SEMANTIC CONGRUITY EFFECTS IN COMPARATIVE JUDGMENTS

William M. Petrusic and Joseph V. Baranski

Carleton University

Semantic congruity and global difficulty contextual effects were examined in two visual extent comparison experiments. In the first, in accord with Vickers' adaptive-accumulator model, response times were longer and accuracy higher for target pairs embedded in a difficult as compared to an easy context. In a second experiment, when accuracy was emphasised and subjects were shifted to a set with a preponderance of very difficult comparisons, relative to control subjects, response times and accuracy increased but confidence decreased. However, for deadline enforced (450 ms) subjects, response time, accuracy and confidence decreased in response to the difficulty shift. These latter findings remain a challenge for the development of models of dynamic, adaptive regulation of the comparison process. Finally, in both experiments, semantic congruity magnitude parallels the macro and the micro speed vs accuracy trade off functions induced by the contextual variations, contrary to the semantic coding theory and in support of an evidence accrual view of the effect.

1. INTRODUCTION

Contextual effects (range effects and sequential dependencies) in psychophysical research are well documented in magnitude estimation (e.g., Green, Luce & Smith, 1980; Ward, 1979), cross-modality matching (e.g., Ward, 1979), and comparative intensity scaling (Garner, 1954). Context effects are also evident in category rating (Parducci & Perrett, 1971) and in absolute judgment (e.g., Nosofsky, 1983; Ward & Lockhead, 1971). Furthermore, elegant and detailed quantitative analyses of these effects are now well developed (see Marley & Cook, 1984; 1986). However, to date, the effects of contextual variations remain unexplored in the classic psychophysical comparison task (but see Restle & Greeno (1970) for applications and extensions of Helson's (1964) adaptation level theory).

The contextual manipulation to be studied here involves the variation of *global task difficulty*. Specifically, we focus on the visual discrimination performance (response time, accuracy, and confidence) of a set of a priori defined *target* stimuli that remain unchanged while varying the relative difficulty of the remaining subset of stimulus pairs.

The issue and study of decisional adaptation is important, since, to date, variations in threshold (criterion) settings, for *unbiased* stimulus presentation, have served as the theoretical basis for performance differences between speed versus accuracy conditions. However, within such *global* criterion settings, changes in the difficulty context of the task should lead to systematic *local* criterion adjustments (adaptation) and, thus, performance changes.

Although all decisional theories would agree that difficulty context manipulations would induce variations in the criterion setting, only Vickers' (1979) adaptive accumulator theory of psychophysical discrimination provides a detailed account of how this might occur. He proposes that the criteria of the "primary decision process" are in turn regulated by a second evidence accrual process which is based on the accumulation of differences in the confidence obtained on each trial from a preset target confidence level. The predictions of this adaptive control decision process module in response to variations of contextual difficulty are straightforward. Vickers (1978) states:

...if a stimulus difference of size m were embedded within a series of very small differences, we should in general expect an observer to make a slower, more careful judgment of m than if it were embedded in a series of very large differences, and we would explain this by arguing that the observer may raise the value of k (the response criterion) when the task becomes more difficult. (pp. 612-613)

Although Vickers and his associates have presented impressive support for the "balance of evidence hypothesis" and the continuous accumulator model (e.g., Smith & Vickers, 1988; Vickers, 1970; Vickers, Burt, Smith & Brown, 1985; Vickers & Packer, 1982; Vickers, Smith, Burt & Brown, 1985), the specific predictions of the "adaptive module" with respect to contextual difficulty manipulations await empirical scrutiny.

There are two major goals to the present research. The first, as discussed, is to study adaptive decision making processes under contextual difficulty manipulations. The second concerns the effects of such global contextual manipulations on the magnitude of the perceptual "semantic congruity" or "cross-over" effect, as it was dubbed by Audley & Wallis (1964), who provided the first demonstration of the effect with perceptual comparisons.

The semantic congruity effect reflects a decisional asymmetry whereby the time required for comparative judgments depends on the relation between the location of the stimuli to be compared and the direction of the instruction. For example, the darker of two relatively dark lights can be chosen more quickly than the brighter. Conversely, the brighter of a pair of bright lights is chosen more quickly than the darker (Audley & Wallis, 1964).

One of the more prominent models of the semantic congruity effect is Banks' semantic coding theory (Banks, 1977; Banks, Fujii, & Kayra-Stuart, 1977). On this view, the effect arises as a consequence of discrete stimulus and instructional code matches or mis-matches which are applied following stimulus discrimination; i.e., the effect has a post-*decisional* locus. However, in support of an evidence accrual theory of the semantic congruity effect, Petrusic (1987) and Petrusic and Baranski (in press) have recently provided evidence that suggests the effect has a decisional locus. They show that the magnitude of the effect is determined by variables that exert their effect exclusively on the discrimination process (such as, the relative demands for speed versus accuracy and the difficulty of the comparison). Although these findings provide considerable support for the decisional locus view, they do not permit the unequivocal rejection of the semantic coding theory.

In the experiments to be reported, we hold constant the relative demands for speed vs accuracy, the location on the attribute, the frequency, and the discriminability of target stimuli, and therefore, the putative semantic codes for the target stimulus pairs also remain constant. As a result, we provide the ideal forum for determining the locus of the semantic congruity effect. Specifically, a post-decisional locus implies that the magnitude of the semantic congruity effect for a set of target stimuli should not change if the above mentioned parameters of that stimulus remain unchanged, when overall global difficulty systematically manipulated. Alternatively, a decisional locus of the effect implies that the magnitude of the effect should mirror changes in base rate response times induced by the contextual manipulations.

2. EXPERIMENT 1

The first experiment attempts to outline the general effects of contextual difficulty manipulations employing a between group design. We define the difficulty context in terms of a probability distribution over the various pair difficulty levels. The easy and hard context conditions were subjected to exactly the same stimuli but the hard context condition received a much larger proportion of the very difficult comparisons. Conversely, subjects in the easy context condition received a much larger proportion of the very easy comparisons and very few difficult comparisons. For both groups, we use a fixed set of pairs, with an a priori defined intermediate difficulty level (target pairs), to gauge the effect of the contextual difficulty manipulation.

The predicted global effects are those outlined earlier by Vickers (1978). Specifically, subjects in the more difficult context should set a higher decisional criterion (more evidence must be accrued) for responding and, consequently, provide longer response times and higher accuracy for all discriminations.

As stated earlier, the predicted effects of the contextual manipulation on the magnitude of the semantic congruity effect differ depending on theoretical perspective. On the semantic coding view we would expect no differences for target pair semantic congruity magnitudes. Alternatively, on the view that the effect has a decisional locus, the magnitude of the effect is predicted to parallel, precisely, the macro trade off function for global, between-group, contextually induced differences, as well as the micro-trade off function for the corresponding relationship between the magnitude of the effect for corrects and errors.

2.1 Method

2.1.1 Subjects

Forty Carleton University undergraduate students with normal or corrected-to-normal vision participated in one experimental session of approximately ninety minutes duration in order to satisfy course requirements. All subjects were naive with respect to the nature and aims of the experiment.

2.1.2 Apparatus

Stimuli and instructions were presented on an Amdek-310A video monitor controlled by an IBM-PC/XT compatible computer which also controlled trial presentation, event sequencing, randomization, and response recordings. A Hercules Monochrome card and MetaWindows software permitted high-resolution graphics (720 pixels horizontally and 348 pixels vertically). Responding was performed on an IBM-PC "Mouse" positioned next to the terminal keyboard on the side of the subject's preferred hand. The PC keyboard, situated directly in front of the subject, was used in the reporting of confidence.

2.1.3 Stimuli and design

On each trial, the vertically-centred visual display consisted of two 5 mm vertical lines presented on the left and right of a central fixation marker (10 mm vertical line). On one half of the trials subjects selected the element that was nearer to the fixation line and farther on the other half. All lines were 1 mm (3.13 pixels) wide and were controlled for brightness and contrast at the outset of each session. In order to preclude using the edges of the screen, the centre line was presented equally often in any one of five possible positions: bisecting the screen, or at 3 or 5 pixels, either left or right of the centre of the screen.

The notation (x,y) will be used to describe a stimulus pair x pixels to the left of the centre fixation point and y pixels to the right. Expressed in pixels, the six stimulus pairs used were: (30,28); (50,48); (70,69); (260,243); (280,269); and (300,296). For convenience of identification, they will be referred to as Pairs 1 through 6, respectively.

Munsterberg (1894), and more recently Petrusic and Jamieson (1979), have shown that the difficulty of comparative judgments can be effectively manipulated by variation of the ratio of the longer to the shorter extent of the comparison pair and the difference in extents; response times are faster with larger ratios and larger differences. Here, the stimulus pairs are expressed, in terms of difficulty, by the ratios: 1.07, 1.04, 1.01, 1.07, 1.04, and 1.01 for pairs 1 through 6, respectively.

The global difficulty contextual manipulation was defined by the frequency with which the various pairs were presented in each of four blocks of 112 trials. For the easy context condition, the two easy pairs were presented a total of 64 times and the two hard pairs were each presented 16 times in the block. Conversely, for the hard context, the hard pairs were presented 64 times and the easy pairs 16 times in each block. For both the hard and the easy context, the intermediate pairs (Pairs 2 and 5) were presented 32 times in every block and they, thus, define the target or critical test stimuli with which to gauge the contextual manipulation.

Subjects were randomly assigned to one of four possible groups: Easy Context / No-Feedback (ECNF), Hard Context / No-Feedback (HCNF), Easy Context / Feedback (ECFB), and Hard Context / Feedback (HCFB). Subjects in the HCFB and ECFB groups were provided with trial-by-trial response feedback (Correct or Incorrect) following each confidence report; subjects in the ECNF and HCNF groups were not.

2.1.4 Procedure

Subjects were seated in a dimly lit room approximately 60 cm from the video screen. Stimuli were presented at eye level and the nearest and farthest stimulus pairs subtended a visual angle of approximately 3 and 14 degrees, respectively.

Each trial began with the presentation of an instruction ("Nearer" or "Farther") followed (1000 ms) by the stimulus pair. The instruction and pair remained on the screen until completion of the comparative judgment. Following the response, the screen was cleared and subjects were prompted to enter their confidence rating on the keyboard using the numbers from 0 to 100. A rating of 100 indicated complete certainty in the correctness of the judgment and the rating of 50 indicated a guess. Since subjects occasionally reported awareness of an error response, ratings below 50 indicated an error response, with 0 denoting complete certainty of an error.

Each session began with 32 practice trials followed by four blocks of 112 trials, each separated by an instructed break period. All pairs were counterbalanced for the left-right presentation order and were randomized within each block. Both instructions appeared equally often within each block and with each stimulus pair.

2.2 Results and discussion

Figure 1 plots mean response time, percent correct, and percent confidence, for each stimulus pair, for the hard versus easy context conditions. The plots show the effectiveness of the a priori difficulty manipulations. For both groups, and for both the near and far pairs, response times increase, while accuracy and confidence decrease as the pairs become more difficult. These plots also show the effect of stimulus difficulty context; response times are considerably longer (500 ms) for all the pairs in the hard as opposed to the easy context condition. As well, accuracy is increased for all pairs in the hard context. However, the lower panels of this figure show no difference in reported confidence between the hard and easy context conditions (cf. Vickers & Packer, 1982).

An analysis of variance, with Greenhouse and Geisser (1959), epsilon-adjusted degrees of freedom, showed the main effect of variations in stimulus pair difficulty was significant with each of the three dependent measures (p<.01). The effects of stimulus difficulty context were also statistically reliable for the response time measure (F(1, 36)=3.45, p<.05). This effect approached (F(1, 36)=2.67) but did not reach significance with the discriminative accuracy measure. The main effect of feedback was significant only with the confidence measure (F(1, 36)=9.09, p<.01) and this factor did not enter into any significant interactions (overall, subjects were more confident with the provision of trial-by-trial feedback).

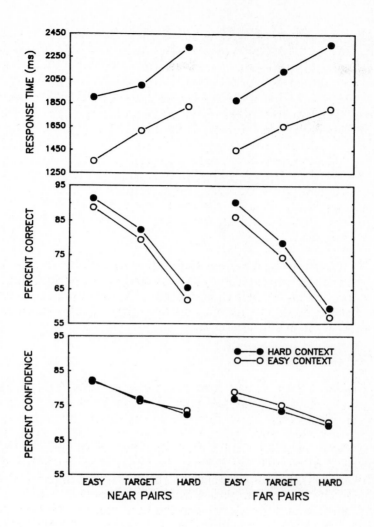

Figure 1. Mean response time, percent confidence and percent correct for each pair in the hard (filled circles) and easy (open circles) context conditions, averaged over the feedback/no feedback groups, in Experiment 1.

Reliable semantic congruity effects were obtained for these confusable stimulus pairs with both the response time ($F(5, 180)=7.57$, $p<.01$)) and the confidence measures ($F(5, 180)=10.14$, $p<.01$) but not with the percent correct accuracy measure. This occurrence of the semantic congruity effect with both the response time and confidence measures but not with the accuracy measure replicates our earlier findings (Petrusic, 1987; Petrusic & Baranski, in press).

The semantic congruity effect for the combined data of all subjects, for both response time and confidence, are depicted by the semantic congruity or cross-over index provided in Figure 2. The plot is positive for the near stimuli, indicating faster responding with the "Nearer" instruction and negative for the far stimulus pairs, indicating that response times for these pairs were faster with the instruction to choose the "Farther". These effects are perfectly paralleled by the Confidence based index.

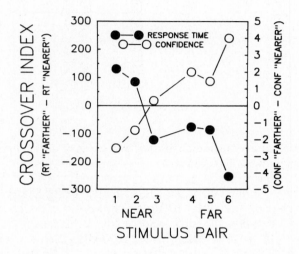

Figure 2. Semantic congruity index for response time in ms (left hand ordinate, filled circles) and confidence (open circles) for the data of all subjects combined over the feedback and the no-feedback conditions. The index plots the difference with each response measure with the instruction "Nearer" subtracted from the measure with the instruction "Farther."

Figure 3 plots cross-over-semantic congruity magnitude as a function of the difficulty of the comparison and shows the magnitude of the effect to mirror the contextually induced macro speed vs accuracy trade-off effects shown in Figure 1. Subjects in the hard context showed much longer response times for each pair and the corresponding semantic congruity cross-over effect magnitudes are increased as well. The clear demonstration of the contextually induced differential semantic congruity effects for the target pairs should be noted.

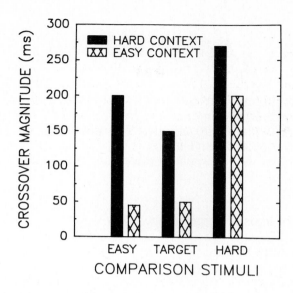

Figure 3. Semantic congruity magnitude for the three levels of difficulty in the hard and the easy context conditions in Experiment 1.

As well, in the hard context, the semantic congruity effect was 284 ms for error responses but only 140 ms for correct responses, paralleling the longer overall times with error responses. In the easy context, where times are generally faster, the difference between correct and error response times was reduced and semantic congruity magnitudes were 85 ms for error responses and 65 ms for correct responses. These findings, taken together with those shown in Figure 3, establish that semantic congruity magnitude parallels the macro *and* the micro speed- accuracy trade off function.

The findings of Experiment 1 provide further support for a decisional locus for the cross-over-semantic congruity effect. As such, the results are problematic for both the pre-decisional, expectancy views (e.g., Kosslyn, Murphy, Bemesderfer & Feinstein, 1977; Marschark & Paivio, 1981) and the post-decisional, semantic coding (Banks, 1977) position.

3. EXPERIMENT 2

Experiment 2 was undertaken to further study the effects of contextual difficulty, this time with a difficulty *shift* conducted within-subjects. As well, and in keeping with more global theoretical considerations, the effect of this context shift was studied under both accuracy and speeded conditions.

3.1 Method

3.1.1 Subjects

Ten Carleton University graduate students with normal or corrected-to-normal vision each participated in eight experimental sessions of approximately 90 minutes duration. Subjects were paid a base rate of $4.00 per session and a bonus depending upon performance. All subjects were naive with respect to the nature and aims of the experiment.

3.1.2 Apparatus

The apparatus of Experiment 1 was used.

3.1.3 Design and procedure

As in the first experiment, visual proximity discriminations were required (on one half of the trials subjects selected the element nearer the fixation point and on the other half, the element farther from the fixation point was selected). In Set 1, the standard set, used for the sessions of pre-shift trials and for three subsequent sessions by the non-shift subjects, Pairs 1 through 4 were assumed a priori to be in the near category and Pairs 5 through 8 were assumed to be in the far category. In pixels, the pairs in Set 1 were: (22,20); (40,37); (58,55); (76,74); (248,242); (266,253); (284,263); and (302,274), for pairs 1 through 8, respectively. As in Experiment 1, the difficulty of each pair was defined by the ratio of the longer to the shorter extent. Thus, Set 1 was defined by the ratios: 1.10, 1.08, 1.05, 1.03, 1.03, 1.05, 1.08, and 1.10 for pairs 1 through 8, respectively.

Set 2, the harder set, used for the contextual-shift subjects, was defined by increasing the difficulty (reducing the ratio) of two of the near pairs (Pairs 1 and 2) and two of the far pairs (Pairs 7 and 8). Hence, Pairs 1, 2, 7, and 8 were the context *induction* pairs and pairs 3, 4, 5 and 6 were the *target* pairs. The following pairs comprise Set 2: (22,21); (40,39); (58,55); (76,74); (248,242); (266,253); (284,277); and (302,289) and they were defined by the ratios: 1.05, 1.03, 1.05, 1.03, 1.03, 1.05, 1.03, and 1.05 for stimulus pairs 1 through 8, respectively.

Subjects in the accuracy condition were rewarded 1 cent for each correct response and penalized 1 cent for incorrect judgments. On the other hand, the payoffs for subjects in the speed condition emphasized beating a 450 ms deadline.

Five subjects were randomly assigned to the speed condition and five to the accuracy condition. Of the five subjects in each group, two were control subjects who participated in six sessions with the standard set and three were experimental subjects performing three pre-shift sessions with the standard set followed by three sessions with the more difficult, post-shift set. As such, the effect of the context shift was evaluated by comparison of pre and post-shift target pair differences, for the experimental and control subjects, for both the speed and accuracy conditions.

3.2.3 Procedure

On each trial, subjects received immediate feedback on accuracy of discrimination ("Correct" or "Incorrect") following provision of the confidence estimate. In addition, subjects in the speed condition received the statement "Too Slow" following responses that failed to meet the deadline.

Each of six experimental sessions and two preceding practice sessions began with 32 practice trials followed by three blocks of 160 trials. The remaining aspects of the procedure were the same as in Experiment 1.

3.3 Results and Discussion

Briefly, we found that under accuracy conditions, the effect of the difficulty context shift was to induce slower, more accurate responding, as in the first experiment. However, in this experiment, target pair confidence actually decreased upon the shift to the more difficult context. Surprisingly, the effect of the shift under speed was to induce faster, less confident, and more inaccurate responding for all pairs. In contrast to the Speed/Control group, whose practice effects decreased response times by 25 ms with no decrement in accuracy, response times decreased by 50 ms and accuracy also decreased for the Speed/Shift subjects.

An analysis of variance restricted to the target pairs revealed significant main effects of speed vs accuracy for response time ($F(1, 6)=31.26$, $p<.01$) and accuracy ($F(1, 6)=12.78$, $p<.05$), but not for confidence (cf. Vickers & Packer, 1982). As well, the main effects of the difficulty shift ($F(1, 6)=20.65$, $p<.01$) and sessions ($F(2, 12)=7.14$, $p<.05$) were statistically reliable for the response time measure.

The important three-way interaction involving the difficulty shift, experimental/control and speed/accuracy conditions ($F(1, 6)=11.66$, $p<.05$) was significant for the response time measure. Thus, relative to the speeded subjects and the Accuracy/Control subjects, the Accuracy/Shift subjects *did not show a decrease* in response time following the difficulty shift.

Figure 4 provides plots of mean response times conditional on the occurrence of a particular response as a function of the probability of that response. These Latency Probability Functions (LPFs) are provided for the pre and post-shift conditions, separately for the accuracy and the speed instructed subjects, and provide a view of the corresponding macro and micro-trade off effects.

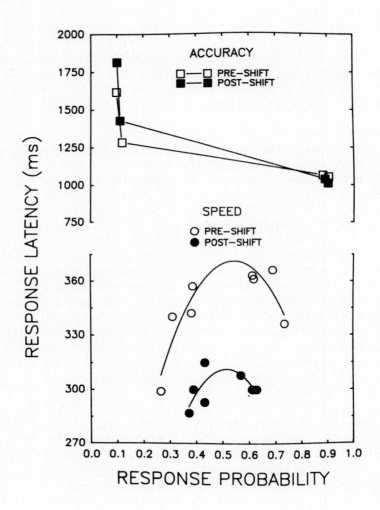

Figure 4. Latency-probability functions for the pre-shift target pairs in the accuracy condition (open squares), target and induction pairs in the pre-shift speed condition (open circles), post-shift target pairs in the accuracy condition (filled squares), and all pairs in the post-shift speed condition (filled circles), in Experiment 2.

The *monotonically decreasing* LPFs for the accuracy subjects are typical of those arising from slow, cautious and accurate responding. On the other hand, the plots for the speed instructed subjects are clearly *non-monotonic*, with nearly equal correct and error response times (cf. Petrusic & Jamieson, 1978; Pike, 1971; see also Luce, 1986, pp. 233-236).

The contextual manipulations are also evident in these LPFs. In the accuracy condition, and considering the large practice effects operating here, the effect of the difficulty shift was to increase error response times more than correct response times (again, suggesting an increase in overall caution), and to slightly increase overall accuracy for the target pairs. Under speed, the effect was to reduce response times and compress the range of probabilities.

The top panel of Figure 5 provides plots of error versus correct response times, with the target pairs, for the pre and the post-shift sessions, separately for the speed and accuracy conditions. The bottom panel of Figure 5 shows semantic congruity (cross-over) magnitude to parallel the macro and the micro trade off effects shown in upper panel. Semantic congruity is greatly reduced under speed as compared to accuracy. Moreover, under accuracy, the magnitude of the semantic congruity effect increases for errors following the difficulty shift but remains constant for correct responses. In addition, and again paralleling the result for overall response times (i.e., the macro-function), the magnitude of the semantic congruity effect is reduced for both error and correct responses under speed following the shift to the more difficult context. Finally, reflecting the micro-trade off shown in the upper panel, the magnitude of the effect is approximately the same for correct and for error responses.

4. GENERAL DISCUSSION

Under conditions emphasising accuracy, Vickers' adaptive module was shown to provide generally accurate predictions with respect to response time and response probability; observers became more cautious when working in the more difficult context and, accordingly responses slowed and became more accurate. However, the finding in Experiment 2 that response time and accuracy increased but confidence decreased upon the shift to a more difficult context is problematic for the "balance of evidence" view of confidence estimation. On this view, an increase in accuracy should be accompanied by an increase in confidence. A similar problem arises for the view of confidence developed by Heath (1984) in the context of the Relative Judgment Theory (Link & Heath, 1975).

Although the results of the contextual difficulty shift under accuracy conditions have important implications for the theoretical basis for confidence estimation, when taken together with those under speed, they also have clear consequences for theories of adaptive-control processes in psychophysical judgment. Instead of slowing down in response to the introduction of a more difficult decisional context, speeded deadline subjects responded even more quickly and made more errors. Viewing this result as simply arising as a consequence of shifts in decisional thresholds, it is unclear why subjects would, logically, increase thresholds under accuracy but decrease thresholds under speed.

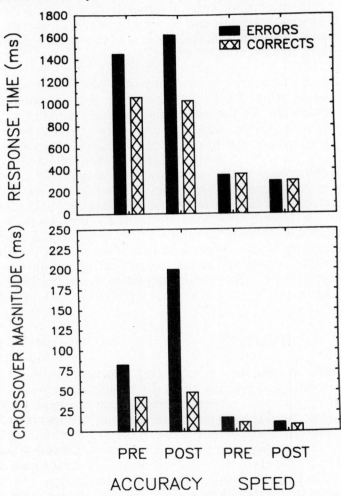

Figure 5. Correct versus error response times (top panel) and semantic congruity (crossover) magnitudes (bottom panel) for the target pairs, prior to and following the shift, in the speed and accuracy conditions in Experiment 2.

Alternatively, a model that permits, on the one hand, slower more accurate responding under accuracy conditions and, on the other hand, faster responding under speed, with both occurring under the assumption of an increase in overall caution, is the slow and fast guessing evidence accrual model, developed originally in the context of binary preferential choice by Petrusic and Jamieson (1978), and since extended to psychophysical comparison (Petrusic, 1987).

The model is similar to the early Laberge (1962) discrete accumulator, with the departure that here occurrences of neutral, or doubtful evidence events (formally identical to a sample from the indifference region) are summed in a separate counter rather than being viewed as merely contributing to "dead time." An overt decision is reached when one of the three counters reaches a preset criterion value: α_1 for A>B, α_2 for B>A, and α_3 for the overt indifference judgment, with partial information favouring the three respective responses with probability p_1 through p_3. Since, typically, overt indifference is not permitted, the observer guesses from the indiscriminant state, responding A>B with probability g and B>A with probability 1-g. This simple three state discrete accumulator permits derivation of explicit quantitative expressions for the probability of the overt response A>B and the expected number of evidence accruals preceding that response (conditional upon its occurrence). We illustrate the main properties of this theory by applying it to the contextual shift data from Experiment 2.

We assume that shifts to a more difficult context induce comparable effects under both speed and accuracy. Such an assumption is permitted under the slow and fast guessing theory if in response to an increase in global difficulty two response regulating parameters are affected. First, the overt response thresholds for the discriminant states increase. Second, the indifference region is expanded, with a consequent increase in the probability of obtaining a sample in this region (i.e., the parameter p_3 increases). As a result, only more "certain" evidence is accrued in favour of either response. Figure 6 provides examples of predicted LPFs for the slow and fast guessing evidence accrual theory upon a slight increase in α_1 and α_2 (the criteria for overt responses from the discriminant state) and extending the width of the indifference region and consequently, increasing p_3. As an example of permissible parameter values for the pre-shift trials in the accuracy condition, we set $p_3 = 0.1$, $\alpha_1 = \alpha_2 = 10$, and $\alpha_3 = 20$ (the slow guessing case) and for speed we set $\alpha_3 = 2$ (the fast guessing case). (Note that at $\alpha_3 = 1$, we have as a special case of the slow and fast guessing theory, the classic fast guess model of Ollman (1966) and of Yellott (1971)). On the other hand, for the post-shift case (more cautious responding) we increment α_1 and α_2 by 1 and p_3 by 0.1.

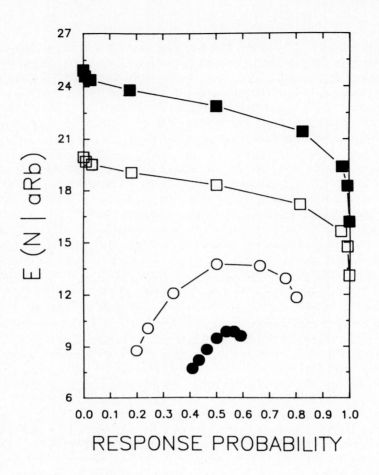

Figure 6. Theoretical Latency Probability Functions (LPFs) derived from the slow and fast guessing evidence accrual theory. Parameter values are $\alpha_1 = \alpha_2 = 10$, $\alpha_3 = 20$, and p_3 = 0.1 for the accuracy pre-shift condition (open squares), $\alpha_1 = \alpha_2 = 11$, $\alpha_3 = 20$, and p_3 = 0.2 for the accuracy post-shift condition (filled squares), $\alpha_1 = \alpha_2 = 10$, $\alpha_3 = 2$, and p_3 = 0.1 for the speed pre-shift condition (open circles) and $\alpha_1 = \alpha_2 = 11$, $\alpha_3 = 2$, and $p_3 = 0.2$ for the speed post-shift condition (filled circles). Each LPF was generated by fixing the relevant parameters and varying $\delta = p_1 / (p_1 + p_2)$, the discriminability parameter.

Examination of the theoretical LPFs shown in Figure 6 shows only slight increases in accuracy and relatively larger increases in error response times than correct response times under an accuracy orientation following the shift to the more difficult context. Alternatively, the effect under speed is faster, more inaccurate responding, with a compression in the observable range of probabilities. Thus, the slow and fast guessing theory is able to account for both the global speed versus accuracy macro and micro-trade off functions and the local contextually induced forms of each these trade off functions. If we make provision for the large practice effect operating in the accuracy condition (i.e. decreasing the intercept of the post-shift LPF), the qualitative similarities between the obtained and theoretically generated LPFs is striking.

In addition to being limited as a model of the perceptual comparison process, the semantic coding theory, in its current form, must now be questioned seriously as an adequate theory of the semantic congruity effect. In light of the present results and those we have provided earlier, a decisional locus of the semantic congruity effect is established.

On the slow and fast guessing theory or, in fact, any evidence accrual model, a decisional locus of the semantic congruity effect is preserved by the following assumption: *The semantic congruity effect occurs at the level of every evidence accrual moment.* In particular, following the reference point theory developed initially by Jamieson & Petrusic (1975) and elaborated later by Holyoak (1978) in the context of a random walk decisional model, we assume that the duration of each evidence accrual moment is directly related to the distance of the stimulus pair from the reference point activated by the presented instruction. Under these assumptions, the average magnitude of the semantic congruity effect is directly proportional to the expected number of evidence accrual events, conditional on the occurrence of a particular response. Thus, the magnitude of the semantic congruity effect must necessarily parallel response time. In particular, semantic congruity magnitude must systematically vary with: a) changes in decision difficulty (following the LPF), b) differential demands for speed versus accuracy (global threshold differences), c) differences between error versus correct response times (micro tradeoffs), and d) contextually induced local variations within global criterion settings, as demonstrated in the present experiments.

The finding of robust and substantial semantic congruity effects with both the response time and the confidence measure but not with the discriminative accuracy measure is of import for the *full* development of existing quantitative theories of decision processing in psychophysical judgment. For example, since both response accuracy and confidence are determined by the "balance of evidence" according to the continuous accumulator theories (Smith & Vickers, 1988; Vickers, 1979), semantic congruity effects are predicted to occur for the accuracy measure whenever the effect is obtained for the confidence measure. Indeed, this asymmetry among measures of the congruity effect remains a challenge for the existing theories of the effect (see Petrusic & Baranski, in press).

Although the findings of the present experiments affirm the occurrence of adaptive regulatory processes upon global contextual variations and although the slow and fast guessing theory provides a viable account of these findings, the ideas sketched here are incomplete. Continued study of this model, especially the difficult problem of estimation of its several parameters, in the context of the adaptive regulatory control processes proposed by Vickers, is the current direction of our work on this problem.

ACKNOWLEDGEMENTS

This research has been supported by grants from the Natural Science and Engineering Research Council of Canada (A8628) to Petrusic.

Correspondence concerning this paper should be addressed to Dr. W.M. Petrusic, Department of Psychology, Carleton University, Colonel By Drive, Ottawa, Ontario, Canada, K1S 5B6.

REFERENCES

Audley, R.J. & Wallis, C.P. (1964). Response instructions and the speed of relative judgments. I. Some experiments on brightness discrimination. British Journal of Psychology, 55, 59-73.

Banks, W.P. (1977). Encoding and processing of symbolic information in comparative judgments. In G.H. Bower (Ed.), The psychology of learning and motivation (Vol. 11). New York: Academic Press.

Banks, W.P., Fujii, M.S. & Kayra-Stuart, F. (1976). Semantic congruity effects in comparative judgments of magnitudes of digits. Journal of Experimental Psychology: Human Perception and Performance, 2, 435-447.

Garner, W.R. (1954). Context effects and the validity of loudness scales. Journal of Experimental Psychology, 48, 218-224.

Green, D.M., Luce, R.D. & Smith, A.F. (1980). Individual magnitude estimates for various distributions of signal intensity. Perception & Psychophysics, 27, 483-488.

Greenhouse, S.W. & Geisser, S. (1959). On methods in the analysis of profile data. Psychometrika, 24, 95-112.

Heath, R.A. (1984). Random walk and accumulator models of psychophysical discrimination: A critical evaluation. Perception, 13, 57-65.

Helson, H. (1964). Adaptation-level theory. New York: Harper and Row.

Holyoak, K.J. (1978). Comparative judgments with numerical reference points. Cognitive Psychology, 10, 203-243.

Jamieson, D.G. & Petrusic, W.M. (1975). Relational judgments with remembered stimuli. Perception and Psychophysics, 18, 373-378.

Kosslyn, S.M., Murphy, G.L., Bemesderfer, M.E. & Feinstein, K.J. (1977). Category and continuum in mental comparisons. Journal of Experimental Psychology: General, 4, 341-375.

LaBerge, D. (1962). A recruitment theory of simple behaviour. Psychometrika, 27, 375-396.

Link, S.W. & Heath, R.A. (1975). A sequential theory of psychological discrimination. Psychometrika, 40, 77-105.

Luce, R.D. (1986). Response times. New York: Oxford University Press.

Marley, A.A.J. & Cook, V.T. (1984). A fixed rehearsal capacity interpretation of limits on absolute identification. British Journal of Mathematical and Statistical Psychology, 37, 136- 151.

Marley, A.A.J. & Cook, V.T. (1986). A limited capacity rehearsal model for psychophysical judgments applied to magnitude estimation. Journal of Mathematical Psychology, 30, 339-390.

Marschark, M. & Paivio, A. (1981). Congruity and the perceptual comparison task. Journal of Experimental Psychology: Human Perception and Performance, 7, 290-308.

Munsterberg, H. (1894). Studies from the Harvard psychological laboratory. A psychometric investigation of the psychophysic law. Psychological Review, 1, 45-51.

Nosofsky, R.M. (1983). Information integration and the identification of stimulus noise and criterial noise in absolute judgment. Journal of Experimental Psychology: Human Perception and Performance, 9, 299-309.

Ollman, R.T. (1966). Fast guesses in simple reaction time. Psychonomic Science, 6, 155-156.

Parducci, A. & Perrett, L.F. (1971). Category rating scales: Effects of relative spacing and frequency on stimulus values. Journal of Experimental Psychology Monograph, 89, 427-452.

Petrusic, W.M. (1987). Semantic congruity in perceptual comparisons: An evidence accrual theory. Paper read at the Fechner Centennial, Leipzig, East Germany, July, 1987.

Petrusic, W.M. & Baranski, J.V. (In press). Semantic congruity in perceptual comparisons. Perception and Psychophysics.

Petrusic, W.M. & Jamieson, D.G. (1978). The relation between probability of preferential choice and the time to choose changes with practice. Journal of Experimental Psychology: Human Perception and Performance, 4, 471-482.

Petrusic, W.M. & Jamieson, D.G. (1979). Resolution time and the coding of arithmetic relations on supraliminally different visual extents. Journal of Mathematical Psychology, 19, 89-107.

Pike, A.R. (1971). The latencies of correct and incorrect responses in discrimination and detection tasks: Their interpretation in terms of a model based on simple counting. Perception & Psychophysics, 9, 455-460.

Restle, F. & Greeno, J.G. (1970). Introduction to mathematical psychology. Reading, Mass.: Addison-Wesley.

Smith, P.L. & Vickers, D. (1988). The accumulator model of two-choice discrimination. Journal of Mathematical Psychology, 32, 135-168.

Vickers, D. (1970). Evidence for an accumulator model of psychophysical discrimination. Ergonomics, 13, 37-58.

Vickers, D. (1978). An adaptive module for simple judgments. In J. Requin (Ed.), Attention and Performance VII. Hillsdale, N.J.: Hillsdale, N.J.

Vickers, D. (1979). Decision processes in visual perception. New York, N.Y.: Academic Press.

Vickers, D., Burt, J., Smith, P. & Brown, M. (1985). Experimental paradigms emphasising state or process limitations: I. Effects on speed-accuracy trade-offs. Acta Psychologica, 59, 129-161.

Vickers, D. and Packer, J.S. (1982). Effects of alternating set for speed or accuracy on response time, accuracy, and confidence in a unidimensional discrimination task. Acta Psychologica, 50, 179-197.

Vickers, D., Smith, P., Burt, J., and Brown, M. (1985). Experimental paradigms emphasising state or process limitations: II. Effects on confidence. Acta Psychologica, 59, 163-193.

Ward, L.M. (1979). Stimulus information and sequential dependencies in magnitude estimation and cross-modality matching. Journal of Experimental Psychology: Human Perception and Performance, 5, 444-459.

Ward, L.M. & Lockhead, G.R. (1971). Response system processes in absolute judgment. Perception and Psychophysics, 9, 73-78.

Yellott, J.I., Jr. (1971). Correction for guessing and the speed-accuracy trade off in choice reaction time. Journal of Mathematical Psychology, 8, 159-199.

Human Information Processing: Measures,
Mechanisms, and Models. D. Vickers and P.L. Smith (eds.)
© *Elsevier Science Publishers B.V. (North-Holland), 1989*

SOME EXPERIMENTAL TESTS OF THE APPLICATION OF AN INTERVAL OF UNCERTAINTY MODEL TO A TIME-LIMITED EXPANDED JUDGMENT TASK.

D. Vickers, E.A. Foreman, M.E.R. Nicholls, N.J. Innes, and R.E. Gott

University of Adelaide

A number of decision models proposed for two choice discrimination have incorporated two sensory cut-offs, defining an interval of uncertainty (IOU). Observations falling within this interval do not contribute to a decision. Prior findings relevant to such a notion are reviewed and results are examined for evidence of the operation of an IOU. In these experiments subjects were presented with a temporal series of observations under two contrasting paradigms. In one paradigm (S), the number of observations was determined by the subject, and, in the other (E), the number was controlled by the experimental program. While the notion of an IOU does appear to be consistent with some qualitative effects, estimated IOUs in E-paradigm experiments do not appear to to be a consistent parameter of performance. Estimation of an IOU does not appear to lead to an improvement in prediction beyond what might be expected with the addition of a further parameter. Implications of an alternative 'random loss' hypothesis are considered briefly.

1. INTRODUCTION

Psychological decision models depend on a variety of initial assumptions. For example, the prospective purchaser of such a model can choose between sensory cutoffs and response thresholds, between discrete and continuous sampling, and between independent and cross-coupled accumulation of evidence for each response. The variety of secondary assumptions, and the number of corresponding parameters, is even greater. For example, one assumption which has been made is that discrete observations can take more or less time to classify, depending on their closeness to a sensory referent. Again, it has been supposed by different theorists that sensory referents and cutoffs, starting points for the accumulation of evidence, sampling rates, and response thresholds can each vary randomly from trial to trial, increase or decrease over a series of trials, or change even within a single trial. It has been proposed that the subject can anticipate the stimulus and begin sampling too soon (or presumably also, too late). It has also been suggested that the subject can abandon one decision rule in favour of another, or transform the sensory input in various ways, depending mainly, it would seem, on his or her allegiance to a particular decision model. In some accounts, the information so laboriously accumulated by the subject can leak away at various rates. Meanwhile, some subjects, it has been suggested (no doubt overcome by the complexity of the psychophysical universe), simply shut their eyes on a certain proportion of trials, and guess.

In each case, the values of the associated parameters are susceptible to change from one subject to another or from one occasion to the next. Yet, apart from certain response bias parameters, few attempts

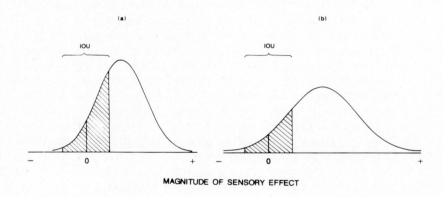

Figure 1. Illustrations of an interval of uncertainty (IOU), as applied to the distribution of differences between a stimulus and a sensory referent. In figure 1a, the mean and standard deviation are small ($\mu = 1$, $\sigma = 1$), while in figure 1b they are both medium ($\mu = 1.41$, $\sigma = 1.41$), while preserving the same μ / σ ratio. With the larger scaling in figure 1b, fewer observations fall within the IOU.

have been made to link variation in these various parameters to other established dimensions of individual differences or developmental change, or to supply some rationale governing variations in parameter values.

For example, one assumption is that subjects in psychophysical judgement tasks may not accumulate information from all observations, but instead register only those falling outside a certain region of sensory indifference or interval of uncertainty (IOU) around some sensory referent as illustrated in figure 1 (Vickers, 1985). Some support for this notion comes from a finding by Smith and Vickers (1989) that a generalized accumulator model, in which only observations greater than a certain absolute magnitude are accumulated, provides a superior fit to response time distributions from an expanded judgement task.

The notion of an IOU has been proposed as long ago as Cartwright and Festinger (1943) and as recently as Hockley and Murdoch (1987). In Smith and Vickers' generalization of the accumulator model, when the response thresholds are so low that they coincide with the upper and lower limits of the IOU, the mechanism becomes a simple, memoryless process of inspecting observations until one of a critical magnitude is encountered. Conversely, when the IOU is set to zero, the process is identical with the simple accumulator model. The extent to which subjects reach decisions either by being insensitive to all except the more striking ones (and then responding quickly), or by a careful accumulation of every observation, seemed likely to be an important dimension of individual differences. Since Warren (1985) has argued that phenomena such as after-effects may be explainable by shifts in a sensory referent, and since susceptibility to after-effects seems to be a correlate of other established dimensions of individual differences, such as extraversion, it seemed plausible to expect IOU values associated with the sensory referent to be similarly related. Consequently, a number of experiments were carried out to see if the IOU was indeed a stable, reliable, and valid measure, and whether it was related to the personality dimensions distinguished by Eysenck & Eysenck (1985).

2. THE EXPANDED JUDGEMENT TASK

The type of experiment that was used has been described in two articles by Vickers et al (1985a,b) and is illustrated in figure 2. The stimulus display is a series of horizontal line segments, presented at a rate of about 3 per second, and projecting to the right or the left of a fixed vertical centre line representing zero. The end point of each segment is determined by sampling from a normal distribution of numbers, and the subject's task is to decide, on the basis of seeing a series of these segments, whether the mean of this distribution is positive or negative. So the task is a so-called 'expanded judgement', which attempts to take psychophysical assumptions about stimulus representation and sampling "out of the head", and give them some kind of external realisation.

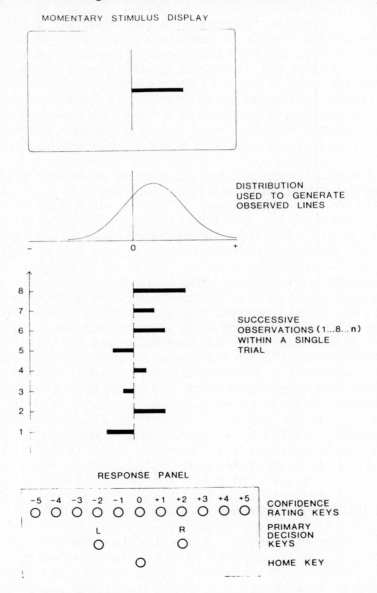

Figure 2. The type of display and the response panel used in Experiments I-IV.

In figure 2, the mean m of the distribution used to generate the segments could be either positive or negative. For example, in many of our experiments, it could be ± 2, with a standard deviations, s, of 6 in each case, so the discriminations were fairly difficult ones. The subject shows whether his decision is positive or negative by moving the index finger of his preferred hand from a home key to press the right- or the left-hand of two primary response buttons. In most experiments, he follows this by a confidence rating, which he gives by using the same finger to press one of 11 buttons, numbered from 0 at the innermost (for 'least confident') up to ±5 at the outermost (for 'most confident').

We have looked at two basic types of condition or paradigm. In the S-(or subject-controlled) paradigm, the subject is free on each trial to look at as many lines as he wishes, and the series is stopped only when he makes a primary decision response. In the E- (or experimenter-controlled) paradigm, with which this paper is concerned, the length of each sequence of observations is controlled by the experimental program, and is varied randomly from one trial to the next.

3. EXPERIMENT I: COMPARISON BETWEEN GROUPS WITH DIFFERENT SCALING LEVELS

If the subject keeps a perfect total of every stimulus magnitude observed except for those smaller than a certain absolute magnitude, and responds according to whether this total is positive or negative, then, as illustrated in figure 1, rescaling these stimulus magnitudes should affect the proportion of discarded line segments. Figure 3 shows the typical decrement in accuracy predicted by such a mechanism for a range of IOU values if stimulus magnitude is rescaled by 1.5 and 2. One aim of the first experiment, carried out by Foreman (1988), was to look for evidence of a decrement of this kind.

Eighteen subjects, all of whom had completed the Eysenck Personality Questionnaire (EPQ), were allocated at random to 2 groups of 9. For subjects in the "Low" group (L), the line segments were drawn from distributions with a mean m = ± 1.5 and a standard deviation s = 4. For those in the "High" group (H), m was ± 3 and s was 8. Each group performed two identical sessions at the same time of day, exactly one week apart. Each session consisted of 240 trials, with an equal number of positive and negative trials. On any trial, the number of line segments presented (n) was 3, 6, 9, 12, 15, or 18, with the value of n varying randomly from one trial to the next.

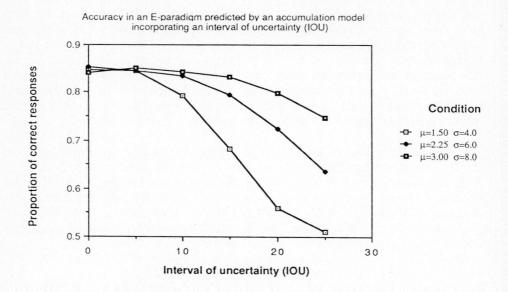

Figure 3. Proportion of correct responses in an E-paradigm predicted by an accumulation model incorporating an interval of uncertainty (IOU).

The number of correct responses is given in table 1. Neither group showed a significant difference in accuracy between the two sessions. For both sessions combined there was no significant difference in accuracy between the two groups. For both groups combined the correlation between accuracy in sessions 1 and 2 was 0.38. However, for both sessions and both groups combined, there was no significant correlation between accuracy and scores on the psychoticism, extraversion, neuroticism, or lie scales of the E.P.Q.

By themselves, these results imply two conclusions. On the one hand, accuracy in this kind of task appears to be a stable, though not highly reliable, dimension of individual differences. On the other hand, there is no evidence for an IOU which is defined in terms of stimulus magnitude. If subjects are operating with an IOU, then it must either be very small and/or it must be set to some relative stimulus magnitude, e.g. one that is normalized in terms of the standard deviation in the presented line segments.

	N	Proportion of correct responses		Correlation between	Difference between
		Session 1	Session 2	Sessions 1 & 2	Sessions 1 & 2
Experiment I					
Group H	9	.82	.82		
Group L	9	.80	.81	.38	n.s.
Experiment II					
Groups LH	9	.80	.80		
Groups HL	9	.81	.80	.53	n.s.
Experiment IV	20	.76	.76	.39	n.s.
Foreman (1988)	22	.82	.82	.49	n.s.

Table 1: Proportions of correct responses made in sessions 1 and 2 of Experiments I, II, and IV, and in a similar experiment by Foreman (1988). In Experiment I the discriminability parameters were $\mu = \pm 3.0$, $\sigma = 8$ for group H (high scaling), while for group L (low scaling) the parameters were $\mu = \pm 1.5$, $\sigma = 4$. For groups LH in Experiment II the discriminability parameters were $\mu = \pm 1.5$, $\sigma = 4$ in session 1, followed by $\mu = \pm 3.0$, $\sigma = 8$ in session 2. Group HL was presented with the same parameters, but in the reverse order. In Foreman's (1988) experiment, $\mu = \pm 2.33$, $\sigma = 6$, while in Experiment IV, $\mu = \pm 2$, $\sigma = 8$ for both sessions. The number of trials for each subject in each session was 240 in Experiments I and II, 288 in Experiment IV, and 200 in the case of Foreman (1988). The number of subjects (N) is given in each case.

4. EXPERIMENT II: COMPARISON BETWEEN SESSIONS AT DIFFERENT SCALING LEVELS

The second experiment, also carried out by Foreman (1988), was designed to explore this second possibility, and to see whether practice at one level of stimulus scaling would affect subsequent performance at a different level of scaling. A different set of 18 subjects were again allocated randomly to 2 groups of 9. Subjects in the "Low-High" group (LH) performed one session in which the line segments were drawn from distributions with $m = \pm 1.5$ and $s = 4$, followed by a second session in which m was equal to ± 3, and s was 8. Subjects in "High-Low" group (HL) performed the two sessions in the reverse order. As in experiment I, both groups performed each session at the same time of day, exactly one week apart, and all other details were unchanged.

The number of correct responses is shown in Table 1. There was no significant effect of session or of group. For both groups combined the correlation in accuracy between the two sessions was r = 0.53 (p < 0.05 , two tails).   For both sessions combined there was again no significant correlation with scores on the psychoticism, extraversion, neuroticism, or lie scales of the E.P.Q.

As with the first experiment, these results show no evidence of an IOU set to some particular stimulus magnitude. If subjects are employing an IOU, then again it must either be very small and/or it must be set very quickly (within just a few trials) to some stimulus magnitude relative to the overall variability in the sample of line segments seen by the subject.

5. EXPERIMENT III: COMPARISON ACROSS TRIALS AT DIFFERENT SCALING LEVELS

An obvious way of testing this last possibility is to vary the stimulus scaling in a random fashion from one trial to the next. So, in experiment III, on any given trial, the sequence of line segments could be drawn from a distribution with m = ± 1.5, s = 4; m = ± 2.25; s = 6, or m = ± 3, s = 8, with each of these three scaling levels being determined at random from one trial to the next.   Experiment III was carried out by Innes (1987). Sixteen subjects performed a total of 288 trials in a single session.

Contrary to the prediction of an IOU model, a repeated analysis of variance carried out between scaling levels across the 16 subjects found no significant effect of scaling level (F(2,30) = 2.38, p = 0.11).

6. EXPERIMENT III: ANALYSIS OF INDIVIDUAL TRIALS

This result again suggests that if subjects are operating with an IOU set to some particular stimulus magnitude then this magnitude must be small relative to the overall variability in the stimulus sequences and also relative to the estimates of IOUs obtained in previous experiments and published by Vickers et al. (1986). Because a record was kept of the line segments presented to the subject on each trial it was possible to look at how well the assumption of an IOU could account for the performance of individual subjects.   In their earlier study, Vickers et al (1986) estimated IOU values by minimising χ^2 values for the difference between predicted and obtained proportions of correct responses. However, while this provided IOU estimates which were reliably related to accuracy, we wished also to test the validity of the IOU measure. To do this, the length values making up each stimulus sequence were totalled, applying each of 51 values of the IOU ranging from 0 to 100 in steps of 2 to "filter" the observations. Whenever the sign of the "filtered" total corresponded to the response made by the subject, the trial was classed as "consistent", and whenever the sign corresponded to the alternative response the trial was classed as "inconsistent". A measure of response consistency was given by the proportion of consistent trials in a session of 288 trials. The IOU which produced the greatest degree of response consistency was selected as the most appropriate. In this way separate IOUs were estimated for each subject and each scaling condition.

Table 2 shows the mean best IOU for each scaling condition, together with the proportion of consistent responses predicted for the best IOU and that predicted for an IOU of zero. From the table, it is obvious that the percentage of consistent trials for a non-zero IOU is minimally different from that predicted by an accumulation process with no IOU whatsoever. Meanwhile, contrary to the supposition of a constant IOU for all trials, the mean IOUs for Levels L and M differed significantly from that for level H (related sample t = 2.64, 3.13, respectively; p < 0.02 in both cases). Only the negative correlation between IOUs in level L and M approached significance at the one-tailed level (p < 0.05), while the average correlation between IOU estimates for different levels was virtually zero (r=0.06).

Scaling level	Prop. of correct responses	Estimated value of IOU	Mean Percentage of consistent responses		
			IOU = 0	Best IOU	Difference
H	.83	8.0	93.44	94.01	0.344
M	.80	8.1	87.24	88.10	0.838
L	.81	20.9	87.96	88.30	0.575
	.81	12.3	89.55	90.14	0.586

Table 2: Proportions of correct responses, mean IOU estimates, and percentages of response consistent trials observed for the three scaling levels in Experiment III. The discriminability parameters were $\mu = \pm 1.5$, $\sigma = 4$; $m = \pm 2.25$, $\sigma = 6$; and $\mu = \pm 3.0$, $\sigma = 8$ for the low (L), medium (M), and high (H) scaling levels, respectively. The numbers of trials for each of the 16 subjects was 288.

In these three experiments there appears to be no evidence for the operation of a single IOU, defined in terms of a specific stimulus magnitude. At the same time, the proportion of correct responses in experiments I, II and III is some 4-5% below the maximum attainable with perfect accumulation. Error rates of this magnitude are consistent with an IOU value of around 12.5, and suggest that a proportion of observations is indeed being lost - if not in a way systematically related to stimulus magnitude, then perhaps at random. Although we had judged the rate of about 3 line segments per second to be sufficiently slow to ensure that each segment would be successfully registered, the presentation rate was also intended to be sufficiently high to discourage or preclude any deliberate cognitive strategy on the part of subjects. So it is possible that observations in these experiments are being lost at random, due perhaps to an inability by some internal sampling mechanism to process them quite as quickly as they are presented.

7. EXPERIMENT IV: PERFORMANCE AT A SPEEDED PRESENTATION RATE

Experiment IV, which was carried out by Nicholls (1988), was intended to look at this last possibility in a situation in which performance would be more clearly limited by the speed at which subjects could sample and process individual observations. The general procedure was the same as in the previous three experiments, except that we used a slightly more difficult level of difficulty (m = ± 2, s = 8), and the rate of presentation was speeded up, with each line segment being shown for only 20 msec, with 20 msec between successive segments. There were 22 subjects, with ages ranging from 18 to 31. In addition to recording their accuracy on the expanded judgement task, we also tested their performance on Raven's Advanced Progressive Matrices (A.P.M.) and measured their inspection times. This last measure is the stimulus exposure duration necessary for subjects to achieve some predetermined (high) level of accuracy in a very easy visual discrimination task where continued sampling from stored traces is precluded by the use of a backward mask (Vickers, Nettelbeck, and Willson, 1972). It has been argued that inspection time is related to the minimum time required by the central nervous system to process a single, discrete sample of sensory input. Over some 50 studies it has been found to have an average correlation of around 0.5 with standard intelligence test scores (Nettelbeck, 1987).

Accuracy scores in this speeded task were again not significantly different between two sessions conducted about one week apart, with a correlation of 0.39 (p < 0.05) between the two sessions. Although there was only a low correlation of r = -0.29 with inspection time, this may well have been due to the high proportion of subjects (12 out of 22) who professed to having deliberately attempted to use apparent movement cues to counteract the effects of the backward mask (cf. Mackenzie and Bingham, 1985). Meanwhile the correlation between accuracy and scores on the A.P.M. was quite reasonable (r = 0.43, p = 0.023). If we measured accuracy for the two longest sequences of 20 and 25 only, the correlation with A.P.M. scores increased to 0.52 (p = 0.007).

8. CONCLUSIONS

Taken together, these results suggest that the notion of an IOU, defined in terms of a specific stimulus magnitude, and indicative of a characteristic bias towards filtering or accumulating observation, does not have much validity in expanded judgement tasks conforming to the E-paradigm. It is perhaps still possible that subjects may employ an IOU which is rescaled from trial to trial, and which is dynamically reset by each observation encountered within a trial. For example, a small line extending to the left may be accumulated if it is preceded by a small line on the right, but discounted if preceded by a large line extending to the right. However, in a further study by Foreman (1988), accuracy was found to be significantly lower when the observation duration was 20 msec than when it was 40. This may, of course, be partly or wholly due to peripheral masking effects operating at the higher presentation speed. On the other hand, it is also consistent with the possibility that observations in this type of task are predominantly lost at random as the result of a failure by the subject to process them as quickly as they are presented.

We have not yet been able to make a direct comparison between performance in the E and in the S paradigms. It is still possible that at the slower rate of 3 per sec, at least some subjects in the S-paradigm can apply a magnitude test to the observations. The S-paradigm differs in that the subject himself determines how many observations he will sample on each trial, and it is possible that this may encourage a different cognitive set on his part. Again, the application of an IOU in the S-paradigm results in accurate performance (albeit at the cost of taking more observations, and assuming that the parameters of any other speed-accuracy tradeoff mechanism remain constant), whereas, in the E-paradigm, it always produces less accurate performance, so there is never any advantage for the subject in operating with an IOU in the latter case.

As can be seen from table 1, the accuracy scores in these and other experiments appear to be stable and fairly reliable indicators of individual differences in performance. Since a previous study (also by Foreman, 1988) had found a significant correlation between accuracy and inspection time - though not this time with intelligence test scores - there are some grounds for thinking that accuracy in this type of task may be largely determined by some quite general limit on information processing performance, such as the time required to process a discrete sample of sensory input.

ACKNOWLEDGMENTS:

The research reported in this paper was supported by an Australian Research Council Grant (A78615464) to D. Vickers.

CORRESPONDENCE:

Correspondence concerning this paper should be sent to Dr. D. Vickers, Department of Psychology, University of Adelaide, Box 498, G.P.O., Adelaide, South Australia, 5001.

REFERENCES

Cartwright, D., and Festinger, L. (1943). A quantitative theory of decision. Psychological Review, 50, 595-621.

Eysenck, H.J. and Eysenck, M.W. (1985) Personality and individual differences: a natural science approach. New York: Plenum Publishing Co.

Foreman, E.A. (1988). Individual differences in decision process parameters. Unpublished research report, University of Adelaide.

Hockley, W.E., and Murdock, B.B. (1987). A decision model for accuracy and response latency in recognition memory. Psychological Review, 94, 341-358.

Innes, N.J. (1987). The effect of an information-limited environment on perceptual processing with respect to an interval of uncertainty. Unpublished honours thesis, University of Adelaide.

Mackenzie, B., and Bingham, E. (1985). I.Q. inspection time, and response strategies in a university population. Australian Journal of Psychology, 37, 257-268.

Nettelbeck, T.J. (1987). Inspection time and intelligence. In: Speed of Information Processing and Intelligence. P.A. Vernon (Ed.). Norwood, N.J.: Ablex,

Nicholls, M.E.R. (1988). The expanded judgement task: an alternative to inspection time? Unpublished honours thesis, University of Adelaide.

Smith, P.L., and Vickers, D. (1989). Modeling evidence accumulation with partial loss in expanded judgement. Journal of Experimental Psychology: Human Perception and Performance. In press.

Vickers, D., Nettelbeck, T.J., and Willson, R.J. (1972). Perceptual indices of performance: the measurement of "inspection time" and "noise" in the visual system. Perception, 1, 263-295.

Vickers, D. (1985). Antagonistic influences on performance change in detection and discrimination tasks. In: Cognition, Information Processing, and Motivation, G. d'Ydewalle (Ed.), Proceedings of XXII International Congress of Psychology, Acapulco, Mexico. Amsterdam: North-Holland, 79-115.

Vickers, D., Burt, J., Smith, P.L., and Brown, M. (1985a). Experimental paradigms emphasising state and process limitations: I. Effects on speed-accuracy tradeoffs. Acta Psychologica, 59, 129-161.

Vickers, D., Smith, P.L. Burt, J. and Brown, M. (1985b). Experimental paradigms emphasising state and process limitations: II. Effects on confidence. Acta Psychologica, 59, 163-193.

Vickers, D., Foreman, E.A., Smith, P.L., and Gott, R.E. (1986). Measures of response threshold and a sensory indifference region in two types of expanded judgement task. In: Current Issues in Cognitive Development and Mathematical Psychology, R.A. Heath (Ed.), Newcastle: University of Newcastle Press, 156-164.

Warren, R.M. (1985). The criterion shift rule and perceptual homeostasis. Psychological Review, 92, 574-584.

Human Information Processing: Measures,
Mechanisms, and Models. D. Vickers and P. L. Smith (eds.)
© Elsevier Science Publishers B.V. (North-Holland), 1989

A DECONVOLUTIONAL APPROACH TO MODELLING RESPONSE TIME DISTRIBUTIONS

Philip L. Smith

University of Adelaide

The accumulator model is a member of one of two broad classes of models of the processes underlying two-choice reaction time. Models of this class typically predict that mean response times for correct responses will be faster than those for errors. This is a frequently reported finding under conditions of accuracy stress and low discriminability, but when discriminability is high and speed is stressed, the reverse relation often obtains. Previously it has been shown that the accumulator model can account for this reversal if augmented with the assumption of criterion variability. This paper extends that treatment from the level of the conditional mean response times to the level of the response time distributions. Two versions of the accumulator model embodying parameter heterogeneity were fitted to the overall response time distributions and to deconvolved estimates of the distributions of decision time. The models performed reasonably well in predicting the form of the response time distributions and the observed proportion of correct responses. However, parameters estimated at the distributional level failed to predict the obtained mean response time ordering. Possible reasons for this failure are discussed.

1. INTRODUCTION

The area of two-choice reaction time is an interesting one for mathematical modelers because it represents a circumscribed and well-established body of experimental data offering diverse points of contact to formal models. Moreover, it constitutes an area of primary theoretical importance, because, dealing as it does with the mechanisms underlying speed and accuracy, it occupies a fundamental nexus between the bottom-up, stimulus-driven aspects of performance and the top-down, cognitively-controlled ones.

In the most general terms, the contact between theory and data is via a collection of N data points, each of which is an ordered pair $(T,R)_j$, $j = 1, 2, ... N$, where the random variable T represents the response time and the binary-valued random variable R represents the category of response. The values assumed by R are generically denoted R_A and R_B. Associated with a given formal model of performance is a theoretical probability distribution $P[T \leq t, R=R_i \mid \Theta]$, $(i=A, B; t > 0)$ on the space of joint events (T,R), which is conditional on a vector of parameters Θ, where Θ includes, but is not restricted to, the stimulus $(S_A$ or $S_B)$ presented.

A formal model of performance is valid to the extent that it can accurately predict the observed distribution of $P[T \leq t, R=R_i \mid \Theta]$ across all relevant and interesting dimensions of variation in Θ. Such dimensions include factors affecting the discriminability characteristics of the stimulus, and those affecting the bias and caution of the response. Among those implicated in the latter are relative stimulus frequency, payoffs, response deadlines, and experimental instructions.

Different approaches to combining estimates of $P[T \leq t, R=R_i \mid \Theta]$ give rise to different ways of viewing the data. Possibilities which have become important in practice include the relationship between mean response time and response probability (either across or within conditions); the relationship between mean response time for correct responses and errors, and the overall form of the response time distribution.

For the investigator seeking to evaluate a formal model of choice reaction processes in this way, two widely-recognized obstacles present themselves. The first is that the obtained response times are not pure measures of decision time, but reflect the duration of operations such as sensory transduction, response activation, and motor transit. The observed distribution of response times therefore contains both decisional and non-decisional components, which, if the decision stage of the process is to be legitimately treated in isolation, must be assumed to be stochastically independent. In addition, the manipulated experimental factors must be assumed to selectively affect only the duration of the decision stage (see Townsend and Ashby, 1983, Ch. 12, for details). It is by no means self-evident that this conjunction of conditions will be satisfied. It would be violated, for example, by a process in which the rate of response activation is a function of the quality of the accumulated stimulus information. However, even when these assumptions appear defensible, there remain serious problems of both a theoretical and methodological nature concerning how the residual component is to be identified and extracted.

The second major obstacle concerns the problem of parameter heterogeneity. To the extent that subsets of a sequence of data points $(T,R)_j$, $j = 1, 2, ... N$, are generated by numerically different values of the parameter vector Θ, the obtained distribution $P[T \leq t, R=R_i \mid \Theta]$ will be a *mixture*, whose precise forms depends on the distribution of Θ, possibly in a quite nonlinear way. When the model under consideration is a sequential sampling model, the vector Θ typically includes one set of parameters describing the sensory characteristics of the stimulus, and another specifying the response characteristics of the subject. Under these circumstances, between-subject variation in one or both of these parameter sets can be expected. This fact has led some investigators to prefer experimental designs in which many observations are collected from each of a small group of subjects, which are then analyzed for individual subjects separately.

While such a technique may be effective in dealing with between-subject variations, there are other sources of parameter heterogeneity which cannot be so easily circumvented. One is the enduring changes in the values of Θ over time, reflecting systematic learning of the experimental task, a phenomenon which has been discussed by Rabbitt (1979). These effects may be minimized by employing the technique of Green, A.F. Smith and von Gierke (1983), of using only highly-practised subjects, and thereby attempting to sample only from a point of asymptotic performance.

However, in addition to systematic long-term trends in parameter values, there remains the problem of fine-grained, trial-by-trial variations in Θ. Compelling evidence for such variation has been adduced by Laming (1979) and Vickers (1985), and is implicit in the rich complexity of the literature on sequential effects (see Kirby, 1980; also Luce, 1986, pp. 253-272). Additional evidence from psychophysical settings is reviewed by Treisman and Williams (1984). The problem with effects of this latter kind is that they suggest that estimates of $P[T \leq t, R=R_i \mid \Theta]$ obtained from pooling data at *any* level of analysis are likely to reflect heterogeneity in the values of the parameter vector Θ. These problems have recently been discussed by Burbeck and Luce (1982).

This paper focuses on one particular model of two-choice performance, the accumulator model, which was proposed by Vickers (1970, 1979) as a generalization of earlier work on unit-increment processes (Audley and Pike, 1965; La Berge, 1962; Pike, 1966, 1968), and mathematically formalized by Smith and Vickers (1988a). In particular, it seeks to extend the empirical treatment of the model provided by Smith and Vickers (1988a,b) from the level of the conditional mean response times to the level of the response time distributions. In so doing, it attempts to take account of the complexities introduced by the problems of parameter heterogeneity and of the residual, non-decisional component of the response time distribution.

2. THE MATHEMATICAL MODEL

The accumulator model assumes that any fixed stimulus magnitude gives rise to a randomly and momentarily varying distribution of activity along an underlying dimension of sensory effect. Samples drawn from this distribution are compared to a sensory referent and the deviation between them computed. The magnitudes of deviations falling above the referent are added into one evidence total, T_A, and those falling below added to another, T_B. Observations are sampled and accumulated in this way at equally-spaced intervals $n = 1, 2, ... $, until $T_A \geq K_A$ or $T_B \geq K_B$, at which point the process terminates, and the response (R_A or R_B) whose threshold has been exceeded is given. Here K_A and K_B represent response threshold or criterion values for the two responses, and are assumed to be under the control of the subject.

If $f(x)$ denotes the conditional density of deviations falling above the referent, and $g(y)$ the conditional density of deviations falling below it, and p the probability of sampling from $f(x)$ rather then $g(y)$, then it may be shown that $P_{A,n}$ and $P_{B,n}$, the probabilities that the process will terminate at response R_A and R_B in exactly n steps, are given by

$$P_{A,n} = \sum_{i=0}^{n-1} \binom{n-1}{i} p^i (1-p)^{n-i-1} \int_0^{K_B} g_{n-i-1}(y)\, dy \; p \int_0^{K_A} f_i(x) \int_{K_A-x}^{\infty} f(z)\, dz\, dx$$

and

$$P_{B,n} = \sum_{i=0}^{n-1} \binom{n-1}{i} p^i (1-p)^{n-i-1} \int_0^{K_A} f_i(x)\, dx \; (1-p) \int_0^{K_B} g_{n-i-1}(y) \int_{K_B-y}^{\infty} g(w)\, dw\, dy \; .$$

Here $f_i(x)$ and $g_{n-i-1}(y)$ are, respectively, the i-fold convolution of densities $f(x)$ and the (n-i-1)-fold convolution of densities $g(y)$. From the above expressions, response probabilities and the conditional and marginal expected number of steps to termination are obtained by summation of terms

$$P_i = \sum_{n=1}^{\infty} P_{i, n}, \qquad\qquad i = A, B,$$

$$E[N_i] = \sum_{n=1}^{\infty} n P_{i, n} / P_i, \qquad\qquad i = A, B,$$

$$E[N] = P_A E[N_A] + P_B E[N_B],$$

where N is a random variable specifying the time at which the process terminates and the subscript denotes the emitted response.

The assumption which is usually made, and the one with the greatest theoretical precedence, is that the distribution of sensory activity generated by the stimulus is normal. However, this leads to analytically intractable expressions for the convolutions of densities $f(x)$ and $g(y)$, and for this reason, the exponential approximation described in Smith and Vickers (1988a) will be employed here instead. A computationally intensive solution for the normal case is described in Smith and Vickers (1989), but in the present setting the exponential approximation is more convenient.

3. RANDOMLY ORIENTED LINES DATA

3.1 Conditional Mean Response Times

The data to which the present model was applied were from an experiment by Vickers and Willson (see Smith and Vickers, 1988a, or Vickers, 1979, pp. 75-76). Each stimulus consisted of a circular array of 300 line segments of equal length and normally distributed orientation, with specified mean and standard deviation 22.5 deg. Subjects were required to judge whether the mean of the orientations fell to the right (clockwise) or left (anti-clockwise) of the vertical, and to make an appropriate keypress response. Five different values of stimulus discriminability were employed, whose nominal values, expressed as a ratio of orientation mean to standard deviation, were $\mu(1) = \pm 0.111$, $\mu(2) = \pm 0.333$, $\mu(3) = \pm 0.556$, $\mu(4) = \pm 0.778$, and $\mu(5) = \pm 1.000$, with an equal number of S_A and S_B stimuli presented at all orientations. (S_A denotes clockwise orientation.) Each of 10 subjects served in five experimental sessions, producing a total of 2500 trials of data per subject, 500 at each discriminability level.

Smith and Vickers (1988a) provide an analysis of the conditional mean response times and response probabilities of the group data, pooled across subjects and days. One interesting feature of the resulting data set is the presence of a reversal in response time orderings across discriminability levels. In the $\mu(1)$, $\mu(2)$ and $\mu(3)$ conditions, correct responses were faster than errors for both R_A and R_B. In the $\mu(5)$ condition, however, errors were faster than correct responses for both R_A and R_B, while in the $\mu(4)$ condition, errors were faster than correct responses for R_A only, this being the faster of the two responses (see Smith and Vickers, 1988a, Table 3).

Orderings of the kind obtained in the latter two conditions are not consistent with the accumulator model in its simple form, which predicts that mean error times will be slower than those for correct responses, or that under certain circumstances, the ordering will reverse for the *slower* of the two responses. However, when augmented with the assumption of criterion variability, as suggested by Pike (1973), the model can predict a reversal in the usual ordering of correct responses and error times, which is more pronounced at higher levels of discriminability.

Specifically, for a distribution of M criterion pairs, with p(m) the probability of the m-th pair, and $T_{ij}(m)$ and $P_{ij}(m)$, respectively, the mean response time and conditional response probability for response j to stimulus i for the m-th criterion pair, then the statistics for the process taken across the distribution of criterion pairs, denoted T'_{ij} and P'_{ij}, will be

$$P'_{ij} = \sum_{m=1}^{M} p(m)\, P_{ij}(m)$$

and

$$T'_{ij} = \left[\sum_{m=1}^{M} p(m)\, P_{ij}(m)\, T_{ij}(m) \right] / P'_{ij}.$$

Smith and Vickers considered a simple version of the distributed criterion model in relation to the randomly-oriented lines data, with M=5 equally-spaced criterion pairs, and $p(1) = p(2) = \ldots p(5)$; that is, where the five criterion pairs were equiprobable. With moderate criterion variability, this model qualitatively predicted a reversal in the orderings for correct responses and errors in the easy discriminability condition, but one which was of insufficient magnitude to explain the observed effects. With increased criterion variability, the magnitude of the reversal likewise increased, but appeared at more difficult discriminabilities also.

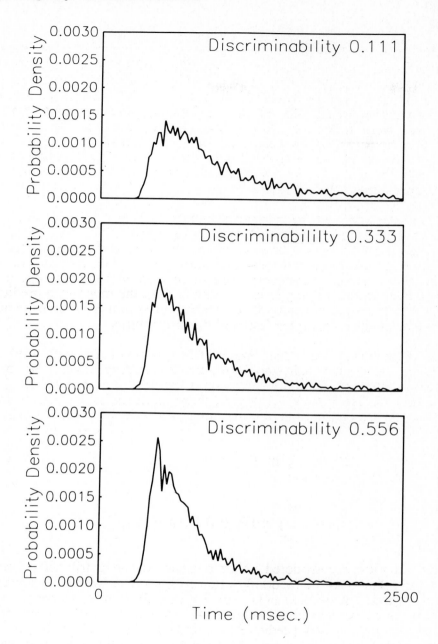

Fig. 1(i) Marginal response time distributions, pooled over subjects and days for the μ(1) to μ(3) conditions.

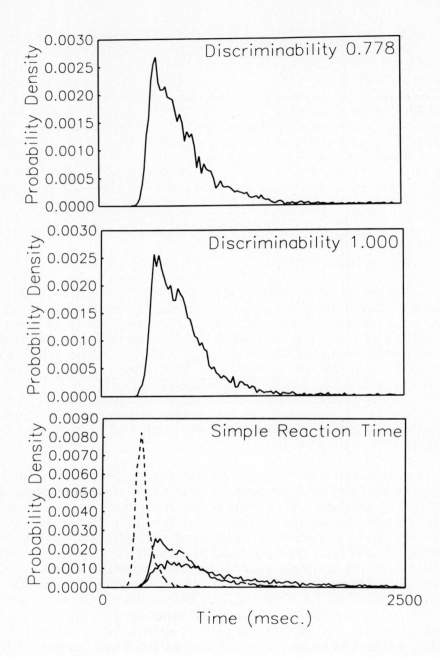

Fig. 1(ii) Marginal response time distributions, pooled over subjects and days for the μ(4) and μ(5) conditions. The lower panel shows the pooled distribution of simple reaction times, with the choice distributions for the μ(1) and μ(5) conditions.

A second model considered by Smith and Vickers made the additional assumption that the values of the discriminability parameters varied *within* each condition, in a manner which was negatively correlated with variations in criterion. This model was motivated by Vickers' (1978) hypothesis of confidence-based self-regulation, which holds that subjects attempt to regulate their performance across changing stimulus conditions by maintaining a target level of response confidence. This translated into the hypotheses that (i) subjects for whom the task is more difficult will tend to adopt higher values of criterion, and (ii) a rise in effective discriminability associated with practice on the task will be accompanied by a decline in criterion values. This discriminability-criterion covariance model, when fitted to the conditional mean response times and correct response probabilities for the five discriminability levels, provided a satisfactory description of the group data.

3.2 Response Time Distributions

Figures 1(i)-1(ii) show marginal density function estimates for each of the five discriminability levels, obtained by pooling over subjects, days and responses.[1] The distributions were obtained by grouping the obtained times into 256 bins of width 19.56 ms, on the range of 0 to 5000 ms, and normalizing. (Only the range 0 to 2500ms is shown.) Each of the distributions shown is based on 5000 trials. While there are advantages to be gained from analyzing distributions of correct responses and errors separately, the number of errors obtained in four of the five discriminability conditions was insufficient to permit construction of error-time distributions, and so the analysis reported here will be of the marginal distributions only.

A striking feature of these data is that, to a considerable degree, they exhibit a fixed mode property. That is, the increase in response time produced by a reduction in discriminability is primarily due to an increase in the skewness of the distribution, rather than to a change in its mode. While this finding is consistent with some sequential sampling models, notably, the diffusion process model of Ratcliff (1978), it immediately suffices to falsify a simple accumulator model, which predicts negative correlations between skewness and marginal mean (see Smith and Vickers, 1988a, Fig. 1). However, computer exploration of the properties of accumulator models with distributed criterion pairs has shown that when the distribution of criterion pairs is approximately lognormal, the model can generate predictions exhibiting the fixed mode property.[2] That is, the distribution of criterion pairs approximates a density of the form:

$$f(x) = (1 / (\sigma x \sqrt{2\pi})) \exp\{-(\ln x - \upsilon)^2 / 2 \eta^2\},$$

whose mean and variance are

$$\text{Mean}(X) = \exp(\upsilon + \eta^2/2),$$

$$\text{Var}(X) = \exp(2\upsilon + \eta^2)(\exp \eta^2 - 1),$$

(Luce, 1986, p. 510). (In the form given above, the lower bound of the lognormal distribution is always zero, but this may be further generalized by incorporating a variable offset parameter.)

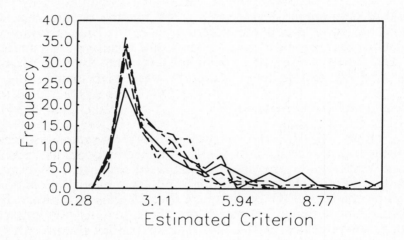

Figure. 2. Estimated distribution of criteria for the five discriminability levels. $\mu(1)$: solid line; $\mu(2)$: dashed line; $\mu(3)$: dotted line: $\mu(4)$ dot-dashed line; $\mu(5)$ long dash line.

The fact that response time distributions of the form of Figure 1 are obtained by assuming a lognormal distribution of criteria is of particular interest in the light of results of an attempt to estimate the distribution of criterion values directly. Lack of space precludes a full account of these findings; but in general terms, estimates of the distribution of criterion values were obtained for each discriminability level by computing the criterion value required to produce the observed proportion of correct responses for each point in the Subject x Day x Lag 1 Stimulus-Dependent Sequential Effect cross classification. Other parameters were fixed at the values estimated by Smith and Vickers (1988a). This yielded five distributions, each of which was based on 100 estimates, as shown in Figure 2. While these estimates relied on a number of simplifying assumptions, making them prone to artifact, and while they ignore other possible sources of heterogeneity in the data, they are nevertheless fairly consistent across discriminability levels. This, coupled with the fact that the distribution of criterion values is theoretically bounded below by zero, suggests that a unimodal positively-skewed distribution may provide a better basis for modelling the distribution of criterion values than the simple mixture employed by Smith and Vickers.

4. DECONVOLUTION OF RESIDUAL RESPONSE COMPONENTS

4.1 Residual Times

As stated in the Introduction, to legitimately treat the decision stage in isolation, it is necessary to assume that decision and residual components are stochastically independent. Even if this assumption is accepted, however, there remains the problem of how the residual component is to be estimated. Here it will be assumed that this component is approximated by the distribution of simple reaction times. This is equivalent to the Donderian assumption that simple and choice reaction times differ by the presence or absence of a processing stage. It is possible that this assumption may be satisfied only approximately; for example, under conditions of simple reaction time the decision stage may not be deleted from the processing sequence, but may be of relatively short duration. Under these circumstances, the duration of the residual processing component would be bounded above by the simple reaction time.

Simple reaction times were collected for 9 of the 10 subjects who served in the randomly oriented lines experiment, 100 for either hand. The lower panel of Figure 1(ii) shows the sample density function for simple reaction times, pooled across subjects and hands, for the 1800 trials.[3] Also shown, for comparison purposes, are the sample densities for the $\mu(1)$ and $\mu(5)$ conditions.

4.2 Fourier Transform Representation

The assumptions outlined above imply that the random variable T, which represents the total observed response time, may be written as the sum of two random variables D and R, which represent, respectively, the duration of the decision and residual stages,

$$T = D + R.$$

If these random variables have associated density functions of h_T, h_D and h_R, respectively, then by the assumption of stochastically independent stages, the density of T can be written as the convolution of the densities of D and R,

$$h_T(t) = \int_0^t h_D(t-s) h_R(s) \, ds.$$

Taking Fourier transforms on both sides we obtain the frequency domain representation

$$H_T(f) = H_D(f) H_R(f).$$

Here upper case symbols denote Fourier transforms of the densities of the subscripted random variables, and are functions of the frequency domain variable f. The frequency domain representation exploits the well-known property of the Fourier transform of converting convolution in the time domain into multiplication in the frequency domain, and vice versa (see e.g. Brigham, 1974). To obtain the density of the decision component, one need only divide through by $H_R(f)$, and take the inverse Fourier transform,

$$h_D(t) = FT^{-1} \left[\frac{H_T(f)}{H_R(f)} \right],$$

where FT^{-1} denotes the inverse transform operator.

Technical problems arise from the direct application of this technique to response time data, because of the presence of noise in the Fourier representation of the sample density estimates, and its amplification by the operation of deconvolution (see Green, 1971; Smith, 1989, for further discussion). Hence some form of filtering is required if the procedure is to recover a reasonable approximation to $h_D(t)$. In the frequency domain, a (low-pass) filter is a function $\phi(f)$ which is applied multiplicatively to the Fourier transform of the deconvolution pair to obtain a smoothed estimate of its true value,

$$\tilde{h}_D(t) = FT^{-1} \left[\frac{H_T(f)\phi(f)}{H_R(f)} \right],$$

where the tilde is used to denote the filtered estimate. In order to produce a smooth time-domain estimate of $\tilde{h}_D(t)$, a "Hanning tapered" filter of the form

$$\phi(f) = \quad 1/2 + 1/2 \cos(\pi f / f_c) \qquad |f| \le f_c$$

$$= \quad 0 \qquad\qquad\qquad |f| > f_c$$

was employed, with $f_c = 25$ (see Smith, 1989, for details).

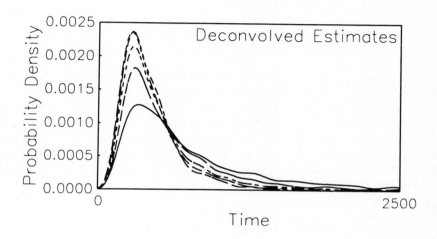

Fig. 3. Deconvolved estimates of the decision component for the five discriminability levels. Curves are $\mu(5)$ to $\mu(1)$ in order of increasing skewness. Modes of the $\mu(4)$ and $\mu(5)$ curves are coincident.

Figure 3 shows the filtered and deconvolved estimates of the decision component $\hat{h}_D(t)$ obtained in this way for each of the five discriminability levels. As may be seen, the fixed mode property which was previously remarked on is strongly apparent in the deconvolved estimates.

4.3 Deconvolved estimates of the decision component

For the purposes of model fitting, it is desirable to have data displaying normal sampling variability characteristics, which are distributed according to the estimates shown in Figure 3. To this end, 5000 trials of simulated "pseudo-data" were constructed for each of the distributions in Figure 3 using the rejection method (Press, Flannery, Teukolsky & Vetterling, 1986). These distributions represent the best estimate of the (unsmoothed) distributions of the latency of the decision stage. As a test of their "statistical typicality", the distributions of the deconvolved estimates were grouped into 25 equal width bins and a chi-square test performed to determine their goodness of fit to the smoothed estimates of $h_D(t)$. For conditions $\mu(1)$ to $\mu(5)$, the obtained chi-squares were 22.0, 26.5, 28.8, 19.9 and 22.2, all of which are acceptably close to the expected value of 24.0.

5. MODEL FITTING PROCEDURES

This section describes the fits of two models, which were fitted to both the undeconvolved data and the simulated distributions of the deconvolved decision stage. In either instance, the basic model of the decision process was the exponential approximation to the accumulator model described by Smith & Vickers (1988a), which was assumed to be unbiased with respect to both sensory and response factors. The difference between the two models lay in their assumptions about parameter heterogeneity. Model 1 assumed that the only source of parameter heterogeneity was in the decision criteria, while Model II assumed negative covariation in criterion and effective (i.e. within-condition) discriminability, as described in Smith and Vickers (1988a).

Model I assumed a lognormal distribution of decision criteria, with parameters υ_K, η_K and ξ_K, where the latter represents the zero-offset. (In making this assumption, no attempt has been made to capture the specific detail of the distributions shown in Figure 2, but only their general qualitative features. This is because, in the light of the simplifying assumptions made there, such results can at best be deemed suggestive.) The discriminability levels had means $\mu(1)$, $\mu(2)$ ... $\mu(5)$. Model II employed a similar distribution of criterion values, but in addition, the discriminability parameters within each condition were also lognormally distributed with common parameters, υ_D and η_D, and variable offsets $\xi(1)$, $\xi(2)$ ... $\xi(5)$. Discrete approximations were used for all distributions, consisting of five point masses, with the values for the discriminability distributions in Model II negatively covarying with those of the criterion distribution, as described in Smith and Vickers (1988a). In addition, both models incorporated a sampling time parameter, λ, describing the time taken to accumulate a single observation, and a residual non-decisional component, t_0. (This parameter was included in the fits to both the undeconvolved and the deconvolved data, although in the latter case its theoretical value is zero).

The models were fitted by minimizing a chi-square statistic defined over both response time distributions and proportion of correct responses. The five response time distributions were each divided into 25 equal-frequency intervals and the following statistic minimized

$$\chi^2 = \sum_{i=1}^{I} \sum_{j=1}^{J} [(O_{ij} - E_{ij})^2 / E_{ij}] + \sum_{i=1}^{I} [(P_i - \hat{P}_i)^2 / \sigma^2 (P_i)],$$

with $I = 5$, $J = 25$. Here, O_{ij} and E_{ij} are, respectively, the observed and expected frequencies for the j-th interval at the i-th discriminability level. P_i and $\hat{P}_i$ are the observed and predicted proportions of correct responses for the i-th discriminability level, and $\sigma^2(P_i)$ is the estimated standard error. To the extent that normality and independence assumptions are satisfied, this statistic will asymptotically possess a chi-square distribution with IJ − n degrees of freedom, where n is the number of estimated parameters.

The fitting was carried out iteratively using two nonlinear minimization routines, the Nelder and Mead (1965) Simplex algorithm, and Powell's direction set method (Press et al., 1986, pp.294-301). Two minimization routines were used, together with a variety of starting values, in an attempt to insure against the problem of local minima, to which such routines are prone.

TABLE 1

Parameter Estimates

Parameter Model I (Model II)			Undeconvolved Data Model I Model II		Deconvolved Data Model I Model II	
Criterion means	μ_K		1.033	1.197	0.870	1.121
Criterion S.D.	σ_K		1.036	1.023	1.133	0.892
Criterion offset	ξ_K		0.512	0.527	1.271	1.231
Sampling time	λ		70.0	61.6	65.5	65.4
Residual time	t_o		372.7	370.4	6.8	7.4
Discriminability	$\mu(1)$	$(\xi(1))$	0.135	0.144	0.153	0.147
(offset)	$\mu(2)$	$(\xi(2))$	0.552	0.515	0.453	0.452
	$\mu(3)$	$(\xi(3))$	0.913	0.898	0.817	0.816
	$\mu(4)$	$(\xi(4))$	1.180	1.163	1.065	1.071
	$\mu(5)$	$(\xi(5))$	1.290	1.281	1.110	1.113
(Discriminability mean)		(μ_D)	-	-6.766	-	-35.904
(Discriminability S.D.)		(σ_D)	-	0.794	-	3.234
	χ^2		498.6	517.4	575.6	575.1
	df		115	113	115	113

Note. Time estimates in ms. Other estimates in stimulus standard deviation units.

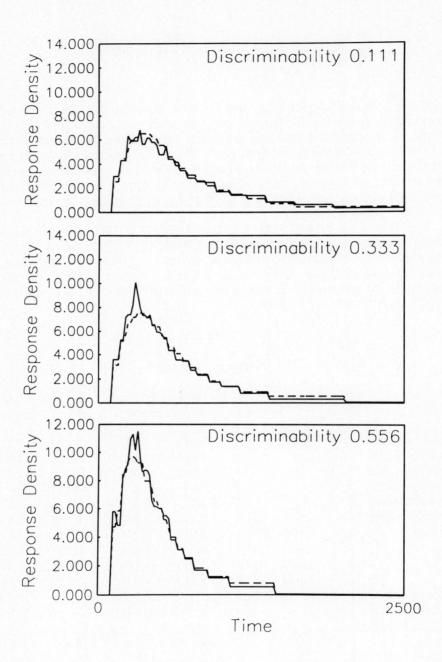

Fig. 4(i)   Fit of Model I to the deconvolved data for the $\mu(1)$ to $\mu(3)$ conditions. The broken lines represent the fitted values.

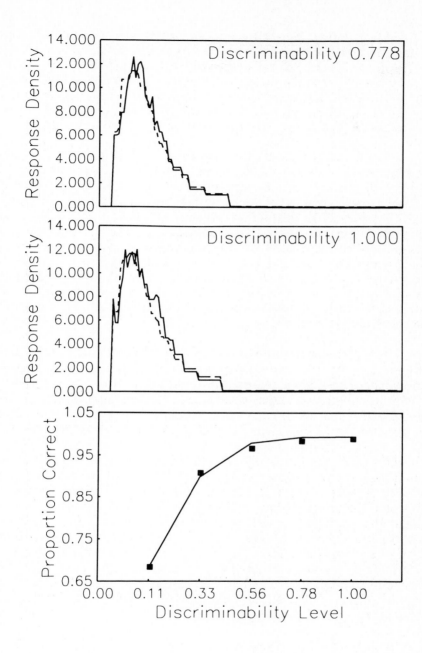

Fig. 4(ii) Fit of Model I to the deconvolved data for the $\mu(4)$ and $\mu(5)$ conditions. The lower panel shows the observed (symbols) and predicted proportions of correct responses.

Table 1 shows the estimated parameters and associated goodness of fit for Models I and II for both the undeconvolved and deconvolved data. The fit of Model I to the deconvolved data is shown in Figures 4(i)-4(ii). The first five panels show the fitted distributions; the lower panel of Figure 4(ii) shows the proportion of correct responses. Although lack of space prevents inclusion of the figure, the fit of Model I to the undeconvolved data shows very much the same qualitative features.

For all of the four fits reported, the data show significant discrepancies at the p = .001 level, although this result should be interpreted in the light of the extremely high power of the chi-square test with large sample sizes. (For the simultaneous fit of the five distributions, N = 25000.) Model II, despite possessing two additional free parameters, performed either no better, or somewhat worse, than Model I. Substitution of the estimated parameters for Model II into the expressions for the lognormal mean and variance reveals that, for both data sets, the estimated distributions of discriminability parameters were effectively singular. Such a result indicates either the inappropriateness of the hypothesis of discriminability-criterion covariation, or the incorrectness of the specific distributional assumptions employed.

The fitted distributions shown in Figure 4 indicate that, in general, the hypothesis of an accumulator model with lognormally distributed criterion pairs provides a reasonably good account of the response time distributions obtained under conditions of changing discriminability. Also, the estimated parameters quite accurately predict the proportion of correct responses, as the lower panel of Figure 4(ii) illustrates.

The main source of systematic discrepancy in the fitted values comes from the fact that the model fails to predict distributions which are as sharply peaked as those in Figures 4(i)-4(ii), particularly for the easier levels of discriminability. Two obvious explanations for these discrepancies suggest themselves. One is that the specific assumption of a lognormal distribution of criterion pairs may be incorrect, particularly in light of the estimates shown in Figure 2. The second is that the fits reported here made use of an exponential approximation to the accumulator model, which generates response time distributions which are rather more symmetrical, and less peaked than those of the corresponding normal increment model.

Both Model I and Model II perform somewhat more poorly when fitted to the deconvolved estimates than when fitted to the raw (undeconvolved) data. This results from the fact that the deconvolved distributions were somewhat more peaked than their undeconvolved counterparts, and, as noted above, the models had difficulty predicting this feature. The prediction of correct response proportions was, however, similarly good in either case. Without knowing how well the distribution of residual times is approximated by simple reaction times, it is difficult to know how to make a comparative assessment of these two results. To the extent that the residual time is bounded above by simple reaction times, the true distribution of the decision component should lie somewhere between that of the undeconvolved and deconvolved estimates. Beyond this, though, one cannot say which of the two fits should be accorded the greater weight.

TABLE 2

Actual and Fitted MRT_E - MRT_C

	$\mu(1)$	$\mu(2)$	$\mu(3)$	$\mu(4)$	$\mu(5)$
Observed	130	313	194	-71	-245
Model I Undeconvolved	-89	-196	-178	-160	-155
Model II Undeconvolved	-105	-208	-108	-168	-164
Model I Deconvolved	-84	-153	-139	-127	-126
Model II Deconvolved	-45	-102	-108	-106	-107

The major shortcoming in the present models lies in their predicted orderings of errors and correct responses. Table 2 shows the actual differences between mean error and correct response times, i.e. MRT_E - MRT_C, together with the predicted values for each of the four fits. As may be seen from the table, the observed response time orderings show a reversal across discriminability levels, whereas the fitted values predict faster errors under all circumstances. This finding is consistent with Smith and Vickers' (1988a) observation that, when fitting conditional mean response times, the hypothesis of criterion variability alone was insufficient to account for both the reversal in response times and the magnitude of the effect observed in the $\mu(5)$ condition, but rather, the stronger hypothesis of discriminability-criterion covariation appeared to be required. Because of the singularity of the distributions of discriminability parameters estimated for Model II, for both deconvolved and undeconvolved data, the fitted values reported here effectively exhibit heterogeneity of criterion values alone, in all four cases. Thus, the result for distributions effectively reproduces that for mean response times.

6. GENERAL DISCUSSION

The work reported here represents an attempt to provide a quantitative account of the response time distributions, the observed proportion of correct responses, and the ordering of correct and error response times in two-choice data using a parameter-heterogeneous accumulator model. In this, it was only partially successful. The model successfully predicted the general manner in which the shape of response time distributions changed over discriminability levels and the observed proportion of correct responses. However, the predicted distributions of response times were somewhat less sharply peaked than those observed empirically in either data set. More seriously, the predicted response time orderings were systematically in error.

Two possibilities obviously need to be considered. One is that the underlying model of the decision process is wrong; the second is that one or more of the subsidiary assumptions concerning the nature of parameter heterogeneity is in error. An alternative model of perceptual recognition which conceivably could be applied to the present data, and whose distributional properties have been extensively investigated, is the diffusion process model of Ratcliff (1978). This model possesses two properties which might make it appealing in the present context. The first is that it predicts that the increases in response time with reduced discriminability will be accompanied by a greater skewing out of the distribution's tail. Second, it predicts faster mean response times for correct responses than for errors. These predictions are qualitatively in accord with the findings reported here, except for the cross-over in response time orderings observed at the easier levels of discriminability.

One of the reasons for not preferring such a description on *a priori* grounds is that the skewness properties observed here are a product of pooling over subjects and days, and are not necessarily characteristic of the individual constituent distributions. In fact, if skewness indices are calculated individually, for the Subject x Day x Discriminability cross-classification, then averaged over subjects and days, the average values are not monotone with discriminability, but increase for $\mu(1)$ to $\mu(3)$ and then decrease. At the level of the data for individual subjects, pooled over days, some distributions exhibit a pattern of skewness which decreases with discriminability, as predicted by the accumulator model, whereas others show a pattern which increases, as predicted by the diffusion model. The predictions of an accumulator model with criterion variance provide one possible way of accounting for these findings: with small amounts of criterion variance the skewness indices will behave like those of a parameter-homogeneous process, and increase with discriminability. With larger levels of criterion variance this pattern reverses. Such an explanation therefore attributes the differences in the pattern of skewness indices for individual subjects to different levels of parameter heterogeneity. This account has some credibility to the extent that individual subjects showed marked differences in their learning curves over days. The discrepancies in the quantitative fits would therefore be attributed either to errors in the assumptions about the form and distribution of parameter variation-covariation, or to the relative crudity with which such variation was approximated in the fitting procedure.

FOOTNOTES

1.The lack of bias in previously reported parameter estimates justifies pooling over responses and permits a lower dimensional parameter solution to be employed. In addition to the results reported here, the analysis was also carried out by fitting across the R_A and R_B distributions simultaneously, with essentially the same outcome. The pooled results are reported in preference as they are more compact.

2.This result was obtained by using a discrete approximation to the lognormal in the manner of the fits reported subsequently.

3. Despite the absence of simple reaction times for one subject, this distribution was treated as an estimate of the group distribution of residual times. Since this distribution is much more symmetrical and less variable by comparison, the omission is unlikely to seriously alter the pattern of deconvolved data.

ACKNOWLEDGMENTS

The research reported in this paper was carried out while the author was supported by a National Research Fellowship (Australia). I would like to thank Douglas Vickers for generously making available computing resources which were indispensible to the completion of this work

Address correspondence to Philip L. Smith, Department of Psychology, University of Otago, PO Box 56, Dunedin, New Zealand.

REFERENCES

Audley, R.J., & Pike, A.R. (1965). Some alternative stochastic models of choice. British Journal of Mathematical and Statistical Psychology, 18, 207-225.

Brigham, E.O. (1974). The Fast Fourier Transform. Englewood Cliffs, N.J.: Prentice Hall.

Burbeck, S.L. & Luce, R.D. (1982). Evidence from auditory simple reaction times for both change and level detectors. Perception & Psychophysics, 32, 117-133.

Green, D.M. (1971). Fourier analysis of reaction time data. Behaviour Research Methods and Instrumentation, 3, 121-125.

Green, D.M., Smith, A.F., & Von Gierke, S.M. (1983). Choice reaction time with a random foreperiod. Perception & Psychophysics, 34, 195-208.

Kirby, N. (1980). Sequential effects in choice reaction time. In A.T. Welford (Ed.), Reaction Times. London: Academic Press.

La Berge, D. (1962). A recruitment theory of simple behaviour. Psychometrika, 27, 375-396.

Laming, D. (1979). Choice reaction performance following an error. Acta Psychologica, 43, 199-224.

Luce, R.D. (1986). Response times. New York: Oxford University Press.

Nelder, J.A., & Mead, R. (1965). A simplex method for function minimization. Computer Journal, 7, 308-313.

Pachella, R.G. (1974). The interpretation of reaction time in information processing research. In B. Kantowitz (Ed.), Human information processing: Tutorials in performance and cognition. Hillsdale, N.J.: Erlbaum.

Pike, A.R. (1966). Stochastic models of choice behaviour: Response probabilities and latencies of finite Markov chain systems. British Journal of Mathematical and Statistical Psychology, 19, 15-32.

Pike, A.R. (1968). Latency and relative frequency of response in psychophysical discrimination. British Journal of Mathematical and Statistical Psychology, 21, 161-182.

Pike, A.R. (1973). Response latency models for signal detection. Psychological Review, 80, 53-68.

Press, W.H., Flannery, B.P., Teukolsky, S.A., & Vetterling, W.T. (1986). Numerical Recipes. Cambridge: Cambridge University Press.

Rabbitt, P.M.A. (1979). Current paradigms and models in human information processing. In V. Hamilton and D.N. Warburton (Eds.) Human Stress and Cognition. Chichester: Wiley.

Ratcliff, R. (1978). A theory of memory retrieval. Psychological Review, 85, 59-108.

Smith, P.L. (1989). Obtaining meaningful results from Fourier deconvolution of reaction time data. Manuscript submitted for publication.

Smith, P.L., & Vickers, D. (1988a). The accumulator model of two-choice discrimination. Journal of Mathematical Psychology, 32, 135-168.

Smith, P.L., & Vickers, D. (1988b). Studies of two-choice reaction time: A cross-paradigmatic validation of the inspection time index. In R.A. Heath (Ed.) Current Issues in Cognitive Development and Mathematical Psychology. Newcastle, Australia: University of Newcastle Psychology Department Publication.

Smith, P.L., & Vickers, D. (1989). Modeling evidence accumulation with partial loss in expanded judgment. Journal of Experimental Psychology: Human Perception and Performance. (in press).

Townsend, J.T., & Ashby, F.G. (1983). The stochastic modeling of elementary psychological processes. Cambridge: Cambridge University Press.

Vickers, D. (1970). Evidence for an accumulator model of psychophysical discrimination. Ergonomics, 13, 37-58.

Vickers, D. (1978). An adaptive module for simple judgements. In J. Requin (Ed.), Attention and Performance VII. Hillsdale, N.J.: Erlbaum.

Vickers, D. (1979). Decision processes in visual perception. London: Academic Press.

Vickers, D. (1985). Antagonistic influences on performance change in detection and discrimination tasks. In G. d'Ydewalle (Ed.), Cognition, Information Processing and Motivation. Proceedings of the XXIII International Congress of Psychology. (Vol. 3). Amsterdam: North Holland.

Vickers, D., Burt, J., Smith, P.L., & Brown, M. (1985). Experimental paradigms emphasising state or process limitations: I. Effects on speed-accuracy tradeoffs. Acta Psychologica, 59, 129-161.

Human Information Processing: Measures,
Mechanisms, and Models. D. Vickers and P. L. Smith (eds.)
©Elsevier Science Publishers B.V. (North-Holland), 1989

CONCENTRATION, SPEED, AND PRECISION IN TIME-LIMITED TASKS

Edward.E.Roskam, Gerard van Breukelen, and Ronald Jansen

University of Nijmegen

This paper reviews a theory, mathematical models and experimental results concerning speed and precision of performance on simple mental tasks, such as in time-limited intelligence tests and so-called concentration- tests. Section 2 introduces the general theory. Section 3 introduces the specific theory, and attempts to explain variability in response times in terms of a stochastic model, which decomposes the response time into 'processing time' and 'distraction time'. The theory explains trends in response times, differences between spaced and massed work, and differences between homogeneous and mixed tasks. Section 4 introduces models concerning the relation between correctness of response and processing time, and elaborates a modified Rasch model for a psychometric theory of intelligence. Section 5 discusses and evaluates the general methodology of the present approach.

1. INTRODUCTION

The patterns of error rates and of mean response times (RT), RT-variance, and RT-trend in performing a series of simple mental tasks of equal difficulty, show that there is no simple trade-off relation between speed and accuracy within an RT series with constant task parameters. Mean RT may increase in the course of a series of trials while error rate also increases.

Increasing RT and error rate is usually explained by something like 'fatigue'. This concept, however, merely labels what is to be explained. Therefore, a model is needed which formalizes the notion that the subject's concentration decreases during, and due to, task performance. This calls for a distinction between time spent in actually processing the task, and time which is 'lost' due to distraction.

A general theory and mathematical models are developed which describe these relations in terms of a stochastic process. Furthermore, the relation between processing time and error rate should be derivable from a psychometric item response model.

2. GENERAL THEORY

The general theory is concerned with performance in terms of speed and error rate in relatively simple mental tasks. Examples of such tasks are lexical identification, identification of rotated figures, and addition of one-digit numbers (see Figures 1 & 2). The theory aims to explain the relation between speed and error rate in terms of subject parameters and task parameters, and particularly to explain trend and variability in response times and in error rate. More generally, the theory embodies what may be called a psychonometric approach to intelligence performance. The research has been motivated originally by the fact that most intelligence tests are time-limited tests. The domain of the theory concerns all tasks where a response is elicited which can be categorized as 'correct' or 'wrong' according to a factual, logical, or semantic rule, as is the case in most intelligence tests. The domain is limited to those tasks for which the subject has all the information needed to produce a correct response (i.e. no specific knowledge is required).

It is a generally accepted fact that error rate increases when response time decreases. This is the so-called speed-accuracy trade-off (cf. Luce, 1986; Pachella, 1974). However, since one can work more slowly without being more accurate, it appears reasonable to assume that subjects may also increase their gross speed without making more errors, at least up to a certain limit. Also, it has been observed (Van Breukelen & Jansen, 1987) that both response times and error rate increase with continuous task performance. Neither of these effects can be explained by the speed-accuracy trade-off function.

A general theory has been developed over the past 15 years by Roskam, Pieters, Van der Ven, Van Breukelen, and Jansen at the Mathematical Psychology Group of the University of Nijmegen. Central to the theory is the idea that the observed (total) response time is the sum of mental processing time and distraction ('lost') time. In what follows, "response time" means "total response time" and "processing time" means "mental processing time", which is the time actually used in processing the task item. The theory is based on the following theoretical hypotheses:

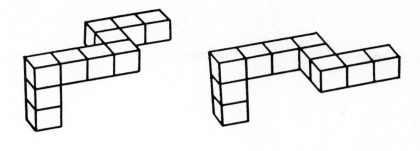

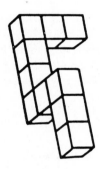 

Figure 1. Two examples of the figure rotation task. The subject must respond by pushing a button for 'same' if the one figure can be rotated into the other, or else push a button for 'different'. (cf. Shepard & Metzler, 1971; Metzler & Shepard, 1974).

2.1 Random Distraction Hypothesis:

During task performance, the processing of the task is interrupted by brief periods of non-processing, called distraction. A distraction is considered as any mental activity which does not itself enhance the probability of a correct response. The occurrence of distraction is supposed to be at least partly under the control of the subject.

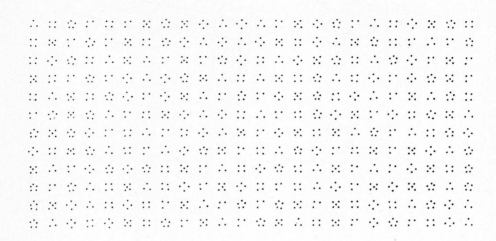

Figure 2. Example of the Bourdon task which was frequently used in our experiments. The subject must mark each pattern of (e.g.) four dots. The dot patterns are presented one at a time in the computerized version. A pencil-and-paper version was also used, where RT's were recorded per line as shown in the figure.

2.2 Constant Processing Time Hypothesis:

The mental processing time necessary to produce a response with a given probability of being correct is constant for each task item, subject, and task condition.

The distraction hypothesis is supposed to hold in general. The processing time assumption is supposed to hold only for simple overlearned mental tasks, where the task itself or the way it is presented does not require some kind of (random) search process (as would be required, for example, with a multiple choice response format, or in tasks involving a memory search). Furthermore, the theory assumes the following hypotheses, which all concern the relations between response time, accuracy, item difficulty, and the effects of task conditions. (For related theories and data, see Brand & Deary, 1982; Jensen, 1982; Spearman, 1927; White, 1973,1982).

2.3 Overload Hypothesis:

The frequency and/or duration of distractions increases with task load. This hypothesis is not very specific, and was initially not incorporated in our formalized models. Our first experiments, however, indicated that parameters governing the distraction time were not independent of the processing time. The overload hypothesis was subsequently incorporated in the inhibition model, to be discussed later.

2.4 Trade-off Hypothesis:

The probability that a correct response is given in the next time interval increases with elapsed actual processing time. This is stronger than the usual trade-off hypothesis, which states only that there is a positive correlation between response time and correctness. What is usually called speed-accuracy trade-off should rather be called time-correctness trade-off, since (mental) speed is better defined as an individual constant. (See also point 6.) Our hypothesis excludes any exponential distribution of the mental processing time, given a certain level of accuracy. It implies that eventually an item can be solved correctly.

2.5 Item Difficulty Hypothesis:

When there are no time constraints, and the subject does not abandon the task item, the processing time which must be invested increases with item difficulty. For a given subject, task condition, and probability of correct response, the processing time which must be invested is a measure of task difficulty.

2.6 Mental Speed Hypothesis:

The rate of increase of the odds of a correct response with increasing mental processing time increases with the subject's mental speed with respect to the kind of task. In other words, mental speed is the rate of gain in correctness of response per unit of mental processing time. In fact, the rate can be taken as the definition of mental speed with respect to the pertinent task domain.

Technical assumptions and auxiliary assumptions are necessary to test the model in an experimental setting, in order to estimate process parameters from a series of response times. These are:

2.7 A series of task items is used which are equal both in the sense of equal item difficulty and in the sense of the process required for their solution.

2.8 The subject maintains a fixed level of precision (i.e. probability of a correct response), and no learning takes place.

By varying subjects, tasks, and experimental conditions, effects on the pertinent process model parameters can be studied in a between-subjects and/or between-tasks design. For example, in several experiments we found that females show lower mental speed than males on a figure rotation task. Also, mixing tasks within a single series produced a decrease in distraction time and consequently in RT mean and variance.

3. PROCESSING AND DISTRACTION

Concerning the frequency and duration of distraction vs. mental processing, a two state Markov process is assumed. Various specifications of this process have been developed, with increasing complexity. Each of these models describes the response time (RT) as the sum of a fixed mental processing time, A, and a variable distraction time, D.

3.1 The GAMMA Model

The simplest assumption, not incorporating the overload hypothesis (see point 3, above), is that distractions occur intermittently during task performance at a constant rate per task trial, and that their durations are independently and exponentially distributed with parameter δ. Consequently, response times are gamma distributed with a shift parameter A (the constant mental processing time per task trial), and parameters n and δ, where n is the number of distractions per task trial. According to this model, learning and/or a shift in the subject's speed-accuracy set will affect A, but not n or δ. Learning during task performance would give a decreasing trend in the expected RT, but not in its variance. This model had to be rejected because of its poor fit (compared to the next model), and because of the trend in the RT variance over successive blocks of trials.

3.2 The Poisson Erlang Model

The Poisson Erlang model (Pieters & Van der Ven, 1982; Pieters, 1985) extends the gamma model in two ways. First, it assumes that the number of distractions is a random variable, and second, it assumes that the hazard rate (per unit of time) of entering into a state of distraction (i.e. interruption of processing), is a constant, λ. Consequently, the response time distribution is a compound Poisson-Erlang distribution (i.e. a gamma distribution with n Poisson distributed), with expectation and variance:

$$E(RT) = A + \gamma / \delta \qquad \text{where } \gamma = \lambda A \qquad (1)$$

and

$$\text{Var (RT)} = 2\gamma/\delta^2. \tag{2}$$

If learning takes place, or if there is a shift in speed-accuracy set, A will change, and so will E(RT) and Var(RT). This model, like the Gamma model, cannot explain an increasing trend in RT, unless by the ad hoc assumption of a trend-like change in the speed-accuracy set toward increasing accuracy over a series of task trials. (Data contradict this, since frequently a small deterioration of accuracy is observed, accompanied by an increase in RT).

3.3 The Inhibition model.

The inhibition model (Van der Ven, Smit & Jansen, 1988; Van Breukelen et al., 1987; Van Breukelen, in prep.) is a formalization of the overload hypothesis. It assumes, in its simplest form, that the hazard rate, $\lambda(t)$ of entering into a state of distraction increases with the accumulated processing time P_t, and decreases with the accumulated distraction time D_t:

$$\lambda(t) = \max [\, 0\,, \lambda(0) + \mu_1 P_t - \mu_2 D_t]. \tag{3}$$

The individual distractions are, as before, assumed to be independently and exponentially distributed with parameter δ. The parameters μ_1 and μ_2 (or their ratio) can be considered as a measure of concentration. They may both be partly under the control of the subject, and partly affected by task conditions.

The inhibition model predicts an increasing or decreasing trend toward stationarity, the sign of the trend depending on $\lambda(0)$. The E(RT) is a function of the trial number, k. Let

$$\mu = \mu_1 / \mu_2\,,$$

$$\alpha = A\,(1 - \mu)\,,$$

$$\theta = \exp\,(-A\mu_2 / \delta)\,,$$

$$\beta = (1 - \theta)\,\{\,\lambda(0) - \delta\mu\,\}\,/\mu_2\,,$$

The expected RT as a function of trial number k is:

$$E\,(RT_k) = \alpha + \beta\theta^{\,k-1}. \tag{4}$$

meaning a negative exponentially increasing or decreasing trend. The stationary Var(RT) is

$$Var(RT) = 2 (1 - \theta) (\mu / \mu_2). \tag{5}$$

Most interestingly, the inhibition model predicts a negative autocorrelation between RT's which, at stationarity, is given by:

$$\rho_m = -1/2 (1 - \theta) \theta^{m-1}, \quad m=1,... \text{ (lag)}. \tag{6}$$

The value of the autocorrelation tends to -.5 when the processing time A increases (e.g. when task units are longer), and when μ_2/δ increases (when there are longer distractions which further reduce λ). Counter-intuitive though it may appear, this means that a fast response on a complicated task is likely to have resulted from an exceptionally small number of short distractions, so that λ is high at the start of the next trial, leading to a longer RT on that trial.

In general, this model appears to fit the data reasonably well, except for the autocorrelation, which was consistently absent or too small. It can be shown, however, that random shifts in the subject's speed-accuracy set, which cause variability in the mental processing time A, increase the RT variance, without affecting the autocovariance, thereby depressing the autocorrelation.

3.4 Parameter estimation and experimental tests

Analysis of real data and simulation studies have both shown that the parameters of these models are difficult to estimate, unless very long RT series are collected from a single subject. Since factors beyond the scope of our theory may affect the subject's performance in prolonged series, with the result that the stability of the subject parameters is not guaranteed, our typical experiments used only series of approximately 35 response times per task type or condition, which is too few for stable parameter estimation. However, the models generate global predictions concerning RT expectation, trend, and variance, and concerning the minimum RT, both over (blocks of) trials within subjects and conditions, and between subjects and conditions, which permit indirect testing of the theory.

3.5 Control of constant processing time

Many factors are known to affect response times in simple mental tasks, e.g. expectancy effects. Moreover, simple tasks which appear homogeneous in the sense of requiring the same solution process, turn out not to be so. For example, in the figure rotation task, mirror-imaged figures appear to elicit a solution process which is different from other figures.

Such factors which violate the assumption of a constant processing time over trials were identified by comparing global RT-statistics. For such comparisons, the model would indicate which statistics to examine, in order to identify violations of the assumption of a constant processing time (cf. Van Breukelen, 1989).

Repetition and related effects were controlled by using groups of single trials as the unit of analysis of response times. Within each group, any factors which might have an effect on the processing time were balanced as much as was possible.

3.6 Massed versus spaced tasks.

The theory implies that intervals between successive task trials can be considered functionally equivalent to a (long) distraction. An interval between task trials will therefore decrease the hazard rate λ of entering into a distraction to a constant value. This means that, in a spaced condition, the model practically reduces to the Poisson-Erlang model. An increasing trend in both E(RT) and Var(RT) will only be observed in a condition of massed work, and not in a condition of spaced work. This was indeed consistently found in two experiments (Van Breukelen et al., 1987), thus strongly corroborating the overload hypothesis. These experiments also indicate that distractions during

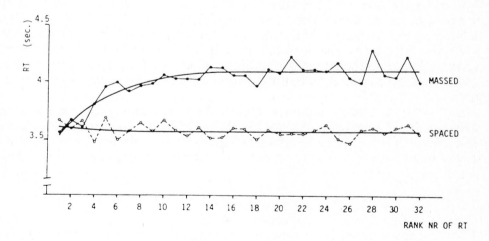

Figure 3. The effect of a massed vs. spaced condition. The task was the Bourdon-task (see figure 2). RT's were recorded per block of six trials which were balanced with respect to e.g. repetition. (figure adapted from Van Breukelen et al., 1987.)

spaced task performance can be small and negligible compared to the mental processing time.

The typical shapes of the response times series in massed and in spaced conditions are shown in figure 3. Similar results were obtained using a paper-and-pencil version of the Bourdon test with primary school children as subjects (Van Breukelen & Jansen, 1987).

3.7   Mixed vs homogeneous tasks

In another experiment, suggested by Dirk Vorberg, a comparison was made between homogeneous tasks and mixed tasks (Jansen & Roskam, in prep.). In the case of mixed tasks, the task consisted of randomly alternating the Bourdon-task of figure 2, a digit-addition task, and/or a letter-matching task (Posner, 1978). Both the homogeneous and the mixed tasks were administered in a massed condition.

To analyze the data of these experiments, an approximation to the inhibition model was used, which simplifies the parameter estimation, and which fits two linear segments to the RT trend curve, instead of the exponential curve of eq. (4). (see figure 4 and figure 5).

Alternating tasks has an effect on RT trend and RT variance which is very similar to (though smaller than) the effect found with a spaced homogeneous task. This result appears to be consistent with a specificity hypothesis concerning the distraction process. It appears to indicate that a task-specific mental processor becomes saturated with prolonged activity, and then is temporarily not active. Alternating tasks, requiring different processors, gives one processor time to recover while another is active, and thus provides what amounts to a spaced condition for each processor.

The data from one experiment (figure 4) clearly demonstrate the effect of mixing tasks on RT trend and on the mean RT. These effects are less clearly visible in the results from another experiment (figure 5). Both experiments, however, showed that the mean RT and the variance of RT, are both significantly lower in the mixed condition than in the unmixed condition.

There was no significant difference in the number of errors. Concerning the processing time, we may assume that the minimum RT is only marginally larger than the mental processing time, A, and thus is a fair estimate of it. The minimum RT was not significantly different between the mixed and the unmixed conditions in experiment 3 (figure 5), indicating that mixing tasks affects the distraction time and not the mental processing time.

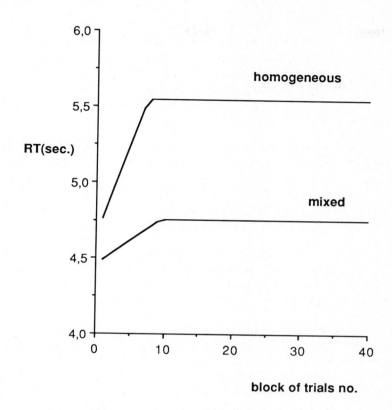

Figure 4. The fitted RT curve of the RT series (averaged over subjects and tasks) for a homogeneous condition, and a mixed condition. The tasks were: letter matching, identification of dot patterns, and digit addition.

3.8 Errors in relation to distractions

According to the theory, distractions are unrelated to error rate. However, some experimental results indicate a small but significant increase in the error rate over trials in a massed condition, which parallels the increasing trend in E(RT) and Var(RT). In a spaced condition, such an increase is not present. This appears to mean that distractions have a deleterious effect on processing efficiency. This can be explained in two ways: (i) When subjects notice that their RT increases (because of distractions), they adjust their speed-accuracy set and sacrifice some

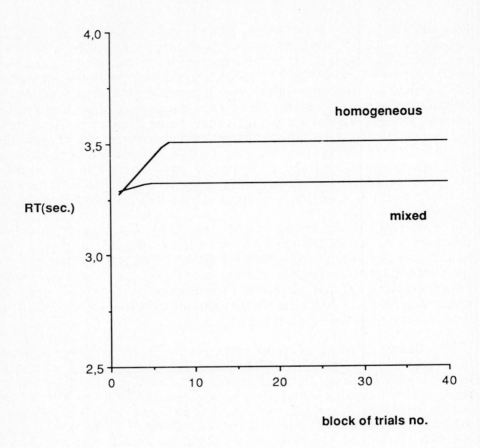

Figure 5. The fitted RT curve of the RT series (averaged over subjects and tasks) for a homogeneous condition, and a mixed condition. The tasks were: letter matching, identification of dot patterns, and lexical decision.

accuracy for increased speed of response; (ii) a distraction, being an interruption of task processing, may lead to loss of information from working memory, and thus increase the probability of an error and/or increase the processing time needed to maintain a certain level of accuracy.

4. PSYCHOMETRIC THEORY OF INTELLIGENCE TASK PERFORMANCE

We may drop the assumption that the subject maintains a constant probability of correct response. Particularly in time-limited tests, a subject may fail on difficult items (even if there is no explicit time limit, the subject may set one for himself). When test items are difficult to solve, the subject may sacrifice correctness for response time, or vice versa. We need a model which writes the probability of correct response, as well as the probability distribution of the mental processing time, as functions of person and item parameters. The person parameters should include at least a mental speed parameter and a persistence parameter. Also, these parameters should be specific for the task domain. For reasons beyond the scope of the present paper, we want models for correct responses and response times which refer to the same parameters and which allow independent estimates of subject and item parameters. This is tantamount to Rasch's (1960) requirement of specific objectivity in measurement.

Roskam (1987) has proposed a modified Rasch model based on the theoretical assumptions given in section 1 of the present paper. That model, however, appeared to suffer from an inconsistency, namely that the expected processing time and the probability of a correct response both decrease in the item parameter (Van Breukelen, 1989) The expected processing time should increase with item difficulty and the probability of a correct response should decrease with it.

Before presenting another model, we will first present the results of a series of experiments (Van Breukelen & Roskam, in prep.) to test the theoretical hypotheses outlined before. The task consisted of figure rotation (see figure 1). Item difficulty was varied by varying the rotation angle. For this task, and the way it was administered, we had reasons to assume that RT variability due to distractions would be relatively small, and that the mental processing time would be well approximated by a constant proportion of the response time. Response time was controlled by controlling the stimulus presentation time and using a backward mask. Due to differences between 'same' and 'different' items, some problems arose in ensuring Rasch homogeneity of the task items (which in this case is an auxiliary assumption as far as subject-item interaction is concerned). This was remedied by presenting a 'same' and a 'different' stimulus pair in succession (in random order), and having the subject indicate which was the 'same' pair.

The data appeared to satisfy the Rasch model for the probability of a correct (+) response:

$$P (+ \mid v, i, t) = \theta_v \, t \, / \, (\theta_v \, t + \varepsilon_i) \qquad\qquad (\theta, \varepsilon > 0) \qquad (7)$$

where θ_v is the subject's ability parameter (in fact to be considered as a compound of mental speed and concentration), ε_i is the item difficulty, and t is the inspection time, that is, the time which the subject allocates to the item (taken as proportional to the mental processing time). In other words, according to the theory, the probability of a correct response decreases with item difficulty, and increases with both the subject's ability and with the mental processing time. These relations are mutually independent for a homogeneous task domain. (One will observe that (7) implies that the probability of a correct response is zero at t=0). This accords with the response time distribution model in eq. (8), below, which excludes the possibility that a response is given at t=0. In other words, we exclude the possibility that the subject does not really process the item and guesses correctly.)

4.1 A modified model

A modified model, proposed by Van Breukelen (1989) consists of a Rasch model for the probability of a correct response as in eq. (7), and the following model for the mental processing time distribution:

$$F_{vi}(t) = 1 - \exp\{-\Lambda_{vi}(t)\}$$

$$f_{vi}(t) = \lambda_{vi}(t) \exp\{-\Lambda_{vi}(t)\} \tag{8}$$

where $\qquad \lambda_{vi}(t) = \theta_v\, t / \delta_v\, \varepsilon_i, \qquad (\theta, \delta, \varepsilon > 0)$

and $\qquad \Lambda_{vi}(t) = \displaystyle\int \lambda_{vi}(t)dt$

$$= \theta_v\, t^2 / 2\, \delta_v\, \varepsilon_i\,.$$

We have as yet no detailed theoretical rationale for the specific form of either (7) or (8). Eq. (7) satisfies the trade-off hypothesis and the principle of specific objectivity in measurement. In eq. (8), the hazard rate, $\lambda_{vi}(t)$, increases with t and with the subject's mental speed θ_v, and decreases with the subject's persistence δ_v, and with the item difficulty ε_i. As in eq. (7), the product θt should be interpreted as the subject's achievement of mental processing at time t, i.e. θ should be interpreted as a function of mental speed and concentration.

The RT distribution of (8) is a Weibull distribution. It is a unimodal density function which is positively skewed, with mean, variance and mode:

$$E(t) = \sqrt{(\pi / 2\kappa)}, \quad \text{where } \kappa = \theta/(\delta\,\varepsilon), \tag{9}$$

$$\text{mode}(t) = 1 / \sqrt{\kappa}, \tag{10}$$

$$\text{Var}(t) = (4 - \pi)/(2\kappa).$$

Consistent with its relationships to the principle of specific objectivity, the model in (8) has the following interesting property. Let t_1 and t_2 be the completion times for different subjects and/or items, with parameters κ_1 and κ_2 (as defined in (9)), respectively. Then:

$$P(t_1 < t_2) = \kappa_1 / (\kappa_1 + \kappa_2). \tag{11}$$

Eq. (11) follows from the fact that, when hazard rates are proportional, the probability of one random variable not exceeding the other is equal to the ratio of the one hazard rate to the sum of both.

For the same subject on different items, we can cancel the subject parameters in κ, and so (11) simplifies into:

$$P(t_{vi} > t_{vj}) = \varepsilon_i / (\varepsilon_i + \varepsilon_j),$$

independent of the subject.

For different subjects on the same item we can cancel the item parameters, and have:

$$P(t_{vi} > t_{wi}) = (\theta_w / \delta_w) / [(\theta_w / \delta_w) + (\theta_v / \delta_v)] \tag{12}$$

which accords with the following, derived from (7):

$$P(- \mid v, i, t) / P(- \mid v, j, t) = \varepsilon_i / \varepsilon_j. \tag{13}$$

The preceding equations demonstrate that, in principle, we can estimate all parameters from response times and accuracy, and test the simultaneous validity of (7) and (8).

To obtain the unconditional probability of a correct response, we must integrate (7) over t, using (8):

$$P(+ \mid v, i) = \int_0^\infty [\theta_v t / (\theta_v t + \varepsilon_i)] \lambda_{vi}(t) \exp\{-\Lambda_{vi}(t)\} \, dt. \tag{14}$$

Numerical integration indicated that the following expression is a fair approximation to (14), the unconditional probability of a correct response:

$$P(+ \mid v, i) = \Theta_v^* / (\Theta_v^* + \varepsilon_i^*), \tag{15}$$

where $\Theta_v^* = \sqrt{(\Theta_v \delta_v)}$, and $\varepsilon_i^* = \sqrt{\varepsilon_i}$.

This formula is obtained by replacing the density function in (14) by its mode, (10). Obviously, eq. (15) is a Rasch model. Thus, even if the probability of a correct response depends on the inspection time, as in (7) and (14), the normal Rasch model of (15) may fit the data quite well. Van den Wollenberg (1979) found that time-limited tests data fitted the common Rasch model acceptably well. From (15), we see that the estimated person parameter Θ_v^* is a function of both the subject's mental speed, his concentration, and his persistence [1].

5. METHODOLOGY OF THEORY CONSTRUCTION AND RESEARCH

The research reported in this paper shows a combination of 'top-down' and 'bottom-up' strategies. There is a close and direct relation between theoretical hypotheses, model formalization, parameter definition and estimation, and the structure of the data. Theoretical quantities, such as mental speed, are not conceptualized a priori but are defined as model parameters governing lawful relations in the observed responses. We avoid the use of concepts which can not be defined as a function of the data. (See also Roskam, 1979, 1982, 1987). Our theoretical hypotheses refer to observable relations in data, or to theoretical concepts which have already been defined as a function of the data. For example, instead of an a priori concept of mental speed, we have the directly testable hypothesis (ignoring technicalities of experimentation and parameter estimation) that the probability of a correct response increases with the presentation time of an item, and that the rate of increase is an individual constant for a given domain of tasks. We call this constant "mental speed". Also, we assume that the probability of a correct response for a given individual, response time, and item domain, depends on an item constant, and we call this the *item difficulty*. Our distraction hypothesis, however, states that part of the gross response time is wasted as described by the Inhibition Model. We also have the hypothesis that the total invested time can vary independently of the subject's mental speed, and independently of the item difficulty, which leads us to introduce *persistence* as a parameter. This does not exclude the possibility of a correlation, over subjects, between mental speed and persistence: subjects with a high mental speed may also be persistent.

A vital element in the construction of the theory is its logical analysis for internal consistency, particularly with respect to the position and definition of its parameters. Because of this, the earlier model of Roskam (1987) had to be rejected, as well as models developed by White (1982) and by Scheiblechner (1979). (For a detailed discussion, see Pieters, 1984; Van Breukelen, 1989).

In testing the theory and the models, it is not sufficient to estimate parameters and assess the goodness-of-fit. We also must test the models experimentally. This means that we test whether the parameter values are in accordance with our theoretical hypothesis when we vary task conditions, such as spaced vs. massed work.

The finding that mixing tasks had an effect similar to a spaced condition was not predicted by our theory (nor was the opposite), although some considerations from cognitive psychology led us to guess that mixing tasks would increase the 'inhibition' effect rather than diminish it. We do not believe that something like 'monotony' explains the increasing RT in a massed homogeneous task. One can not explain a phenomenon by labelling it. Monotony may be defined as a task condition. The explanation of its effect must be found in a theory and model which formalizes a lawful relation between monotony and trend in RT. At present we can say no more than that changing tasks is functionally equivalent to a distraction or a resting interval. We can use this to define a task processor: tasks are related to different processors to the extent that changing tasks is equivalent to a distraction.

In conclusion, we feel that our models and experiments will lead to more detailed theory and explanation of individual differences and *task effects* in cognitive performance, such as those encountered in the usual intelligence tests.

FOOTNOTE

1. Guessing is another possibility to consider. The usual models for guessing assume that the subject guesses with a certain probability of being correct, or else responds to the best of his ability. However, Kemp(1976) has shown that a specifically objective model with guessing leads to a model where the guessing probability is inversely proportional to the item difficulty, and that guessing effects a non-identifiable shift in the parameters. This appears reasonable: a multiple choice format makes all items easier to answer correctly, and makes a subject appear to have a higher ability. In our models we have, at the present stage, left out 'guessing', even though we consider it a matter for further consideration.

ACKNOWLEDGEMENT

This research was supported by grant no. 560-267-003 from the PSYCHON foundation of the Netherlands Organization for Scientific Research (N.W.O.).

Correspondence concerning this paper should be addressed to Edw. E. Roskam, Psychological Laboratory, University of Nijmegen, P.O. Box 9104, 6500 HE Nijmegen, The Netherlands.

REFERENCES

Brand, C.R. & Deary, I.J. (1982). Intelligence and "Inspection time". in: H.J. Eysenck (ed.). A model for intelligence. Berlin: Springer-Verlag

Jansen, R.W. & Roskam, E.E. (1988, in prep.). Mental processing and distraction.

Jensen, A. R. (1982). Reaction time and psychometric *g*. In H.J.Eysenck: A model for intelligence, Berlin: Springer-Verlag.

Kempf, W.F. (1976). Zur Einbeziehung von Ratewahrscheinlichkeiten im Testmodel von Rasch. In W.F. Kempf, B. Niehausen & G.Mach: Logistische Testmodelle mit additiven Nebenbedingungen. IPN Arbeitsberichte. Institut fuer Paedagogik der Naturwissenschaften, Universitaet Kiel.

Lewin, K. (1936). Principles of topological psychology. New York: McGraw-Hill (paperback ed. 1966).

Luce, R.D. (1986). Response times: their role in inferring elementary mental organization. New York: Oxford University Press.

Metzler, J. & Shepard, R.N. (1974). Transformational studies of the internal representation of three-dimensional objects. in: R.L. Solso (ed.). Theories in cognitive psychology: the Loyola Symposium. Potomac (Maryland): Erlbaum.

Pachella, R.G. (1974). The interpretation of RT in information processing research. In: B.H. Kantowitz (ed.). Human information processing. Hillsdale (N.J.): Erlbaum.

Pieters, J.P.M. (1984). Components of response latency in simple mental tasks. Doct. Diss. University of Nijmegen.

Pieters, J.P.M. (1985). Reaction time analysis of simple mental tasks: a general approach. Acta Psychologica, 59, 227-269.

Pieters, J.P.M. & Van der Ven, A.H.G.S. (1982). Precision, speed and distraction in time-limit tests. Applied Psychological Measurement, 6, 93-109.

Posner, M.I. (1978). Chronometric explorations of the mind. Hillsdale (N.J.): Erlbaum.

Rasch, G. (1960). Probabilistic models for some intelligence and attainment tests. Copenhagen: Danish Institute for Educational research (reprinted by the University of Chicago press, 1980).

Roskam, E.E.Ch.I. (1979). Eine Fallstudie ueber Forschungsmethodik (A case study of research methodology). Zeitschrift fuer Sozialpsychologie, 10, 114-133.

Roskam, E.E.Ch.I. (1982). Hypotheses non fingo. Nederlands Tijdschrift voor de Psychologie, 37, 331-359.

Roskam, E.E.Ch.I. (1987). Toward a psychometric theory of intelligence test scores. in: E.E.Ch.I. Roskam & R. Suck (Eds.). Progress in mathematical psychology, Vol.1. Amsterdam: North-Holland Publ. Co.

Scheiblechner, H. (1979). Specific objective stochastic latency mechanisms. Journal of Mathematical Psychology, 19, 18-38.

Shepard, R.N. & Metzler, J. (1971). Mental rotation of three-dimensional objects. Science, 171, 701-703.

Spearman, C.E. (1927). The abilities of man. London: McMillan.

Townsend, J.T. & Ashby, F.G. (1983). The stochastic modeling of elementary psychological processes. London/Cambridge: Cambridge University Press.

Van Breukelen, G.J.P. (1989). Concentration, speed and precision in mental tests. Nijmegen (the Netherlands): unpublished doctoral dissertation.

Van Breukelen, G.J.P. & Jansen, R.W.T.L. (1987). The role of concentration in simple mental tasks: an experimental test of some models. Nijmegen (the Netherlands), Department of psychology, internal report 87 MA 08. (submitted for publication).

Van Breukelen, G.J.P., Jansen, R.W.T.L., Roskam, E.E.Ch.I., Van der Ven, & A.H.G.S., Smit, J.C. (1987). Concentration, speed, and precision in simple mental tasks. In: E.E.Ch.I. Roskam & R. Suck (Eds.). Progress in mathematical psychology, Vol.1. Amsterdam: North-Holland Publ. Co.

Van Breukelen, G.J.P. & Roskam, E.E.Ch.I. (1988, in prep.). The speed-precision trade-off in mental rotation.

Van Breukelen, G.J.P., Van der Ven, A.H.G.S. & Van den Wollenberg A.L.(1987). Decomposing response times with the Poisson-Erlang model. Nijmegen: Department of Psychology, internal report 87 MA 02.

Van der Ven, A.H.G.S. (1974). The correlation between speed and precision in time-limit tests. Nederlands Tijdschrift voor de Psychologie, 29, 447-456.

Van der Ven, A.H.G.S. & Pieters, J.P.M. (1978). The Poisson-Erlang model: a probabilistic approach to the response latency in routine mental tasks. Nijmegen (the Netherlands), unpublished paper.

Van der Ven, A.H.G.S., Smit, J.C. & Jansen, R.W.T.L. (1988). Inhibition in prolonged mental tasks. Applied Psychological Measurement, in press.

Van den Wollenberg, A.L. (1979). The Rasch Model and Time-limit tests. Unpubl. Doct. Dissertation. University of Nijmegen.

White, P.O. (1973). Individual differences in speed, accuracy and persistence: a mathematical model for problem solving. in: H.J. Eysenck (ed.). The measurement of intelligence. Lancaster (U.K.): Medical and Technical Publ. Co.

White, P.O. (1982). Some major components in general intelligence. In H.J. Eysenck (Ed.) A model for intelligence. Berlin: Springer, p. 44-90.

Human Information Processing: Measures,
Mechanisms, and Models. D. Vickers and P.L. Smith (eds.)
© Elsevier Science Publishers B.V. (North-Holland), 1989

SUBTRACTIVE DECOMPOSITION OF PERCEPTUAL-MOTOR REACTIONS AFTER DONDERS

Robert Gottsdanker

University of California

Two very different behavioral approaches now exist for testing the validity of subtractive isolation of operations in reaction-time tasks. One is through presence-absence applications of the additive factors method. The other is through the method of brief PSIs (precue-to-stimulus intervals). Presence-absence additivity has been tested in respect to stimulus discrimination and response selection, and for the programming of response dimensions. The occurrence of only discrimination or selection on a task may be tested further through comparative influence analysis. In the method of brief PSIs, a -1 slope of RT against PSI is evidence that some operations are delayed until others have been completed. Applications have included the relation between choice and simple reactions, the programming of response dimensions, and the programming of serial responses. The main scientific advantage of this method stems from the use of time as the independent variable.

1. INTRODUCTION

Donders' (1869) idea of measuring the mean duration of a mental operation by subtracting the mean reaction time (RT) on a less inclusive task (e.g. the simple reaction) from the mean RT on a more inclusive task (e.g., the choice reaction) has considerable appeal. To a great extent, progress in science has come about through such isolation of entities. There are two requirements for using the subtraction method of decomposing a perceptual-motor reaction. The first is that there is, in fact, the stipulated seriality of operations in the minuend task. The second is that the subtractive tasks differ only in respect to the inclusion of particular operations. The demonstration of serial operations in itself would be of great current interest, with ever more complex processing models being developed. Certainly progress has been made in satisfying the assumption of seriality for several kinds of task following Sternberg's

(1969) introduction of the additive-factors method, even though equivocality of interpretation has been pointed out (e.g. D. A. Taylor, 1972). More direct evidence would seem to be called for.

Since Donders' presentation of the subtraction method, two basic ways have emerged for dealing with the seriality and compositional requirements in combination. D. H. Taylor (1966), in an anticipation of the additive factors method, used four tasks in a presence-absence paradigm relative to stimulus discrimination and response selection, and reported additivity. Gottsdanker & Shragg (1985) found that RT to a tone decreased by the duration of brief precue-to-stimulus interval when the precue indicated the correct response (if the tone occurred). This indicated that response actualization is delayed in a choice reaction until previous operations have been completed. The results are shown in Figure 1.

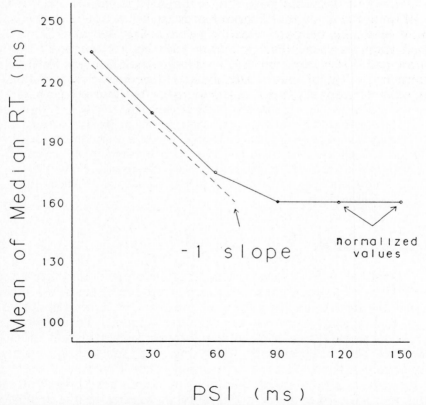

Figure 1. Effect of full response-specification precue (Gottsdanker & Shragg, 1985)

2. TESTS OF PRESENCE-ABSENCE ADDITIVITY

The four tasks used by D. H. Taylor may be described in terms of the combinations of two levels, 1 and 0, of two variables: response-selection requirement and stimulus-discrimination requirement. In the choice (b) reactions, the subject responded with the right hand to one colour of stimulus and with the left hand to the other colour. In the contingent (c) reaction, the subject responded with the preferred hand to only one of the two colours. In the simple reaction (here c′ instead of c because of 50% catch trials) the subject responded with the preferred hand on the trials on which a stimulus occurred and made no response on the other trials. In the pure-selection (b′) reaction – which Taylor added to the three foregoing tasks used by Donders – the subject responded with one hand when a stimulus occurred after the warning signal, and with the other hand when no stimulus occurred. Thus, the choice (b) reaction was at the 1 level of both variables; the contingent (c) reaction was at the 1 level of required stimulus discrimination and the 0 level of required response selection; the pure-selection (b′) reaction was at the 0 level of required stimulus discrimination and at the 1 level of required response selection; and finally, the simple (c′) reaction was at the zero level of both requirements. Taylor tested stochastic independence as well as the assumption of seriality (and composition). As Sternberg (1969) has

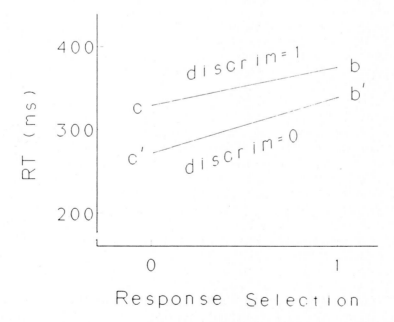

Figure 2. Effect of hypothesized discrimination and selection requirements (Taylor, 1966)

stressed, these issues may advantageously be addressed separately, and I will not consider stochastic independence here. When Taylor's results with mean values are cast in the form of the familiar two-factor graph, the result is as shown in Figure 2.

If additivity is shown, the hypothesized operations are serial and the inclusion of stimulus discrimination or response selection is in accord with the labels that were assigned. Thus, there is a basis for accepting the subtractions as indicative of the mean durations of the stimulus-discrimination and response-selection operations. Essentially, Taylor did not find sufficient interaction to reject the null hypothesis. Sternberg (1969, p. 280) comments "Taylor's test cannot be said to have succeeded, mainly because his experiment was insufficiently precise." The negative interaction in Figure 2 does seem sufficiently large to be significant with reliable data.

Another use of additive-factors methodology with tasks which presumably differ by the presence or absence of required operations is found in Rosenbaum's (1980) study of the specification of response dimensions. Rosenbaum employed a task in which one arm or the other, was moved forward or backward, a short or a long distance to press the appropriate button, in accordance with a learned S-R code. A letter precue indicating values (e.g. R or L for right or left arm) on from one to all three of the response dimensions – or Xs indicating the dimensions not precued – was presented 3.5 secs. in advance of the response stimulus. Coloured dot stimuli were assigned to the eight possible responses. Rosenbaum's main argument for the identification of response-specification time was based on the consistent sequence of arm specification adding more time to the reaction than did direction specification, which in turn added more time than did extent specification. However, this dimensional difference in outcome may be regarded as a fortuitous circumstance; the assumptions of seriality and composition are most unequivocally tested in the standard additive-factors way. This is shown in Figure 3, which was obtained from the graph of mean values Rosenbaum presented. The 0 or 1 levels indicate whether a dimension still remained to be specified after the appearance of the precue. Simple RT is excluded from the graph, as a considerable amount of time appeared to be required for the choice-reaction operations other than dimensional specification. Overall there is an impressive display of additivity. The three amounts of time added by arm specification are found to be about 130, 140, and 150 ms; the amounts added by direction specification are about 90, 100, and 90 ms; and those added by extent specification are about 60, 80, and 70 ms. On the basis of this demonstration of additivity, it could be argued that the values do, in fact, represent the durations of the indicated specifications.

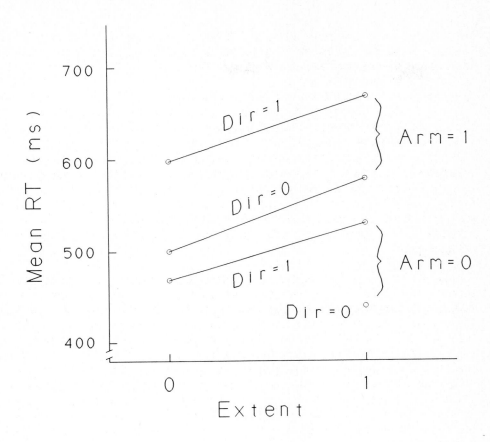

Figure 3. Effect of hypothesized dimensional programming operations (Rosenbaum, 1980).

3. COMPARATIVE-INFLUENCE ANALYSIS

Let us assume that both the Taylor and Rosenbaum experiments have passed the additivity test, and ask whether there are further steps that might be taken to strengthen the validity of the subtractions. In the case of Taylor's study, in which the reactions supposedly differed in respect to inclusion of two stages, the conclusions could be strengthened by the application of Salthouse's comparative influence analysis (1981). The experiment would be conducted at different levels of variables that have differential effects on the four tasks. Suppose it had already been demonstrated on a choice reaction that signal quality and time uncertainty are additive, and presumably do not affect any stage in common. A hypothetical set of effects is shown in Table 1. The difference in RT for

Table 1

Hypothetical Comparative Influence analyses

Comparative Influence of Stimulus Quality (ms difference)

Operation

Reaction	Total Effect	Stimulus Encoding	Stimulus Discrim.	Response Selection	Response Actualization
		*	*		
Simple	30	30 +			+
Contingent	60	30 +	30 +		+
Pure Sel.	30	30 +		+	+
Choice	60	30 +	30 +	+	+

Comparative Influence of Time Uncertainty (ms difference)

Operation

Reaction	Total Effect	Stimulus Encoding	Stimulus Discrim.	Response Selection	Response Actualization
				*	*
Simple	30	+			30 +
Contingent	30	+	+		30 +
Pure Sel.	60	+		30 +	30 +
Choice	60	+	+	30 +	30 +

Note.   * Operation influenced by the variable
         + Operation hypothesized to be present in the reaction

the two levels of signal quality are 30, 60, 30, and 60 ms for the c′, c, b′, and b reactions respectively. The corresponding differences for time uncertainty are 30, 30, 60, and 60 ms. This set of effects is in accordance with the model shown in Table 1. The + marks indicate the operations hypothesized as present in each task; the asterisks indicate the operations hypothesized to be influenced by the given variables. The value in each cell indicates the effect of the variable on each of the hypothesized operations. Thus, stimulus quality influences stimulus encoding, which is common to all the tasks and stimulus discrimination which is common to only the c and b tasks. Time uncertainty influences response selection, which is common to only the b and b′ tasks, and response actualization, which is common to all the tasks.

4. THE METHOD OF BRIEF PSIs

While comparative-influence analysis is applicable to subtractions based on inclusion of whole operations, as in Taylor's study, it does not seem applicable to Rosenbaum's study, in which choice reactions are compared in respect to the inclusion of sub-operations within a response-specification stage. The method of brief precue-to-stimulus intervals (PSIs) (Gottsdanker & Shragg, 1985) is applicable to both cases. In this procedure an informative precue is presented briefly before the response signal. If, over a brief time span, with an increment in PSI there is the same decrement in median or mean RT, i.e. a minus 1 slope between RT and PSI (as seen in Figure 1), it indicates that the operations dependent on the precue go to completion before any other operation is initiated. An alternative statement is that the latency between precue onset and response is constant. This outcome of an executory delay in utilizing the additional information satisfies the assumption of seriality on the precued task. Thus, direct evidence is provided of serial operations in the precued response. Moreover, the inference may be drawn that there is the same seriality in the choice reaction performed in the usual way, without a precue.

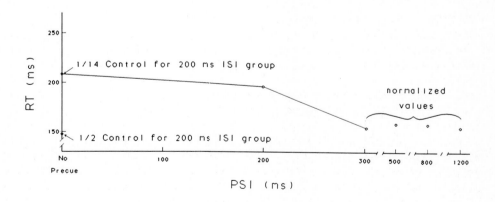

Figure 4. Effect of probability changing precue (Gottsdanker, 1975).

A model of how the brief PSIs procedure is applied to the subtraction method is presented in Figure 4. The diagram at the top shows the procedure and results which have just been described: the subject has full information on the required response, but there is time or event uncertainty in regard to the response stimulus. Although the events are represented for single trials, the application is to mean values. RT with a very short PSI is the sum of the following durations: I, encoding of the discriminative stimulus (i.e. preliminary processing of the stimulus); II, operations on the discriminative stimulus (e.g. stimulus discrimination and response selection); and III, remaining operations (e.g. premotor actualization of the response) minus the value of PSI. The middle diagram represents the events with a somewhat longer (but not very long) PSI. If RT remains at a constant value here, a suitable subtrahend for subtractional analysis is provided. It is obtained under conditions providing a "mental set" for the more inclusive task, but without the additional discrimination-choice requirements. Now, RT is the sum of the durations of I, encoding, and of III, other operations. The obtaining of the minuend for the subtraction is shown in the bottom part of the figure. This is seen to be an ordinary discriminative response, without a precue. The alternative discriminative stimuli form a set of which the response stimulus in the foregoing examples is a member. RT in this case is seen to be the sum of the durations of I, encoding; II, operations on the discriminative stimulus; and III, other operations. The subtraction of mean RT of equation 2 from the mean RT of equation 3, is indicated as providing the mean duration of II, operations on the discriminative stimulus. It is assumed that a precue study has been performed on discrimination B, comparable to that shown in the two upper diagrams on discrimination A. The generalizing of the outcome with short PSIs to the unprecued reaction is indicated in the executory delay between the encoding and remaining operations. Similar experimental paradigms are suitable for other applications of brief PSIs.

Thus far, support has been given to Donders' choice reaction minus simple reaction subtraction (Gottsdanker and Shragg, 1985; and Semjen & Gottsdanker, in press). The results of the first study were shown in Figure 1. No clear way has emerged to test the further decomposition of the choice reaction by brief PSIs. Precueing the contingent (c) reaction would not provide the answer, as it would beg the question of whether the contingent reaction really is a choice between execution and inhibition as has been suggested over the years following Donders' study (e.g. Watt, 1907). More recently it has been suggested from pupilometric analysis that there is an active motor process associated with not responding to the no-response stimulus (Richer, Silverman, & Beatty, 1983). A different approach has been to augment the choice reaction with an advance discrimination. The minus-one slope obtained in this study (Gottsdanker, 1986) at least suggests that discrimination can operate as a self-contained stage.

In a study patterned on the procedure of Rosenbaum (Reed, 1984), but with the precue presented very briefly before the response stimulus, the minus-one slope was not found with either hand or directional precues, casting some doubt on the occurrence of serial specification of response dimensions. A typical result is shown in Figure 5. A problem there

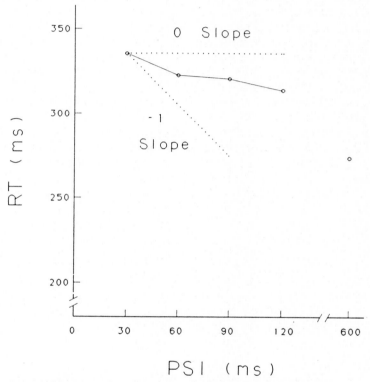

Figure 5. Effect of hand precue on hand-direction choice (Reed, 1984).

might have been the difficulty in quickly identifying one among eight possible precues. However, it was also found in the Semjen and Gottsdanker (in press) study that precuing hand for a series of responses, did not provide a minus-one slope between RT and PSI, when information on mode of first response (weak or strong) was not known in advance. That is, it was provided by the stimulus for response. This suggests that a movement is programmed as an entity rather than dimensionally. However, it was possible to decompose the programming of the individual responses, which took place before response actualization. The results with the brief-PSI method are clearest when a minus 1 slope is obtained. Two other patterns have been obtained. One is essentially a

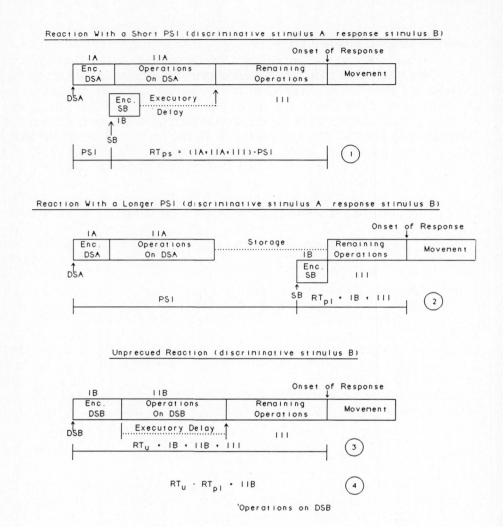

Figure 6. Model of the application of brief PSIs to the subtraction method.

zero slope until a rather long PSI (over 200 ms) is reached. This result might be attributed to a cognitive reorganization corresponding to the subject's comprehension of the new status. Such a result, shown in Figure 6 was found when an occasional precue informed the subject on a simple reaction that the probability of stimulus occurrence on the forthcoming trial was 1/2 rather than 1/14 (Gottsdanker, 1975). A slope less steep than minus-one, probably has different meanings in different circumstances. When the precue gives complete response information, a shallow slope could be indicative of the overlap between response selection and response actualization, with capacity divided between the two operations. When the precue gives partial response information, a shallow slope, such as that in Figure 5, could indicate a preparation effect for subsequent operations rather than a start on the processing sequence (Requin, 1980).

In order to avoid the increasing of momentary expectation of the response stimulus with lengthening of PSI, the subject must be provided with precise knowledge of one of the following points in time: (1) The instant when the precue will occur, (2) the instant when the response stimulus will occur, or (3) the first possible instant of response-stimulus presentation with nonaging waiting intervals (Gottsdanker, 1986). Moreover, PSI itself should not provide an increasing expectation of the response stimulus, as is the case with a rectangular distribution of PSIs. Such temporal knowledge has been successfully provided by both the transit-signal method (Gottsdanker, 1970) in four studies (Gottsdanker, 1975, 1986; Gottsdanker & Shragg, 1985; Reed, 1984); and by a countdown method (Semjen & Gottsdanker, in press).

A further precaution is that of testing for the possibility of a mixture distribution (Gottsdanker & Perkins, 1987). Thus, RT might decrease with PSI simply because of the increase in the probability of a prepared state as compared with an unprepared state rather than because of reduction in delay in the start of a processing operation. If the hypothesis of a mixture distribution is falsified, the delay explanation remains tenable.

5. SOME CONCLUSIONS

Without disparaging the use of the additive-factors method for identifying serial processing stages, and of the presence-absence variants here described for subtractive decomposition, I would like to point out some unique advantages of the method of brief PSIs. First, there is direct intervention into the reaction process, with time itself used as a manipulated variable to test the hypothesis of seriality. The provision of a critical test may be contrasted with the accumulative approach of testing many variables in the additive-factors method and the intuitive identification of the constituents of tasks in D. H. Taylor's four-task paradigm. Second, because of the reduction in procedural differences for the more and less inclusive tasks (especially when within-block variation of PSI is possible) quite comparable subtractive tasks may be obtained.

ACKNOWLEDGEMENTS

This research was supported by Grant No. BBP 5 MH 39359 to the University of California from the National Institute of Mental Health.

Correspondence concerning this paper should be addressed to Robert Gottsdanker, Department of Psychology, University of California, Santa Barbara, CA 93106, U.S.A.

REFERENCES

Donders, F.C. (1868). Die Schnelligkeit Psychischer Prozesse. Archive für Anatomie und Physiologie, 657-681.

Gottsdanker, R. (1970). A transit-signal methodology for studying reaction time. Behaviour Research Methods and Instrumentation, 2, 6-8.

Gottsdanker, R. (1975). The attaining and maintaining of preparation. In P. Rabbitt & S. Dornic (Eds.), Attention and Performance V, (pp. 33-49). New York: Academic Press.

Gottsdanker, R. (1986). The isolation of visual discrimination in a speeded decision. In Berglund, B., Berglund, U., and Teghtsoonian, R. (Eds.) Fechner Day 86. Stockholm, Sweden: International Society for Psychophysics.

Gottsdanker, R., & Perkins, T. (1987). Testing Donders' subtraction method with nonaging precue-to-stimulus intervals. Paper presented at the 23rd meeting of the Psychonomic Society, Seattle, WA.

Gottsdanker, R., Perkins, T., & Ahab,J. (1986).Studying reaction time with nonaging intervals: an effective procedure. Behaviour Research Methods, Instruments, and Computers, 18, 287-292.

Gottsdanker, R. & Shragg, G.P. (1985). Verification of Donders' subtraction method. Journal of Experimental Psychology: Human Perception and Performance, 11, 765-776.

Reed, P.S. (1984, June). A timecourse analysis of movement precue utilization. Unpublished doctoral dissertation, University of California, Santa Barbara.

Requin, J. (1985). Looking forward to moving soon: Ante factum selective processes in motor control. In M.I. Posner & O. Marin (Eds.), Attention and Performance XI, (pp. 147-167), Hillsdale, NJ: Erlbaum.

Richer, F., Silverman, C., & Beatty, J. (1983). Response selection and initiation in speeded responses: A pupilometric analysis. Journal of Experimental Psychology: Human Perception and Performance, 9, 360-370.

Rosenbaum, D. (1980). Human movement initiation: Specification of arm, direction, and extent. Journal of Experimental Psychology: General, 109, 444-474.

Semjen, A., & Gottsdanker R. (in press). Rapid serial movements: Relation between the planning of sequential structure and effector selection. In M. Jeannerod (Ed.), Attention and Performance XIII, Hillsdale, NJ: Erlbaum.

Sternberg, S. (1969). The discovery of processing stages: Extensions of Donders' method. In W. Koster (Ed)., Attention and Performance II (pp.276-315). Amsterdam: North-Holland.

Taylor, D.A. (1976). Stage analysis of reaction time Psychological Bulletin, 83, 161-191.

Taylor, D.H. (1966). Latency components in two-choice responding. Journal of Experimental Psychology, 72, 481-487.

Watt, H.J. (1905). Experimentelle Beitrage zu einer Theorie des Denkens [Experimental contributions to a theory of thinking]. Archiv für die Gesamte Psychologie, 4, 289-436.

Human Information Processing: Measures,
Mechanisms, and Models. D. Vickers and P.L. Smith (eds.)
©Elsevier Science Publishers B.V. (North-Holland), 1989   *325*

INFERRING MENTAL PROCESS ORGANIZATION FROM REACTION TIMES

Richard Schweickert, Cynthia Dahn & Kimberly McGuigan

Purdue University

Pieron's Law relates simple reaction time to stimulus intensity via a power function. We investigated whether Pieron's Law applies to choice reaction time, or whether Nakka-Rushkin or logistic functions would do better. We also investigated the relationship between stimulus intensity and number of alternative responses. These factors had additive effects on reaction time which were consistent with the hypothesis that processes prolonged by them are in series. If each process produces an output which can be categorized as correct or incorrect, given its input, the factors would have additive effects on log percent correct. Additivity was not found, so the processes are not categorical. Summarizing, the processes are serial and non-categorical. A final result is theoretical. PERT networks provide an alternative to the assumption that processes are in series. Simulations of processes in a Wheatstone bridge demonstrate that additivity fails, but there is a pattern in the interactions.

1. INTRODUCTION

Stimulus intensity is of interest to cognitive psychologists because it serves as a kind of bench mark. Intensity is thought to affect early processing, and its neuronal effects are relatively well understood, compared with those of higher cognitive factors such as semantic relatedness.

Functions which have been proposed to relate stimulus intensity, I, to neuronal response, a(I), include the power function (e.g., Werner & Mountcastle, 1965),

$$a(I) = k(I - c)^p,$$ (1)

the Michaelis, or Naka-Ruston (1966), function,

$$a(I) = kI^p/(I^p + c^p),$$ (2)

and the logistic function (e.g., Hinton & Sejnowski, 1986),

$$a(I) = k/(1 + \exp[-p(I - c)]).$$ (3)

In these equations, k, p and the threshold, c, are positive constants. We investigated whether these functions, proposed for neurons, would give reasonable accounts of the rate of accrual of information as measured by reaction time.

In principle, intensity could have effects throughout the neural sequence from stimulus to response, since the receptor response increases with intensity, and the output of each successive neuron is monotonic with the net input from its predecessors. Indeed, effects of intensity are sometimes reported near the response end of the system (see Luce, 1986 for a review). But usually, the effects of intensity on reaction time are found to be additive with the effects of other factors (Everett, Hochhaus, & Brown, 1985). Usually, the additivity is interpreted as evidence that intensity affects one process in a series of discrete processes, and the other factor affects another process (Sternberg, 1969).

We investigated the joint effects of intensity and the number of alternatives in a hue identification task. One possibility is each of these factors affects a separate process in a series of processes, so the factors would have additive effects on reaction time. Another possibility is that intensity affects the rate, a(I), at which evidence accrues, and the number of alternatives affects the amount of evidence, b(j), required for a response to be selected. That is, the time required to make a decision is b(j)/a(I) (e.g., Luce, 1986, pp. 84-87). This predicts an interaction between the effects of intensity and number of alternatives (Grice, 1968; Luce, 1986; Nissen, 1977).

In short, the reaction time for intensity I with number of alternatives j is

$$t(I,j) = r/a(I) + b(j),$$

according to the additive model, and

$$t(I,j) = r + b(j)/a(I),$$

according to the multiplicative model. The parameter r is assumed to depend on minor details of the experiment.

2. METHOD

Each rate of accrual, a(I), in Equations 1, 2 and 3 was considered in each of the above equations. Two experiments were run, with 18 subjects in the first and 6 in the second. On each trial a coloured rectangle of red, orange, green or blue was presented on a computer monitor. In each block of trials, the number of alternative colours was either 2 or 4. In each experiment there were three levels of intensity produced by covering the screen with appropriate neutral density filters. The intensities (candelas per meter squared) were 28.55, 5.70, and .72 in experiment 1, and 26.49, .26, and .04 in experiment 2.

3. RESULTS AND DISCUSSION

3.1 Reaction times

The results are described in detail in Schweickert, Dahn, and McGuigan (1988). In each experiment, intensity and the number of alternatives had additive effects on reaction time. The power function in Equation 1 gave the best fit for the accrual function. The estimate of the power, p, was .7 and the estimate of the threshold, c, was .04, very close to 0. The power function as a predictor of simple reaction times is known as Pieron's Law (Pieron, 1914, 1920). Investigations of it for choice reaction times seem to be rare (see Luce, 1986; Nissen, 1977 for reviews).

3.2 Errors

Let us call a process categorical if its output can be classified as correct or incorrect, given its input. For example, a process given as input a percept of the word red, and producing the internal speech "red", is categorical. But a process producing as output strength of evidence that the word red was presented is not categorical, because the strength, in itself, cannot be classified as correct or incorrect. If each of the factors, intensity and the number of alternatives, affects a different process that is categorical, and all the processes in the task are in series, then the factors are predicted to have additive effects on log percent correct (Schweickert, 1985).

In experiment 1, there was not a significant interaction between intensity and number of alternatives for log percent correct. However, there was no main effect of the number of alternatives on log percent correct, so the lack of an interaction is not particularly meaningful. In experiment 2, intensity and the number of alternatives each had a significant effect on reaction time, and their interaction was significant (see Schweickert, Dahn, & McGuigan, 1988 for details). The processes affected by the two factors are not categorical.

4. THEORETICAL DEVELOPMENTS

4.1 The Logistic Function and the Hyperbolic Tangent

The logistic equation for a(I) in Equation 3 has been proposed to relate the input and output of neural units in some connectionistic models. It is an S shaped curve, with domain the set of all real numbers, and range those between 0 and 1, when the constant k is 1. Although this curve gave the worst fit to the data, it does have a notable mathematical property: the equation for the upper arm of the logistic function can be expressed in terms of the hyperbolic tangent. The upper arm is of interest because intensities are non-negative, so it is worth asking what the equation of the logistic function would be if it were rescaled to take on values between 0 and 1 as I takes on values at the threshold and above it.

Equation 3 gives the logistic function. Assume $k = 1$. As I approaches negative infinity, a(I) approaches 0, and, as I approaches infinity, a(I) approaches 1. The upper arm is the portion of the curve above $I = c$, where a(I) = 1/2. To rescale this part of the curve, let

$$h(I) = 2a(I) - 1.$$

When $I = c$, $h(I) = 0$, and, as I approaches infinity, h(I) approaches 1. Now,

$$h(I) = 2/(1 + \exp[-p(I - c)]) - 1$$

$$= (1 - \exp[-p(I - c)])/(1 + \exp[-p(I - c)])$$

$$= \tan h[p(I - c)/2].$$

4.2 Prolonging processes in PERT Networks

Sternberg (1969) noted that if the processes required to perform a task are all in series, then two processes affecting different processes will have additive effects on reaction time. Schweickert (1977, 1978) considered the effects of prolonging separate processes when the processes are not in series, but are partially ordered in a PERT network.

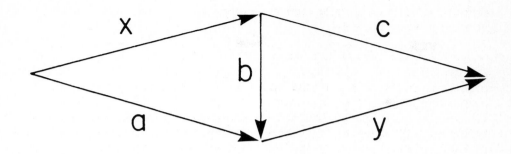

Figure 1. A Wheatstone Bridge PERT Network

An example of such a network is in Figure 1. Each arrow in the network represents a process. A process begins execution when and only when all the processes immediately preceding it are completed. A path is a sequence of processes such that the terminal vertex of one process is the starting vertex of its successor. The duration of a path is the duration of all the processes on it. The time to complete the task on a given trial is the duration of the longest path through the network, called the critical path.

Several people have contributed to understanding the case in which the durations of the processes are random variables (Fisher & Goldstein, 1983; Schweickert, 1977, 1982; Schweickert & Townsend, in press; Townsend & Ashby, 1983; Townsend & Schweickert, 1985, in press; Vorberg, 1988). In the following, we assume the process durations are random variables.

The network in Figure 1 is a Wheatstone bridge. Schweickert (1982) showed that factors prolonging the processes x and y will have interactions which are negative or, when the baseline durations of the processes x and y are very long, interactions which are zero. Schweickert and Townsend (in press) found conditions under which the interactions will be strictly negative.

Let $T(ij)$ be the reaction time when the factor prolonging x is at level i and the factor prolonging y is at level j. The interaction contrast at levels i and j, with respect to the baseline $T(11)$ is defined as

$$I(ij) = T(ij) - T(1j) - T(i1) + T(11).$$

We assume every level of the factor prolonging x produces an increase in reaction time over the baseline reaction time $T(11)$. Suppose the levels of the factor prolonging x are numbered so that $i < i'$ if and only if $T(i1) < T(i'1)$. Let the levels j of the factor prolonging process y be numbered analogously.

If $i < i'$ and $j < j'$, then $I(ij) < I(i'j)$, $I(ij)' < I(i'j')$. One of us (Schweickert) has demonstrated that this relation holds by simulating processes with normal distributions. Donald L. Fisher (personal communication, 1986) has demonstrated this relationship with exact calculations for processes with exponential distributions, using the algorithm in Fisher and Goldstein (1983). The interactions tend to be smaller in magnitude for the exponential distributions, but the overall qualitative pattern is the same. More details will be given in a later paper.

Table 1

Effects of Prolonging Processes in a Wheatstone Bridge

Simulated Reaction Times

E(Y)

E(X)	25	100	150	200	250
50	527.4	602.2	654.0	701.9	756.2
200	557.1	616.3	651.6	706.9	750.7
250	579.4	618.7	668.0	706.9	755.1
300	598.3	640.4	675.4	718.3	761.3
400	669.7	693.8	720.9	749.1	793.9
450	715.8	733.4	754.2	781.0	814.2
500	760.2	770.8	782.6	808.6	843.6

Interactions

E(Y)

E(X)	25	100	150	200	250
50	-	-	-	-	-
200	-	-15.6	-32.1	-24.8	-35.2
250	-	-35.5	-38.1	-47.1	-53.1
300	-	-32.7	-49.5	-54.5	-65.8
400	-	-50.7	-75.5	-95.1	-104.6
450	-	-57.2	-88.2	-109.2	-130.3
500	-	-64.2	-104.2	-126.1	-145.3

Table 1 gives the results of one of the simulations using normal distributions. For each process the coefficient of variation, that is, the standard deviation divided by the mean, is 1/4. This is in the range usually found for the coefficient of variation for reaction times themselves (Luce, 1986). The means for processes a, b, c, x and y were, respectively, 500, 10, 250, 50 and 25. The distribution of each process was a normal distribution, truncated so that values were non-negative. The distributions were pairwise independent. One thousand simulated trials were run in each condition using MICROSAINT.

Three relationships are immediately apparent in Table 1. First, the reaction times themselves are monotonically increasing across the rows and down the columns. Secondly, all the interaction contrasts are negative. Third, the interaction contrasts are monotonically decreasing. The occasional small deviations from this pattern do not occur when larger sample sizes, of 10,000 trials, are used.

ACKNOWLEDGEMENTS.

This research was supported by NIMH grants MH38675 and MH41452. We thank George Adams, Brian Boruff, Jerry Busemeyer, Donald L. Fisher, Cathrin Hayt, Leslie Kane, Barry Kantowitz, Robert Macmillian, Philip Smith, James T.Townsend, David Tumenoksa, Gerald Wasserman and Alex Wilkinson for help with various aspects of this work.

CORRESPONDENCE

Correspondence concerning this paper should be addressed to Richard Schweickert, Department of Psychological Sciences, Purdue University, West Lafayette, IN 47907, USA.

REFERENCES

Everett, B. L., Hochhaus, L., & Brown, J. R. (1985). Letter-naming as a function of intensity, degradation, S-R compatibility, and practice. Perception & Psychophysics, 37,467-470.

Fisher, D. L., & Goldstein, W. M. (1983). Stochastic PERT networks as models of cognition: Derivation of mean, variance, and distribution of reaction time using order-of-processing (OP) diagrams. Journal of Mathematical Psychology, 27, 121-151.

Grice, G. R. (1968). Stimulus intensity and response evocation. Psychological Review, 75, 359-373.

Hinton, G. E., & Sejnowski, T. J. (1986). Learning and relearning in Boltzmann machines. In D. E. Rumelhart & J. L.McClelland (Eds.), Parallel distributed processing: Explorations in the micro-structure of cognition (pp. 282-317). Cambridge, MA: MIT Press.

Luce, R. D. (1986). Response times: Their role in inferring elementary mental organization. New York: Oxford University Press.

Naka, K. I., & Rushton, W. A. (1966). S-potentials from luminosity units in the retina of fish (Cyprinidae). Journal of Physiology, 185, 587-599.

Nissen, M. J. (1977). Stimulus intensity and information processing. Perception & Psychophysics, 22, 338-352.

Pieron, H. (1914). Recherches sur les lois de variation destemps de latence sensorielle en fonction des intensites excitatrices. L'Annee Psychologique, 20, 17-96.

Pieron, H. (1920). Nouvelles recherches sur l'analyse du temps de latence sensorielle et sur la loi qui relie le temps a l'intensite d'excitation. L'Annee Psychologique, 22, 58-142.

Schweickert, R. (1977). A generalization of the additive factor method. (Technical Report MMPP 77-2). Ann Arbor, MI: The University of Michigan.

Schweickert, R. (1978). A critical path generalization of the additive factor method: Analysis of a Stroop task. Journal of Mathematical Psychology, 18, 105-139.

Schweickert, R. (1982). The bias of an estimate of coupled slack in stochastic PERT networks. Journal of Mathematical Psychology, 26, 1-12.

Schweickert, R. (1985). Separable effects of factors on speed and accuracy: Memory scanning, lexical decision, and choice tasks. Psychological Bulletin, 97, 530-546.

Schweickert, R., Dahn, C., & McGuigan, K. (1988). Intensity and number of alternatives in hue identification: Pieron's law and choice reaction time. Perception & Psychophysics, 44, 383-389.

Schweickert, R., & Townsend, J. T. (In press). A trichotomy method: II. Interactions of factors prolonging sequential and concurrent processes in stochastic PERT networks. Journal of Mathematical Psychology.

Sternberg, S. (1969). The discovery of processing stages: Extensions of Donders' method. Acta Psychologica, 30, 276-315.

Townsend, J. T., & Ashby, F. G. (1983). The stochastic modelling of elementary psychological processes. Cambridge: Cambridge University Press.

Townsend, J. T., & Schweickert, R. (1985). Interactive effects of factors prolonging processes in latent mental networks. In G.d'Ydewalle (Ed.), Cognition, information processing, and motivation. Amsterdam: Elsevier.

Townsend, J. T., & Schweickert, R. (In press). A trichotomy method: I. Journal of Mathematical Psychology.

Vorberg, D. (1988, August). Network models of reaction times. In S. W. Link & H. C. Micko (Chairs), Response latency: Theories of psychological processes. Symposium presented at the XXIV International Congress of Psychology, Sydney, Australia.

Werner, G., & Mountcastle, V. B. (1965). Neural activity in mechano-receptive cutaneous afferents: Stimulus-response relations, Weber functions, and information transmission. Journal of Neurophysiology, 28, 359-397.

SECTION 6

COMPUTATIONAL MODELS OF REPRESENTATION, RECOGNITION, AND RECALL

Human Information Processing: Measures,
Mechanisms, and Models. D. Vickers and P. L. Smith (eds.)
© Elsevier Science Publishers B.V. (North-Holland), 1989

CROSS MODAL TRANSFER OF GEOMETRIC FIGURES: ARE PROTOTYPES FORMED IN ONE MODE RECOGNIZED WHEN PRESENTED IN ANOTHER ?

Robert L. Solso, Brian Oppy and Curt Mearns

University of Nevada

The issue of the transfer of abstract memory representations (prototypes) from one modality to another was examined. In one experiment ("Haptic Experiment"), subjects were asked to feel a series of geometric figures which had been derived from a base figure or prototype figure. Following familiarization with items, subjects were asked to identify either visual or tactual figures which included likenesses of some of the original figures, some new figures, and the prototype figure. Cross modality transfer of prototypes exceeded transfer of exemplars. The results indicated (1) a robust prototype formation of haptic experiences with geometrically presented figures and (2) prototypes formed haptically transfer to visual recognition of figures. The specific locus of the transfer seemed to be more between exemplars rather than between prototypes.

1. INTRODUCTION

Interest in memories based on a class of sensory experiences has occupied a central position in the study of man's intellectual make-up for many centuries. Recently, the study of memory representations has become an intriguing puzzle for many cognitive psychologists.

The particular memory representations of interest here are known in the psychological literature under an assortment of labels; and although the distinctions between terms range from large to insignificant, all seem to be related to the concept of abstract memories. Some of these terms include prototypes, schemas, abstract memory representations, pseudo-memory (Solso & McCarthy, 1981), schemata, schema abstractions (Hintzman, 1986), blended memory, (Galton, 1883), generic memory systems (Tulving, 1983), schemata-abstractions, and sometimes even concept formation.

In order to distinguish precisely the phenomenon under inquiry from other, similar concepts, we shall use the term "prototype" to mean an abstract memory trace which develops out of experience with a class of sensory events. It is suggested that through the perception of everyday experiences or experimental stimuli, these "events" operate as exemplars out of which memory traces are formed. Through experience with exemplars of the same class, an abstract memory representation is developed, which is commonly called a prototype. Furthermore, it is hypothesized that prototype formation is basically a function of the frequency with which features of events are perceived. Thus, it is possible for a subject to form a prototype solely on the basis of experience with frequently perceived features of a class of stimuli rather than through direct experience with a stimulus which represents the embodiment of that class of information. This memory representation, or prototype, may be functionally equivalent to actual perceived events and, in the cognitive life of a person, is understood as an accurate expression of reality. Some evidence (see Solso & McCarthy, 1981) has appeared in the psychological literature which suggests that abstract visual memories derived from exemplar information may form a memory trace which is subjectively more graphic than memories for perceived stimuli.

1.1 Transfer of Prototypes.

An intriguing puzzle about abstract memory representations is the question of cross modal transfer. Such a question deals not with an isolated and circumscribed issue, as might be initially thought given the narrow title, but appears to be an integral component of the larger picture of human cognition vis-a-vis the representation of knowledge.

What is the relationship between memory representations formed through one modality and their corresponding representations in another modality? And, of related interest, what is transferred between modalities - features, exemplars, or prototypes, or a combination of these?

Some effort has been directed toward the solution of these questions (see Rumelhart & McClelland, 1986, Shepard, 1975, and Solso & Raynis, 1982). Of particular relevance to the current experiment is the theoretical model of isomorphism and second order isomorphism suggested by Shepard in which external and internal representations are lawfully related, as demonstrated in the now famous "mental rotation" experiment which indicated a linear relationship between the degree of rotation of a geometric figure and reaction time. According to Shepard "...the principle of second-order isomorphism has really to do with the relationship between the internal representation and the objects to which they correspond in the external world - regardless of the modality through which these objects may have been perceived" (p. 107). Several empirical questions are raised by theories of isomorphism, including the question of how internal representations experienced in one modality may subsequently be recognized when presented in another. Data addressing this question were presented by Solso and Raynis (1982) for geometric figures which were initially presented in the visual, tactual or kinesthetic modality and then presented for transfer recognition in one of the three modalities. For example, if the stimulus was initially presented in the visual mode, then the transfer recognition could be to visual, tactual, or kinesthetic modalities. In general, Solso and Raynis found support for transfer effects of geometric figures experienced in one modality and then presented in another.

A larger issue is raised by the theory of isomorphism. That is the question of cross modal transfer of abstract memory representations which may be formed in one mode and then presented for recognition in another mode. To illustrate this point, consider a subject who has learned about a geometric figure which has been presented tactually. Data indicate that abstract memories are formed on the basis of tactually presented geometric forms (see Solso & Raynis, 1982). However, the question is whether these abstract memories form the basis of transfer to another modality. If so, one would expect a high degree of correspondence between prototype formation in one modality when tested in another modality. The current research addresses this issue with the modalities in question being visual and haptic.

1.2 Model.

We approach prototype formation by way of a structural interpretation which holds that a prototype is the derived embodiment of a set of exemplars. Conceptually, prototypes can be envisioned as possessing a tree structure as shown below:

$$P_1$$

$$/ \quad | \quad \backslash$$

$$E_1 \quad E_2 \quad ...E_n$$

in which Prototype P_1 is formed through experiences with Exemplars E_1, E_2, and a continuing number of Exemplars, E_n. In the basic model, P_1 is formed on the basis of experience with Exemplars of a single modality (e.g., vision). In a cross-modal transfer condition, the possibilities of exemplar/prototype combinations become much more complex as shown below:

Modality A   Modality B   Modality C...

P_1 P_2 P_3

/ | \   / | \   / | \

E_1 E_2 ...E_n E_1 E_2 ...E_n E_1 E_2 ...E_n

in which each explicit exemplar (by modality) represented in memory may transfer its value to other exemplar representations associated with another modality (solid lines). That is, it implies that some sub-routing of information is possible in which recognition of specifically encoded information is recognizable in another modality. Thus, a subject may experience a geometric figure in the haptic mode and at the same time form a mental image of that figure. It is commonly accepted that such transfer may occur. When one feels a surface and then is asked to visually recognize the object felt, the response is usually correct. However, if one forms a prototype of an object in one modality, then whether that prototype will be accessible for recognition of stimuli presented in another modality is less obvious. Similar cross modal prototype transfer problems may exist for other types of material.

Another possibility might be that the formation of a prototype by means of one modality (e.g., visual) would also be stored in another modality (e.g., auditory) or, as in the case of exemplar storage, be accessible through some sub-routine which would approximate the initial storage of the prototype. Other possibilities exist. It is conceivable that exemplars from one modality contribute to the formation of prototypes of another modality directly.

1.3 Previous Results.

The most direct test of the hypothesis of cross-modal transfer of prototype information was done by Solso and Raynis (1982) in which geometric exemplars were presented either visually, tactually, or kinesthetically and then transfer data was collected in which recognition was tested both within the same and betwen different modalities. Their data indicated that transfer between visually experienced geometric figures and (1) visually experienced transfer figures, (2) tactually experienced geometric figures and (3) kinesthetically experienced geometric figures, was high for exemplar information. Less reliable transfer effects were noted for prototype transfer between modalities. These data provide clear support for the transfer of specific, exemplar information between modalities, but the evidence for transfer of abstract memories is equivocal. Only in the transfer between kinesthetically experienced geometric figures and their recognition in visual and tactile modalities did the correspondence between exemplar information break down.

These results have encouraged us to extend these findings to haptic information. The experiment reported here is part of an ongoing series which are all tied to the general model presented earlier.

2. METHOD

2.1 Subjects

Twenty students at the University of Nevada-Reno participated; approximately one-half were male and one-half were female. All subjects were run individually.

2.2 Stimuli and Apparatus

Stimuli were the Series 1 set of geometric figures described by Solso and Raynis (1979), composed of a central prototype figure and several exemplar figures which were derived from the prototype. The rules for similarity posited by Solso and Raynis were followed in the construction of the prototype and exemplars.

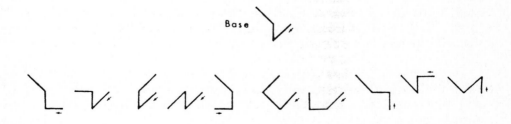

Figure 1. Base figure and exemplars.

Haptic stimuli were created with a raised line drawing kit, which produced a raised image of the figures on a plastic sheet. (Each figure was drawn on a separate sheet). Visual stimuli were exactly equal in size to the haptic stimuli, and consisted of black images on white paper. A cardboard screen was used to conceal haptic stimuli, and subjects reached through a small aperture to explore figures.

2.3 Procedure

Two groups were run, with ten subjects in each group. The first group was haptic-haptic (H-H), in which acquisition stimuli and recognition stimuli were both presented in the haptic modality. The second group was haptic-visual (H-V), in which acquisition was haptic, but recognition was visual. The training phase was identical for both groups.

For the training phase, each subject was told that they would be presented with a number of figures, one at a time, by touch, and that after all figures had been presented, they would be presented a second time to facilitate learning. Subjects were also told that there would be a recognition task after the learning trials. They were then asked to reach through the aperture with their dominant hand where the figures would be placed under their fingers for ten seconds.

Stimuli were presented in random order to each subject. After all stimuli had been presented, they were presented again in the same order for an additional ten seconds. Acquisition was always in the haptic modality. After a short pause, recognition items were presented.

In the recognition phases, subjects were told that they would be presented with some new items and some old items, to which they were to respond "new" or "old", as appropriate. For each response they were also asked to give a confidence rating from 1 to 5: 1 represented low confidence, and 5 represented high confidence. At this point, if they were in the H-V condition they were told that the items would be presented visually, instead of by touch. No time limit was set for recognition.

Subjects in H-H were haptically presented with three (old) items from the acquisition trials, three new items (one each of high, medium, and low similarity), and the prototype figure, in random order. The experimenter recorded a "+" for each response of "old", or a "-" for the response "new", regardless of the correctness of the response. Confidence ratings were scored as they were reported by the subject, resulting in a possible value range of +1 to +5 for old judgments, and -1 to -5 for new judgments.

Subjects in the H-V condition performed the same task as H-H, except that recognition items were displayed visually, at approximately the same distance as haptic stimuli had been presented.

3. RESULTS

The transfer effects between haptic-haptic and haptic-visual tasks is shown in Figure 2.

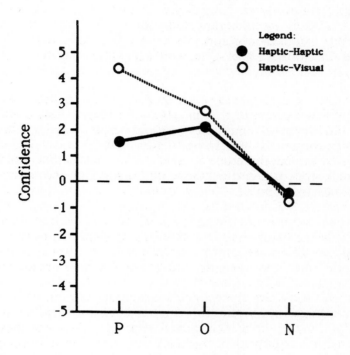

Figure 2. Confidence ratings for transfer between haptic-haptic and haptic-visual conditions for prototypes (P), old items (O), and new items (N).

A repeated measures MANOVA was performed on the data which yielded overall significant difference between the six recognition stimuli (Prototype, Old figures, and New figures) $F (5,80) = 10.45$, $p < .001$. The effect of condition type (H-H vs. H-V) by recognition stimuli was also significant, $F (5,80) = 5.17$, $p < .001$. Gender effects were nonsignificant, $F (5,80) = .62$, $p > .05$ so male and female data were combined for all contrasts. A series of univariate F tests were performed on the following combinations: Haptic-Haptic condition: prototype vs. old items, $F (1,9) = .31$, $p > .05$; prototype vs. new items, $F (1,9) = 3.16$, $p > .05$. Haptic-

Visual condition: prototype vs. old items, F (1,9) = 17.19, p < .005; prototype vs. new items, F (1,9) = 84, p < .001. Finally, a one way ANOVA performed on the prototype ratings for the two groups (H-H vs. H-V) showed a significant difference, F (1,18) = 8.15, p < .05.

4. DISCUSSION

Initially, several issues were raised regarding the breadth of prototype formation among various modalities and the transfer effects between modalities. First, consider the question of prototype formation with haptic stimuli. Results indicated a tendency to make false alarms on the prototype item when contrasted with other new items. Thus, some support for the formation of a haptic prototype was found. Four findings will now be discussed and considered with reference to the transfer model.

Of particular interest, both from a theoretical and empirical stand point, are the data which indicate (1) a very high level of false alarms for the visually-presented prototype figure when the exemplars were presented in the haptic mode. Also (2) prototype recognition in the haptic-visual mode is significantly more robust than exemplar recognition in the haptic-visual mode. Thus, prototype recognition in the haptic-visual transfer condition meets the criterion for "pseudo-memory." In addition, (3) significant differences were found between prototype recognition in the haptic-haptic condition and the haptic-visual condition. Finally, (4) no differences were obtained between the old items from the haptic-haptic and haptic-visual exemplars. These four results, taken together, suggest that the false alarm data in the haptic-visual mode for a geometric prototype may be considered due to cross-modal transfer in the exemplar storage of haptic information rather than being attributed exclusively to the cross-modal transfer between haptic and visual prototypes. This argument is based on the robust effect of haptic-visual prototype recognition and the less robust haptic-haptic prototype recognition data. The route of transfer would appear to be between exemplar modes (e.g., haptic-visual) with the abstraction process taking place in the visual mode after the transfer.

These conclusions are tentative and must rely on further empirical work for validation. However, on the basis of the data presented here, it appears that the mechanism of transfer between modalities is local rather than global or abstract. This finding contradicts those theorists who hold that the encoding of information is analogous to a tree structure, in which information is encoded in higher and higher order structures, and which suggests that at some high level of abstraction in the ascending notion of abstract memory representations, modality-specific information encoded and structured in a tree pattern, is connected to another modality-specific tree pattern. Our results suggest that the transfer effects may occur at a far more local level in the abstraction process.

CORRESPONDENCE

Correspondence concerning this paper should be addressed to Robert L. Solso, Department of Psychology, University of Nevada-Reno, Reno, Nevada, U.S.A 89557-0062

REFERENCES

Galton, F. (1883/1907). Inquiries in human faculty and its development. London: Macmillan.

Hintzman, D. L. (1986). "Schema abstraction" in a multiple-trace memory model. Psychological Review, 93, 411-428.

Rumelhart, D. E. & McClelland, J. L. (1986). Parallel Distributed Processing, Cambridge, MA: MIT.

Shepard, R. N. (1975). Form, formation and transformation of internal representations. In R. Solso (Ed.), Information Processing and Cognition: The Loyola Symposium, Potomac, Md: Erlbaum.

Solso, R. L. & McCarthy, J. E. (1981). Prototype formation of faces: A case of pseudomemory. British Journal of Psychology, 72, 499-503.

Solso, R. L. & Raynis, S. A. (1982). Transfer of prototypes based on visual, tactual, and kinesthetic exemplars. American Journal of Psychology, 95, 13-29.

Solso, R. L., and Raynis, S. A., (1979) Prototype formation from imaged, kinesthetically, and visually presented geometric figures. Journal of Experimental Psychology: Human Perception and Performance, 5, 701-712.

Tulving, E. (1983). Elements of episodic memory. London: Clarendon Press/Oxford University Press.

Human Information Processing: Measures, Mechanisms, and Models. D. Vickers and P.L. Smith (eds.) ©*Elsevier Science Publishers B.V. (North-Holland), 1989*

COGNITIVE ARITHMETIC: LEARNING AND PERFORMANCE IN AN ARTIFICIAL MATHEMATICS DOMAIN

D. Jeffrey Graham

University of Waterloo

Single-digit multiplication performance yields four robust effects: large problems have longer solution times than small ones, tie problems (squares) require less time overall and do not show a problem-size effect, errors tend to be multiples of one of the operands, and correct RTs are predicted by problem and product error rates. Current accounts of these effects are demonstrated to be insufficient in an experiment using an artificial mathematics domain that uses letters as operands. The task is called "alphaplication" due to formal similarities with multiplication (a x e = K). Two groups of grade three children were trained on 25 items for two sessions, and tested during the third session. One group was given a subset (A) to learn on session 1, and a subset (B) on session 2. The other group were given set B first and then set A. This teaching order manipulation was used to test the hypothesis that order of acquisition is a determinant of the problem-size effect in mental arithmetic. Training frequency was held constant for all problems. Mean correct RT and error rates were shown to be functions of teaching order. The four target effects were observed in a context that rules out traditional accounts. These results are problematic for any models of cognitive arithmetic that base their explanations on the numeric properties of arithmetic stimuli. The network-interference model (Campbell and Graham, 1985) is presented to account for these data.

1. INTRODUCTION

Cognitive arithmetic research has revealed at least four standard reaction time and error phenomena that demand explanation. First and foremost is the finding that the difficulty of single-digit problems (e.g., generating an answer to 7 x 8 = ?) increases with the sizes of the digits employed for both children and adult samples (Ashcraft & Fierman, 1982;

Campbell & Graham, 1985; Resnick & Ford, 1981; and Siegler & Shrager, 1984). In simple multiplication this "problem-size" effect appears as a monotonic increase in mean correct reaction time (RT) for the problems from 2 x 2 to 9 x 9, as a function of the size of the digits' product (Campbell & Graham, 1985). The second phenomenon, called the "tie" effect, is an error and RT advantage for the tie problems (those that involve repeated operands, e.g., 3 x 3 or 8 x 8) relative to nontie problems of similar sizes. Tie problems are reliably solved faster and are less prone to error than nontie problems (Campbell & Graham, 1985; Miller, Perlmutter, & Keating, 1984). Third, the kinds of errors generated are systematically related to the size of the operands. For example, most errors in simple multiplication are multiples of one of the operands in the problem (Graham, 1987; Norem & Knight, 1930). Finally, there is conclusive evidence that arithmetic retrieval is subject to associative priming and interference effects typical of classic semantic memory effects (Campbell, 1987a; 1987b; Graham, 1987; Kreuger & Hallford, 1985; Lefevre, Bisanz & Mrkonjic, 1988; Stazyk, Ashcraft, & Hammon, 1982; and Winkelman & Schmidt, 1974).

It is of both theoretical and practical interest to understand the cognitive factors that underlie these determinants of problem difficulty. Both the problem-size effect and the tie effect have been the focus of much theoretical analysis and have received explanations couched in procedural terms as well as in declarative fact retrieval frameworks (Parkman, 1972; Stazyk et al., 1982; Woods, Resnick, & Groen, 1975). Early procedural accounts of the problem-size effect proposed counting models that assumed incrementing mechanisms were the direct causal link between difficulty and problem-size (see Parkman, 1972). Tie problems were special cases whose answers were accessed via direct retrieval. Recent associative models such as Ashcrafts (1987) network-distance model, and Siegler's (1986) strategy choice model (also referred to as the distribution of associations model) have emphasized associative strength constructs based on training frequency, and error learning during the time when children adopt counting procedures as a backup strategy when retrieval fails. These training assumptions are invoked to account for the presence of the problem-size and tie effects in adult samples in which performance is presumably based on a fact retrieval strategy.

These classes of models share one attribute that is the focus of this paper. Each model accounts for one or more of the standard phenomena by explicitly or implicitly employing mechanisms that are governed by the size of the numbers in the arithmetic problem. The experiment reported below will show that all four phenomena can be observed in a problem domain that is devoid of numeric attributes, supporting the network-interference model of mental arithmetic first proposed by Campbell and Graham (1985). Network-interference theory is an elaboration of Ashcraft's network retrieval approach, and will be presented in more detail in the discussion.

Although much experimental work has focussed on correct response RTs to true items in a verification paradigm (e.g., 3 x 8 = 24, true or false?), correct RTs in a generation paradigm (e.g., 4 x 6 = ?) are more ecologically valid and allow the analyses of frequencies and types of errors which reveal important regularities. A useful error classification scheme distinguishes among four classes: 1) naming and adding errors, (e.g., 4 x 2 = 4, or 4 x 2 = 6); 2) table-related errors, which are correct responses in one of the times-tables specified by the operands in the problem (e.g., 4 x 7 = 32); 3) table-unrelated errors, which are multiplication responses that are not members of the given operands' times-tables (e.g., 4 x 7 = 25); and finally, 4) miscellaneous errors, which are not answers to any simple multiplication problem (e.g., 4 x 7 = 31). Campbell and Graham (1985) compared error patterns in three grade 3 samples (tested every 6 weeks) and in adult samples and observed that naming and adding errors are relatively rare (less than 5% of all errors). The proportion of errors categorized into the three remaining error classes indicated that table-related errors became the most common error by the end of 12 weeks (56.2%), and were well above chance even in the first month of training (43.2%). If subjects were guessing randomly approximately 14 percent would be table-related, 19 percent would be table-unrelated, and 67 percent would be miscellaneous (see Graham, 1987).

In adult samples, between 70 and 90 percent of errors are answers to other multiplication problems, and usually, about 90 percent of these are table-related errors (Campbell and Graham, 1985; Miller, Perlmutter & Keating, 1984; Norem & Knight, 1930). Network-distance theory (Ashcraft, 1987) accounts for such errors by assuming that each operand activates its own times-table responses, entailing that selected errors would be divisable by one of the operands. The distributions of associations model accounts for table-related errors by assuming that beginners make incrementing errors in which a counting procedure stops too soon or too late in the counting sequence, producing a number that was a multiple of the counting step size. These errors would gain strength through repetition, and reappear in adult's speeded retrieval performance.

Retrieval interference effects in arithmetic tasks provide a fourth class of effects that any model of cognitive arithmetic must deal with. The mental arithmetic literature reports a variety of interference effects in both verification tasks (Stazyk et al., 1982; Campbell, 1987b) and production tasks (Campbell & Graham, 1985; Campbell, 1987a). For present purposes the relevant interference effect to discuss is the empirical finding that in production tasks, correct reaction time for a problem is well predicted by two error measures. Independently, percentage error rates for each problem (called total errors or TE), and the frequency of errors involving that problem's product (called product errors or PE), account for a total of 55 to 75 percent of the variance in RT across the problems 2 x 2 to 9 x 9. Neither network-distance nor distributions of associations models can explain the inhibitory relationship between product error rates (PE) and correct retrieval RT. Both could argue that high-frequency error responses would have elevated "resting strengths" due to recent retrievals, however this would lead to the opposite prediction that products with high PE rates would be faster.

The network-interference model argues that the TE and PE error measures reflect associative structures that actively inhibit the accumulation of activation at the response node, thereby delaying its selection during retrieval. Retrieval time in arithmetic production is correlated with these independent error measures because these two error rates operationalize two sources of network interference: inhibition of the correct node by competing candidates, and inhibition of the correct node by other problem nodes to which it is a candidate. Problem error rates (TE) provide an estimate of the number (or strength) of competing candidates (set size effects), and product error frequencies (PE) provide an estimate of how strongly that response is falsely linked to other problems (fan effects). The model is elaborated upon in the Discussion (see Figure 3).

The importance of these error measures as predictors of correct performance is evident when one compares the developmental trends in the amount of RT variance they can account for with traditional problem-size predictors. Simple correlations predicting correct RT from these error measures (TE and PE) are contrasted with problem-size predictors of RT in Figure 1. These include the minimum operand (MIN), the maximum operand (MAX), the sum of the operands (SUM), and the product of the operands (PROD). Three successive sessions of grade three data and a single grade five sample (Campbell and Graham, 1985) show a dramatic decrease in the size of the problem-size correlations with experience (with perhaps the exception of MAX). The set size correlation (TE x RT) is always the largest of the predictors, and the fan measure correlation (PE x RT) grows steadily through the three grade-three sessions to become the second best predictor. Moreover, these two indices of interference (TE and PE) cannot be said to be measuring the same process since they contribute independently in multiple regression analyses (see Graham, 1987).

While training frequency is most likely an operative factor in determining the relative difficulty of problems, it is by no means the sole explanatory construct. The network-interference model was proposed by

Campbell and Graham (1985) to provide an associative account for a

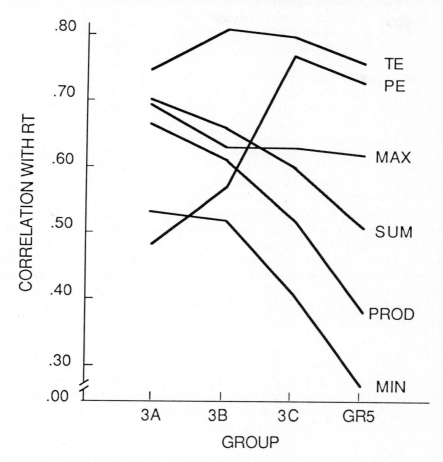

Figure 1. Correlation coefficients for the operand-size measures and the error measures (TE, PE) predicting correct response time. Data from Campbell and Graham(1985).

wide range of priming and interference effects observed in the literature. The model consists of both operand "parent nodes" and unitary "problem nodes" that have associative links to the 100 response integers from 0 to 99 (for single-digit multiplication). Learning is accomplished by strengthening the links between (correct or incorrect) responses and the components of the stimulus problem each time the problem is attempted. Retrieval is described as a selection process that is triggered dynamically as activation converges on particular candidates within the network. Correct retrieval RT is a function of both candidate set size and fan-like relations (Anderson, 1983) that evolve with experience. Large problems are more difficult because of interfering associations that small problems do not encounter. Therefore, the "problem-size effect" is a misnomer. Some problems are more difficult, not because they have large operands, but rather because they were learned later in the learning sequence. Typically, large problems are learned in a context in which previous learning proactively interferes with new fact acquisition.

The network-interference model has a unique account for the problem-size effect as a consequence of training order and the tie effect as a function of the size of the active candidate set, and imports Ashcraft's assumptions about operand-specific pathways to explain table-related errors. Thus, the network-interference model can account for all of the four target effects. The main purpose of the experiment reported below is to bring into question all explanations based solely on training frequency or the use of numerically based procedures.

In contrast to models attributing difficulty directly to problem size, to testing frequency, or to the use of procedural strategies, the network-interference model attributes differences in problem difficulty to a dynamic interaction of the organization and history of the encoding-retrieval structure. A straightforward way to test these two accounts is to examine learning of arithmetic-like facts under conditions that eliminate problem-size factors, differences in testing frequency, and the opportunity to use procedural strategies.

1.1 An artificial mathematics domain

The experiment reported in this paper examines the network-interference account of multiplication performance in a new task called "alphaplication", a memory task with 25 arithmetic-like "facts" and a training regimen that controls for practice frequency. The task is a cued-recall task in which subjects are given a pair of vowels (separated by a comma, e.g., A , U) and asked to produce the consonant that occurred with that pair during training (A , U = m). The paradigm was constrained to be similar to multiplication: 10 stimulus pairs were commutative (e.g., A , U = U , A = m), 5 of the 15 operand combinations were ties (E , E = j), there were 5 times-tables (A, E, I, O, U) or alpha-tables, and 15 unique answers. If the four major effects (problem-size/order-of-learning, tie, related errors, and interference) can be observed with alphabetic stimuli then current models would have to be flexible enough to account for the new task as well. No model based on a causal link between numerical attributes of the operands and RT (e.g., operands specify the number of iterations to sum over, or the distance to be searched in memory) can be modified to account for the data from the new task.

The experiment was designed to compare two groups who learned two sets of problems under reversed teaching orders, so that all problems were trained equally often. If the problem-size effect in arithmetic is due to the order in which problems are taught, then the second set learned by both groups should be more error prone and have longer RTs than the first set learned. If, however, RT is primarily determined by some other intrinsic properties of the stimuli (e.g., the ease with which a convenient mnemonic can be created for each problem trigram), then relative problem difficulty will be invariant across teaching orders. If the only determinant of the problem-size effect in multiplication is differential practice frequency, then there should be no difference between the problem sets for either group in this task. The cumulative interference hypothesis predicts an interaction of problem-set and acquisition order. Although there is no aspect of the alpha stimuli that corresponds to problem size, the experiment controls a factor that is confounded with problem size in simple arithmetic and potentially will show that order of learning, on a short-term basis at least, contributes to differences in problem difficulty.

Alpha tie problems should show both speed and accuracy advantages over nonties. If the tie advantage in simple arithmetic is caused by extra training exposure, then there should be no tie effect in alphaplication since experience on tie problems will be equated with experience on nontie problems. Evidence that ties have fewer competing candidates will be obtained if the tie effect is fully accounted for once the interference measures are partially out in a multiple regression analysis.

Errors in alphaplication should be answers in one of the "alpha-tables" specified by the operands. Any model that accounts for this error effect in terms of the numeric properties of simple multiplication facts is forced to predict that such an effect would not be observed in alphaplication.

Finally, regression analyses should reveal that both problem error rates (TE) and product error rates (PE) will account for correct retrieval RTs in the alphaplication paradigm. This would support the network-interference claims that 1) the size of the candidate set activated by a pair of operands (either letters or digits) inhibits correct retrieval RT, and 2) when the "solution" to a problem has many false links to other problems its retrieval is delayed. On the other hand, if both error measures are simply indicators of problem difficulty than only one should enter the regression equations.

2. METHOD

2.1 Subjects

The sample consisted of 45 children (23 females) in grades 3 and 4 from a rural school in southwestern Ontario. Ages ranged from 8.2 to 10.7 years with a mean of 9.4.

2.2 The problem set

Fifteen problems were created using a format similar to single digit multiplication in which two operands are paired with a single response. Five uppercase vowels (A,E,I,O,U) were used as operands, and fifteen lowercase consonants were used as responses (b,c,d,g,j,k,m,n,p,r,s,t,v,x,z). There are ten unique combinations of the five operands plus 5 tie problems (i.e., repeated operands as in A,A). A comma was employed as the operator sign, and both operand orders were introduced at the same time (e.g., E,I=p and I,E=p). The responses were randomly assigned to the problems with the constraint that no problem-answer pair could form an English word (e.g., E,A=t).

Over the entire set of fifteen problems each operand occurs in five problems constituting the members of that vowel's "times-table" or "alpha-table". In order to counterbalance teaching order, the fifteen problems were divided into two subsets, Set 1 (N=7) and Set 2 (N=8). Set 1 consisted of mainly the A and E "alpha-tables". Set 2 consisted of mainly the I, O and U "alpha-tables".

2.3 The training schedule

Each set of problems was introduced on a fact sheet for initial study and copying into the students' mathematics workbooks. Drill sheets containing only the operands were given to provide practice at generating the answers. The grade 3 class was trained for 3 days (approximately 30 minutes/day) and tested on the fourth. The grade 4 class was trained for 2 days (45 minutes/day) and tested on the third. Both grades were split into two groups, matched for general mathematical ability by their teacher. Within each grade, one group (A) was given problem Set 1 to learn first while the other group (B) received Set 2. The difference in length of training between grades was due to scheduling difficulties. However this is crossed with teaching order groups A and B, which consist of students in both grades.

Drill sheets were designed so that all nontie problems would be tested equally often. On each drill sheet each nontie problem was tested 5 times and ties were tested 3 times. Therefore, across two versions of the drill sheets used for training purposes, each nontie problem occurred 10 times (5 times in each operand order), and tie problems appeared 6 times. Since there would be considerable transfer across operand orders, the nontie combinations were trained 1.67 times more often than tie problems making a tie advantage more difficult to obtain.

2.4 Apparatus and procedure

Each student was tested in a quiet office using a PET 2001 microcomputer connected to a black and white CRT screen. The problems were presented horizontally at the centre of the screen in a five character field (e.g., "E , E"). Subjects sat facing the screen at a distance of approximately 50 cm and were instructed to respond verbally as quickly and accurately as possible. Both speed and accuracy were emphasized.

All 15 problems were tested in each of four blocks. On each trial a flashing fixation point appeared twice and was replaced by the operation sign flanked by the operands on what would have been the third flash. The problem remained on the screen until the subject responded. If no response was given within 7 seconds, a prompt "can you guess" appeared on the screen. When subjects responded the problem was re-presented with the correct response at the same location on the screen in order to provide immediate feedback. Response times were measured by means of a software clock. Timing began when a problem appeared and the experimenter stopped the timer by pressing a button when a response was given. Manual timing was employed in order to avoid trials being spoiled by extraneous vocalizations. The set of 60 trials required approximately 10 minutes to complete.

3. RESULTS

Of the 45 children in the classes employed in this study, 5 subjects were dropped due to excessive error rates (58 to 67 percent). Data analyses were based on mean correct RTs with an outlier exclusion rule of 2.5 standard deviations beyond a subject's mean. Overall, there were 57 outliers (2.4 percent of 2400 trials), 1 spoiled trial, and 725 errors (30.2 percent). The 20 subjects in Group A learned Set 1 before Set 2, and 20 subjects in Group B learned the problems in the reverse order. In most of the analyses to be reported the groups are analyzed separately. Preliminary analyses indicated that there was no effect of operand order (i.e., A,E=k vs. E,A=k) on RT or on error rates, and thus it was dropped as a factor.

Mean response time (RT) and total errors were calculated for each subject, for each problem, collapsing over blocks 1 and 2 and blocks 3 and 4 (and thus over operand order). For the RT analyses, 8 means were calculated for each subject: one mean for ties and nonties, in each of the problem sets 1 and 2, for the first and second halves of the experiment. These data were analysed in an ANOVA of the following design: Group (2) x Set (2) x Tie (2) x Block (2). Group was the only between-subjects factor.

Group B was marginally faster than Group A overall, $F(1,38)=2.61$, p=.114. There were no main effects of SET or of BLOCK, while the TIE effect was substantial, $F(1,38)= 164.7$, p<.001. Nonties had a mean RT of 3706 msec, and ties were almost twice as fast at 2005 msec. Figure 2 shows correct RT for tie and nontie problems in SET 1 and SET 2 for each teaching order group.

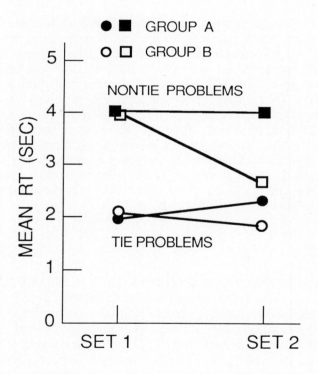

Figure 2. Mean correct RT in each of the teaching order groups for tie and nontie problems in each of the problem sets.

The most important result of this ANOVA was the significant interaction between GROUP (i.e., learning order) and SET, $F(1,38)= 7.16$, p=.011. These results, shown in Figure 2, confirm the teaching order prediction, since the set of problems learned second (set 2 for group A, and set 1 for group B) required on average 658 msec more time to be answered correctly. Under the assumption that the practice regimen maintained an equal frequency for both problem sets, it appears that teaching order has a strong effect on the relative difficulty of problems. At first glance, the RT data in Figure 2 suggest that there was no teaching order effect for Group A, and a large effect for Group B. However, an examination of the error data plotted in Figure 3 confirms that the lack of a set effect on RT was entirely due to a speed-accuracy trade-off. Group A's exceptionally low error rates on set 1 indicated that set 1 problems were easier than set 2, even though there were no differences on RT.

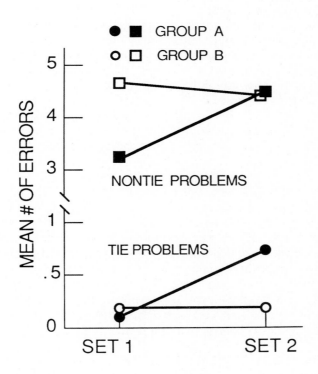

Figure 3. Mean number of errors in each of the teaching order groups for tie and nontie problems in each of the problem sets.

An ANOVA of the same design was performed on error rates. Figure 3 illustrates the effects on the number of errors in SET 1 and SET 2 for each teaching order group. The only main effects were for SET, $F(1,38)=5.79$, p=.021, and for TIE, $F(1,38)=201.3$, p=.001. The critical interaction between SET and GROUP was found for errors as well,

F(1,38)=7.13, p=.011. In this instance, Group B exhibited a minimal SET effect on error rates (while exhibiting large SET effects on RT), and Group A (who maintained constant speed across SETs) made many more errors on the set they learned second.

A classification analysis of the errors revealed a very strong trend for errors to be table-related, i.e., answers that were correctly associated with one of the problem's operands in the context of another problem (e.g., t is a table-related error for A,E since it is correct for A,A). Both groups had very similar error rates (29% and 32% for groups A and B, respectively) and will be collapsed in the following discussion. Overall, there were 725 errors in 2400 trials, 547 of which were table-related (75.4 %), 168 were table-unrelated (23.2 %), 10 were vowels as responses (1.4 %), and there were no instances of the miscellaneous letters (f,h,l,w,and y). These observed proportions were tested against the expected proportions of errors that fall into the error categories (expected under a random guessing strategy). On an error trial there are 25 possible error responses, of which 8 would be table-related (32%), 6 would be table-unrelated (24%), 5 would be vowels (20%), and 6 would be miscellaneous (24%). It is clearly the case that operand-driven associations are influencing the nature of errors observed, since well over twice as many table-related errors occur than could be expected by chance alone.

The final analyses were designed to examine the relative importance of the interference predictors established in the context of multiplication. Specifically, it was of interest to observe whether or not both total error rates (TE) and product-error rates (PE) would correlate with RT. As an additional predictor, the set number of each problem was used (SET) to correspond roughly with problem-size measures whose predictive power in arithmetic may be due to the order in which problems were learned. The simple correlations predicting RT with the SET, TIE and interference variables, TE and PE, were calculated for each group across the 15 problems. These are displayed in Table 1.

At the bottom of Table 1 are the regression equations based on these 4 predictors in a stepwise entry procedure. Group A reaction times for the 15 problems were predicted by TE and PE independently (R squared was .928) replicating the effects observed in the multiplication data. Once these interference variables entered there was no residual tie advantage. The multiple R squared for Group B was .932. Both TE and SET captured unique variance. The PE variable was only marginally predictive of residual variance (p=.12) and therefore did not enter the equation, probably because in this sample TE and PE were highly correlated (r(TExPE)=0.90, p<.001). Moreover, the TIE variable did not capture unique variance after TE entered the equation.

Table 1.

Summary of the regression analyses for the two teaching-order groups.

Sample		Correlations		
	TE	PE	TIE	SET
Group A	.93	.92	-.78	.14
Group B	.91	.89	-.78	-.42

Regression Equations

Group A	RT = 1645 + 45.6 (TE) + 44.0 (PE)
Group B	RT = 2235 + 50.0 (TE) - 719 (SET)

Note. TE=Total Errors. PE=Product Errors. TIE=Tie/nontie. SET=problem set. Correlations predict mean correct RT across the 15 problems in the task. Critical r(13)=0.51.

4. DISCUSSION

The alphaplication task provides very good evidence in support of the hypothesis that differential problem difficulty is a function of the order in which problems are first learned, and not due to differential practice frequency. The pattern of error rates and RTs for the two groups indicated that performance was worse for problems learned in the second set, relative to those learned first. Since problems were counterbalanced across teaching orders, the effect could not be due to intrinsic properties of the stimuli (e.g., approximation to English word fragments).

The alphaplication study also demonstrated a very strong tie effect (repeated operand problems), even when the training frequency for those problems was less than that for nontie problems. The tie advantage is proportionally larger than in simple arithmetic, but this seems to be entirely due to reduced competition from the smaller candidate sets activated by the tie's functional operand. This conclusion is warranted by the fact that the TIE vector does not enter the regression equation once the effects of the interference measures have been removed. The tie effect is not merely a frequency effect, since ties were studied less often than nontie problems. This seriously challenges any model of arithmetic retrieval that explains tie effects as a function of training exposure.

Table-related errors (error responses that are correct in the context of one of the operands in the problem) were the predominant class of error in alphaplication, suggesting that operand specific associations were functioning in this task. Since the task precludes the use of reconstructive strategies (e.g., backup counting in multiplication), it is assumed that these errors are caused by the simultaneous activation from each operand at the time of encoding (i.e., on-line), rather than as the result of error learning during non-retrieval trials. In other words, the only alternative strategy in alphaplication is random guessing. Errors made on the basis of this strategy could not have produced the predominance of table-related errors observed. This result is inconsistent with any model that explains table-related errors in multiplication on the basis of the numeric properties of the stimulus (e.g., where an operand specifies the number of operations needed to compute or retrieve an answer).

Candidate set size interference and response fan effects appear to predict RT in alphaplication, just as they do in simple arithmetic. While this was clearly observed for the Group A data, it was not observed for Group B. The fact that product error rates contributed only marginally because of the high correlation with total error rates suggests that the effect is present, though statistically weak. The interference effects that are inferred from the problem and product error rate predictors (TE, and PE) have been replicated in both simple multiplication, and in the artificial arithmetic task.

4.1 The network-interference model of cognitive arithmetic

In the network-interference theory the intimate relation between error rates and RT is interpreted as evidence of inhibition during the response selection process. The theoretical account of this retrieval process involves the construct of a candidate set activated by encoding the problem. Consider the two schemas presented in Figure 4 which illustrate the associative architecture and the retrieval processes involved in solving a problem like 5x9=45. In the top panel, encoding the operands in the context of a multiplication goal serves to activate individual operand nodes ("parent nodes" on the periphery of the problem plane) as well as a "problem node" stored on the problem plane at the intersection of the parents' row and column. Each of these three nodes have associative links with as many as 100 integer values within a reasonable range (i.e., the 100 responses from 0 to 99). The initial activation level of any one integer on the response plane is assumed to be proportional to the summation of the associative weights between that response node and the activated nodes on the problem plane. The majority of the response nodes will have very low activation levels. However a few will have accumulated some activation and will thereby begin to compete for selection. A response node will enter the candidate set when it has sufficient activation to exceed some minimum threshold.

The selection process (retrieval), illustrated in the bottom panel of Figure 4, is assumed to involve a stabilization stage where the activities of candidate nodes are positively and negatively adjusted depending on the set of associative pathways involved (referred to as the local network structure). On correct trials the correct response will have the highest activation level (after stabilization), but if it does not and no other node has reached threshold, the system will wait in order to accrue sufficient evidence for a particular candidate to fire. Fast and accurate trials will be observed when the size of the candidate set is small (as shown with 3 x 7 relative to 5 x 9) and when the correct node has a small number of false links with other problems (e.g., 21 linked with 4 x 7 vs. 45 linked with 5 x 8, 6 x 9, and 7 x 9). Response nodes compete for a limited activation resource, a resource whose allocation is further modulated by positive and negative associative pathways in the arithmetic fact network.

The network-interference model hypothesizes that the response selection process depends on the size of the candidate set activated by a problem, which is determined by the strength of links between problem nodes and response nodes and a fan-like effect of associative interference (cf. Anderson, 1983) which is determined by the number of links the correct response has to other problem stimuli. The name of the network-interference theory is in part due to the central role percentage error rates (both TE and PE) play as measures of the size and strength of competing associations. Product Error frequencies directly reflect a second sort of interference that occurs simultaneously with the first. Both of these theoretical constructs are the consequence of one spreading activation process, but the former reflects forward associations from problems to responses, and the latter represents backward associations from the responses to specific problems.

Campbell and Graham (1985) claim that cumulative proactive interference may be responsible for the pattern of problem difficulty called the problem-size effect. Problems encountered later in the learning sequence would be influenced by the pre-existing associations established by the problems learned earlier. These competing associations would make the items more difficult to master and more error prone, ultimately creating relatively large candidate sets due to the formation of erroneous associative links. Similarly the tie advantage could be accounted for by the relatively small candidate sets activated by the one unique operand in tie problems.

THE NETWORK - INTERFERENCE MODEL

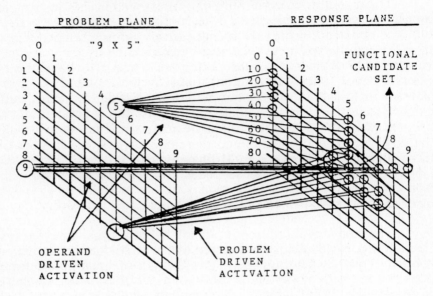

LOCAL NETWORK STRUCTURE

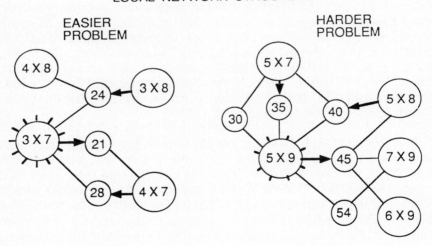

Figure 4. Schematic representations of the functional associative connections in the network-interference model

5 CONCLUSION

The alphaplication results support the hypothesis that the problem-size effect in multiplication is at least partially due to the order in which problems are traditionally taught. In alphaplication, the set of problems that is learned second has longer correct RTs and/or is more error prone than the problem set learned first. There was a very strong trend for errors to be intrusions from correct associations formed in the context of other problems (i.e., 75% of the errors were table-related). Moreover, there was a very strong advantage for ties, paralleling and even exceeding the same effect in multiplication. Finally, the interference measures derived from multiplication performance (TE, PE) were found to be relevant in explaining alphaplication performance. Given these effects of teaching order, table-relatedness, ties, and associative interference, all of which were observed in the context of a task completely free of numeric attributes, the causal account of such numeric properties in simple multiplication performance is in need of revision.

Since automatic counting models and network-distance models account for variance in correct retrieval time in terms of the numerical properties of the problem set, these results in alphaplication appear to be problematic for both classes of models. The generalizability of network-interference across arithmetic operations and artificial tasks such as alphaplication legitimizes this theoretical approach.

ACKNOWLEDGMENTS

This research was supported by a Natural Sciences and Engineering Research Council of Canada Postgraduate Scholarship awarded to the author and by NSERC grant A0790 to Dr Neil Charness, Department of Psychology, University of Waterloo. I would like to thank Janice Graham, Neil Charness, and Jamie Campbell for their interest and support.

Correspondence concerning this paper should be addressed to Jeff Graham, Department of Psychology, University of Otago, Box 56, Dunedin, New Zealand

REFERENCES

Anderson, J.R. (1983). A spreading activation theory of memory. Journal of Verbal Learning and Verbal Behaviour, 22, 261-295.

Ashcraft, M.H. (1982). The development of mental arithmetic: A chronometric approach. Developmental Review, 3, 231-235.

Ashcraft, M.H. (1987). Children's knowledge of simple addition: A developmental model and simulation. In J. Bisanz, C.J. Brainerd, & R. Kail (Eds.), Formal methods in developmental psychology: Progress in cognitive development research (pp.302-338). New York: Springer-Verlag.

Ashcraft, M.H., & Battaglia, J. (1978). Cognitive Arithmetic: Evidence for retrieval and decision processes in mental addition. Journal of Experimental Psychology: Human Learning and Memory, 4, 527-538.

Ashcraft, M.H., & Fierman, B.A. (1982). Mental addition in third, fourth, and sixth graders. Journal of Experimental Child Psychology, 33, 216-234.

Ashcraft, M.H., Fierman, B.A., & Bartalotta, R. (1984). The Production and verification tasks in mental addition: An empirical comparison. Developmental Review, 4, 157-170.

Campbell, J.I.D. (1987a). Network interference in mental multiplication. Journal of Experimental Psychology: Learning, Memory, and Cognition, 13 (1), 109 -123.

Campbell, J.I.D. (1987b). Production, verification, and priming of multiplication facts. Memory and Cognition, 15 (4), 349-364.

Campbell, J.I.D., & Graham, D.J. (1985). Mental multiplication skill: Structure, process, and acquisition. Canadian Journal of Psychology, 39, 338-366.

Findlay, J.M., & Roberts, M.A. (1985, March). Knowledge of the answer and counting algorithms in simple arithmetic addition. Paper presented at the Keele Conference on Maths and Maths Learning, University of Keele, England.

Geary, D.C., Widaman, K.F., & Little, T.D. (1986). Cognitive Addition and Multiplication: Evidence for a single memory network. Memory and Cognition, 14(6), 478-487.

Graham, D.J. (1987). Simple multiplication performance in grades two through five: Retrieval processes and associative structure. In J. Sloboda, & D. Rogers (Eds.) Cognitive Processes in Mathematics (pp. 123-141). Oxford, England: Oxford University Press.

Groen, G.J., & Parkman, J.M. (1972). A chronometric analysis of simple addition. Psychological Review, 79, 329-343.

Krueger, L.E., & Hallford, E.W. (1985). Why 2+2=5 looks so wrong: On the odd-even rule in sum verification. Memory and Cognition, 12, 171-180.

LeFevre, J.A., Bisanz, J., & Mrkonjic, L. (1988). Cognitive arithmetic: Evidence for obligatory activation of arithmetic facts. Memory and Cognition, 16 (1), 45-53.

McCloskey, M., Caramazza, A., & Basili, A. (1985). Cognitive mechanisms in number processing and calculation: Evidence from dyscalculia. Brain and Cognition, 4, 171-196.

Miller, K., Perlmutter, M., & Keating, D. (1984). Cognitive arithmetic: Comparison of operations. Journal of Experimental Psychology: Learning, Memory, and Cognition, 10, 46-60.

Norem, G.M., & Knight, F.B. (1930). The learning of the 100 multiplication combinations. National Society for the Study of Education: Report on the Society's Committee on Arithmetic. Vol. 15, Yearbook 29, 551-567.

Parkman, J.M. (1972). Temporal aspects of simple multiplication and comparison. Journal of Experimental Psychology, 95, 437-444.

Resnick, L.B., & Ford, W.W. (1981). The Psychology of Mathematics for Instruction. Hillsdale, NJ: Lawrence Erlbaum Associates.

Siegler, R.S. (1986). Unities in strategy choice across domains. In M. Perlmutter (Ed.), Minnesota Symposium on Child Development Vol 21 (pp. 229-294). Minneapolis: University of Minnesota Press.

Siegler, R.S., & Shrager, J. (1984). A model of strategy choice. In C. Sophian (Ed.), Origins of cognitive skills (pp.229-294). Hillsdale, NJ: Erlbaum.

Stazyk, E.H., Ashcraft, M.H, & Hamann, M.S. (1982). A network approach to simple multiplication. Journal of Experimental Psychology: Learning, Memory, and Cognition, 8, 320-335.

Woods, S.S., Resnick, L.B., Groen, G.J. (1975). An experimental test of five process models for subtraction. Journal of Educational Psychology, 67(1), 17-21.

Human Information Processing: Measures,
Mechanisms, and Models. D. Vickers and P. L. Smith (eds.)
©Elsevier Science Publishers B.V. (North-Holland), 1989

A FUZZY LOGICAL MODEL OF SPEECH PERCEPTION

Dominic W. Massaro

University of California

Speech perception is viewed as having available multiple sources of information supporting the identification and interpretation of the language input. The results from a wide variety of experiments can be described within a framework of a fuzzy logical model of perception (FLMP). The assumptions central to the model are 1) each source of information is evaluated to give the degree to which that source specifies various alternatives, 2) the sources of information are evaluated independently of one another, 3) the sources are integrated to provide an overall degree of support for each alternative, and 4) perceptual identification and interpretation follows the relative degree of support among the alternatives. The model is tested against the results of a novel expanded factorial design of the audible and visible characteristics of the syllables /ba/ and /da/. These two sources of information are synthesized and manipulated independently of one another in both factorial combination and in isolation. Identification judgments reveal that subjects are influenced by both auditory and visual information. The two sources of information appear to be evaluated, integrated, and identified in an optimal manner, as described by the FLMP. These same results reject an alternative categorical model of speech perception. The good description of the results by the FLMP indicates that the sources of support provide continuous rather than categorical information. The integration of the multiple sources results in the least ambiguous sources having the most impact on processing. These results provide major constraints to be met by other theories of speech perception and language processing.

1. INTRODUCTION

Speech perception is a human skill that rivals our other impressive achievements. Even after decades of intense effort, speech recognition by machine remains far inferior to human performance. The central thesis of the present proposal is that there are multiple sources of information supporting speech perception, and the perceiver evaluates and integrates all of these sources to achieve perceptual recognition. Consider recognition of the word *performance* in the spoken sentence .

The actress was praised for her outstanding performance.

Recognition of the critical word is achieved via a variety of bottom-up and top-down sources of information. Top-down sources include semantic, syntactic, and phonological constraints and bottom-up sources include audible and visible features of the spoken word.

According to the present framework, well-learned patterns are recognized in accordance with a general algorithm, regardless of the modality or particular nature of the patterns (Massaro, 1987). The model has received support in a wide variety of domains and consists of three operations in perceptual (primary) recognition: feature evaluation, feature integration, and decision. Continuously-valued features are evaluated, integrated, and matched against prototype descriptions in memory, and an identification decision is made on the basis of the relative goodness of match of the stimulus information with the relevant prototype descriptions. The model is called a fuzzy logical model of perception (abbreviated FLMP).

Central to the FLMP are summary descriptions of the perceptual units of the language. These summary descriptions are called prototypes and they contain a conjunction of various properties called features. A prototype is a category and the features of the prototype correspond to the ideal values that an exemplar should have if it is a member of that category. The exact form of the representation of these properties is not known and may never be known. However, the memory representation must be compatible with the sensory representation resulting from the transduction of the audible and visible speech. Compatibility is necessary because the two representations must be related to one another. To recognize the syllable /ba/, the perceiver must be able to relate the information provided by the syllable itself to some memory of the category /ba/.

Prototypes are generated for the task at hand. In speech perception, for example, we might envisage activation of all prototypes corresponding to the perceptual units of the language being spoken. For ease of exposition, consider a speech signal representing a single perceptual unit, such as the syllable /ba/. The sensory systems transduce the physical event and make available various sources of information called features. During the first operation in the model, the features are evaluated in terms of the prototypes in memory. For each feature and for each prototype, featural evaluation provides information about the degree to which the feature in the speech signal matches the featural value of the prototype.

Given the necessarily large variety of features, it is necessary to have a common metric representing the degree of match of each feature. The syllable /ba/, for example, might have visible featural information related to the closing of the lips and audible information corresponding to the second and third formant transitions. These two features must share a common metric if they eventually are going to be related to one another. To serve this purpose, fuzzy truth values (Zadeh, 1965) are used because they provide a natural representation of the degree of match. Fuzzy truth values lie between zero and one, corresponding to a proposition being completely false and completely true. The value .5 corresponds to a completely ambiguous situation whereas .7 would be more true than false and so on. Fuzzy truth values, therefore, not only can represent continuous rather than just categorical information, they also can represent different kinds of information. Another advantage of fuzzy truth values is that they couch information in mathematical terms (or at least in a quantitative form). This allows the natural development of a quantitative description of the phenomenon of interest.

Feature evaluation provides the degree to which each feature in the syllable matches the corresponding feature in each prototype in memory. The goal, of course, is to determine the overall goodness of match of each prototype with the syllable. All of the features are capable of contributing to this process and the second operation of the model is called feature integration. That is, the features (actually the degree of match of each feature) corresponding to each prototype are combined (or "conjoined" in logical terms). The outcome of feature integration consists of the degree to which each prototype matches the syllable. In the model, all features contribute to the final value, but with the property that the least ambiguous features have the most impact on the outcome.

The third operation during recognition processing is decision. During this stage, the merit of each relevant prototype is evaluated relative to the sum of the merits of the other relevant prototypes. This relative goodness of match gives the proportion of times the syllable is identified as an instance of the prototype. The relative goodness of match could also be determined from a rating judgment indicating the degree to which the syllable matches the category. The pattern classification operation is modelled after Luce's (1959) choice rule. In pandemonium-like terms (Selfridge, 1959), we might say that it is not how loud some demon is shouting but rather the relative loudness of that demon in the crowd of relevant demons. An important prediction of the model is that one feature has its greatest effect when a second feature is at its most ambiguous level. Thus, the most informative feature has the greatest impact on the judgment.

Figure 1 illustrates the three stages involved in pattern recognition. Auditory and visual sources of information are represented by uppercase letters. The evaluation process transforms these into psychological values (indicated by lowercase letters) that are then integrated to give an overall value. The classification operation maps this value into some response, such as a discrete decision or a rating. The model confronts several important issues in describing speech perception. One issue has to do with whether multiple sources of information are evaluated in speech perception. Two other issues have to do with the evaluation of the sources, in that we ask whether continuous information is available from each source and whether the output of evaluation of one source is contaminated by the other source. The issue of categorical versus continuous perception can also be raised with respect to the output of the integration process. Questions about integration assess whether the components passed on by evaluation are integrated into some higher-order representation and how the two sources of information are integrated.

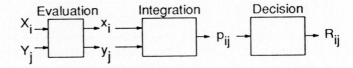

Figure 1. Schematic representation of the three operations involved in perceptual recognition.

The theoretical framework of the FLMP has proven to be a valuable framework for the study of speech perception. Experiments designed in this framework have provided important information concerning the sources of information in speech perception, and how these sources of information are processed to support speech perception. The experiments have studied a broad range of information sources, including bottom-up sources such as audible and visible characteristics of speech and top-down sources, including phonological, lexical, syntactic, and semantic constraints (Massaro, 1987).

Watching a speaker's face and lips provides important information in speech perception and language understanding (Sumby & Pollack, 1954). This visible speech is particularly effective when the auditory speech is degraded, because of noise, bandwidth filtering, or hearing-impairment. In a noisy environment with -12 dB S/N ratio using a continuous prose background, accuracy of sentence perception with a view of the speaker's face was 65% correct versus 23% correct when no visual information was presented (Summerfield, 1979). The perception of short sentences that have been bandpass filtered improves from 23% to

79% correct when subjects are permitted a view of the speaker (Breeuwer & Plomp, 1985). For hearing-impaired adults, lip-reading the speaker improves consonant recognition from 55% to 80% correct (Walden, Prosek, & Worthington, 1975).

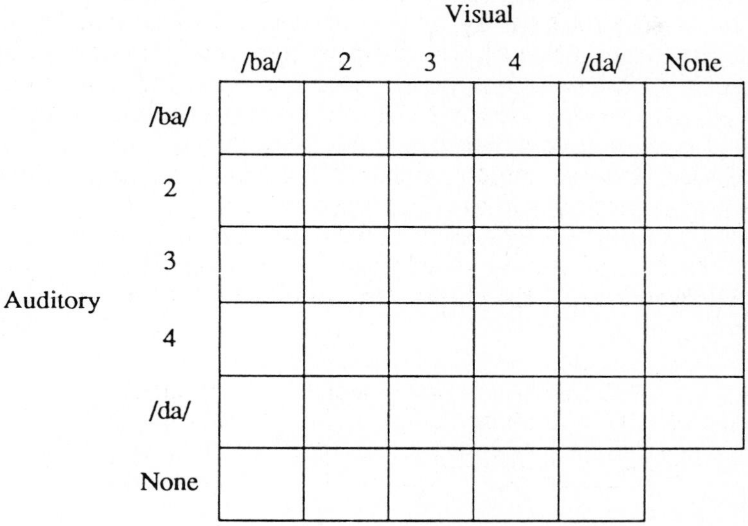

Visual

	/ba/	2	3	4	/da/	None
/ba/						
2						
3						
4						
/da/						
None						

Auditory

Figure 2. Expansion of a typical factorial design to include auditory and visual conditions presented alone. The five levels along the auditory and visible continua represent auditory and visible speech syllables varying in equal steps between /ba/ and /da/.

The strong influence of visible speech is not limited to situations with degraded auditory input, however. McGurk and MacDonald (1976) demonstrated that visual articulation has an important influence even when paired with perfectly intelligible speech sounds. We have all noticed the discrepancy of sight and sound in dubbed movies, but McGurk and MacDonald modified the situation to illustrate the power of visible speech. They dubbed a visible articulation such as /pa-pa/ with the speech sounds /na-na/. This dubbed speech event gives a situation with perfectly intelligible auditory speech presented with a contradictory visual articulation. The surprising perceptual experience has come to be known as the McGurk effect. Even though subjects were asked to indicate what they heard, a strong effect of the visual source of information was observed. Faced with the visible articulation /pa-pa/, paired with the sounds /na-na/, subjects often reported hearing /ma-ma/. A perceiver's recognition of an auditory-visual syllable reflects the contribution of both sound and sight. If an auditory syllable /ba/ is dubbed onto a videotape of a speaker saying /da/, subjects often perceive the speaker to be saying /tha/ (Massaro, 1987).

An expanded factorial design offers the potential of addressing important issues in speech perception. I will describe an experiment manipulating auditory and visual information in a speech perception task. The novel design illustrated in Figure 2 provides a unique method of addressing the issues of the evaluation and integration of audible and visible information in speech perception. In this experiment, five levels of audible speech varying between /ba/ and /da/ are crossed with five levels of visible speech varying between the same alternatives. The audible and visible speech also are presented alone giving a total of $25 + 5 + 5 = 35$ independent stimulus conditions.

2. METHOD

2.1 Subjects

Eleven college students from the University of California, Santa Cruz, participated for one hour in the experiment.

2.2 Test Stimuli

Auditory tokens of a male speaker's /ba/ and /da/ were analyzed using linear prediction to derive a set of parameters for driving a software formant serial resonator speech synthesizer (Klatt, 1980). By altering the parametric information specifying the first 80 msec of the consonant-vowel syllable, a set of five 400 msec syllables covering the range from /ba/ to /da/ was created. During the first 80 msec, the first formant (F1) went from 250 Hz to 700 Hz following a negatively accelerated path. (Formants are bands of energy in the syllable that normally result from natural resonances of the vocal tract in real speech.) The F2 followed a negatively accelerated path to 1199 Hz, beginning with one of nine values equally spaced between 1000 and 2000 Hz from most /ba/-like to most /da/-like, respectively. The F3 followed a linear transition to 2729 Hz from one of nine values equally spaced between 2200 and 3200 Hz. All other stimulus characteristics were identical for the nine auditory syllables. These stimuli were stored in digital form for play-back during the experiment.

The visible speech synthesis was based on the work of Parke (1982), who developed an animated face by modelling the facial surface as a polyhedral object composed of about 900 small surfaces arranged in three dimensions and joined together at the edges. The surface was shaded to achieve a natural appearance of the skin. The face was animated by altering the location of various points in the face under the control of 50 parameters. About 11 parameters control speech animation. These specify the duration of the segment, the manner of articulation, jaw opening angle, mouth x and z values, width of the lip corners, mouth corner x, y, and z offsets, lower lip /f/ tuck, degree of upper lip raise, and x and z teeth offset. There is no tongue in the current version. Software provided by Pearce, Wyvill, Wyvill, and Hill (1986) was implemented and modified on a Silicon Graphics Inc IRIS 3030 computer to create synthetic visible speech syllables. The control parameters were changed over time to produce a realistic articulation of a consonant-vowel syllable. By modifying the parameters appropriately, a five-step /ba/ to /da/ visible speech continuum was synthesized.

The synthetic visible speech was created frame by frame and recorded on a Betacam video recorder which was later transferred to 3/4" U-matic video tape. The five levels of visible speech were edited to a second 3/4" tape according to a randomized sequence in blocks of 35 trials. There was a 28 sec interval between blocks of trials. Six unique test blocks were recorded with the 35 test items presented in each block. The edited tape was copied to 1/2" VHS tape for use during the experiment. It was played on a Panasonic NV-9200 and fed to individual NEC C12-202A 12" colour monitors. The auditory speech was presented over the speaker of the NEC monitor. The presentation of the auditory synthetic speech was synchronized with the visible speech for the bimodal stimulus presentations. This synchronization gave the strong illusion that the synthetic speech was coming from the mouth of the speaker.

Subjects were instructed to listen and to watch the speaker, and to identify the syllable as /ba/ or /da/. Each of the 35 possible stimuli were presented a total of 12 times during two sessions of six blocks of trials in each session. The subjects identified each stimulus during a 2 second response interval.

3. RESULTS AND DISCUSSION

The observed proportion of /da/ identifications was computed for each subject for each of the 35 conditions. The mean proportion of /da/ identifications across subjects is shown by the points in Figure 3. As can be seen, the proportion of /da/ responses significantly increased across the visual continuum, both for the unimodal, $F(4,40) = 74.78$, $p < .001$, and bimodal, $F(4,40) = 16.50$, $p < .001$, conditions. Similarly, the proportion of /da/ responses significantly increased across the auditory continuum, for both the unimodal, $F(4,40) = 61.23$, $p < .001$, and bimodal, $F(4,40) = 30.82$, $p < .001$, conditions. There was also a significant auditory visual interaction, $F(16,160) = 4.61$, $p < .001$, in the bimodal condition, because each stimulus dimension had its greatest effect to the extent that the other was most ambiguous.

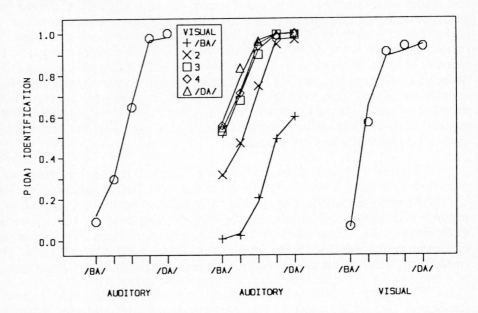

Figure 3. Observed (points) and predicted (lines) proportion of /da/ identifications for the auditory alone (left panel), bimodal (centre panel), and visual alone (right panel) conditions as a function of synthetic auditory and visual stimulus conditions. The lines give the predictions for the FLMP.

Applying the model to the present task using auditory and visual speech, both sources are assumed to provide continuous and independent evidence for the alternatives /ba/ and /da/. Defining the onsets of the second (F2) and third (F3) formants as the important auditory feature and the degree of initial opening of the Lips as the important visual feature, the prototype for /da/ would be:

/da/   :   Slightly Falling F2-F3 & Open Lips.

The prototype for /ba/ would be defined in an analogous fashion,

/ba/   :   Rising F2-F3 & Closed Lips,

and so on for the other response alternatives. Given that a prototype has independent specifications for the auditory and visual sources, the value of one source cannot change the value of the other source at the prototype matching stage. The integration of the features defining each prototype is evaluated according to the product of the feature values. If aD_i represents the degree to which the auditory stimulus A_i supports the alternative /da/, that is, has Slightly Falling F2-F3; and vD_j represents the degree to which the visual stimulus V_j supports the alternative /da/, that is, has Open Lips, then the outcome of prototype matching for /da/ would be:

$$/da/ \quad : \quad aD_i\, vD_j$$

where the subscripts i and j index the levels of the auditory and visual modalities, respectively. Analogously, if aB_i represents the degree to which the auditory stimulus A_i has Rising F2-F3 and vB_j represents the degree to which the visual stimulus v_j has Closed Lips, the outcome of prototype matching for /ba/ would be:

$$/ba/ \quad : \quad aB_i\, vB_j$$

Given the contrasting alternatives /da/ and /ba/, it is reasonable to assume that the feature values for /ba/ are the negation of those for /da/. Following fuzzy logic (Zadeh, 1965), negation is implemented as the additive complement. In this case, aB_i is one minus aD_i and vB_j is one minus vD_j. Thus, the outcome of prototype matching for /ba/ would be:

$$/ba/ \quad : \quad (1 - aD_i)\, (1 - vD_j)$$

The decision operation would determine their relative merit leading to the prediction that

$$P(/da/ \mid A_i\, V_j) = aD_i\, vD_j / \Sigma \tag{1}$$

where Σ is equal to the sum of the merit of the /ba/ and /da/ alternatives.

The important assumption of the FLMP is that the auditory source supports each alternative to some degree and analogously for the visual source. Each alternative is defined by ideal values of the auditory and visual information. Each level of a source supports each alternative to differing degrees represented by feature values. The feature values representing the degree of support from the auditory and visual information for a given alternative are integrated following the multiplicative rule given by the FLMP. The model requires 5 parameters for the visual feature values and 5 parameters for the auditory feature values.

The FLMP was fit to the individual results of each of the 11 subjects. The quantitative predictions of the model are determined by using the program STEPIT (Chandler, 1969). The model is represented to the program in terms of a set of prediction equations and a set of unknown parameters. By iteratively adjusting the parameters of the model, the program minimizes the squared deviations between the observed and predicted points. The outcome of the program STEPIT is a set of parameter values which, when put into the model, come closest to predicting the observed results. Thus, STEPIT maximizes the accuracy of the description of each model. The goodness-of-fit of the model is given by the root mean square deviation (RMSD) - the square root of the average squared deviation between the predicted and observed values. The lines in Figure 3 give the average predictions of FLMP. The model provides a good description of the identifications of both the unimodal and bimodal syllables with an average RMSD of .0574 across the individual subject fits.

Table 1 gives the average best fitting parameters of the FLMP. As can be seen in the table, the parameter values change in a systematic fashion across the five levels of the audible and visible synthetic speech.

Table 1

The average best fitting parameters of the FLMP. The values lie between 0 and 1 and represent the degree to which the alternative /da/ is supported by auditory and visual sources of information.

Dim	/ba/	2	3	4	/da/
aD_i	.1206	.3054	.6653	.9667	.9805
vD_j	.0623	.6525	.8880	.9129	.9452

It is essential to contrast one model with other models that make alternative assumptions. One alternative is a categorical model of perception (CMP). It assumes that only categorical information is available from the auditory and visual sources and that the identification judgment is based on separate decisions to the auditory and visual sources. Considering the /ba/ identification, the visual and auditory decisions could be /ba/-/ba/, /ba/-/da/, /da/-/ba/, or /da/-/da/. If the two decisions about a given speech event agree, the identification response can follow either source. When the two decisions disagree, it is assumed that the subject will respond with a decision based upon the auditory source on some proportion p of the trials, and with a decision based upon the visual source on the remainder $(1-p)$ of the trials. The weight p reflects the relative dominance of the auditory source.

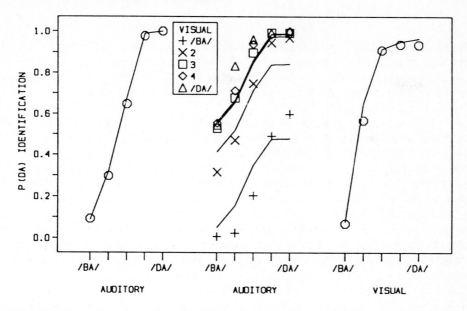

Figure 4. Observed (points) and predicted (lines) proportion of /da/ identifications for the auditory alone (left panel), bimodal (centre panel), and visual alone (right panel) conditions as a function of synthetic auditory and visual stimulus conditions. The lines give the predictions for the CMP.

The probability of *a* /ba/ identification response, $P(/ba/)$, given a particular auditory/visual speech event, A_iV_j, would be:

$$P(/ba/|\ A_i\ V_j) = (1)\ aB_i\ vB_j + (p)\ aB_i\ (1-vB_j) + (1-p)(1-aB_i)\ vB_j + (0)\ (1-aB_i)(1-vB_j)$$

$$(2)$$

where i and j index the levels of the auditory and visual modalities, respectively. The aB_i value represents the probability of *a* /ba/ decision given the auditory level i, and vB_j is the probability of *a* /ba/ decision given the visual level j. The value p reflects the bias to follow the auditory source. Each of the four terms in the equation represents the likelihood of one of the four possible outcomes multiplied by the probability of *a* /ba/ identification response given that outcome. To fit this model to the results, each unique level of the auditory stimulus requires a unique parameter aB_i, and analogously for vB_j. The modeling of /ba/ responses thus requires 5 auditory parameters plus 5 visual parameters. The additional p value would be fixed across all conditions for a total of 11 parameters. Thus, we have a fair comparison to the FLMP which requires 10 parameters.

The CMP was fit to the individual results in the same manner as in the fit of the FLMP. Figure 4 gives the average observed results and the average predicted results of the CMP. As can be seen in the figure, the CMP gave a poor description of the observed results. The RMSD was .1047, compared to the average RMSD of .0574 for the FLMP.

In summary, the present framework provides a valuable approach to the study of speech perception. We have learned about some of the fundamental stages of processing involved in speech perception by ear and eye, and how multiple sources of information are used in speech perception. Given the potential for evaluating and integrating multiple sources of information in speech perception and understanding, no single source should be considered necessary. There is now good evidence that perceivers have continuous information about the various sources of information, each source is evaluated, and all sources are integrated in speech perception. Future work should address the nature of the variety of sources of information, and how they function in recovering the speaker's message. Finally, it is of interest that the present theoretical framework and the FLMP also provide an account of decision making (Massaro, 1989).

ACKNOWLEDGMENTS

The research reported in this paper and the writing of the paper were supported, in part, by grants from the Public Health Service (PHS R01 NS 20314) and the graduate division of the University of California, Santa Cruz. The author would like to thank Michael Cohen for eclectic assistance.

Correspondence concerning this paper should be addressed to Dominic Massaro, Program in Experimental Psychology, University of California, Santa Cruz, CA 95064.

REFERENCES

Breeuwer, M., & Plomp, R. (1985). Speech reading supplemented with formant-frequency information for voiced speech. Journal of the Acoustical Society of America, 77, 314 - 317.

Chandler, J. P. (1969). Subroutine STEPIT - finds local minima of a smooth function of several parameters. Behavioural Science, 14, 81-82.

Luce, R. D. (1959). Individual choice behaviour. New York: Wiley.

Massaro, D. W. (1987). Speech perception by ear and eye: A paradigm for psychological inquiry. Hillsdale, NJ: Lawrence Erlbaum Associates. .

Massaro, D. W. (1989). A pattern recognition account of decision making. Proceedings of the XXIV International Congress of Psychology.

McGurk, H., & MacDonald, J. (1976). Hearing lips and seeing voices. Nature, 264, 746-748.

Parke, F. I. (1982). Parametized models for facial animation. IEEE Computer Graphics, 2(9), 61-68.

Pearce, A., Wyvill, B., Wyvill, G., & Hill, D. (1986). Speech and expression: A computer solution to face animation. Graphics interface "86.

Selfridge, O. G. (1959). Pandemonium: A paradigm for learning. In Mechanization of thought processes (pp. 511-526). London: Her Majesty's Stationery Office. .

Sumby, W. H., & Pollack, I. (1954). Visual contribution to speech intelligibility in noise.Journal of the Acoustical Society of America, 26,\f1 212-215.

Summerfield, A. Q. (1979). Use of visual information for phonetic perception. Phonetica, 36, 314-331.

Walden, B. E., Prosek, R. A., & Worthington, D. W. (1975). Auditory and audiovisual feature transmission in hearing-impaired adults. Journal of Speech and Hearing Research, 18, 272-280.

Zadeh, L. A. (1965). Fuzzy sets.Information and Control, 8, 338-353.

Human Information Processing: Measures,
Mechanisms, and Models. D. Vickers and P.L. Smith (eds.)
© *Elsevier Science Publishers B.V. (North-Holland), 1989*

A DISTRIBUTED MEMORY MODEL FOR ASSOCIATIVE LEARNING

Stephan Lewandowsky

University of Western Australia

and

Bennet B. Murdock

University of Toronto

A version of Murdock's Theory of distributed Memory is presented and is applied to data on associative learning. It is shown that this distributed memory model, which uses a feedback loop to regulate learning, can handle some classic data on associative learning and interference with few parameters and at a quantitative level. In addition, some list discrimination data can be explained by simple manipulation of a response criterion and without requiring separate item-to-list associations.

1. INTRODUCTION

In a distributed memory model, all information in memory is stored in one common location, without maintaining a one-to-one mapping of stimulus items to representations in memory. In comparison with the common 'looks-in-the-library' localized storage view, a distributed memory model has various advantages: search is not required for retrieval, and local damage can be sustained without complete failure.

Distributed memory models have been applied in a number of areas, for example, memory for serial order (Lewandowsky & Murdock, 1989) or item and associative information (Murdock, 1982). In this article we present a version of Murdock's (1982) Theory of distributed Associative Memory (TODAM) and show that it can account for a number of classic data in associative learning.

2. TODAM

In TODAM, items are represented as vectors consisting of a large number (N) of elements, each drawn from a Gaussian distribution. Item information, as required for a recognition decision, is represented by the addition of each item vector to the common memory vector, called M. Associative information, such as the associations between A and B members in a list of paired associates, is represented by the *convolution* of the two constituent items. Convolution is an operation defined for functions or vectors that combines two items into a single vector, which is then also added to M. Thus the storage equation in TODAM is given by

$$M_j = M_{j-1} + A_j + B_j + A_j * B_j, \tag{1}$$

where $A_j * B_j$ represents the convolution of items A and B, and M_{j-1} and M_j represent the state of the memory vector before and after the jth pair has been added. Note that encoding of new information does not result in a new memory trace, or a change in size of M, but only in an update of the memory vector.

During paired associate recall, the subject is presented with item A and must recall item B. In TODAM, A is *correlated* (correlation is the approximate inverse of convolution) with M, which results in an approximation (B′) to the desired response, B. If B′ bears more resemblance (has a greater dot product) to B than to any other possible response member, and if that resemblance falls between two tolerance criteria (ax and bx), a correct response is scored.

The above, simplified model is quite capable of handling some basic item and associative phenomena, but not learning (Murdock, 1982). Several learning mechanisms were suggested in Murdock (1989); here we explore one. It turns out that learning can be induced quite readily by installing a feedback loop that regulates the encoding of new information by what has already been added to memory. A simple version of this *closed-loop* model was used in Lewandowsky and Murdock (1989), but for the present application a more robust, albeit more complicated, model was used. Its storage equation is given by

$$M_j = M_{j-1} + k E \tag{2}$$

where k is a parameter and E represents the 'error', or the discrepancy between what needs to be learned and what has already been encoded:

$$E \quad = \quad (A_j * B_j) - (A_j * B_j') \text{ or}$$

$$(3)$$

$$= \quad A_j * (B_j - B_j').$$

B is the to-be-learned response member, and B′ is the currently retrievable approximation to that item. Consider the situation at the outset of learning: B′ is approximately 0, since no information has thus far been acquired. Thus, on the average, the information added on the first learning trial is simply the pair A-B weighted by k. Now consider a trial late in learning: B′ may resemble B very closely, reducing E almost to 0, and leading to very little new information being added. It can be appreciated how this feedback loop keeps M 'within bounds'; as learning proceeds, less and less new information is added to M.

3. THE SIMULATIONS

To demonstrate the general feasibility of this model, we applied TODAM to a number of classic data in associative learning by way of computer simulations. The simulations required somewhere between two and four parameters. The size of the memory vector was specified by the number (N) of elements and, to minimize computing time, was kept as small as possible without sacrificing the level of performance required by the particular empirical data. The parameter k determined the rate of learning, and typically ranged from 0.02 to 0.05. The lower tolerance criterion ax was always zero, and bx (upper criterion) was set to infinity, unless otherwise mentioned. In consequence, with bx set to infinity, errors would only occur in the simulations if the greatest dot product was between B′ and a response member other than B. Another parameter, ρ, was required to implement similarity relations between study items. The parameter ρ was the theoretical correlation coefficient between the distributions for corresponding pairs of features in any two items. Thus, for sampling of independent items ρ would be zero, whereas a ρ of unity would result in a pair of identical items. Different values of ρ were used to describe pairwise within-list similarity (i.e., all items share a semantic category) or pairwise between-list similarity (i.e., responses used in two different lists all come from the same category). As in previous applications (Lewandowsky & Murdock, 1989), the goodness of fit of the predicted points to the data is shown by juxtaposition of the patterns in the figures below.

3.1 Barnes and Underwood

In 1959, Barnes and Underwood studied unlearning and

interference between lists of paired associates. Subjects learned a first list (A-B) to a criterion of one perfect recall of all eight responses and were then given a second list for further study. Stimulus members were the same on the second list, and response members either were similar to those used on the first list (usually called A-B′ we use A-B* to avoid confusion with the retrieved approximation B′; see Eq (3)), or were unrelated (A-C). It will come as no surprise that subjects had greater difficulty learning the unrelated new responses (C) to the old stimuli than learning the related responses (B*). After varying degrees of learning of List 2, subjects had to recall *both* responses to each cue (B and B* or B and C, depending on condition) and assign each response to a list. This MMFR procedure was chosen to rule out response competition, which to that date had been considered to be a major factor in interference and forgetting. The top panels of Figures 1 and 2 show the MMFR data for the A-C and A-B* condition, respectively.

In both conditions, the (negatively accelerated) learning curve for List 2 is parallelled by a (positively accelerated) forgetting curve for List 1. It is of interest that virtually no forgetting occurs for List 1 in the A-B* condition, whereas substantial forgetting results from studying a second list with unrelated, new response members. One popular explanation for the absence of forgetting in the A-B* condition has invoked *response mediation* (Barnes & Underwood, 1959, p. 104). According to this explanation the subject does not replace each A-B association with the corresponding A-B* association, but instead associates B* to the existing bonds to form a triplet A-B-B*. Perhaps TODAM, which only contains associations between *pairs* of items, can provide an alternative interpretation for these data.

Simulation of the experiment was quite straightforward, once a scoring mechanism for the MMFR procedure had been agreed upon. When A is presented as cue during retrieval, the retrieved approximation (B′/C′) resembles both responses that have previously been associated with A. There are two possible ways of disambiguating the retrieved information. The maximum resemblance between B′/C′ and the possible responses could either be computed by comparing across both lists simultaneously, or by establishing a separate maximum for each list. In the former case, the two largest resemblance values would be output as responses regardless of list membership, whereas in the latter case each list-wise maximum would be the response for that particular list. It turned out that both scoring procedures led to nearly identical predictions, and we chose the latter, simpler, scheme.

The bottom panels of Figures 1 and 2 show the simulation results. The values for $\underline{k}$ and N were 0.06 and 149, respectively, for both conditions, whereas the value of ρ was 0.2 for the A-C condition and 0.8

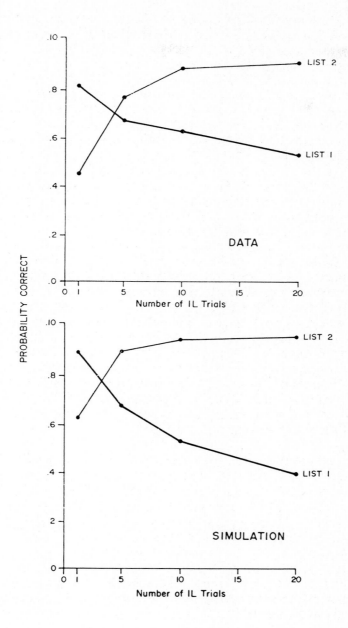

Figure 1. Observed (top panel) and simulated (bottom) results from the A-C condition in Barnes and Underwood (1959).

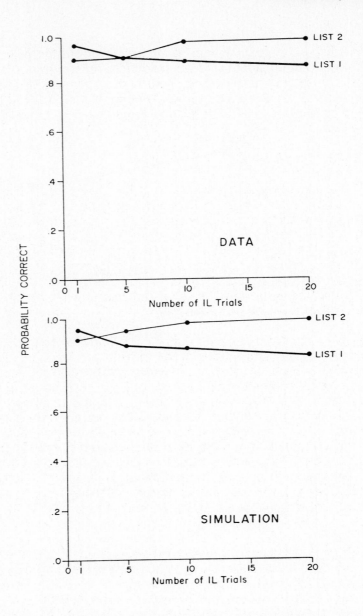

Figure 2. Observed (top panel) and simulated (bottom) results from the A-B* condition in Barnes and Underwood (1959).

for the A-B* condition. That is, each C was similar to the corresponding B by a value of 0.2, whereas each B* was similar to its B by 0.8. Within each list, on the other hand, items were independent. TODAM clearly captures the pattern of the data, although the unlearning of List 1 responses is somewhat too rapid in the A-C condition (Figure 1, bottom panel). It turns out that the rate of unlearning depends directly on the value of ρ, with independent C items leading to unlearning of B items in a few trials, and related items being more resistant to unlearning. In fact, the results of the A-B* condition fell out of the simulation simply by choosing a greater value of ρ: no response mediation or triple associations were required.

3.2 Thune and Underwood

What happens if, instead of using the more liberal MMFR procedure, subjects are required to report the appropriate response only? For example, during relearning of an original list, all responses from the intervening List 2 can be counted as intrusions. This procedure differs from Barnes and Underwood (1959) only in the instructions given to subjects during recall (or relearning), and was reported by Thune and Underwood (1943). Subjects had to learn List 1 for five trials, then received a varying number of interpolated learning (IL) trials on List 2 (A-C), and relearned List 1 to criterion.

When simulating these data, care had to be taken that no fundamentally new assumptions were introduced from the Barnes and Underwood simulation, since the only major difference between the two experiments was subjects' instructions. Thus, B′/C′ was compared to responses from both lists simultaneously, and the response associated with the maximum resemblance was scored as correct only if it was from List 1, and if it fell between $\underline{ax}$ and $\underline{bx}$. The value for $\underline{ax}$ was always zero, whereas that of $\underline{bx}$ was moved from infinity to approximately 0.10 during relearning, to model subjects' ability to reject overlearned responses from List 2. Although the pattern of predictions is unaffected if $\underline{bx}$ remains unchanged across levels of IL, we report the best-fitting simulation in which the exact magnitude of $\underline{bx}$ varied with the number of IL trials (see Figure 3).

Figure 3 shows relearning performance on Trials 1 and 4. The behavioural data show clear evidence of retroactive interference (RI) on Trial 1, where RI is proportional to the degree of IL, and also a release from RI by Trial 4, where performance is unaffected by IL. In the simulation (N=499, $\underline{k}$=0.015), even though it predicts RI at the outset of relearning, no release from RI occurs; List 2 training has a detrimental effect even after four relearning trials. It is unclear why TODAM did not make the correct predictions.

Figure 4 presents a more in-depth analysis of the first relearning trial. The total RI is computed as the difference in performance between the condition that received no IL, and the conditions that received a varying number of List 2 trials. Data and simulation results are very similar in pattern. Intrusions (List 2 responses) were generated in the simulation if the greatest resemblance of B′/C′ was to an item from List 2

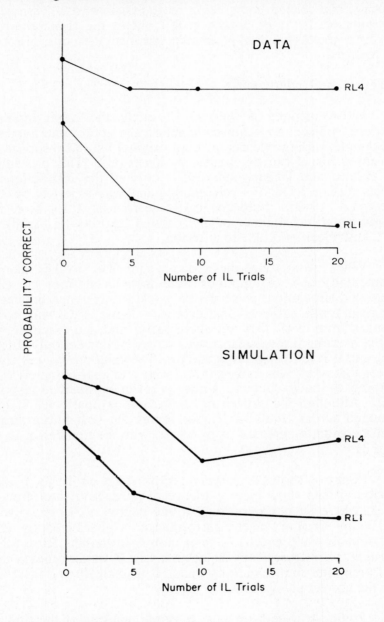

Figure 3. Observed (top panel) and simulated (bottom) results for the relearning phase in Thune and Underwood (1943). Values of bx for the simulation were .14, .13, .10, and .10 for 0,...,20 IL trials.

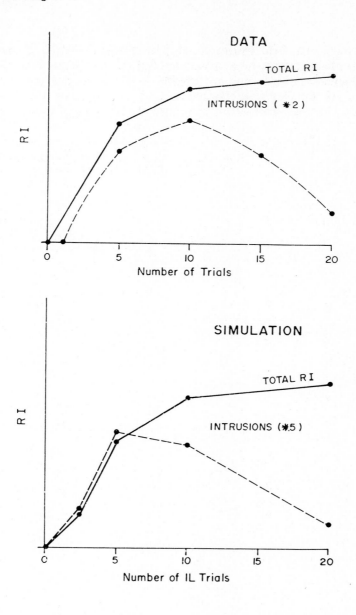

Figure 4. Observed (top panel) and simulated (bottom) total RI and intrusions in Thune and Underwood (1943).

and if it fell between <u>ax</u> and <u>bx</u>. The simulated pattern of intrusions is of the same inverted U-shape as the empirical data, although, owing to computing time restrictions and the consequent limitation on the magnitude of N, the absolute values for intrusions are too large by a factor of four. The qualitative pattern of the prediction derives from the placement of bx: early during List 2 learning, few List 2 responses are learned well enough to be given as intrusions. Later on, as learning progresses, more intrusions are made. With large amounts of IL, List 2 responses are overlearned relative to List 1 items, and their resemblance falls above the bx cutoff - thus reducing the number of intrusions.

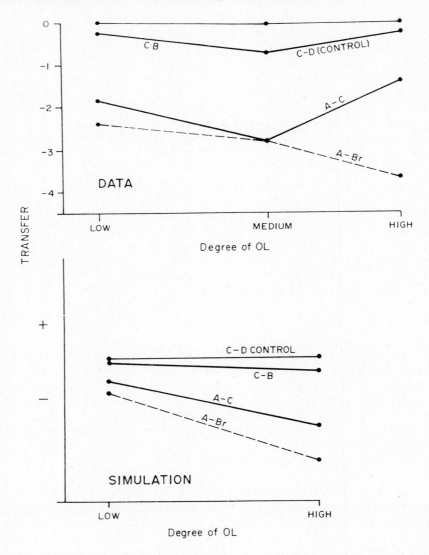

Figure 5. Observed (top panel; Postman, 1962) and simulated (bottom) transfer effects as a function of degree of original learning.

3.3 Degree of learning and transfer

Transfer to a second list can be observed after varying degrees of original learning (OL) on List 1. The top panel of Figure 5 shows a representative pattern obtained by Postman (1962).

It is clear from this figure, and many other studies, that transfer to a list in which the original response members and the original stimuli are re-paired (A-Br) is most disruptive, and increasingly so with increasing degrees of OL. At the other extreme, changing to new stimuli (C-B) shows little effect in relation to the C-D control, regardless of degree of OL. The exact behaviour of the A-C transfer condition, on the other hand, is unknown. Whereas some authors have confirmed the U-shaped function of Figure 6, others (e.g., Mandler & Heinemann, 1956) have obtained linearly increasing negative transfer with increasing degree of OL.

TODAM's simulation of the transfer data is shown in the bottom panel of Figure 5. Degree of OL on an eight-pair list was either low (5 trials) or high (15 trials), and in addition to the standard two parameters (N=299, k=0.03) $\rho(0.5)$ was needed to generate lists with a pairwise intra-list similarity structure. On each list, each response (or stimulus) member resembled every other response (or stimulus) member to the degree specified by ρ. With this assumption about similarity, TODAM predicts the correct pattern and rank ordering in the data.

3.4 Transfer surfaces

The data from the foregoing application, and indeed many others, can be summarized by plotting transfer as a function of the similarity between stimuli and responses across the two lists. If the two types of similarity are plotted along the two dimensions of the plane, and transfer is plotted as vertical deflection from the baseline (C-D), a surface results that provides a good description of many experiments on transfer. This is the Osgood surface (Osgood, 1949) and is a comprehensive summary of the empirical data existing at the time.

The results of the corresponding simulation ($\underline{k}$=0.03, N=299) are shown in Figure 6, together with the values for the pairwise between-list similarity for stimuli and responses. The surface plotted in the figure is very similar to the empirically observed pattern, which is therefore omitted.

4. DISCUSSION

The foregoing simulations demonstrate that a distributed memory model can capture some of the more important associative learning phenomena. Moreover, beyond merely describing the data, the simulations provided some interesting conceptual insights. For example, the simulation of the Barnes and Underwood (1959) data showed that response mediation is not required to account for their A-B* transfer data. This is an interesting conclusion, given the popularity the mediation view once enjoyed. Furthermore, TODAM can handle at least some list discrimination problems (e.g. Thune & Underwood, 1943) without requiring item-to-list associations. The inverted U-shaped function for

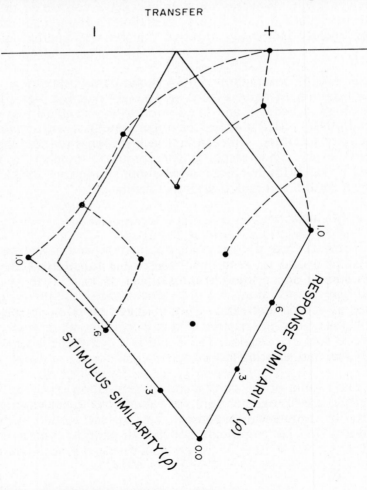

Figure 6. Osgood transfer surface predicted by TODAM.

intrusions fell out of the model simply by introducing an upper response criterion (bx). Similarly, the ordering of transfer conditions and the linear relation of transfer to degree of OL, were obtained without parameter manipulation. Finally, the Osgood transfer surface was also obtained with no manipulation other than changing the values of ρ, which is a straightforward implementation of the experimental procedure.

In closing, it must be pointed out that other theories (e.g., ACT; Anderson, 1983, or SAM; Mensink & Raaijmakers, 1989) can also handle a variety of associative effects. SAM in particular has been applied to an impressive array of phenomena, and thus TODAM's contribution must be seen as providing an alternative interpretation to classic interference data.

ACKNOWLEDGEMENT

This research was supported in part by grant APA 146 to the second author from NSERC Canada, and a CTEC equipment grant to the department of Psychology at the University of Western Australia.

Address correspondence to the authors at the department of Psychology, University of Toronto, Toronto, Ontario M5S 1A1, Canada.

REFERENCES

Anderson, J R (1983). A spreading-activation theory of memory Journal of Verbal Learning and Verbal Behaviour, 22, 261-295.

Barnes, J M., & Underwood, B J (1959). "Fate" of first-list associations in transfer theory Journal of Experimental Psychology, 58, 97-105.

Lewandowsky, S., & Murdock, B B (1989). Memory for serial order Psychological Review, in press.

Mandler, G., & Heinemann, S H (1956). Effect of overlearning of a verbal response on transfer of training Journal of Experimental Psychology, 57, 39-46.

Mensink, G.J., & Raaijmakers, J G W (1989). A model for interference and forgetting Psychological Review, in press.

Murdock, B B (1982). A theory for the storage and retrieval of item and associative information Psychological Review, 89, 609-626.

Murdock, B B (1989). Learning in a distributed memory model In C. Izawa (Ed.),
       Current issues in cognitive processes: The Tulane Flowerree symposium in
       cognition. Hillsdale, NJ: Erlbaum, in press.

Osgood, C E (1949). The similarity paradox in human learning: A resolution.
       Psychological Review, 56, 132-143.

Postman, L (1962). Transfer of training as a function of experimental paradigm and
       degree of first-list learning Journal of Verbal Learning and Verbal Behaviour,
       1, 109-118.

Thune, L E., & Underwood, B J (1943). Retroactive inhibition as a function of degree of
       interpolated learning Journal of Experimental Psychology, 32, 185-200.

Human Information Processing: Measures,
Mechanisms, and Models, D. Vickers and P.L. Smith (eds.)
© Elsevier Science Publishers B.V. (North-Holland), 1989

RECOGNITION IN A DISTRIBUTED-MEMORY MODEL

Bennet B. Murdock and William E. Hockley

University of Toronto

In this paper we review MIM, a Memory Interrogation Model for the decision processes involved in recognition memory, and show how it can be extended to judgments of frequency. MIM assumes that the output from the memory comparison stage is mixed with extraneous random noise and fed into a two-criterion decision stage which can respond "new," "old," or wait. After a wait outcome the noise is resampled and the distance between the decision criteria is reduced. This model is able to describe much of the accuracy and latency data from several recognition-memory paradigms with a relatively small number of free parameters. In the application to judgments of frequency, multiple strength distributions corresponding to presentation frequencies are assumed. A counter is associated with each frequency band and one of these counters is incremented after each loop of the decision cycle. The process terminates when a criterion value is reached. This extension of MIM is able to account for several aspects of the data from an experiment on absolute judgments of frequency.

1. INTRODUCTION

In this paper we review MIM, a Memory Interrogation Model for recognition memory (Hockley & Murdock, 1987) and show how it can be extended to JOF (Judgments of Frequency). This later development is due to Hockley (1989) but we include it here to show that MIM can be generalized to tasks other than recognition memory. MIM is a decision model after Swets and Green (1961) and it can be interfaced with a distributed-memory model. However, it could also be coupled to other models as well (e.g. the SAM model of Gillund & Shiffrin, 1984, or the Minerva model of Hintzman, 1988).

The basic model is shown in Fig. 1. The results from the memory comparison process are mixed with extraneous random noise and fed into the decision system. The decision system has three options. If the (combined memory plus noise) input is less than the lower criterion (a), it responds "new." If it is greater than the upper criterion (b), it responds "old." Otherwise, it waits. During the wait interval the random noise fluctuates. There is no new memory comparison, but a new sample of extraneous noise is added to the original output from the memory comparison process. Given the presence of random noise, a single evaluation of the input will be error prone. Having a wait interval for ambiguous evaluations serves to decrease uncertainty. As we shall show, the wait option results in a reasonable speed-accuracy trade-off function and does so without any need to postulate the accumulation of information over time.

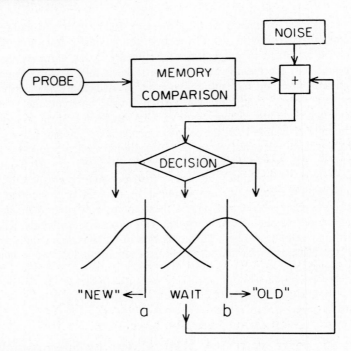

Figure 1. Decision model for item recognition.

The decision latency depends upon the number of cycles, or loops, that the decision system takes to reach a decision. This could be 1, 2, 3,.... cycles, and to avoid an infinite loop we assume the criteria come together, or converge, after each iteration. More specifically, the distance between a and b is reduced by CCR (Criterion Convergence Rate) after each iteration. CCR is one of the parameters of the model, and generally it is of the order of .10. We also have to specify the starting value of a (Astart) and the starting value of b (Bstart), and these are two more parameters of the model.

We need a function to map number of cycles into real time, and this mapping is given by

$$t = (k^2 + k + 2)BCT \qquad (1)$$

where t is time in msec, k is number of previous cycles, and BCT is Base Cycle Time (in msec). In the present applications BCT is set to 17.5 msec. Thus, the first loop of the decision cycle takes 35 msec.

The effect of this mapping function (Eq. 1) is to produce a progressive slow-down in the operation of the decision system. Each cycle takes longer than the previous cycle, and the increase is progressive. One can think of this as reactive inhibition. Also, there should be probably some variability in BCT if one is to avoid scalloping in the reaction-time distributions (Gronlund & Ratcliff, 1988).

We assume that decision latency is only one component of reaction time; there are other stages as well. We lump these together into a TOS (Time for Other Stages) distribution, and this is assumed to be a normal distribution with some mean and some variance. Finally, since this is a general decision model, we must assume some mean and variance for the underlying strength distributions of new and old items as well, and these can vary with experimental conditions. These parameters would be supplied by the memory model that MIM is interfaced with, but to keep the decision model general we have not yet coupled MIM to a memory model.

This then is MIM and, given the numerical values of the parameters, one can generate the reaction-time distributions for "yes" and "no" responses to old and new items (see Hockley & Murdock, 1987, for details). Using the fitting program of Ratcliff and Murdock (1976) one can then estimate the numerical values of the distributional parameters μ, σ and τ for any given set of data. We have done that for the four standard recognition-memory paradigms (Sternberg, study-test, continuous task, and prememorized lists), and we turn now to these applications.

2. APPLICATIONS OF MIM TO DATA

Figure 2 shows the fit of the model to data from a Sternberg task. The left panel shows the latency and accuracy data for correct rejections while the right panel shows the same for hits. As can be seen, the change in latency with set size is appreciably larger (about 4:1) for μ than for τ.

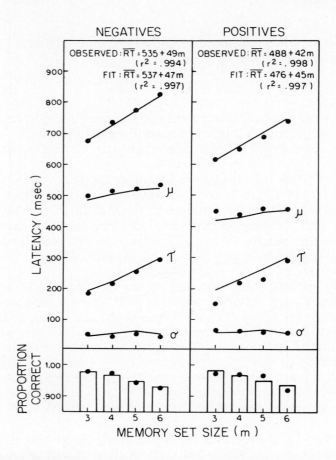

Figure 2. Observed (data points) and fitted (solid lines) correct mean response times, distribution parameter estimates, and proportion of correct responses for negative and positive responses as a function of memory set-size for the Sternberg paradigm (Hockley, 1984a, Exp. 1)

In the application of the ex-Gaussian to latency distributions, μ is the mean of the normal component and τ is the parameter of the exponential component. Thus, more of the change with set size is in the latter than the former.

Figures 3 and 4 show the fit of the model to data from a study-test paradigm. Fig. 3 shows the mean response time (top panel) and accuracy (bottom panel) as a function of output position for new, 1P (once-presented), and 2P (twice-presented) items. Fig. 4 shows the change in the distributional parameters with output position for these same three

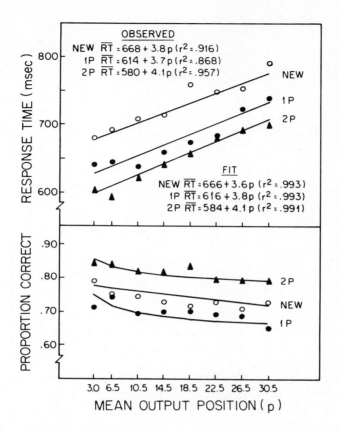

Figure 3. Observed (data points) and fitted (solid lines) correct mean response times and proportion of correct responses for new, once-presented (1P) and twice-presented (2P) items as a function of blocked output position for the study-test paradigm (Ratcliff & Murdock, 1976, Exp. 4).

item types. Again, more of the change with output position is in μ than in τ. The model misses out somewhat on the intercept of these functions for 1P and 2P items, but does seem to capture the slope relatively well.

Figures 5 and 6 show the fit of the model to data from a continuous recognition-memory task. Fig. 5 shows the changes in response time (top panel) and accuracy (bottom panel) for 2P and 3P items as a function of test lag. Items on their first presentation have no lag. Fig. 6 shows the changes in the distributional parameters with lag. Here μ and τ change about equally with test lag, and in general the fit of the model to the data is quite satisfactory.

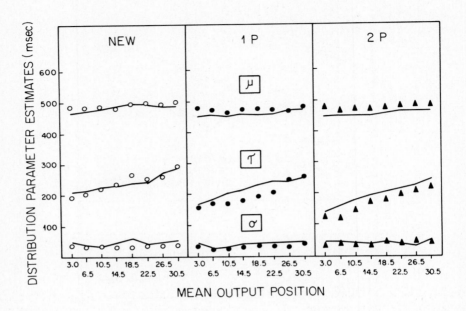

Figure 4. Observed (data points) and fitted (solid lines) distribution parameter estimates for the mean response times presented in Figure 3.

Fig. 7 shows the results from a study using the prememorized-lists paradigm. Here the results are essentially error-free so the only results we present are latencies. The left panel shows mean reaction time as a function of list length while the right panel shows how μ and τ change with list length. As in the study-test case, the model is somewhat off on the intercepts but fairly accurate for the slopes.

What are the processes in the model that produce these fits? A summary is shown in Table 1 (see Hockley & Murdock, 1987, for details) and the dots (i.e., ...) indicate that the parameters are yoked. Thus, as trace strength decreases with set size in the Sternberg paradigm so does (the lower) criterion starting value, and similarly in the pre-memorized lists paradigm. For the study-test paradigm both change with output position but at different rates. The criterion values cannot change with lag in the continuous task because lag information is not independently available to the subject, but TOS does vary with repetition.

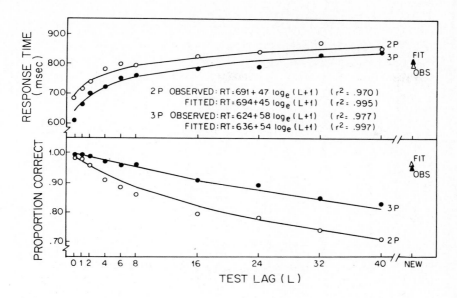

Figure 5. Observed (data points) and fitted (solid lines) mean correct response times and proportion of correct responses for old items presented twice (2P) and three times (3P) as a function of test lag and for new items for the continuous recognition paradigm (Hockley, 1982, Exp. 1).

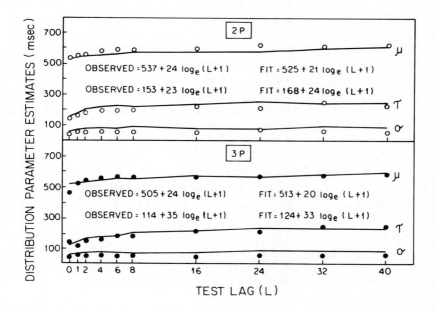

Figure 6. Observed (data points) and fitted (solid lines) distribution parameter estimates for the mean response times presented in Figure 5.

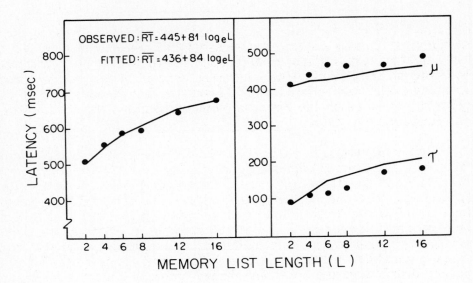

Figure 7. Observed (data points) and fitted (solid lines) mean correct response times (left panel) and distribution parameter estimates (right panel) as a function of list length for the prememorized-lists paradigm (Hockley & Corballis, 1982, Exp. 1).

Table 1.

Parameters involved in fitting MIM to data from four different recognition-memory paradigms.

Paradigms	Memory Trace Strength	Criteria Starting Values	TOS
Sternberg	X...............................X		X
Study-Test	X	X	
Continuous	X		X
Prememorized	X...............................X		

Selected speed-accuracy trade-off functions generated by the model are shown in Fig. 8. The value of d' is plotted as a function of decision time for three different values of the (mean) old-item strength. The increased spacing along the decision-time axis reflects the operation of the mapping function given in Equation 1, and in each case the asymptotic d' value is considerably below these mean values.   This difference reflects both the assumed variability in the memory trace-strength distributions and the extraneous random noise (always set to 2.25 times the new-item variance in all the fits shown here). As pointed out by Gronlund and Ratcliff (1988), there are some problems with the speed-accuracy explanation offered by MIM, but the fact remains that we can generate not unreasonable functions without assuming the accumulation of information over time.

To summarize, as a model for the decision system in recognition memory MIM assumes separate "yes" and "no" criteria which converge over time and the iteration continues until a combined signal plus noise observation falls outside the "wait" zone. The interrogation process undergoes reactive inhibition so each iteration takes more time than its predecessor. Given new- and old-item strength distributions, the model is able to fit accuracy and latency data from the four major recognition-memory paradigms including the μ, σ and τ parameters of the ex-Gaussian latency distribution and how they change with experimental conditions. In addition, it can generate reasonable speed-accuracy tradeoff functions which will vary according to the mean strength value of the old-item distribution.

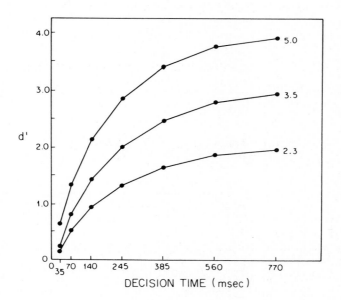

Figure 8. Predicted d′ values as a function of decision time. Decision time is based on Equation 1. The parameter is the mean of the old-item strength distribution.

3. JUDGMENTS OF FREQUENCY

The extension of MIM to Judgments of Frequency (JOF) is shown in Fig. 9. This extension is described more fully in Hockley (1989) and can only be summarized here. There are multiple strength distributions corresponding to 1P, 2P, 3P,... items and they are assumed to differ in mean and variance. (Again, these parameters would be provided by the appropriate memory model.) As before, the output from the memory comparison process is mixed with a random sample from the extraneous noise distribution, and this result will fall between two criteria (C1 and C2 in this case) that partition the strength distributions.

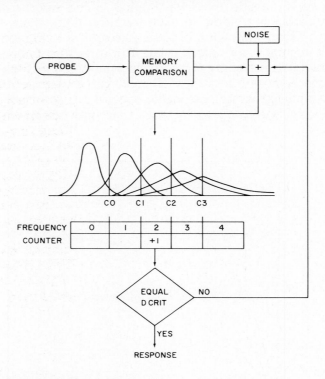

Figure 9. Decision model for absolute judgments of item frequency.

We assume multiple counters, one for each possible frequency judgment. On each loop the appropriate frequency counter is incremented, and the process recycles or not depending on whether the value of that counter exceeds a decision criterion (DCRIT) value. (In the present application DCRIT has a value of 4.) If it does not exceed that value then, as before, the noise is resampled and the process continues. It ends when the value of the incremented criterion equals the value of DCRIT, and the decision latency depends upon the number of iterations.

There are similarities and differences between the application of MIM to recognition memory and JOF. The front end is the same, and we use the same parameter values for the extraneous random noise. Again we use Eq. 1 to map number of cycles into real time, so reactive inhibition is involved in both. We also use the same value of BCT; namely, 17.5 msec. There are no converging criteria in JOF, but there are multiple frequency counters. We do not have the parameters CCR, Astart, or Bstart but we do have DCRIT and the four criteria C0-C3.

One might ask why the differences between the two cases? Basically the reason is that this difference is task dependent. Clearly with JOF one must have multiple criteria, and an extreme value cannot trigger a response because then the decision-time distribution would have no variability. One might argue that recognition memory is just the special case of JOF in that the only two frequencies are 0 and 1, but we need a wait option in recognition memory to provide the variability there. However, we should also point out that this is a first attempt to model recognition and JOF accuracy and latency data within the same conceptual framework, and further work may result in a better synthesis.

4. APPLICATION TO DATA

One application of this model to JOF data is shown in Figs. 10 and 11. (For details, see Hockley, 1989.) The top panel of Fig. 10 shows the mean frequency judgment for 0P, 1P, 2P, 3P, and 4P items; clearly, judged frequency is a linear function of presentation frequency. The middle panel shows proportion correct as a function of presentation frequency, and the bottom panel shows mean response time as a function of presentation frequency. The model over-predicts the bowing in the response-time functions, but otherwise the fits are quite good.

The JOF distributions are shown in Fig. 11 for 0P, 1P, 2P, 3P, and 4P items. Naveh-Benjamin and Jonides (1986) have argued that JOF performance should be evaluated with respect to the absolute magnitude of the mean estimates, the slope of the function relating mean estimates to actual frequencies, and the variability of the estimates. We have added proportion correct and mean response time to this list, and in general the extension of MIM to JOF seems to be able not only to capture the general pattern of data but also fit the details quite closely.

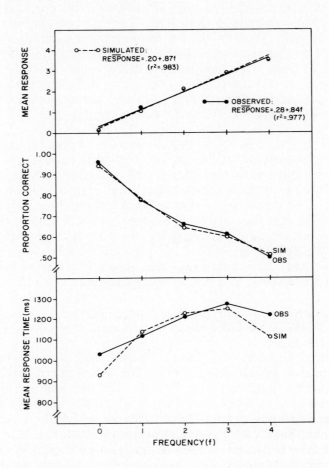

Figure 10. Observed (solid data points and lines) and fitted (open data points and dashed lines) mean responses (top), proportion of correct responses (middle) and mean latency of correct responses (bottom) as a function of presentation frequency for a continuous frequency judgment task (Hockley, 1984b, Exp. 3).

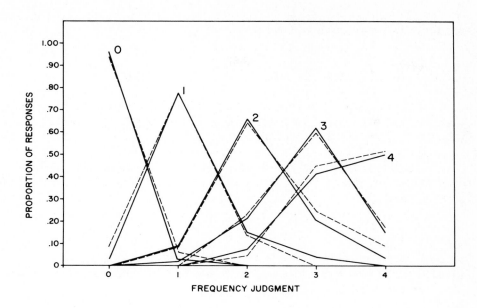

Figure 11. Observed (solid lines) and fitted (dashed lines) frequency judgment distributions for the continuous frequency judgment task. The parameter is the presentation frequency.

5. SUMMARY

We have presented a brief account of MIM, a decision model reported more fully in Hockley and Murdock (1987) and Hockley (1989), and shown how it can be applied to recognition memory and frequency-judgment data. Memory and decision processes are clearly separated. MIM is a decision model, and all it needs from a memory model is the result of the memory comparison process. We assume that extraneous random noise enters into the decision process, but we do not assume that there is accumulation of information over time. There is reactive inhibition in the decision process so each iteration takes longer than the prior one, and the first loop is assumed to take 35 msec. There are converging criteria for recognition but separate frequency counters for JOF, so the applications are somewhat different in these two cases.

The model seems to provide a reasonable fit to selected data sets in both recognition and JOF, but the critical variables which change with experimental conditions vary with the application. Two further areas of application we would like to explore are Judgments of Recency and list discrimination. Then we could claim to have a fairly general decision model. Also, we would like to interface MIM with a distributed memory model but this too remains to be done.

ACKNOWLEDGMENTS

This research was supported by Grant APA 146 from the Natural Science and Engineering Research Council of Canada. We would like to thank our colleagues for many helpful comments.

Requests for reprints should be sent to Bennet B. Murdock, Department of Psychology, University of Toronto, Toronto, Ontario Canada, M5S 1A1.

REFERENCES

Gillund, G., & Shiffrin, R. M. (1984). A retrieval model for both recognition and recall. Psychological Review, 91, 1-67.

Gronlund, S. D., & Ratcliff, R. (1988, July 30). The time course of item and associative information: Implications for global memory models. Paper presented at Mathematical Psychology Meetings, Northwestern University.

Hintzman, D. L. (1988). Judgments of frequency and recognition memory in a multiple-trace model. Psychological Review, 95. 528-551.

Hockley, W. E. (1982). Retrieval processes in continuous recognition. Journal of Experimental Psychology: Learning, Memory, and Cognition, 8, 497-512.

Hockley, W. E. (1984a). The analysis of reaction time distributions in the study of cognitive processes. Journal of Experimental Psychology: Learning, Memory, and Cognition, 10, 598-615.

Hockley, W. E. (1984b). Retrieval of item frequency information in a continuous memory task. Memory & Cognition, 12, 229-242.

Hockley, W. E. (1989, in press). Interrogating Memory: A decision model for recognition and judgment of frequency. In M. C. Corballis, K. G. White, and W. Abraham (Eds.), Memory mechanisms: A tribute to G. V. Goddard. Hillsdale, NJ: Erlbaum.

Hockley, W. E., & Corballis, M. C. (1982). Tests of serial scanning in item recognition. Canadian Journal of Psychology, 36, 189-212.

Hockley, W. E., & Murdock, B. B. (1987). A decision model for accuracy and response latency in recognition memory. Psychological Review, 94, 341-358.

Naveh-Benjamin, M., & Jonides, J. (1986). On the automaticity of frequency coding: Effects of competing task load, encoding strategy, and intention. Journal of Experimental Psychology: Learning, Memory and Cognition, 12, 378-386.

Ratcliff, R., & Murdock, B. B., Jr. (1976). Retrieval processes in recognition memory. Psychological Review, 83, 190-214.

Swets, J. A., & Green, D. M. (1961). Sequential observations by human observers of signals in noise, In C. Cherry (Ed.), Information theory: Proceedings of the fourth London symposium (pp. 177-195). London: Butterworths.

Human Information Processing: Measures,
Mechanisms, and Models, D. Vickers and P. L. Smith (eds.)
© *Elsevier Science Publishers B.V. (North-Holland), 1989*

AN AUTOASSOCIATIVE MODEL FOR HUMAN
MEMORY BASED ON AN ADAPTIVE KALMAN FILTER

Richard A. Heath

University of Newcastle

A mathematical model for the storage and retrieval of item and associative information in human memory is proposed. Simultaneously presented items are represented by a concatenated input vector and are stored in an associative memory matrix using an autoassociative scheme based on an adaptive Kalman filter memory modification algorithm. The stability of the adaptive memory update and the predictions of the model for the retrieval of item and order information are investigated. The predictions of the model are compared with relevant experimental data using discriminability indices derived from a random walk model for the decision process in recall tasks.

1. INTRODUCTION.

The human information processing (HIP) system may be characterized as a dynamic mechanism for transforming externally and internally generated inputs into action sequences. External inputs are those which are generated by changes in the physical environment and are transduced by the relevant sensory modalities, whereas internal inputs are generated within the nervous system. The HIP system is required to assimilate environmental changes which are distributed over time as random perturbations in a structured series of events. Appropriate behaviour is then emitted in order to minimize any mismatch between the environmental demands and the subsequent action sequence. Hence an important property of the HIP system is its ability to adapt to environmental change.

When an appropriate behaviour sequence is not contained in the organism's behaviour repertoire, the HIP system's internal functional parameters must be altered to accommodate these novel environmental demands. This requires a structural change in the information processing mechanisms, generating a modified memory representation. When expressed in an adaptive behavioural sequence, this modification is interpreted as evidence that the organism has learned.

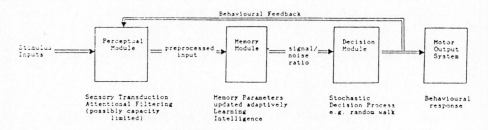

Figure 1. A representation of the human information processing system in terms of interacting perceptual, memory and decision modules.

The HIP system may be represented as an interacting set of modules as shown in Figure 1. External inputs are processed by sensory transducers in the perceptual modules. This information is then filtered by an attentional system so that the components of the input are weighted in proportion to their importance for the organism. In a limited capacity system, the sum of these weights will be fixed, so that there is a trade-off between the amount of attention paid to the competing input components. This sum may vary with time to accommodate changes in arousal caused by fatigue or loss of vigilance over time.

The output from the perceptual module is processed by the memory module which generates an adaptive modification to the memory representation. The performance of this module depends on the subject's memory parameters which generate a wide variety of individual differences in information processing capacity. The memory module provides a signal-noise ratio measure which is then input to the decision module.

The decision module uses an input from the memory module to generate an output which permits the motor system to produce a response. The environmental consequences of this response can then be fed back as an input to the perceptual module, thus allowing the HIP system to control its behavioural output.

All three modules operate in parallel as cascaded processes (McClelland,1979). Information flows from the perceptual module into the memory module and then to the decision module in such a way that a response can be generated while an external input is still being filtered by the perceptual system and generating an output from the memory module. Depending upon task demands, the decision module can regulate, or gate, the information flow from the memory module so that only necessary responses are generated.

2. AN ADAPTIVE FILTER MECHANISM FOR INFORMATION STORAGE

The adaptive filter mechanism is based on control theory techniques which compute the parameters of a time-varying dynamic process so that future states of the system can be predicted. These techniques are particularly useful when the system parameters vary with time. In this case the new values of the system's parameters need to be "learned" so that any error between the predicted value of the system's output and the actual output can be minimized. If the learning process is controlled by the sequence of external inputs then this is an example of unsupervised learning, or learning without a teacher. If a goal or teaching input is provided, then supervised learning occurs. Both types of learning can be accommodated by the adaptive filter mechanism.

Heath (1982,1984) has described an optimal linear estimator for a series of observations occurring over time which is known as the Kalman filter. In these applications of the Kalman filter the observations are scalar quantities such as the total neural activity in a sensory system at each observation period (Heath, 1982), or a measure such as the heart inter-beat-interval when a physiological measure is being tracked (Heath, 1984). In the more general model described in this paper, the observations are multivariate vectors representing the filtered output from perceptual modules. The parameters of the system are represented by the elements of a memory matrix which is updated following the input of each new observation vector. Unlike the conventional Kalman filter in which information is derived from a time series of observations, this application in the memory module of the HIP system involves a dynamic update of parameters representing spatial interactions in the neural substrate involved in information storage. How a spatial representation of information can code the temporal information in a sequence of inputs is an important problem for such a memory system to solve.

Figure 2 depicts the operation of the adaptive Kalman filter in a memory module of the HIP system. In the sequel, vectors and matrices are printed in boldface type, with vectors being in lower case and matrices in upper case. All inputs to the memory module occur at time t and any values updated in the tth observation period which are retained for use in the next observation period are labelled (t+1). Transposed vectors are indicated by a superscript T.

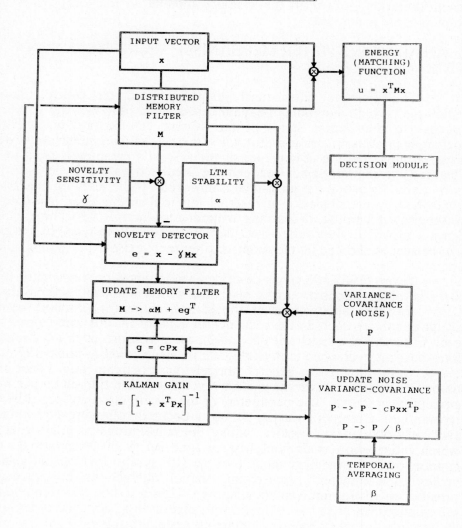

Figure 2. The update of an associative memory matrix based on an adaptive Kalman filter.

The input vector during the tth observation period, $x(t)$, enters the memory module from the perceptual modules. It contains m components, $x_i(t)$, i=1, m, which represent the simultaneous activity in the perceptual module during the tth observation period. This information must reside in a sensory memory buffer long enough to

(a) be filtered through the memory matrix, $M(t)$, to generate an output vector $M(t)x(t+1)$;

(b) premultiply the output vector to generate a scalar matching function given by:

$$u(t+1) = x^T(t+1)M(t)x(t+1) \qquad (2.1)$$

which can be accessed by the decision module;

(c) compute the prediction error vector during the tth observation period given by:

$$e(t+1) = x(t+1) - \gamma M(t) x(t+1) \qquad (2.2)$$

where γ is a novelty sensitivity parameter; and

(d) be used in the update of the memory matrix for use in the next time period. Since all these processes can occur in parallel, the information need only reside in the sensory memory for a relatively brief time.

The input vector is also used to compute a Kalman gain vector and to update the error (or residual) variance-covariance matrix, $P(t)$. This matrix contains the variance of the prediction error for each component of the input vector down its main diagonal and the product of the correlation and standard deviations of the prediction errors for pairs of stimulus components in the off-diagonal elements. The error variance-covariance matrix is symmetric and positive semi-definite, i.e. it has real positive eigenvalues. Since the memory matrix, $M(t)$ stores terms of the form $x(t)$ $x(t)^T$, it stores the covariance of the input vectors. Hence the error variance-covariance matrix, $P(t)$, is an appropriate noise referent for the memory matrix.

If the linear function

$$L(t) = x_1e_1 + x_2e_2 + ... + x_me_m$$

$$= x^Te \qquad (2.3)$$

representing the covariance of the input and output of the novelty detector in the memory module, is estimated during each observation period, then the variance of L(t) is given by $\mathbf{x}(t)^T P\mathbf{x}(t)$. A simple transformation of L(t) yields the Kalman gain coefficient, c(t+1), computed by

$$c(t+1) = 1 / [1 + \mathbf{x}(t+1)^T \mathbf{P}(t+1) \mathbf{x}(t+1)] \qquad (2.4)$$

Hence, a measure of signal-to-noise ratio can be computed as the product of u(t+1) and c(t+1).

The error variance-covariance matrix is updated according to the equation

$$\mathbf{P}(t+1) = [\mathbf{P}(t) - c(t+1)\mathbf{P}(t)\mathbf{x}(t+1)\mathbf{x}(t+1)^T\mathbf{P}(t)] / \beta \qquad (2.5)$$

where β is an exponential averaging parameter which has the effect of distributing the changes in the error variance-covariance matrix over time. This represents a type of short-term memory in the memory module.

Finally, the memory matrix is initially multiplied by a memory permanence parameter, α, $0 \le \alpha \le 1$, and then a component proportional to the prediction error variance is added. The final equation for the memory update is

$$\mathbf{M}(t+1) = \alpha\mathbf{M}(t) + \mathbf{e}(t+1)\mathbf{g}^T(t+1) \qquad (2.6)$$

where the Kalman gain vector is given by

$$\mathbf{g}(t+1) = c(t+1)\mathbf{P}(t+1)\mathbf{x}(t+1)$$

and e(t+1) is given in (2.2).

Hence

$$\mathbf{M}(t+1) = \alpha\mathbf{M}(t) + c(t+1)[\mathbf{I} - \gamma\mathbf{M}(t)] \mathbf{x}(t+1)\mathbf{x}^T(t+1)\mathbf{P}(t+1)$$

The updated memory matrix is then available for filtering the output of the perceptual modules in the (t+1)[th] observation period.

If the off-diagonal terms of $\mathbf{P}(t+1)$, representing error covariance, are negligible when compared with the variance terms down the main diagonal, then $\mathbf{P}(t+1)$ is approximately equal to $\sigma^2 (t+1)\mathbf{I}$ and c(t+1) is approximately equal to $1 / [1 + \sigma^2 (t+1)]$. Hence Eq. (2.6) can be rewritten as

$$\mathbf{M}(t+1) = \alpha \mathbf{M}(t) + \beta (t+1)[\mathbf{I} - \gamma\mathbf{M}(t)] \mathbf{x}(t+1) \mathbf{x}^T(t+1) \qquad (2.7)$$

where $\beta(t+1) = \sigma^2(t+1) / [1 + \sigma^2(t+1)]$.

Equation (2.7) is equivalent to the stochastic approximation memory update described in Heath and Fulham (1988).

3. HABITUATION OF THE ADAPTIVE FILTER MEMORY SYSTEM TO CONSTANT STIMULUS INPUT

When an input stimulus with constant signal-noise ratio is processed by the memory module, the output of the adaptive filter stabilizes as the system habituates to the constant input. In order to evaluate the extent of this habituation in the memory module, the signal-noise ratio, $s(t) = u(t)c(t)$, was computed as a function of the stimulus duration, t, for several values of long-term memory (LTM) permanence, α, short-term memory (STM) temporal averaging parameter, β, novelty sensitivity, γ, and input noise. For convenience, we assume that β does not depend on t.

The input stimuli were the pair of lower-case letter strings, "abcdefgh" and "ijklmnop" in the form of a single 80-element vector. The letter subvectors were the coordinates of points representing the location of the lower-case letter in a five-dimensional perceptual space obtained by multidimensional scaling of a similarity judgment matrix contained in Geyer (1977). The input vectors were corrupted by the addition of zero-mean Gaussian noise and normalized before being processed by the memory module.

Figure 3 shows the effects of variation in each of the four parameters when three of the parameters are fixed at $\alpha=1.0$, $\beta=0.8$, $\gamma=0.8$ and noise $=0.25$ and the fourth parameter is allowed to vary. Figure 3(a) shows that the exponential decay rate (coefficient), does not depend on LTM permanence but that the intercept increases with LTM permanence. This result suggests that the signal-noise ratio may be depressed for "leaky" memory systems such as those affected by age, e.g. in senile dementia and Altzheimer's syndrome, and brain damage, e.g. Korsakoff patients. The plot attains a maximum at $\alpha=0.9$, suggesting that the optimal LTM permanence is not 1.0, especially when γ is not equal to 0.

Figure 3(b) shows the effect of variation in STM exponential averaging on $\log[s(t)]$. The exponential decay rate increases as β decreases, so that habituation is more rapid the less the extent of temporal exponential averaging. The larger the value of β, the longer information can be retained in the memory system before being interrupted by a novel input. In this way the memory module generates the illusion of a short-term memory buffer with limited capacity due to the temporal averaging property of the STM parameter. Now, if we define STM "capacity" as $B = 1/(1-\beta)$, then B is the mean number of items being processed by the temporal averager per unit time. As β decreases, items deplete more

rapidly and the STM "capacity" decreases. When β =1, B is not defined
and information remains available to the memory module as long as it is

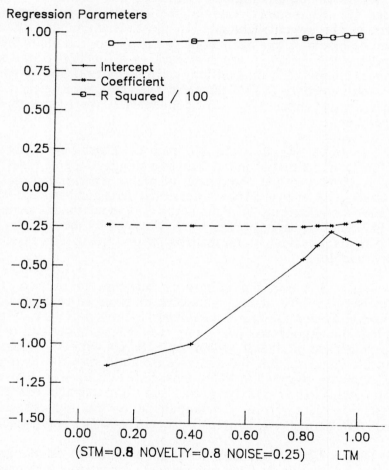

Regression of LOGe(S/N) on Time
The Effects of Long Term Memory

Figure 3 (a). The effects of variation in LTM permanence

needed.   As shown in Figure 3(b), as ß approaches 1, the simple
exponential decay model no longer applies, and s(t) attains a maximum
value at some nonzero value of t.

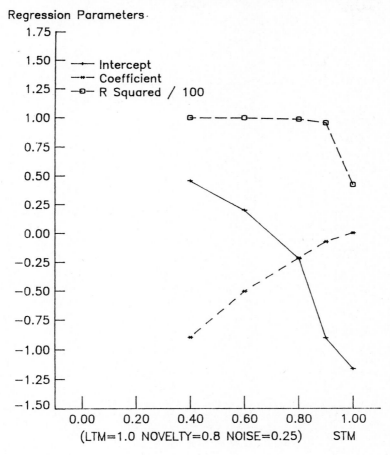

Regression of LOGe(S/N) on Time
The Effects of Short Term Memory

Figure 3(b) The effect of variation in STM exponential averaging on log[s(t)].

Figure 3(c) shows the effect of variation in the novelty sensitivity parameter, γ, on the habituation process. Although changes in this parameter do not affect the rate of decay of information in storage, the initial signal-noise ratio is non-monotonic.

Figure 3(d) shows a clear effect of input noise on the initial signal-noise ratio at time t=0. As the noise variance increases to 0.5, there is a rapid decline in the fidelity of the input information to the memory system. However, there is no effect of input noise on the time course of information in memory.

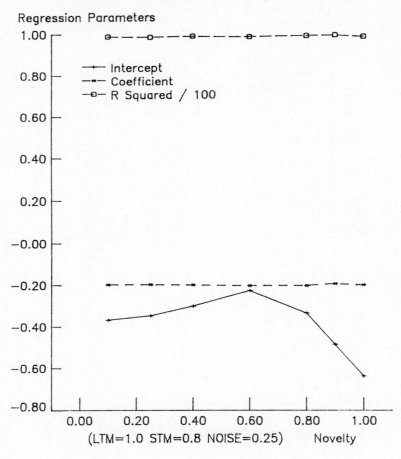

Regression of LOGe(S/N) on Time
The Effects of Novelty Sensitivity

Figure 3(c) The effect of variation in the novelty sensitivity parameter, γ, on the habituation process.

As the STM parameter increases, there is a decrease in initial signal-noise ratio yielding a tradeoff between the amount of information entering the memory (the value of s(t) at t=0) and the time that information is available for processing. Hence weak inputs habituate slowly so that conservation of information occurs.

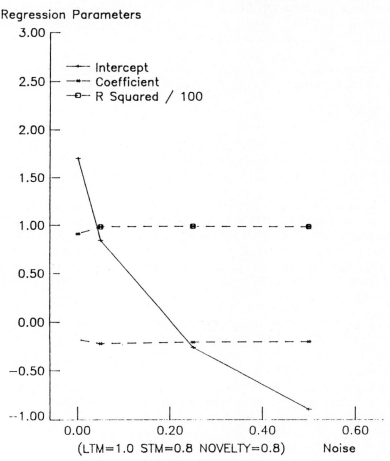

Figure 3(d) The effect of input noise on the initial signal-noise ratio at time t=0.

A canonical correlation analysis was performed on the slope and intercept of the regression of log[s(t)] on t (variable set 1) and the Kalman filter parameters, LTM (α), STM (β), Novelty (γ) and Noise (variable set 2). It was shown that the regression slope was affected by the STM parameter, β, [$F(4,18)=21.93$, $p<.001$], and the regression intercept increased with both an increase in the LTM parameter, α, and a decrease in Noise, [$F(4,18)=163.54$, $p<.001$]. This analysis provided statistical verification for the trends observed in Figure 3.

4. AN AUTOASSOCIATIVE MODEL FOR HUMAN MEMORY

A mathematical model for the storage and retrieval of simultaneously presented information is described. Unlike the models of Murdock (1982) and Eich (1982), simultaneously presented items are represented by the same input vector to the memory module.

On each experimental trial a set of stimuli is presented for storage. On the tth trial this set consists of n items in the extended vector

$$\mathbf{x}(t) = [w_1(t)\mathbf{x}_1{}^T(t),...,w_i(t)\mathbf{x}_i{}^T(t),...,w_n(t)\mathbf{x}_n{}^T(t)]^T \qquad (4.1)$$

Each of these items is represented by an m-element vector of neural activity, $\mathbf{x}_i(t)$, i=1,n, which is weighted by $w_i(t)$ to represent the attention accorded this item when all n items are processed simultaneously.

New information impinging on the memory module, represented by the vector product $\mathbf{x}(t)\mathbf{x}^T(t)$ may be expanded in terms of submatrices $\mathbf{X}_{ij}(t) = \mathbf{x}_i(t)\mathbf{x}_j{}^T(t)$, i,j = 1,n. The diagonal submatrices, $w_i{}^2(t)\mathbf{X}_{ii}(t)$, i=1,n, represent item information and the off-diagonal submatrices, $w_i(t)w_j(t)\mathbf{X}_{ij}(t)$, represent associations between simultaneously presented items. Since $\mathbf{X}_{ij}(t) \neq \mathbf{X}_{ji}{}^T(t)$, the memory is sensitive to the spatial location of the component items, unless $\mathbf{X}_{ii}(t) = \mathbf{X}_{jj}(t)$, i.e. the items are identical.

5. RESPONSE OF THE ADAPTIVE MEMORY MODULE TO EXEMPLAR PATTERNS DERIVED FROM A SINGLE PROTOTYPE PATTERN.

Suppose that the tth stimulus presented to the memory module, $\mathbf{x}(t)$, is an exemplar pattern generated by adding uncorrelated zero mean gaussian noise to a prototype stimulus, $\mathbf{x}$. So

$$\mathbf{x}(t) = \mathbf{x} + \mathbf{n}(t)$$

where $E[\mathbf{n}(t)] = \mathbf{0}$ and $Var[\mathbf{n}(t)] = \sigma^2 \mathbf{1}$, where $\mathbf{1}$ is the vector with all elements set equal to 1. We assume that $\mathbf{x}^T(t)\,\mathbf{n}(t) = 0$ for all t.

If $\mathbf{P}(j) = \beta(j)\,\mathbf{x}(j)\,\mathbf{x}^T(j)$, then Heath and Fulham(1988) have shown that the solution to the stochastic approximation memory update equation (2.7) is

$$\mathbf{M}(1) = \mathbf{P}(1)$$

$$\mathbf{M}(t) = \mathbf{P}(t) + \sum_{j=1}^{t-1} \mathbf{P}(j) \prod_{i=j+1}^{t} [\alpha\mathbf{I} - \gamma\mathbf{P}(t-i+1)], \quad t > 2. \qquad (5.1)$$

This memory update algorithm is a modification of the Widrow-Hoff, or delta, rule (Widrow & Hoff, 1960). The technique described in Stone (1986) can be used to evaluate the stability of the memory update represented by Eq. (2.7). Taking expectations of each side of Eq. (2.7) yields

$$E[\mathbf{M}(t+1)] = \alpha\, E[\mathbf{M}(t)] + \beta(t+1)\mathbf{R} - \gamma\, \beta(t+1)E[\mathbf{M}(t)]\mathbf{R}$$

$$\text{where } \mathbf{R} = E[\mathbf{x}(t+1)\mathbf{x}^T(t+1)]$$
$$= E[(\mathbf{x}+\mathbf{n}(t+1))\,(\mathbf{x}+\mathbf{n}(t+1))^T]$$
$$= \mathbf{x}\mathbf{x}^T + \sigma^2\mathbf{I}$$

$$\text{Hence } E[\mathbf{M}(t+1)] = E[\mathbf{M}(t)]\,[\alpha\,\mathbf{I} - \gamma\,\beta(t+1)\mathbf{R}] + \beta(t+1)\mathbf{R}$$
$$= \alpha\, E[\mathbf{M}(t)] + \beta(t+1)\,\{\mathbf{I} - \gamma\, E[\mathbf{M}(t)]\}\mathbf{R}$$
$$= \alpha\, E[\mathbf{M}(t)] + \{\mathbf{I} - \gamma\, E[\mathbf{M}(t)]\}\mathbf{P}(t+1)$$

$$\text{where } \mathbf{P}(t+1) = \beta(t+1)\mathbf{R}.$$

Using Eq. (5.1) yields

$$E[\mathbf{M}(t)] = \beta(t)\mathbf{R} + \sum_{j=1}^{t-1} \beta(j)\mathbf{R} \prod_{i=j+1}^{t} [\alpha\,\mathbf{I} - \gamma\,\beta(t-i-1)\mathbf{R}], \quad t>2$$

$$= \mathbf{R}\{\beta(t) + \sum_{j=1}^{t-1} \beta(j)\mathbf{R} \prod_{i=j+1}^{t} [\alpha\,\mathbf{I} - \gamma\,\beta(t-i+1)\mathbf{R}]\}.$$

If $\beta = \beta(t)$ is fixed for all t, then

$$E[\mathbf{M}(t)] = \beta\mathbf{R}\,[\mathbf{I} + \sum_{j=1}^{t-1} (\alpha\,\mathbf{I} - \gamma\beta\mathbf{R})^{t-j}] \qquad (5.2)$$

The expected matching function for the prototype at time t, $E[u(t)]$, can be computed by

$$E[u(t)] = \mathbf{x}^T E[\mathbf{M}(t)]\mathbf{x}$$

$$= \beta[(1+\sigma^2) + \sum_{j=1}^{t-1} \delta^{t-j}]$$

$$= \beta(1+\sigma^2) + \delta\,(1-\delta^{t-1})\,/\,(1-\delta)$$

where $\delta = \alpha - \beta \gamma(1 + \sigma^2)$.

Now when $t \to \infty$, $E[u(\infty)] = \beta[(1 + \sigma^2)(1 - \delta) + \delta] / [1 - \alpha + \gamma\beta(1 + \sigma^2)]$ and the algorithm is stable provided $\alpha - \gamma\beta(1 + \sigma^2) < 1$. If the novelty sensitivity parameter, γ, equals 0, then stability occurs provided $\alpha < 1$.

6. A STOCHASTIC MODEL FOR PROCESSES IN THE DECISION MODULE

The input to the decision module consists of a scalar matching function, $u(t)$, and a scalar noise term represented by the reciprocal of the Kalman gain coefficient, $c(t)$. Both terms are stochastic quantities with expected values which vary with time. A possible stochastic decision model for a two-choice task is a nonstationary generalization of the two-boundary random walk model (Heath, 1981).

A pictorial representation of the nonstationary random walk model is shown in Figure 4. Before the beginning of each trial of a two-choice task, the subject sets two response thresholds at values A and -A on a scalar dimension representing the total accumulated information. When the total accumulated information reaches or exceeds A, the response R(A) is initiated by means of the appropriate motor system, whereas when it reaches, or is less than, -A, the response R(-A) is elicited. The subject's choice of A will depend on the task instructions, being small when speed is emphasized and large when accuracy is required. Hence it is proposed that the parameter, A, represents the subject's response caution which, when varied, generates a speed-accuracy tradeoff. The starting point of the random walk, C, -A<C<A, can be controlled by the subject from one trial to the next depending upon the expected correct response for that trial.

During each sampling period of arbitrarily brief duration, an increment to the random walk occurs. At the tth observation period, this increment is a normally distributed random variable with mean equal to the matching function, $u(t)$, and variance equal to the reciprocal of the Kalman gain constant, $c(t)$. Since both the mean and the variance of the step size distribution are time-dependent, the random walk is nonstationary and cannot be analyzed by the conventional stationary models such as that of Link and Heath(1975).

The general nonstationary random walk model can be fit to response proportion and mean RT data using a suitable parameter estimation program such as FITTRW (Heath, 1983). This analysis provides estimates of the signal-noise ratios for a memory task which can be identified with the scalar matching function, $u(t)$. A memory model, such as the stochastic approximation model of Eq.(2.7), can be fit to the u(t) values to provide estimates of the memory parameters, α, $\beta(t)$ and γ.

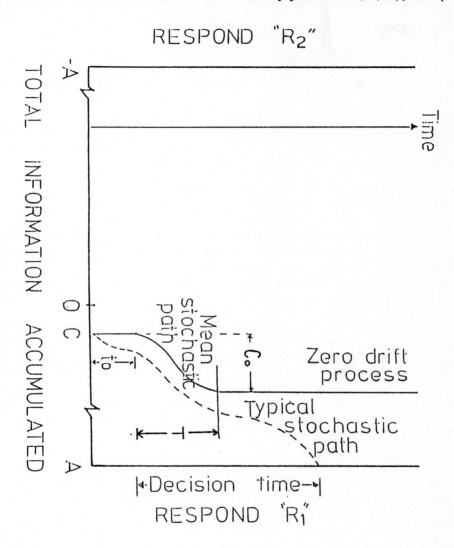

Figure 4. A nonstationary random walk model for a two- choice decision process driven by information derived from an adaptive memory module.

7. APPLICATIONS OF THE AUTO-ASSOCIATIVE MEMORY MODEL

Applications of the autoassociative memory model in several experimental contexts will be described. These applications include (a) the item-recognition paradigm; (b) a continuous recognition task; (c) serial position effects for single items and paired associates; (d) the study-test paradigm and (e) recency and order judgements.

7.1 The Item-recognition Paradigm.

Heath and Fulham(1988) have applied the adaptive filter model to analyse data obtained in a task requiring subjects to indicate whether a probe item belonged to a small set of previously presented items. The probe item was equally likely to have been presented, or not presented, in the memorised sequence. The stimuli were the set of two-dimensional Walsh patterns (Heath & Fulham,1988, Figure 2).

Several versions of the adaptive filter memory model were fit to serial position curves using a discriminability parameter estimated from an analysis of the response accuracy and mean RT data for correct and erroneous responses using the FITTRW parameter estimation program for general random walk models (Heath,1983). The best fitting model, derived in the Appendix of Heath & Fulham(1988), provided parameter estimates, $\hat{\alpha} = 0.40$, $\hat{\gamma} = 0.84$, $\hat{r} = 0.32$ and $ß(k) = 1.2 \exp(-0.71k)$, where r is the average inter-item correlation.

Although this model fit the nonmonotonic serial position curves quite adequately, it was difficult to distinguish it from a model which assumed that the memory update was not adaptive, i.e., the novelty sensitivity parameter, γ, equals 0, and the memory system has a superimposed lateral inhibitory mechanism which generates inhibition between temporally adjacent items.

7.2 The Continuous Recognition Paradigm.

Heath and Fulham(1985) presented subjects with random dot exemplar patterns derived by perturbing the locations of points in a small number of random dot prototype patterns. Subjects were required to judge the familiarity of each exemplar on an 18 point confidence scale ranging from "No-certain" to "Yes-certain". The subject's familiarity judgement was assumed to be proportional to the norm of the novelty detector error vector, $e(t) = [I - \gamma M(t-1)] x(t)$. Adaptive filter parameter estimates were computed so that the mean squared error between observed and predicted familiarity judgements was minimized. When RT measures are available, a discriminability index can be computed which accommodates the trade-off between speed and accuracy (Casey & Heath,1989).

Figure 5 depicts the observed (solid lines) and predicted (dotted lines) change in discriminability of exemplar stimuli over trials in a continuous recognition task. For the example data depicted in Figure 5 which demonstrate an increase in discriminability over trials, the predicted curve followed the general learning change but did not track accurately any sudden changes in observed discriminability. For most subjects the memory permanence parameter, α, was close to 1 and the novelty sensitivity parameter, γ, was not equal to 0, suggesting an adaptive memory update.

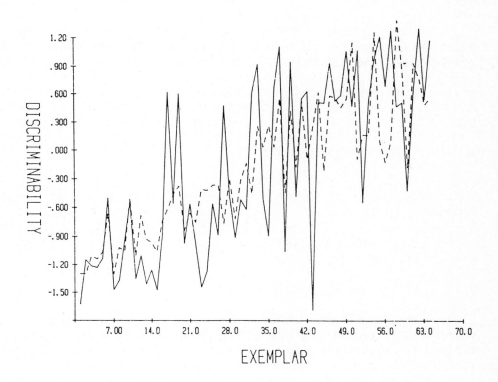

Figure 5. Predicted (dotted lines) and observed (solid lines) discriminability of exemplar stimuli derived from a small set of random dot prototypes in a continuous familiarity judgement task.

7.3 Recall of Memorised Lists of Related Items.

The autoassociative memory model provides a parsimonious account of performance in tasks requiring the storage and subsequent recall of independent presentations of related items. For example, in the study-test paradigm, the subject may be presented with a sequence of paired associates e.g. bird-sparrow, during a study period, and be required to recognize these items in a subsequent test period. Other tasks require the subject to recall, or recognize, item and associative information, such as the position of single items, or the order of more than one item, in the study list.

When the input vectors, representing simultaneously presented items, are independent and normalized then the memory update equation simplifies since $M(t) x(t+1) = 0$. Hence Eq. (2.7) becomes

$$M(t+1) = \alpha M(t) + \beta(t+1) x(t+1) x^T(t+1)$$

and

$$M(t) = \sum_{i=1}^{t} \alpha^{t-i} \beta(i) x(i) x^T(i)$$

If item $x(k)$ is presented in the test phase then the matching function, $u(k,t)$ is given by

$$u(k,t) = x^T(k) M(t) x(k)$$

$$= \sum_{i=1}^{t} \alpha^{t-i} \beta(i) r^2 (k, i)$$

where $r(k,i) = x^T(k) x(i)$ is the correlation between the probe vector and the ith vector stored in memory.

Suppose that pairs of simultaneously presented items are presented for memorization and then probed for recall using partial cues, e.g. one item in a pair is used as the cue for recall of the associated item. If successive pairs are unrelated then the matching functions for various contingencies involving familiar items can be computed as follows:

a) Recall of Paired Associates

(i) First Item in the kth Pair

$$u(k,t;1) = \alpha^{t-k} \beta(k) (w_{1k} + \rho_k w_{2k})^2$$

(ii) Second Item in the kth Pair

$$u(k,t;2) = \alpha^{t-k} \text{ß}(k) (\rho_k w_{1k} + w_{2k})^2$$

where w_{ik}, $i=1,2$, is the attention allocated to the ith item in the kth paired associate and ρ_k is the correlation (similarity) between the items in the kth pair.

b) Recall of the kth Single Item

When single items are presented, they can be considered as perfectly correlated "paired associates" so that

$$u(k, t) = C(k) \alpha^{t-k} \text{ß}(k)$$

where $C(k)$, a scale factor equal to $w_{1k}^2 + w_{2k}^2$, measures the information processing capacity allocated to the kth item.

Any difference in the recall of individual items in associated item pairs is given by

$$u(k, t; 1) - u(k, t; 2) = \alpha^{t-k} \text{ß}(k) (1- \rho_k^2)(w_{1k}^2 - w_{2k}^2).$$

If the associated items are uncorrelated and one of the items in a pair, e.g. the left item of a horizontal display, is afforded greater attention then $w_{lk} > w_{2k}$ implies that $u(k, t; 1) > u(k, t; 2)$. This generates better recall and a shorter RT for the left item in each pair and produces zig-zag serial position curves like those observed by Murdock and Franklin (1984).

This model also generates order sensitive recall within each paired associate since

$$u(k, t; 1, 2) = \alpha^{t-k} \text{ß}(k) (w_{lk} + w_{2k})^2$$

when the probe items are presented in the same order as in the original presentation and

$$u(k, t; 2, 1) = \alpha^{t-k} \text{ß}(k) \rho_k^2(w_{ik} + w_{2k})^2$$

when the probe items are presented in the opposite order. As the similarity between items within a pair increases, the recall becomes less sensitive to the order of the items within a pair since ρ_k^2 increases and the difference, $u(k, t; 1, 2) - u(k, t; 2, 1)$, decreases.

An interesting implication of the model is that the recall of paired associates should improve the greater the similarity of the component items (Eich,1985), but the recall accuracy of item order within a pair should be reduced when the item similarity increases (Murdock,1983).

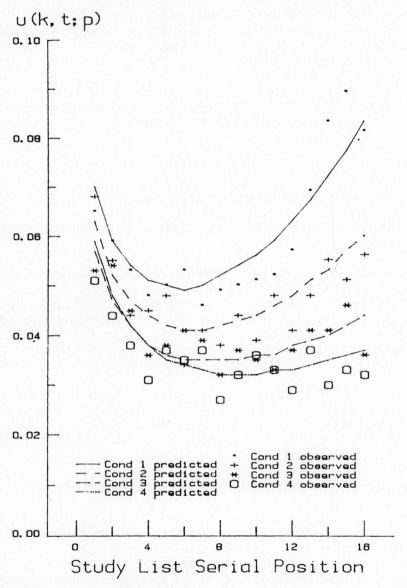

Figure 6. The fit of the adaptive memory model to discriminability indices derived from the data in Table 2 of Ratcliff (1978). The indices were computed for four positions of the study items in the test list as a function of the original position of these items in the study list.

7.4. The Study-Test Paradigm.

The study-test paradigm involves the presentation of a supraspan set of items at a uniform rate during the study phase, followed by an equal number of study and novel items during the self-paced test phase (Ratcliff,1978). Since this paradigm has been studied extensively by Murdock and others, it provides an ideal vehicle for evaluating the autoassociative memory model.

Figure 6 shows the trends in a discriminability index computed by using the mean RT and accuracy data in Figure 10 of Ratcliff (1978), and the following formula derived from a random walk model for decision making:

$$d(k, t) = \{[2P(c)-1]\log[P(c) / (1-P(c))] / (RT-RT_0)\}^{1/2} \quad (7.4.1)$$

where $P(c)$ is the proportion of correct responses, RT is the mean RT, RT_0 is the mean residual RT (set equal to 350 msecs [Ratcliff(1978) Table 2, p 80]), t is the test position of the item and k is the location of the item within the study list.

According to the autoassociative model with independent items, $u(k,t) = \alpha^{t-k} \beta(k)$, where $\beta(k)$ includes an arbitrary scale factor. A modification of this equation permits the prediction of recall discriminability as a function of input position, k, and output position, p, in a study list of t items, since

$$u(k, t; p) = \beta(k, p) \, \alpha \, (p)^{t-k+p} \quad (7.4.2)$$

where $\beta(k, p) = (\beta + \beta_0 p) / (k + \lambda)$ and $\alpha (p) = \alpha + \alpha_0 p$.

An excellent fit of Eq. (7.4.2) was obtained using the BMDP program PAR, yielding a pseudo multiple correlation of 0.88. The prediction equation was

$$u(k, 16; p) = (1.548 + 0.248p) (0.868 + 0.0016p)^{16-k+p} /(k + 1.84)$$

where p was set at the middle output test list locations of 4,12,20 and 28. The observed and predicted values for the four output ranges employed in Ratcliff's data analysis are shown in Figure 6. The increase in the memory permanence parameter with output position may reflect the operation of rehearsal generated by the spontaneous repetition of study items in the recall list.

7.5 Memory for Recency and Order.

The simplest mechanism for the recall of the order of memorised items involves a comparison of the matching functions generated by the probe items. When two items are presented at locations k_i and k_j, $i<j$, in the original study list containing t items, this difference is given by

$$d(k_i, k_j; t) = \beta(k_i)\, \alpha^{t-k_i} - \beta(k_j)\, \alpha^{t-k_j} = \alpha^{t-k_j}\, [\beta(k_i)\, \alpha^{k_j-k_i} - \beta(k_j)]$$

which depends on both the recency of the later item, $t-k_j$, and the time interval between the items, $k_j - k_i$. For example, if $\beta(k) = \beta$, a constant, then $d(k_i, k_j; t)$ increases as the study position of the more recent item increases and the time delay between the two items increases, a result commonly observed in the literature (Hockley, 1984).

8. CONCLUSION

An adaptive model for human information processing has been proposed to accommodate the complex control processes required to adjust to environmental changes. It has been shown that a model based on adaptive control theory can be used to model memory processes in a variety of standard experimental paradigms. The distinguishing features of the model are its assumption that item and associative information can be stored by means of the same autoassociative storage operation and that parameters representing the memory performance of individual subjects can be estimated using a suitable stochastic model for the decision process.

There remain many unanswered questions about the ability of the parallel distributed processing models (Rumelhart and McClelland, 1986) to explicate complex cognitive processes. It is hoped that the use of parameter estimation procedures can complement the extensive research findings revealed by the use of computer simulation, and so help bridge the gap between the work of experimental psychologists and cognitive scientists.

ACKNOWLEDGEMENTS

This research was supported by a grant from the Australian Research Grants Scheme. I wish to thank Christopher Willcox and Ross Fulham for assistance in the preparation of the paper. The painstaking job of typing the paper was performed by Helen Finegan and Sharon Harris.

Correspondence concerning this paper should be addressed to Richard A. Heath, Department of Psychology, The University of Newcastle, N.S.W. 2308, Australia.

REFERENCES

Casey, P. & Heath, R.A. (1989). A semantic memory sentence verification model based on Relative Judgment Theory. Memory and Cognition (in press).

Eich, J.M. (1982). A composite holographic associative recall model. Psychological Review, 89, 627-661.

Eich, J.M. (1985). Levels of processing, encoding specificity, elaboration and CHARM. Psychological Review, 92, 1-38.

Geyer, L.H. (1977). Recognition and confusion of the lowercase alphabet. Perception & Psychophysics, 22, 487-490.

Heath, R.A. (1981). A tandem random walk model for psychological discrimination. British Journal of Mathematical and Statistical Psychology, 34, 76-92.

Heath, R.A. (1982). A model for signal detection based on an adaptive filter. Biological Cybernetics, 45, 95-100.

Heath, R.A. (1983). FITTRW: A parameter estimation program for a general random walk analysis of two choice response time (2CRT) data. Behaviour Research Methods and Instrumentation, 15, 95-96.

Heath, R.A. (1984). The detection of change in physiological measures using an adaptive Kalman filter algorithm. Psychological Bulletin, 96, 581-588.

Heath, R.A. & Fulham, R. (1985).Applications of system identification and adaptive filtering techniques in human information processing. In G. d'Ydewalle (Ed.), Cognition, information processing and motivation. Amsterdam: Elsevier Science, pp. 117-147.

Heath, R.A. & Fulham, R. (1988). An adaptive filter model for recognition memory. British Journal of Mathematical and Statistical Psychology, 41, 119-144.

Hockley, W.E. (1984). Analysis of response time distributions in the study of cognitive processes. Journal of Experimental Psychology: Learning, Memory and Cognition, 10, 598-615.

Link, S.W. & Heath, R.A. (1975). A sequential theory of psychological discrimination. Psychometrika, 40, 77-105.

McClelland, J.L. (1979). On the time relations of mental processes in cascade. Psychological Review, 86, 287-330.

Murdock, B.B., Jr. (1982). A theory for the storage and retrieval of item and associative information. Psychological Review, 89, 609-626.

Murdock, B.B., Jr. (1983). A distributed memory model for serial order information. Psychological Review, 90, 316-338.

Murdock, B.B., Jr. & Franklin, P.E. (1984). Associative and serial-order information: Different modes of operation? Memory and Cognition, 12, 243-249.

Ratcliff, R. (1978). A theory of memory retrieval. Psychological Review, 85, 59-108.

Rumelhart, D.E. & McClelland, J.L. (1986). Parallel distributed processing: Explorations in the microstructure of cognition, Volume 1: Foundations. Cambridge, Mass.: The MIT Press.

Stone, G.O. (1986). An analysis of the delta rule and the learning of statistical associations. In D.E. Rumelhart & J.L. McClelland (Eds.) Parallel distributed processing: Explorations in the microstructure of cognition. Volume 1: Foundations. Cambridge, Mass.: MIT Press, pp. 444-459.

Widrow, G. & Hoff, M.E. (1960). Adaptive switching circuits. Institute of Radio Engineers, Western Electronic Show and Convention, Convention Record, Part 4, 96-104.

Human Information Processing: Measures,
Mechanisms, and Models, D. Vickers and P.L. Smith (eds.)
© Elsevier Science Publishers B.V. (North-Holland), 1989

STOCHASTIC GENERAL RECOGNITION THEORY

F. Gregory Ashby

University of California

General recognition theory assumes that the perceptual effect of a stimulus is random and that on any single trial it can be represented as a point in a multidimensional space. The theory successfully accounts for many important categorization, identification, and perceived similarity results. The present study provides a stochastic interpretation of the static theory. Each stimulus component is assumed to provide input into a parallel distributed processing system consisting of a set of mutually interacting perceptual channels. The channel outputs describe a point that moves through a multidimensional perceptual space during processing. General recognition theory is shown to describe the equilibrium behaviour of this system and thus the stochastic version can account for all results of the older static theory. In addition, the stochastic version is shown to have the potential to make response time predictions and to account for the effects of tachistoscopic stimulus presentation.

1. INTRODUCTION

General recognition theory is a general perceptual theory that successfully accounts for many important results of perceived similarity, identification, categorization, and preference (Ashby & Gott, 1988; Ashby & Perrin, 1988; Perrin, 1986). In addition, it has been used to formalize and interrelate a variety of concepts that are associated with perceptual independence (Ashby, 1988; Ashby & Townsend, 1986). The fundamental assumption of general recognition theory is that the perceptual effect of a stimulus is random and on any single trial it can be represented as a point in a multidimensional space. Essentially, the theory is a multivariate generalization of signal detection theory (e.g., Green & Swets, 1966; Tanner, 1956).

One current limitation of the theory is its static nature. Like signal detection theory it makes no response time predictions, nor does it describe the dynamic nature of processing as it unfolds during the course of an experimental trial. In this article, I will describe a stochastic version of general recognition theory, which I believe has the potential to unify results from a wide variety of experimental paradigms.

2. GENERAL RECOGNITION THEORY

General recognition theory assumes that the identification or categorization process is composed of sensory and perceptual subprocesses, and a separate decision subprocess. The sensory and perceptual processes encode the stimulus and abstract a perceptual representation. On any single trial, the perceptual effect can be represented as a point in a multidimensional space. Stimulus and perceptual noise cause the perceptual effect to vary from trial to trial. With two perceptual dimensions, x_1 and x_2, let $f_i(x_1,x_2)$ be the joint probability distribution (i.e., joint density function) of the perceptual effects elicited by stimulus i (constructed from stimulus dimensions, X_1 and X_2).

The decision process uses the perceptual effect to select a response. For example, consider an identification experiment. On each trial, the subject's task is to uniquely identify the single presented stimulus. General recognition theory assumes that, through experience with the stimuli, the subject comes to learn which regions of the perceptual space are associated with which responses. To respond on a given trial, the subject only needs to determine into which region the perceptual effect associated with the presented stimulus happened to fall. The decision bound is the line or curve separating the response regions.

Ashby and Gott (1988) used general recognition theory to characterize large classes of existing decision models according to the type of decision bound the models predict. For example, independent decisions models (e.g, feature analytic models; see Blackwell, 1963; Shaw, 1982; Townsend & Ashby, 1982) predict decision bounds that are parallel to the coordinate axes. Minimum distance models, which are associated with multidimensional scaling, prototype models of categorization, and many distributed memory models, predict a linear decision bound that bisects and is perpendicular to the chord connecting the means of the perceptual distributions. On the other hand, ideal observer or optimal models generally predict curved decision bounds.

To discriminate empirically between the alternative decision models, Ashby and Gott developed an experimental paradigm, called the randomization technique, in which the normally unobservable perceptual space is approximated by the observable stimulus space. The randomization technique is a categorization task but it is meant also to mimic the decision processes involved in identification.

In a two stimulus identification task, general recognition theory assumes there are two relevant multivariate perceptual distributions. In the randomization technique, numerical parameter values that specify a pair of multivariate distributions are chosen by the experimenter. On each trial, a random sample is drawn from one of the two distributions. The numerical sample values on each dimension are then used to construct a stimulus, which is presented to the subject. The subject's task is to categorize the stimulus as a member of class A or B. In the prototypical experiment, error-free performance is impossible and the subject is given feedback about the correct response on every trial.

As a specific instantiation, suppose the stimuli of both categories consist of a vertical and horizontal line segment joined at an upper left corner and that categorization is possible because the line segments in the different categories tend to differ in length. For example, samples from category A might tend to have long vertical segments and short horizontal segments whereas samples from B might tend to have short vertical and long horizontal segments. In this case, on every trial a random sample (X_1, X_2) is drawn from one of the two bivariate distributions and a stimulus with horizontal length X_1 and vertical length X_2 is presented to the subject.

The stimulus category, the actual line lengths, and the subject's response are all recorded on every trial. The actual line lengths correspond to a point somewhere in the X_1, X_2 plane. Stimulus contrast is high and displays are response terminated so that the X_1, X_2 stimulus plane should correspond monotonically to the x_1, x_2 perceptual plane. A subject's decision bound can be estimated by observing the pattern of his or her responses throughout the plane. For example, independent decisions can be ruled out if the subject's A and B responses can be partitioned by a single curve or diagonal line.

Using the randomization technique with stimuli of this type, Ashby and Gott obtained strong evidence that their subjects used deterministic decision rules. For a given location in the perceptual space and a fixed value of the decision bound, most subjects appeared to always give the same response. Such deterministic responding is incompatible with many popular categorization models (e.g., the context theory of Medin & Schaffer, 1978). The experiments also demonstrated that there are few natural constraints on the decision process. In particular, subjects were not constrained to make independent decisions, they were not constrained by minimum distance classification and, although the evidence was not as clear-cut on this point, they apparently were not constrained to use linear decision bounds. Instead, subjects appeared first to choose simple decision rules that place a minimal burden on available cognitive resources. If these prove inadequate however, subjects apparently have the ability to learn more complex rules.

In general recognition theory, the probability of confusing a pair of stimuli in an identification task is determined by the amount their perceptual distributions overlap, rather than by something like the distance between their prototypical perceptual effects. More specifically, with two stimuli, A and B, the probability of confusing B for A is equal to the proportion of the A perceptual distribution falling in the response region assigned to B. Therefore, under the assumption that confusability and similarity covary, Ashby and Perrin (1988) showed that perceived similarity is functionally determined by distributional overlap, or in particular, that the perceived similarity of A to B is proportional to the probability of confusing B for A in an unbiased identification task.

Ashby and Perrin (1988) showed that this theory of perceived similarity contains Euclidean multidimensional scaling models (e.g., Torgerson, 1958; Shepard, 1962a, b; Kruskal, 1964a, b) as a special case; even those that allow the subject to place differential weights on oblique psychological dimensions (e.g., Carroll & Chang, 1972; Tucker, 1972). Unlike the distance-based similarity theories however, general recognition theory is not constrained by any of the distance axioms. In a natural way, it is also able to account for contextual effects. Ashby and Perrin (1988) also reported several empirical tests that supported the general recognition theory of similarity.

In addition to these empirical applications, Ashby and Townsend (1986) used general recognition theory to investigate the theoretical relation between several varieties of perceptual independence. These included sampling independence (a condition that is critical to many feature models of letter recognition), dimensional orthogonality, stimulus separability and integrality, and performance parity. They began by using general recognition theory to obtain a precise definition of perceptual independence.

Consider a stimulus $A(i)B(j)$ constructed from a physical component A at level i and a component B at level j. Suppose x_1 is the perceptual dimension associated with component A and x_2 is the dimension associated with B. Perceptual independence occurs if and only if the perceptual effects of A and B are statistically independent, or in other words, if and only if for all values of x_1 and x_2

$$f_{ij}(x_1,x_2) = g_{ij}(x_1)\, g_{ij}(x_2) ,$$

where $g_{ij}(x_k)$ is the marginal distribution of perceptual effects on dimension x_k when the stimulus is $A(i)B(j)$. Perceptual separability occurs if and only if the perceptual effect of one component does not depend on the level of the other, or equivalently if, for example

$$g_{i1}(x_1) = g_{i2}(x_1) \qquad (1)$$

for all values of x_1 and for all levels of i. Similarly, decisional separability occurs if the decision about one component does not depend on the level of the other, that is, if the decision bounds are parallel to the coordinate axes.

Using these definitions, Ashby and Townsend (1986) showed that none of the concepts they investigated are equivalent to perceptual independence but that if decisional separability holds, then sampling independence is equivalent to perceptual independence. They suggested several simple tests of separability and they showed that dimensional orthogonality is a valid test of perceptual independence only if some strong distributional assumptions are made about the perceptual effects of stimuli. Recently I (Ashby, 1988) extended the results of Ashby and Townsend (1986) to an experimental paradigm used in the spatial vision literature called the concurrent rating task (e.g., Hirsch, Hylton, & Graham, 1982; Olzak, 1986).

Ashby and Townsend (1986) also briefly examined response time tests of independence and separability but they concluded that "it is impossible to specify the exact relationship between the two (i.e., response time and accuracy tests) without an explicit theory relating the perceptual representation to the processing time of a stimulus" (p. 172). Because response time separability tests are so widely used (e.g., Garner, 1974), this problem is especially important. Developing such a theory is a major goal of this article.

General recognition theory is a powerful and general perceptual theory that can provide a unified description of categorization, identification, concurrent ratings, perceived similarity, and preference. Even so, its ultimate potential is limited by its static nature. A dynamic version of general recognition theory would make many contributions. First, it would make response time predictions in each of the above tasks. Second, it would allow the tests of independence and separability developed by Ashby and Townsend (1986) and Ashby (1988) to be generalized to include response time measures. It would also allow the response time tests of Garner (1974) to be related theoretically to the accuracy tests developed within the general recognition theory framework. Third, it would provide a theory of the speed-accuracy tradeoff that could be applied to each of the above experimental paradigms. Fourth, it would provide an explicit account of the effects of limiting stimulus exposure duration on each of these tasks. A related benefit is that such a theory would account for instances of dynamic stimulus presentation. This might include forward and backward masking as well as situations in which a series of stimuli is presented on each trial. Finally, a dynamic general recognition theory would attempt to provide an account of trial by trial sequential effects that are frequently observed when the response stimulus interval (RSI) is small.

3. STOCHASTIC GENERAL RECOGNITION THEORY

A processing structure that has long been associated with signal detection theory and therefore that is compatible with general recognition theory is the notion of a processing channel. Classical signal detection theory has traditionally limited itself to single channel models because of its emphasis on unidimensional stimulus representations. General recognition theory is concerned primarily with stimuli composed of several separate components and therefore a dynamic version of general recognition theory based on the notion of processing channels would involve an array of such channels, each tuned to a different stimulus component and all mutually interacting. The outputs of these channels would determine the location of the perceptual effect in the perceptual space. The decision process could operate on the perceptual effects just as it does in the static general recognition theory.

A natural way to model such an array of mutually interacting channels is as a parallel distributed processing (PDP) system of the type proposed by Anderson (e.g., Anderson & Mozer, 1981; Anderson, Silverstein, Ritz, & Jones, 1977), Kohonen (e.g., Kohonen, 1977; Kohonen, Lehtio, & Oja, 1981), Rumelhart and McClelland (1986; McClelland & Rumelhart, 1986), and others. A diagram of the proposed network is given in Figure 1 for the case in which the stimulus is composed of two separate components, which activate two separate processing channels.

The system is composed of three parts; input lines (with weights represented by the b_{ij}), the interacting channels (with interaction weights represented by the a_{ij}), and output lines (with weights represented by the c_{ij} and the d_i). The inputs to the system at time k are denoted by $u_1(k)$ and $u_2(k)$. The ith input is assumed to represent the ith stimulus component. For example, with stimuli constructed from horizontal and vertical line segments of varying length, $u_1(k)$ might be the length of the horizontal segment at time k and $u_2(k)$ the length of the vertical segment [i.e., so that $u_i(k) = X_i(k)$].

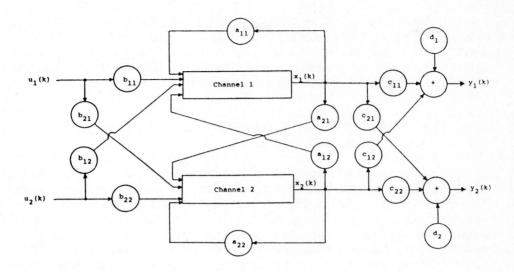

Figure 1: Schematic illustrating the connections between two hypothetical processing channels as postulated by stochastic general recognition theory.

The neural transduction of many stimulus dimensions involves response compression, so that receptor output is a negatively accelerating function of stimulus input (e.g., as with light and sound intensity). In the case of noxious stimuli, the transducer function may even be positively accelerated. Thus, in general I will assume that the network input $u_i(k)$ is related to the stimulus value $X_i(k)$ by Stevens' (1960) law, or in other words, that

$$u_i(k) = [X_i(k)]^{p_i}$$

for some positive constant p_i. The stimulus dimensions in many experiments that have been run to test general recognition theory involve line length, and the Stevens' exponent for perceived length is very close to 1.0 (e.g., Stevens, 1975). Therefore, in these cases $p_i = 1.0$.

The outputs of the channels at time k, denoted by $x_1(k)$ and $x_2(k)$, represent the momentary perceptual effects. With stimuli constructed from horizontal and vertical line lengths, the $x_i(k)$ correspond to the perceived vertical and horizontal lengths. Finally, the outputs of the system are denoted by $y_1(k)$ and $y_2(k)$. Because of decision processes, the system outputs might not equal the perceptual effects.

The channels will be assumed to respond one time unit later with the sum of their inputs. Although at some point it may be necessary to incorporate thresholds and other nonlinearities, for now the simplifying assumption of linear channels will be retained. A major advantage of linearity is that it allows analytic predictions to be obtained. Note that the output of each channel feeds back both as input to itself (multiplied by the weight a_{ii}) and laterally, as input to the other channel (multiplied by the weight a_{ij}). We might expect these lateral interactions to disappear in the presence of perceptual independence (i.e., $a_{12} = a_{21} = 0$).

The nature of the input lines is determined by the b_{ij}. If b_{21} and b_{12} are nonzero, then each stimulus component is at least partially processed by both channels. We might expect both b_{21} and b_{12} to equal zero if perceptual separability holds. Finally, the nature of the output lines is determined by the c_{ij} weights. If c_{21} and c_{12} are nonzero then each output is affected by the perceptual effect of both stimulus components. Under decisional separability we might expect both c_{12} and c_{21} to equal zero. The weights d_1 and d_2 represent potential response criteria or biases.

Note that the behaviour of the channels is described by the equations

$$x_1(k+1) = a_{11} x_1(k) + a_{12} x_2(k) + b_{11} u_1(k) + b_{12} u_2(k)$$

$$x_2(k+1) = a_{21} x_1(k) + a_{22} x_2(k) + b_{21} u_1(k) + b_{22} u_2(k)$$

and that the output is described by the equations

$$y_1(k) = c_{11} x_1(k) + c_{12} x_2(k) + d_1$$

$$y_2(k) = c_{21} x_1(k) + c_{22} x_2(k) + d_2$$

If we define the matrices A, B, and C and the vectors $\underline{u}(k)$, $\underline{x}(k)$, $\underline{y}(k)$, and $\underline{d}$ in the following fashion:

$$A = \begin{bmatrix} a_{11} & a_{12} \\ a_{21} & a_{22} \end{bmatrix} \qquad B = \begin{bmatrix} b_{11} & b_{12} \\ b_{21} & b_{22} \end{bmatrix} \qquad C = \begin{bmatrix} c_{11} & c_{12} \\ c_{21} & c_{22} \end{bmatrix}$$

$$\underline{u}(k) = \begin{bmatrix} u_1(k) \\ u_2(k) \end{bmatrix} \qquad \underline{x}(k) = \begin{bmatrix} x_1(k) \\ x_2(k) \end{bmatrix}$$

$$\underline{y}(k) = \begin{bmatrix} y_1(k) \\ y_2(k) \end{bmatrix} \qquad \underline{d} = \begin{bmatrix} d_1 \\ d_2 \end{bmatrix}$$

then the network equations can be rewritten as

$$\underline{x}(k+1) = A\,\underline{x}(k) + B\,\underline{u}(k) \qquad (2)$$

$$\underline{y}(k) = C\,\underline{x}(k) + \underline{d} \qquad (3)$$

Of course, there is no reason to constrain the network to only two inputs, two channels, and two outputs. In general, we can consider the case in which there are q inputs or stimulus components, r processing channels, and s outputs. In this case, the matrix A is of order r x r, the matrix B is r x q, the matrix C is s x r, and the vector $\underline{d}$ is s x 1.

Equation 2 is a difference equation. Its solution, which is easily found through iteration, can be used to obtain an equation describing the output of the network in terms of the inputs

$$\underline{y}(k) = C\,A^k\,\underline{x}(0) + \underline{d} + C \sum_{i=1}^{k} A^{k-i}\,B\,\underline{u}(i-1) \qquad (4)$$

where $\underline{x}(0)$ is the initial state of the system. By allowing $\underline{x}(0)$ to be nonzero this model can account for sequential effects. Equation 4 makes it possible to obtain exact analytical predictions.

One especially appealing property of the Figure 1 network is that it performs a feature analysis of the input vector (e.g., Anderson et al., 1977). The features are the eigenvectors of the matrix A and the associated eigenvalues measure the sensitivity of the network to that particular feature. The greater the sensitivity of the network to a particular feature (i.e., the larger the associated eigenvalue), the more persistent is the response of the network to that feature.

Next, consider an identification experiment in which we present the subject with response terminated displays. Suppose the stimuli are represented by the vectors $\underline{u}_1, \underline{u}_2, ..., \underline{u}_n$. Then on trials when stimulus i is presented, the input sequence is $\underline{u}(k) = \underline{u}_i$, for all $k > 0$. In this case, the output of each channel initially rises but eventually it will reach and then maintain an equilibrium value, as long as there is no change in the stimulus. On trials when stimulus i is presented, the equilibrium state $\underline{x}_i$ is found by letting $\underline{x}(k+1) = \underline{x}(k) = \underline{x}_i$ in Equation 2 and then solving for $\underline{x}_i$:

$$\underline{x}_i = (I - A)^{-1} \, B \, \underline{u}_i$$

A natural decision strategy is for the subject to associate a different response with each equilibrium state and then on each trial to just wait until an equilibrium state is reached. This strategy will, in general, guarantee perfect performance, but only in the absence of noise.

So far, the model is deterministic. In reality we know that human perceptual processing must overcome several noise sources. Stochastic general recognition theory allows three separate sources of noise: stimulus noise, perceptual noise, and criterial noise. Stimulus noise includes noise masks that the experimenter presents simultaneously with the stimulus as well as uncontrolled stimulus noise, such as quantal fluctuations in light sources. Stimulus noise can be modelled by replacing the input vector $\underline{u}(k)$ in Equation 2 with $\underline{u}(k) + \underline{e}_s(k)$, where $\underline{e}_s(k)$ is a random vector of order q with a multivariate normal distribution with mean $\underline{0}$ and covariance matrix Σ_s For simplicity I will assume that the noise added to different components is statistically independent and therefore that Σ_s is diagonal. Note that the stimulus noise gets dispersed over the input lines according to the weights in the matrix B.

Perceptual noise is generated within the network, specifically within each processing channel. In addition to the other inputs, channel i therefore receives a perceptual noise input represented by the normally distributed random variable $e_{ip}(k)$. Since there are r channels, the perceptual noise is represented by the r-dimensional random vector $\underline{e}_p(k)$ that has a multivariate normal distribution with mean $\underline{0}$ and covariance matrix Σ_p. I assume that the perceptual noise input to different channels is statistically independent and therefore that Σ_p is diagonal. Of course, interactions between channels could lead to a statistical dependence of the outputs of different channels.

Finally, criterial noise may be generated in the decision end of the network, specifically at the last "plus" nodes in Figure 1. Let the effects of criterial noise be represented by the s-dimensional random vector $\underline{e}_c(k)$, which is assumed to have a multivariate normal distribution with mean $\underline{0}$ and diagonal covariance matrix Σ_c . The most general possible model therefore, with all three noise sources, is described by the equations

$$\underline{x}(k+1) = A\,\underline{x}(k) + \underline{e}_p(k) + B\,[\underline{u}(k) + \underline{e}_s(k)] \tag{5}$$

$$\underline{y}(k) = C\,\underline{x}(k) + \underline{e}_c(k) + \underline{d} \tag{6}$$

The noise sources will not affect the qualitative behaviour of the model. When a stimulus is presented to the network, activity on the channels will still tend to increase. This activity can be represented as a point in a multidimensional space in which the output of each channel corresponds to a dimension. If the noise does not depend on time (i.e., on k), then with response terminated displays the output will still achieve an equilibrium state, but the equilibrium point will vary from trial to trial. Specifically the equilibrium state on trials when stimulus $\underline{u}_i$ is presented is given by

$$\underline{x}_i = (I - A)^{-1}\,B\,[\underline{u}_i + \underline{e}_s] + (I - A)^{-1}\,\underline{e}_p \tag{7}$$

Because both $\underline{e}_s$ and $\underline{e}_p$ are normally distributed, the equilibrium point is also normally distributed, with mean vector

$$E(\underline{x}_i) = (I - A)^{-1}\,B\,\underline{u}_i \tag{8}$$

and covariance matrix

$$\mathrm{Cov}(\underline{x}_i) = (I - A)^{-1}\,[B\,\Sigma_s\,B^T + \Sigma_p]\,[(I - A)^{-1}]^T \tag{9}$$

Thus, with response terminated displays, the perceptual effects of each stimulus are represented by a multivariate normal distribution and so all predictions of the model, with the exception of latencies, can be obtained from general recognition theory. This is an important advantage of this approach. Because general recognition theory has been extensively studied, we know that stochastic general recognition theory is able to accurately describe detection, identification, categorization, similarity, and preference.

3.1 Decision Rules in Stochastic General Recognition Theory

With response terminated displays and instructions that emphasize accuracy over speed, it is natural for the subject to select a response on the basis of the equilibrium state of the perceptual processing system. However, under instructions that emphasize speed over accuracy the subject might choose to respond before equilibrium is reached, and with tachistoscopic presentation, no nonzero equilibrium state may exist. In these cases, the decision problem facing the subject is more difficult than with response terminated displays and no speed stress. In the next two subsections, the unique decision problems accompanying speed stress and tachistoscopic presentation are considered in some detail.

3.1.1 Speed stress.

Consider first the case in which subjects are instructed to respond as quickly and accurately as possible. For simplicity suppose there are only two possible responses and that the perceptual distributions are such that in the absence of speed stress the subject uses the bound $x_2 = x_1$. This situation might occur either in a two stimulus identification task or in a categorization task that employs the randomization technique. Within stochastic general recognition theory this implies

$$y(n) = [-1 \ 1] \, \underline{x}(n)$$

and thus $y(n) > 0$ if and only if $x_2(n) > x_1(n)$. Ashby and Gott (1988) showed that when the stimulus dimensions are line length, subjects easily learn this rule and that they apply it in an accurate and reliable fashion.

Given the bound $x_2 = x_1$, stochastic general recognition theory assumes that as the point representing the output of the channels moves through the perceptual space, the evidence favours response A whenever the point is above the bound. Let $d(n)$ be the distance from the point $\underline{x}(n)$ at time n to the bound and let $d^*(n) = d(n)$ when the point is above the bound and $d^*(n) = - d(n)$ when it is below. When $d^*(n)$ is large and positive, note that category A is strongly indicated and when it is negative, category B is indicated. In a task where the subject is under some time pressure, a plausible strategy is to accumulate the $d^*(n)$ and to wait until this sum either exceeds some criterion α and then to respond A or until it falls below a criterion $- \beta$ and then to respond B.

This process describes a random walk in time (e.g., Ashby, 1983; Link & Heath, 1974; Luce, 1986; Townsend & Ashby, 1983). The position of the walk at time n is

$$w(n) = \sum_{i=1}^{n} d^*(i)$$

At each time point, the subject is assumed to terminate and respond A if $w(n) \geq \alpha$, to respond B if $w(n) \leq - \beta$ and otherwise to wait one more time unit.

Suppose $\underline{x}(n)^T = [x_1(n), x_2(n)]$ and that the subject is using the bound $x_2 = x_1$. Then the normal through $\underline{x}(n)$ is

$$x_2 = x_2(n) + x_1(n) - x_1$$

and the Euclidean distance from $\underline{x}(n)$ to the bound is

$$d(n) = \{ [x_2(n) - x_1(n)]^2 / 2 \}^{1/2}$$

and therefore

$$d^*(n) = [x_2(n) - x_1(n)]/\sqrt{2}$$

$$= [-1/\sqrt{2} \quad 1/\sqrt{2}] \; \underline{x}(n)$$

$$\Rightarrow \quad w(n) = [-1/\sqrt{2} \quad 1/\sqrt{2}] \sum_{i=1}^{n} \underline{x}(i)$$

Since $\underline{x}(i)$ has a bivariate normal distribution, $w(n)$, the position of the walk at time n is normally distributed and so it should be possible to generate categorization time predictions from this model.

3.1.2 Tachistoscopic stimulus presentations.

To examine the decision problem facing the subject in the case of tachistoscopic stimulus presentation, consider the identification experiment reported by Townsend, Hu, and Kadlac (1988). In this study, eight stimuli were constructed by factorially combining three components, A, B and C. The stimuli can be designated as A (A alone), B, C, AB (A and B present), AC, BC, ABC (all components present), and Blank (all components absent). In the Townsend et al. experiment, the components were a horizontal (A), a vertical (B), and a diagonal (C) line segment all joined at an upper left corner.

On each trial, one of these stimuli was tachistoscopically presented to the subject, whose task was to uniquely identify the presented stimulus. Three different exposure durations were used. The shortest duration was selected so that each subject's averaged overall accuracy was about 50%. With the intermediate duration, accuracy was about 70% and with the longest duration, accuracy was about 85%. Two subjects each participated in 20 one-hour experimental sessions. The first five sessions were regarded as practice but each subject still experienced 400 presentations of each stimulus at each exposure duration. Data from such an identification experiment are conveniently catalogued in a confusion matrix, which contains an estimate of $P(R_j|S_i)$ in row i and column j.

Within stochastic general recognition theory, limiting the exposure duration of a stimulus S_i can be represented by assuming that the stimulus sequence is $\underline{u}(j) = \underline{u}_i$ for $j = 1, 2, ..., N$ and $\underline{u}(j) = 0$ for all $j > N$, where N is proportional to the exposure duration. In this case, if the network is at rest when the stimulus is presented (i.e., there are no residual effects of prior stimuli), the state vector will initially begin to move away from the origin. Activity will continue to grow as long as the stimulus is present. After it is removed, however, activity will eventually begin to wane, until finally the network will again come to rest. With tachistoscopic presentation therefore, no nonzero equilibrium point will exist and so the decision problem facing the subject is more difficult than with response terminated displays.

Under the conditions of the Townsend et al. experiment, it is reasonable to suppose that the subject divides the perceptual space into eight regions and assigns a different response to each. Logically, the origin will be included in the region assigned to the Blank response. On trials when the Blank is presented, noise may cause some activity in the channels but the state vector will tend to remain near the origin and so a Blank response will be likely.

Because subjects in these experiments are typically under no time pressure to respond, one plausible decision rule is for the subject to wait until activity in the network is at its maximum and then to emit the response associated with the region containing the state vector. In the typical identification experiment of this sort, exposure duration is limited but no external noise is added to the stimulus. Therefore, for simplicity I will assume only time-invariant perceptual noise. In this case Equation 5 reduces to

$$\underline{x}(k+1) = A\,\underline{x}(k) + \underline{e}_p + B\,\underline{u}_i \qquad \text{for } 1 \le k \le N$$

$$= A\,\underline{x}(k) + \underline{e}_p \qquad \text{for } k > N$$

In this model, activity will tend to be greatest one time unit after the stimulus is removed, or in other words at $k = N+1$. Therefore, one natural possibility is for the subject to base his or her response on the location of $\underline{x}(N+1)$.

In the case of the Townsend et al. (1988) experiment, it is natural to assume one channel for each of the three stimulus components as well as decisional separability (i.e., $C = I$ and $\underline{d} = -\underline{x}_0$), or in other words that the subject constructs the eight response regions by placing decision bounds parallel to each coordinate axis. In the absence of sequential effects, on trials when stimulus i is presented, the state vector at time $N+1$ is given by

$$\underline{x}_i(N+1) = \sum_{j=1}^{N+1} A^{j-1} \underline{e}_p + \sum_{j=1}^{N-1} A^j B \underline{u}_i$$

$$= [I + A^{(N)}] \underline{e}_p + A^{(N-1)} B \underline{u}_i$$

where

$$A^{(k)} = \sum_{j=1}^{k} A^j$$

Thus $\underline{x}_i(N+1)$ is normally distributed with mean vector

$$\underline{\mu}_i = A^{(N-1)} B \underline{u}_i$$

and with covariance matrix

$$\Sigma_i = [I + A^{(N)}][I + A^{(N)}]^T.$$

Therefore, for example, the probability that the subject responds ABC on trials when stimulus i is presented is given by

$$P(ABC|S_i) = \int_{x_{o3}}^{\infty} \int_{x_{o2}}^{\infty} \int_{x_{o1}}^{\infty} N(\underline{\mu}_i, \Sigma_i) \, dx_1 \, dx_2 \, dx_3$$

where $N(\underline{\mu}_i, \Sigma_i)$ represents the multivariate normal probability density function with mean vector $\underline{\mu}_i$ and covariance matrix Σ_i.

The Appendix shows that this multiple integral reduces to

$$P(ABC \mid S_i) = P(a_{11} Z_1 > x_{01} - \mu_1, a_{21}Z_2 + a_{22}Z_3 > x_{02} - \mu_2, a_{31}Z_1 + a_{32}Z_2$$

$$+ a_{33}Z_3 > x_{03} - \mu_3) \tag{10}$$

where the Z_1 are independent and identically distributed random variables with a standard normal distribution and the a_{ij} are entries in the so-called Cholesky matrix A. For any covariance matrix Σ, there exists a unique lower triangular matrix A, called the Cholesky matrix, such that $\Sigma = A\ A^T$ (e.g. Graybill, 1976). The advantage of Equation 10 is that the coefficients of the matrix A can be easily computed and since the Z_i are mutually independent, the equation can be quickly evaluated using numerical integration.

3.2 Perceptual Independence and Separability

Several of the operational tests of separability that were proposed by Garner (1974) involve response time measures. For example, with stimuli A(1)B(1), A(1)B(2), A(2)B(1), and A(2)B(2), Garner suggested that if components A and B are separable then the time to categorize the stimuli according to the level of component A should not depend on whether there is variation in the level of component B. This separability criterion is widely used, but was established operationally and lacks a theoretical foundation. For example, it is not clear under what conditions perceptual separability, as defined in Equation 1, implies this response time invariance. In particular, it is unclear whether perceptual independence is required.

Stochastic general recognition theory can be used to investigate the theoretical relation between speeded classification and perceptual separability (and independence). The first requirement for investigating these concepts is to determine their influence on the connections between lines in the network. Specifically, what form must the matrices A, B, and C of Equations 2 and 3 take to ensure perceptual independence and/or perceptual separability? From Ashby and Townsend (1986) we know that on trials when stimulus A(i)B(j) is presented, components A and B are perceived independently if the covariance matrix associated with the equilibrium point, $\mathrm{Cov}(\underline{x}_{ij})$, is diagonal. Suppose there is no stimulus noise. Then we see from Equation 9 that

$$\mathrm{Cov}(\underline{x}_{ij}) = (I - A)^{-1} \Sigma_p [(I - A)^{-1}]^T .$$

Since Σ_p is diagonal it is easy to see that perceptual independence holds, as we intuited, if A is diagonal, or in other words, if there is no interaction between channels. However, the Appendix shows that independence can occur even if A is not diagonal. It can occur, for example, if $\Sigma_p^{-1/2} (I - A)$ is orthogonal.

Perceptual separability holds if:

$$Cov(\underline{x}_{i1}) = Cov(\underline{x}_{i2}) \qquad \text{for } i = 1 \text{ and } 2$$

and
$$Cov(\underline{x}_{1j}) = Cov(\underline{x}_{2j}) \qquad \text{for } j = 1 \text{ and } 2$$

and if
$$[1 \ 0] \, E(\underline{x}_{i1}) = [1 \ 0] \, E(\underline{x}_{i2}) \qquad \text{for } i = 1 \text{ and } 2$$

and
$$[0 \ 1] \, E(\underline{x}_{1j}) = [0 \ 1] \, E(\underline{x}_{2j}) \qquad \text{for } j = 1 \text{ and } 2 \, .$$

From Equations 8 and 9 it is clear that a sufficient condition for perceptual separability is that the matrices A and B are diagonal. This makes sense. There is no crossing of the input lines and no crosstalk between channels. On the other hand, the diagonality of A and B are not necessary conditions. For example, perceptual separability will occur if $(I - A)^{-1} B$ is diagonal. One way for this to occur is if $B = (I - A)$. In this case the input lines may cross and there may be crosstalk between channels but these two effects, in a sense, cancel each other out and so this particular possibility seems unlikely.

If perceptual separability and independence occur then decisional separability results if the subject simply sets a criterion on the output of each channel, or in other words if

$$\underline{y}(n) = \underline{x}(n) - \underline{x}_o \qquad (11)$$

where $\underline{x}_o$ is a vector containing the criteria. In this case, the first entry in $\underline{y}(n)$ is positive if and only if the output of the first channel exceeds a criterion value, irrespective of the activity on any other channels. Note that Equation 11, and hence decisional separability, holds if C is diagonal. Again, this is as we intuited. The off-diagonal elements in the C matrix represent the integration of information across channels and because there is no such integration with decisional separability, we expect C to be diagonal.

If perceptual separability or independence fail then the diagonality of C is of interest because it still implies a sort of decisional separability. However, in this case it is a decisional separability of the perceptual dimensions and not the experimenter defined dimensions. In stochastic general recognition theory, the matrix C is under the subject's control (as is the vector $\underline{d}$) since it is part of the decision process. Because of specific instructions from the experimenter, the subject might try to decisionally separate the experimenter defined dimensions, even if these do not correspond to the perceptual dimensions.

From Equations 6 and 7, it can be seen that at equilibrium, the decision vector is given by

$$\underline{y}_i = C(I - A)^{-1} B \underline{u}_i + C(I - A)^{-1} [B \underline{e}_s + \underline{e}_p] + \underline{e}_c + \underline{d} .$$

Therefore, because each of the noise vectors has zero mean and a diagonal covariance matrix, decisional separability will occur if and only if $C(I - A)^{-1} B$ is diagonal. The most obvious way for this to happen is if A, B, and C are all diagonal. This corresponds to the case of perceptual and decisional separability and perceptual independence. However, even if perceptual separability and independence fail, we see that the subject can decisionally separate the stimulus components by constructing C so that, for example, $C = [(I - A)^{-1} B]^{-1}$.

Once the concepts of separability and independence have been translated into conditions on the A, B, and C matrices, it becomes possible to test the validity of the operational definitions of separability that use response times. For example, if perceptual separability holds but perceptual independence fails, will variation on an irrelevant dimension slow categorization? In addition, it allows the possibility of developing response time tests of perceptual independence. Unfortunately, a solution to each of these problems is beyond the scope of this article.

4. APPENDIX

4.1 Derivation of Equation 10

By the properties of the lower triangular Cholesky matrix A, $\Sigma_i = A\ A^T$. Therefore, the multivariate random vector $\underline{X}$ can be represented as $\underline{X} = A\underline{Z} + \underline{\mu}_i$, where $\underline{Z}$ is a random vector with a multivariate Z distribution. Thus

$$P(ABC \mid S_i) = P(X_1 > x_{01}, X_2 > x_{02}, X_3 > x_{03})$$

$$= P([1\ 0\ 0]\ \underline{X} > x_{01}, [0\ 1\ 0]\ \underline{X} > x_{02}, [0\ 0\ 1]\ \underline{X} > x_{03})$$

$$= P\{[1\ 0\ 0]\ (A\underline{Z} + \underline{\mu}) > x_{01}, [0\ 1\ 0]\ (A\underline{Z} + \underline{\mu}) > x_{02},$$

$$[0\ 0\ 1]\ (A\underline{Z} + \underline{\mu}) > x_{03})\}$$

$$= P([1\ 0\ 0]\ A\underline{Z} > x_{01} - \mu_1\ [0\ 1\ 0]\ A\underline{Z} > x_{02} - \mu_2,$$

$$[0\ 0\ 1]\ A\underline{Z} > x_{03} - \mu_3)$$

$$= P(a_{11}\ Z_1 > x_{01} - \mu_1, a_{21}Z_2 + a_{22}Z_3 > x_{02} - \mu_2, a_{31}Z_1 + a_{32}Z_2$$

$$+ a_{33}Z_3 > x_{03} - \mu_3)$$

4.2 Proof that diagonality of A is not required for perceptual independence

Perceptual independence occurs if

$$(I - A)^{-1} \Sigma\ [(I - A)^{-1}]^T = D$$

where D is diagonal. But since

$$[(I - A)^{-1}]^T = [(I - A)^T]^{-1}$$

this requirement can be rewritten as

$$(I - A)^{-1} \Sigma\ [(I - A)^T]^{-1} = D$$

which implies

$$(I - A)^T \Sigma^{-1} (I - A) = D^{-1}$$

and

$$[\Sigma^{-1/2}(I - A)]^T [\Sigma^{-1/2}(I - A)] = D^{-1/2} D^{-1/2}$$

and

$$D^{1/2} [\Sigma^{-1/2}(I - A)]^T [\Sigma^{-1/2}(I - A)] D^{1/2} = I$$

and finally

$$[\Sigma^{-1/2}(I - A) D^{1/2}]^T [\Sigma^{-1/2}(I - A) D^{1/2}] = I$$

Therefore, perceptual independence implies that $\Sigma^{-1/2}(I - A) D^{1/2}$ is orthogonal. Orthogonal matrices need not be diagonal. Since Σ, I and D are diagonal, $\Sigma^{-1/2}(I - A) D^{1/2}$ is not diagonal only if A is not diagonal.

CORRESPONDENCE

Correspondence concerning this paper should be addressed to F. Gregory Ashby, Department of Psychology, University of California, Santa Barbara, CA 93106, U.S.A

REFERENCES

Anderson, J.A., & Mozer, M.C. (1981). Categorization and selective neurons. In G.E. Hinton and J.A. Anderson (Eds.), Parallel models of associative memory (pp. 213-236). Hillsdale, N.J.: Lawrence Erlbaum Associates.

Anderson, J.A., Silverstein, J.W., Ritz, S.A., & Jones, R.S. (1977). Distinctive features, categorical perception, and probability learning: Some applications of a neural model. Psychological Review, 84, 413-451.

Ashby, F.G. (1983). A biased random walk model for two choice reaction times. Journal of Mathematical Psychology, 27, 277-297.

Ashby, F.G. (1988). Estimating the parameters of multivariate signal detection theory from simultaneous ratings on separate stimulus components. Perception and Psychophysics, 44, 195-204.

Ashby, F.G., & Gott, R.E. (1988). Decision rules in the perception and categorization of multidimensional stimuli. Journal of Experimental Psychology: Learning, Memory, and Cognition, 14, 33-53.

Ashby, F.G., & Perrin, N.A. (1988). Toward a unified theory of similarity and recognition. Psychological Review, 95, 124-150.

Ashby, F.G., & Townsend, J.T. (1986). Varieties of perceptual independence. Psychological Review, 93, 154-179.

Blackwell, H.R. (1963). Neural theories of simple visual discriminations. Journal of the Optical Society of America, 53, 129-160.

Carroll, J.D., & Chang, J.J. (1972, March). IDOSCAL (individual differences in orientation scaling): A generalization of INDSCAL allowing IDIOsyncratic reference systems as well as analytic approximation to INDSCAL. Paper presented at the meeting of the Psychometric Society, Princeton, NJ.

Garner, W.R. (1974). The processing of information and structure. New York: Wiley.

Graybill, F.A. (1976). Theory and Application of the Linear Model. North Scituate, MA: Duxbury Press.

Green, D.M., & Swets, J.A. (1966). Signal detection theory and psychophysics. New York: Wiley.

Hirsch, J., Hylton, R., & Graham, N. (1982). Simultaneous recognition of two spatial-frequency components. Vision Research, 22, 365-375.

Kohonen, T. (1977). Associative memory - A system theoretical approach. Berlin: Springer-Verlag.

Kohonen, T., Lehtio, P., & Oja, E. (1981). Storage and processing of information in distributed associative memory systems. In G.E. Hinton and J.A. Anderson (Eds.), Parallel models of associative memory (pp. 105-143). Hillsdale, N.J.: Lawrence Erlbaum Associates.

Kruskal, J.B. (1964a). Multidimensional scaling by optimizing goodness of fit to a nonmetric hypothesis. Psychometrika, 29, 1-27.

Kruskal, J.B. (1964b). Nonmetric multidimensional scaling: A numerical method. Psychometrika, 29, 115-129.

Link, S.W., & Heath, R. (1974). A sequential theory of psychological discrimination. Psychometrika, 40, 77-105.

Luce, R.D. (1986). Response times. New York: Oxford University Press.

Medin, D.L., & Schaffer, M.M. (1978). Context theory of classification learning. Psychological Review, 85, 207-238.

McClelland, J.L., & Rumelhart, D.E. (Eds.) (1986). Parallel distributed processing: Explorations in the microstructure of cognition. Volume 2: Psychological and Biological Models. Cambridge, Massachusetts: The MIT Press.

Olzak, L.A. (1986). Widely separated spatial frequencies: Mechanism interactions. Vision Research, 26, 1143-1153.

Perrin, N.A. (1986). The general recognition theory of preference: A new theory of choice. Unpublished doctoral dissertation, Ohio State University.

Rumelhart, D.E., & McClelland, J.L. (Eds.) (1986). Parallel distributed processing: Explorations in the microstructure of cognition. Volume 1: Foundations. Cambridge, Massachusetts: The MIT Press.

Shaw, M.L. (1982). Attending to multiple sources of information: I. The integration of information in decision making. Cognitive Psychology, 14, 353-409.

Shepard, R.N. (1962a). The analysis of proximities: Multidimensional scaling with an unknown distance function I. Psychometrika, 27, 125-140.

Shepard, R.N. (1962b). The analysis of proximities: Multidimensional scaling with an unknown distance function II. Psychometrika, 27, 219-246.

Stevens, S.S. (1960). Psychophysics of sensory function. American Scientist, 48, 226-252.

Stevens, S.S. (1975). Psychophysics: An introduction to its perceptual, neural and social prospects. New York: Wiley.

Tanner, W.P. (1956). Theory of recognition. Journal of the Acoustical Society of America, 28, 882-888.

Torgerson, W.S. (1958). Theory and methods of scaling. New York: Wiley.

Townsend, J.T., & Ashby, F.G. (1982). Experimental test of contemporary mathematical models of visual letter recognition. Journal of Experimental Psychology: Human Perception and Performance, 8, 834-864.

Townsend, J.T., & Ashby, F.G. (1983). Stochastic modeling of elementary psychological processes. New York: Cambridge University Press.

Townsend, J.T., Hu, G.G., & Kadlac, H. (1988). Feature sensitivity, bias, and interdependencies as a function of energy and payoffs. Perception & Psychophysics, 43, 575-591.

Tucker, L.R. (1972). Relations between multidimensional scaling and three-mode factor analysis. Psychometrika, 37, 3-28.

SECTION 7

DECISION MAKING

Human Information Processing: Measures,
Mechanisms, and Models, D. Vickers and P. L. Smith (eds.)
© Elsevier Science Publishers B. V. (North-Holland), 1989

AN ADAPTIVE THEORY OF HUMAN DECISION MAKING

Jerome R. Busemeyer and In Jae Myung

Purdue University

How do humans learn to improve their decision strategies through experience with the outcomes of previous decisions? Three decision strategy learning principles are proposed - worth-estimation, hill-climbing, and error-correction. Worth-estimation is used to select the best strategy from a discrete set of qualitatively different strategies (e.g., choosing a diagnostic categorization procedure). The basic idea is that subjects keep track of the running average payoff produced by each strategy, and they tend to choose the strategy producing the greatest average payoff. The other two principles are used to select the best parameters from a continuous set of policies corresponding to a given strategy (e.g., choosing cutoff criteria for a particular diagnostic categorization procedure). According to the hill-climbing principle, parameters are changed a small amount in the direction that previously produced improved payoffs.   According to the error-correction principle, parameters are changed a small amount in the direction that reduces the probability of repeating a previous error. All three principles operate simultaneously after each feedback trial to guide the evolution of strategies.

1. AN ADAPTIVE THEORY OF HUMAN DECISION MAKING

Human decision making is a highly adaptive cognitive skill. Previous research (see Payne, 1983 for a review) indicates that different individuals will display different strategies when confronted with the same situation. Furthermore, the same individual will display different strategies when confronted with different situations. In fact, the past ten years of research can be characterized as a vast program designed to estimate the cell frequencies within the following hypothetical situation × strategy table. The cells represent the frequency that each strategy is selected under each situation.

Table 1

Hypothetical Strategy × Situation Table

Environmental Situation

	E_1	E_2 ...	E_j...	E_N
S_1				
.				
Strategy S_i			P_{ij}	
.				
S_M				

P_{ij} = proportion of individuals choosing strategy i under environmental situation j.

Theoretically, this is an unsatisfactory state of affairs. What is needed is a theoretical mechanism that can be used to predict the frequencies in the above hypothetical table. The present work is based on the premise that decision strategies are evolve from experience, and this evolution can be described by a small set of learning principles. Three learning principles of human decision making are proposed and supporting evidence for each principle is reviewed briefly. The first, called worth-estimation, is used to estimate the worth of each strategy within a discrete set of strategies. The next two, called error correction and hill-climbing, are used to search continuous parameter spaces within each strategy. All three principles are assumed to operate simultaneously, but they are described one at a time below.

2. LEARNING PRINCIPLES

2.1 Worth-Estimation.

This principle is used to learn the best strategy from a finite set of qualitatively different strategies. The basic idea is that individuals keep track of the estimated worth of each strategy (producing a vector of estimates), and they tend to choose the strategy with the highest estimated worth.

Assume that there is a set of N different strategies under consideration $R = \{R_1, ..., R_i, ..., R_N\}$, where R_i is the ith strategy in the set. Each strategy R_i produces a sequence of payoffs which can be ordered in terms of recency $\{V_i(1), V_i(2), ...\}$, where $V_i(1)$ is the most recently experienced payoff produced by strategy i, and $V_i(2)$ is the second most recent payoff. The integer n_i represents the frequency that strategy i was selected from a total of $t = n_1 + ... + n_N$ feedback trials.

The estimated worth of strategy i (denoted W_i) is a forecast about the future payoffs of strategy i, which is generated from the following dynamic linear system. Define $W_i(1)$ as the previous estimate before feedback and define $W_i(0)$ as the new estimate after feedback on trial t. If strategy i was not chosen on trial t, then $W_i(0) = W_i(1)$. If strategy i was chosen on trial t and the payoff $V_i(1)$ was received, then the new estimate equals a linear combination of the previous estimate and the new payoff:

$$W_i(0) = \alpha(n_i) \cdot W_i(1) + \gamma(n_i) \cdot V_i(1) \tag{1}$$

The weights, $\alpha(n_i) > 0$ and $\gamma(n_i) > 0$, may or may not depend on past choice frequency. For example, setting $\alpha(n_i) = (n_i-1)/n_i$ and $\gamma(n_i) = 1/n_i$, produces a mean model, and in this case W_i is the average of all the previous payoffs produced by strategy i. Both averaging and summation models can be defined in terms of the weights in Equation 1. A weighted averaging model is defined by the restriction $\alpha(n_i) + \gamma(n_i) = 1.0$, and a weighted sum model is defined by the restriction $\alpha(n_i) = 1.0$.

The probability of choosing strategy i from the set of N strategies is assumed to follow the monotonic decomposability principle (see Krantz, Luce, Suppes, and Tversky, 1971, p. 317):

$$P[\, R_i \mid R \,] = F_i[W_1, ..., W_i, ..., W_N], \tag{2a}$$

where F_i is an increasing function of the current estimated worth for strategy i, W_i, and a decreasing function of the current estimated worth of each of the other strategies, W_j, $j \neq i$. An important special case of Equation 2a is the familiar ratio rule:

$$P[R_i \mid R\,] = \exp[\beta \cdot W_i] / \Sigma \exp[\beta \cdot W_j], \quad j = 1, ..., N \tag{2b}$$

The parameter β determines the sensitivity of choice to differences in estimated worth. When $\beta = 0$, strategy selection is random, and when β approaches infinity, strategy selection becomes deterministic. In the latter case, the strategy with the highest estimated worth is always chosen.

Equations 1 and 2b are equivalent to Luce's (1959) learning model applied to decision strategies rather than simple responses. More recently, Estes (1987) used Equations 1 and 2b to explain human performance on decision tasks involving uncertainty. Yovits, Foulk, and Rose (1981) have proposed a model that is essentially the same as

Equations 1 and 2b, except that they allow the sensitivity parameter to increase with training. Adaptive production rule models use rule strength principles similar to those proposed here for worth-estimation (e.g., Anderson, 1983).

2.2 Error-Correction.

This principle is used to learn the best set of parameters for problems which provide binary-valued correct/incorrect feedback following each response. Suppose that θ_i is a point within the parameter space of strategy i, and $\{\theta_i(1), \theta_i(2), ...\}$ is the sequence of parameter vectors used with strategy i ordered in terms of recency, where $\theta_i(1)$ is the parameter vector used on the most recent previous application of strategy i, and $\theta_i(2)$ is the vector used on the second most recent application of strategy i. The new parameter vector to be used on the next future application of strategy i is denoted $\theta_i(1)$.

If the strategy was not applied on a particular trial, or if the strategy was applied and a correct decision was made, then no change is made and $\theta_i(0) = \theta_i(1)$. Following an incorrect application of a strategy, a small adjustment is made in the direction of reducing the probability of repeating the previous error. More precisely, if strategy i incorrectly produced response j on the preceding trial, then a new point $\theta_i(0)$ is selected such that the probability of incorrectly producing response j is smaller when the decision is based on $\theta_i(0)$ as compared to a decision based on $\theta_i(1)$.

One advantage of this learning principle is simplicity. Its use only requires recalling the previous type of error and the previous parameter vector. One disadvantage is that it is insensitive to payoff magnitude. This could be overcome by allowing the magnitude or probability of adjustment to vary depending on the magnitudes of the payoffs. However, this extension requires adding a new (and as yet unknown) principle for relating adjustment and payoff magnitudes. The hill-climbing principle described below overcomes this problem without introducing any new parameters.

The error-correction principle was developed to account for uni-dimensional criterion learning in signal detection tasks (Kac, 1962; Thomas, 1973; Dorfman and Biderman, 1971; Norman, 1972). Experimental tests of the error-correction principle have been carried out within the signal detection paradigm with unequal prior probabilities (see Dusoir, 1980, for a review). Myung and Busemeyer (in press) used the error-correction principle to describe how stopping criteria are learned in a sequential sampling decision task.

2.3 Hill-Climbing.

This principle is used to learn the best set of parameters for decision problems which provide continuously valued payoffs as feedback after each trial. Once again, $\{\theta_i(1), \theta_i(2), ...\}$ represents the sequence of parameter vectors used with strategy i ordered in terms of recency and $\theta_i(0)$ represents the parameter vector to be used with the next application of strategy i. The payoffs $V_i(k)$ are assumed to vary in a continuous manner across trials.

According to the hill-climbing principle, a small adjustment is made in the direction of improvement. More specifically, a new point $\theta_i(0)$ is selected to satisfy the property (where $X'X$ denotes the inner product of two vectors):

$$[V_i(1) - V_i(2)] \cdot [\theta_i(1) - \theta_i(2)]'[\theta_i(0) - \theta_i(1)] > 0.$$

The main advantage of the hill-climbing principle is that it provides a simple way to find the maximum of a smooth unimodal objective function based solely on recently experienced (local) information. The main disadvantage is that hill-climbing search algorithms can easily get stuck on local maximuma or get lost in flat regions. Also note that this learning principle requires substantially more memory than the error-correction principle. Hill-climbing requires recall of events from two previous trials whereas error-correction only requires recall of events from the previous trial.

The basic idea of hill-climbing comes from the stochastic gradient ascent algorithms used in adaptive control theory (Tsypkin, 1971). The hill-climbing principle has been experimentally investigated by Busemeyer, Swenson, and Lazarte (1986) and Busemeyer and Myung (1987) using a resource allocation decision task. Hill-climbing was used by Connolly and Wholey (1988) to describe learning with an information purchasing task.

Recently, Busemeyer and Myung (1989) reported a series of three experiments using a diagnostic categorization task that were designed to provide more direct tests of the proposed learning principles. The first experiment provided empirical support for the worth-estimation principle in a task requiring only strategy learning. The second experiment provided empirical evidence for the simultaneous operation of both error-correction and hill-climbing principles in a task requiring only criterion learning. The third experiment provided empirical evidence for the simultaneous operation of all three principles in a task requiring both strategy and criterion learning. In general, these principles provided reasonably accurate predictions regarding both rate of learning and asymptotic performance using a relatively small number of parameters. However, qualitative tests as well as quantitative tests of the models in each experiment revealed systematic deviations. Therefore, we concluded that these three principles are necessary but not sufficient for understanding decision strategy learning.

3. EXTENSIONS FOR FUTURE RESEARCH

Potential applications of the proposed principles reaches far beyond the previously mentioned studies using categorization, sequential sampling, resource allocation, and signal detection tasks. It is quite easy to see how these same principles could be applied to other new tasks. Consider, for example, the common multi-attribute, multiple-alternative decision task. Several qualitatively different strategies have been discussed, including the weighted additive rule, the elimination by aspects rule, and the satisficing rule (e.g., Payne, Bettman, and Johnson, 1988). Each of these strategies involve parameters such as importance weights, thresholds, and cutoff criteria. Worth-estimation may be used to learn to choose among the qualitatively different strategies, while hill-climbing and error-correction may be used for parameter learning. Thus, there are good reasons to believe that these principles are very general and pervasive.

Production rule learning is an important topic in problem solving, and a number of learning models have been proposed (Klahr, Langley, and Neches, 1987). However, problem solving learning tasks (e.g., geometry proofs) typically involve deterministic, binary-valued (correct/incorrect) feedback. In contrast, decision strategy learning tasks (e.g., the tasks used in the present study) typically involve feedback that is probabilistically distributed across a large number of payoff values. Thus, the learning principles developed for problem solving must be modified before they are applicable to decision strategy learning.

One simple way to modify production rule learning models is to define production rule strength (see Anderson, 1983, Ch. 6) as the estimated worth of a rule (using Equation 1). In fact, the worth-estimation principle is essentially the same as the rule-strengthening principle proposed by Anderson (1983). Another way to modify production rule learning models is to use hill-climbing and error-correction principles to adjust the quantitative parameters of a production rule.

Connectionistic learning models provide an alternative approach to rule learning (cf. Rumelhart & McClelland, 1986). From this point of view, all learning is represented by changes in a weight vector, where each weight represents the strength of connection between two nodes in the network. The weights are continuous parameters that are adjusted on the basis of trial by trial outcome feedback.

One successful learning rule for adjusting the weight vector is the delta rule (Rumelhart, Hinton, and Williams, 1986). Essentially, the delta rule is a stochastic descent algorithm designed to search for a weight vector that minimizes the expected value of the squared deviations between the actual and the desired output of the network. The hill-climbing rule is an alternative stochastic descent algorithm that could be used to adjust the weight vector of connectionistic networks. The hill-climbing rule may be slower than the delta rule when the objective is to minimize mean square error, but it has the advantage of being applicable to arbitrary objective functions.

Further research is needed to address the following issues. First, the strategies investigated up to this point have been relatively simple. Each strategy can be described by a single production rule or condition-action statement. Further research is needed to test the applicability of these principles to more complex strategies involving a large set of production rules and a long sequence of actions on each feedback trial.

Second, more research is needed on the question of generalization or transfer of knowledge across decision tasks. Prior knowledge or past experience can be represented by the initial worth assigned to each possible strategy.

Third, more research is needed on the question of discrimination. A particular strategy may perform very well under some environmental conditions but perform very poorly under other conditions (see, e.g., Payne et al., 1988). One direct way to incorporate discrimination learning is to substitute the Rescorla & Wagner (1972) learning algorithm for the linear model represented by Equation 1.

Finally, new learning principles are needed for searching large but finite sets of strategies that have a weakly organized similarity structure. The proposed learning rules are designed for two extreme cases: (a) a small set of strategies with no apparent similarity structure (e.g., the clinical trials task) or (b) a continuous set of decision policies with a well defined distance function (e.g., the criterion selection task). Although the experiments by Busemyer and Myung (1989) show that the proposed rules can operate simultaneously to learn within a domain that is constructed from a mixture of these two extreme cases, these principles may not be very efficient for searching an intermediate case involving a large number of weakly organized strategies (e.g., the individual paths of a large decision tree).

ACKNOWLEDGEMENTS

This research was supported by NSF Grant BNS # 8710103. Correspondence concerning this paper should be sent to Jerome R. Busemeyer, Psychological Sciences, Purdue University, West Lafayette, Indiana, 47907.

REFERENCES

Anderson, J. R. (1983) The architecture of cognition. Cambridge, Mass.: Harvard University Press.

Beach, L. R., & Mitchell, T. R. (1978) A contingency model for the selection of decision strategies. Academy of Management Review, 3, 439-449.

Busemeyer, J. R., Swenson, K. N., Lazarte, A. (1986) An adaptive approach to resource allocation. Organizational Behavior and Human Decision Processes, 38, 318-341.

Busemeyer, J. R., and Myung, I. (1987) Resource allocation decision making in an uncertain environment. Acta Psychologica, 66, 1-19.

Busemeyer, J. R. & Myung, I. J. An adaptive approach to human decision making: Learning theory, decision theory, and human performance. Manuscript under review.

Connolly, T., and Wholey, D. R. (1988) Information mispurchase in judgment tasks: A task-driven causal mechanism. Organizational Behavior and Human Decision Processes.

Christensen-Szalanski, J. J. J. (1978) A mechanism for strategy selection and some implications. Organizational Behavior and Human Decision Processes, 22, 307-323.

Dorfman, D. D., and Biderman, M. (1971) A learning model for a continuum of sensory states. Journal of Mathematical Psychology, 8, 264-284.

Dusoir, A. E. (1980) Some evidence on additive learning models. Perception and Psychophysics, 27, 163-175.

Estes, W. K. (1987) Application of a cognitive-distance model to learning in a simulated travel task. Journal of Experimental Psychology: Learning, Memory, and Cognition, 13, 380-386.

Kac, M. (1962) A note on learning signal detection. IRE Transactions on Information Theory, IT-8, 126-128.

Klahr, D., Langley, P., & Neches, R. (1987) Production system models of learning and development. Cambridge, Mass.: MIT Press.

Krantz, D. H., Luce, R. D., Suppes, P., and Tversky, A. (1971) Foundations of Measurement. N. Y.: Academic Press.

Luce, R. D. (1959) Individual Choice Behavior. N. Y. : Wiley.

Myung, I. J., & Busemeyer, J. R. (1989) Criterion learning in a deferred decision making task. American Journal of Psychology.

Norman, M. F. (1972) Markov Processes and Learning Models. N. Y. Academic Press.

Payne, J. W. (1982) Contingent decision making. Psychological Bulletin, 92, 382-402.

Payne, J. W., Bettman, J. R., & Johnson, E. J. (1988) Adaptive strategy selection in decision making. Journal of Experimental Psychology: Learning, Memory, and Cognition, 14, 534-552.

Rescorla, R. A., & Wagner, A. R. (1972) A theory of Pavlovian conditioning: Variations in the effectiveness of reinforcement and nonreinforcement. In A. H. Black and W. F. Prokasy (Eds.) Classical Conditioning II: Current Research and Theory. New York: Appleton-Century-Crofts. Pp. 64-99.

Rumelhart, D. E., and McClelland, J. L. (1986) Parallel Distributed Processing: Explorations in the Microstructure of Cognition. Volume 1: Foundations. Cambridge, Mass.: MIT Press.

Rumelhart, D. E., Hinton, G. E., & Williams, R. J. (1986) Learning internal representations by error propagation. In Rumelhart, D. E., and McClelland, J. L. (Eds.) Parallel Distributed Processing: Explorations in the Microstructure of . Cognition. Volume 1: Foundations. Cambridge, Mass.: MIT Press. Ch. 8, 318-362.

Thomas, E. A. C. (1973) On a class of additive learning models: Error correcting and probability matching. Journal of Mathematical Psychology, 10, 241-264.

Tsypkin, Y. Z. (1973) Foundations of the theory of learning systems. N. Y. : Academic Press.

Yovits, M. C., Foulk, C. R., & Rose, L. L. (1981) Information flow and analysis: Theory, simulation, and experiments. 1. Basic theoretical and conceptual development. Journal of the American Society for Information Science, 32, 187-202.

Human Information Processing: Measures,
Mechanisms, and Models, D. Vickers and P. L. Smith (eds.)
© *Elsevier Science Publishers B.V. (North-Holland), 1989*

THE SEARCH FOR A DOMINANCE STRUCTURE: SIMPLIFICATION VERSUS ELABORATION IN DECISION MAKING

Henry Montgomery

University of Göteborg

According to the dominance search model a decison maker attempts to structure or restructure the representation of the choice alternatives in such a way that one alternative becomes dominant (i. e. a dominance structure is created). In this paper a scheme is presented which distinguishes between different dominance structuring operations by relating them to particular psychological determinants of evaluative judgments. In terms of this scheme it is shown that violations of dominance could be obviated either by *simplifying* or *elaborating* the representation of a decision situation. Simplifying may be achieved by selecting suitable attributes for describing the choice alternative and by defining crude enough response categories. Elaboration may be achieved by changing or activating links between specific attributes and more general values or goals. Another possibility is to find appropriate anchors for relevant evaluative judgments.

1. INTRODUCTION

After many years of research in human decision making not very much is known about how people actually make their decisions. In particular, we know very little about how a decision process as a whole is organized. In the present paper I present a model which may serve as a source of inspiration for research on human decision processes. The model is called the dominance search model. It may be compared with Beach and Mitchell's (1987) Image theory, which has aims similar to those of the dominance search model (see Montgomery, 1987).

The dominance search model was originally described by Montgomery (1983). Empirical tests of the models are reported in Montgomery and Svenson (1983/1989) and in Dahlstrand and Montgomery (1984/1989). Several other empirical studies have been inspired by the model and some of these studies will be referred to in this paper. A recent discussion and development of the model is presented in Montgomery (1989, see also Montgomery, 1987). The present paper develops further some of the ideas in the Montgomery (1989) paper. As a start I will give a brief overview of the model.

2. THE DOMINANCE SEARCH MODEL

The key idea of the dominance search model is that a decision maker attempts to structure or restructure the representation of the choice alternatives in such a way that one alternative dominates the other alternatives. Put differently, the decision maker searches for a representation in which one alternative is better than the others on at least one attribute and not worse on all other attributes. This is the ideal. In reality, decision makers may be satisfied with more or less good approximations to this ideal as a basis for their decision.

The search for a dominance structure is assumed to go through four stages, viz. pre-editing, finding a promising alternative, dominance testing, and dominance structuring. Figure 1 gives an overview of how the decision process is organized in terms of the four phases. In the *pre-editing* phase, which primarily occurs in the beginning of the decision process, the decision maker selects those alternatives and attributes that should be included in the final representation of the decision problem. The activities associated with *finding a promising alternative* aim at finding an alternative that has a reasonable chance to be seen as dominant. An alternative which is more attractive than the other alternatives on an important attribute may be selected as a promising alternative. In the *dominance testing* phase, the decision maker tests whether a promising alternative dominates the other alternatives.

If the decision maker finds that a promising alternative violates dominance he/she continues to the *dominance structuring* phase. The goal of this phase is to restructure the given information in such a way that a dominance structure is obtained. A number of operations are used in these attempts. The decision maker may *de-emphasize* a given disadvantage or may *bolster* the advantages of a promising alternative, which in turn may reduce the importance of the disadvantages of that alternative, if any. A seemingly more rational operation is *cancellation* which implies that the decision maker counterbalances a disadvantage by relating it to an advantage having some natural connection to the disadvantage in question (e. g., in terms of similarity). Another seemingly more rational operation is *collapsing* which implies that two or more attributes are collapsed into a new more comprehensive attribute (e.g., different types of monetary cost may be collapsed into total cost).

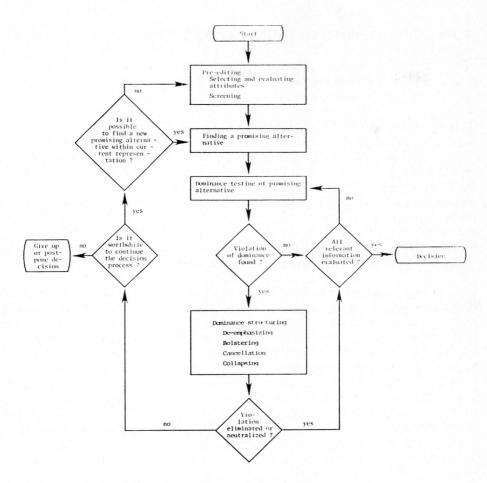

Figure 1. A dominance search model of decision making.

If the decision maker fails in the attempt to find a dominance structure it may be necessary to return to a previous phase in order to make a fresh start in the search for dominance. Alternatively, it may be necessary to postpone the decision, if this is possible.

The dominance structuring phase is the crucial component of the dominance search model. If this phase has no reality it would be pointless to describe decision making as a search for dominance. In the present paper a scheme is presented which distinguishes between different dominance structuring operations by relating them to particular determinants of evaluative judgments. In the following section these determinants are introduced. It is also discussed how these determinants relate to each other (see Figure 2).

3. PSYCHOLOGICAL DETERMINANTS OF EVALUATIVE JUDGMENTS

Necessarily, evaluative judgments concern one or more *objects* (or alternatives in a decision situation). The objects to be evaluated have to be selected in one way or another. Figure 2 indicates that this selection is dependent on previous evaluative judgments inasmuch as a positive or negative judgment of an object may determine whether it will be further considered or not. There is ample research evidence that such selection processes occur in decision making processes (e. g., Payne, 1976; Wright & Barbour, 1977). In the dominance search model these processes are associated with the screening of alternatives (in the pre-editing phase) and with finding a promising alternative.

As is traditionally assumed in judgment and decision making research, evaluative judgments are assumed to be expressed on *attributes* or *dimensions*. The evaluation of objects on an attribute as well as the selection of an attribute is assumed to result from how the attribute is linked to more general *values* or *goals* (e g. togetherness or freedom). It is

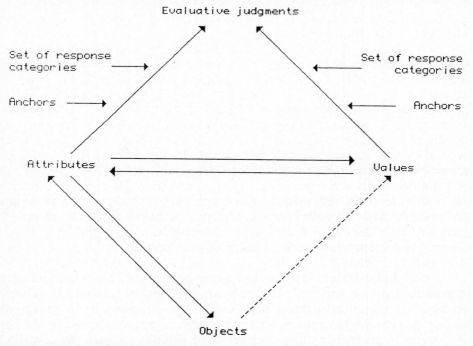

Figure 2. Psychological determinants of evaluative judgments.

also conceivable that people see direct links from objects to values (Lindberg, Gärling, & Montgomery, 1988). In this case the values will function as attributes, the evaluation of which may depend on perceived links between the pertinent values and other values (e.g. togetherness leads to happiness, cf. Montgomery, 1984). Obviously, the more an attribute is perceived as related to important values the more importance will be attached to the attribute itself and the more likely it will be that the attribute is considered in further evaluative judgments. In addition, the more a given level of an attribute is seen as related to positive values the more positive will the evaluation of the attribute level be. Correspondingly, the evaluation will be more negative if there are perceived relations to negative "values" or states. Evidence for links between evaluative judgments and values have been presented in the research of Lindberg et al on housing preferences (e.g, Lindberg, Gärling, & Montgomery, 1987, 1988, Lindberg, Gärling, Montgomery, & Waara, 1988).

The evaluation of an object is expressed in an *evaluative response* (e.g. very good, rather bad). The responses are selected from a *set of response categories*. These categories may be more or less fine-grained and they may distributed in various ways along a given attribute or dimension. The response distribution along an attribute is not static but is rather affected by context factors such as the frequency of different attribute levels (Parducci, 1965).

Judgments are relative. There is an abundance of research showing that judgments of a given object are made in relation to other objects or stimuli (e. g., Hellström, 1984; Helson, 1964; Parducci, 1965). Obviously, this is also true for evaluative judgments (Parducci, 1968). More specifically, I assume that an evaluative judgment reflects the perceived distance to one or more *anchors*. The anchors may correspond to the typical or normal level of an attribute (cf. Helson, 1964) or to perceived maximum and minimum levels of the attribute (cf. Parducci, 1965). Aspiration levels are a particular type of anchors which in turn may be equivalent to other definitions of anchors such as the maximum level or the typical level of an attribute (cf. Campbell, Converse & Rogers, 1976).

The framework described above implies that there will be a multitude of possibilities for an individual to *construct* his or her evaluative judgments of objects in a given situation. Different objects and attributes may be selected, different values may be activated, different anchors may be used, and different response categories may be defined. In this way, the judgments may be more or less guided by how the individual expects or wishes objects to be evaluated and, hence, not only by how the objects, in some sense, really are constituted. More specifically, there may be many potential roads to a dominance structure in a given decision situation. In the following section, I will suggest that these roads may be classified into two broad categories.

4. SIMPLIFICATION VERSUS ELABORATION IN DOMINANCE SEARCH

Consider a decision situation in which a violation of dominance is found for a promising alternative. Let us assume that the decision maker, in line with the dominance search model, attempts to "repair" the violation. Logically speaking, there are two possible ways of doing so. The decision maker may either *simplify* or *elaborate* his/her representation of the decision situation. More precisely, the decision maker may eliminate or ignore information which blocks dominance (simplification) or he/she may find new information which neutralizes or falsifies the dominance violation (elaboration).

Table 1 presents an overview of operations associated with simplifying and elaboration in dominance search. Corresponding dominance structuring operations as described in previous accounts of the dominance search model also given in Table 1.

Let me now first discuss the role of simplification in decision making and how it relates to dominance structuring. The notion of simplification is a cornerstone of several descriptive theories of decision making (e.g, Simon, 1955; Tversky, 1969, 1972). Many decision rules for choices among multiattribute alternatives represent various possibilities of simplifying a decision problem (e.g., by ignoring attributes or by using crude attractiveness evaluations, cf. Montgomery & Svenson, 1976; Svenson, 1979). In particular, this is true for the so-called non-compensatory decision rules which release the decision maker from the problem of weighing advantages in relation to disadvantages. For example, consider the lexicographic decision rule. According to this rule the decision maker will select the most important attribute on which one, and only one, alternative is better than all other alternatives. This alternative will be chosen regardless of how much worse it is on less important attributes.

How is the simplification yielded by non-compensatory decision rules related to dominance structuring? The answer is simple, at least for those rules I know of. The pattern of attractiveness values which according to these rules is required for making a decision fulfils the requirements of a dominance structure. In other words, the chosen alternative has no disadvantages as compared to other alternatives in terms of the representation of the decision situation that these rules require. Obviously, this is the case for the attributes considered in the lexicographic decision rule discussed above. As further examples, consider the conjunctive and disjunctive decision rules. The conjunctive

Table 1

Operations Associated with Simplification and Elaboration in Dominance Structuring

Basic operation	Simplification	Elaboration
Select attributes	Restrict number of attributes (de-emph.)	—
Activate values	Restrict number of values (de-emph.)	Weaken/strengthen value links (de-emph., bolst.)
		Work forwards (bolst., collaps.)
		Work backwards (cancell.)
Find anchors	—	Find alternative anchors
		(de-emph., bolst.)
Define response categories	Use broad categories (de-emph.)	—

rule states that if only one alternative exceeds a certain criterion on *all* attributes then this alternative should be chosen. The disjunctive rule requires the choice of an alternative that exceeds a certain criterion on *at least one* attribute, provided that this is not true for any other alternative. Both rules imply that the attractiveness of aspects is reduced to two attractiveness levels, viz. attractiveness below and above the criterion. It is easily realized that in terms of this simplified representation the chosen alternative will dominate when one of the two rules is applicable. The reader is invited to verify for him/herself that a corresponding type of reasoning is applicable to other non-compensatory decision rules such as the the elimination by aspects rule (Tversky, 1972) and the semi-order lexicographic rule (Tversky, 1969).

It can be concluded that the simplification yielded by non-compensatory decision rules is achieved in terms of two of the factors described in our scheme for evaluative judgments, viz., selection of attributes (e.g., the lexicographic rule and the the elimination by aspects rule) and definition of (crude enough) response categories (e.g., the conjunctive, disjunctive and elimination by aspects rules). It may also be concluded that the empirical evidence for the use of these rules simultaneously is possible evidence for dominance structuring via simplification. (In order to show that data on simplification constitute clear evidence for dominance structuring the data should indicate that the simplification occurred in an attempt to *re*structure a given representation of the decision problem. As far as I know, it is not possible to know whether this was the case or not from previous studies of non-compensatory decision rules.)

Let me now briefly discuss another operation considered in the scheme shown in Figure 2, viz., activation of values. In a series of experiments Lindberg, Gärling and Montgomery (1987, 1988) compared how values relate to attractiveness judgments of single alternatives (preferences) and to choices among several alternatives. It was consistently found that preferences seemed to be based on a greater number of values than was the case for choices, which often were significantly related to just one value. Obviously, the fewer values that are activated the greater is the chance that the activated values are distributed in line with a dominance structure. However, so far we have not examined whether activated values in fact follow a dominance structure.

Table 1 shows that simplification generally is related to the de-emphasizing operation, inasmuch as simplification implies that counterevidence to dominance is ignored.

The notion of elaboration in decision making may be associated with attempts to generate more or less complex scenarios of events that could result from choosing a certain alternative (cf. Thüring & Jungermann, 1986). Biel and Montgomery (1986) found that scenarios in energy politics could be described in terms of instrumental attributes which lead to or block the attainment of favorable levels of goal attributes (e.g, large scale of energy systems leads to or impedes security). In terms of the scheme in Figure 2, instrumental attributes correspond to attributes and goal attributes to values. The scenarios analyzed by Biel and Montgomery sometimes included long chains of causally connected events. Hence, the links between attributes and values may actually consist of fairly long causal chains (e.g, orders to domestic industry - development of domestic technology - increased export - a good economy, see Montgomery & Biel, 1984).

The scenarios analyzed by Biel and Montgomery had one thing in common. The pattern of values associated with the scenarios imagined in a given decision situation usually were almost perfect examples of dominance structures. For example, some politicians argued that a district heating system leads to a good environment, a good economy and high safety whereas electrical heating leads to a bad environment, a bad economy and low   safety. Other politicians had exactly the reverse opinions. Common to both groups were that their favored alternative dominated other alternatives with respect to long term values or goals.

How may elaborating the links between attributes and values lead to a dominance structure? In order to answer this question it is necessary to distinguish between dominance violations on the level of attributes (e.g. flat A has lower rent but smaller size than flat B) and dominance violations on the level of values (e.g., flat A is better for your health but leads to reduced togetherness with other people as compared to flat B). Dominance violations on the level of attributes may be obviated simply by activating values linked to the attributes (e.g. lower rent and smaller size may lead to altogether more freedom and unreduced comfort). This corresponds to the so-called collapsing operation in earlier accounts of the dominance search model.

Consider now how dominance violations on the level of values may be obviated. One possibility is simply to *weaken* links to values associated with rejected alternatives and/or to *strengthen* links to values associated with a favored alternative. This could be done if the decision maker finds some means of changing the relation between an attribute and a value. In politics there is a large arsenal of policy measures like laws, taxes, subsidies, and organizational endeavors that may be used for creating links to desired values (Montgomery & Biel, 1984). In everyday day life people may imagine means like asking other people for help, borrowing money, studying, working harder in order to attain important values from the attributes of a to-be-chosen alternative (e.g. to build a house). Weakening or strengthening could be associated with the de-emphasizing or bolstering operations, depending on whether the result of the operation is reduction of drawbacks or an intensification of advantages, respectively.

Another possible way of obviating dominance violations on the level of values is to *search forwards* from activated values in order to find more general values which will yield dominance. A common way of finding more general values is to widen the time perspective. In this way a dominance structure may be attained inasmuch as short term losses with respect to certain values are compensated by long term value gains with respect to the same values. Obviously, the notion of searching forwards is applicable to dominance violations on the level of attributes. In this case the search implies that the decision maker activates links from attributes to values. It may be noted that both types of searching forwards correspond to the collapsing operation discussed earlier. If the search is biased in favor of strong links to positive values the search will also be an example of bolstering.

A third possibility is to *search backwards*. With this I mean attempts to find alternative links to a given value that will change the activation of that value. For example, if a person fails to activate the value "good economy" because of high investment costs of a certain alternative, he or she may change the activation of that value if it is found that the running costs are low. It is worth noting that searching backwards corresponds to the cancellation operation in the dominance search model.

Biel and Montgomery's (1986, 1989; Biel & Montgomery, 1984) studies of decision making in energy politics provide ample evidence for possibilities of finding or rescuing dominance by elaborating on attribute-value links and value-value links. It seems that within a given domain a decision maker may have access to a network of ideas which almost guarantees that a dominance structure could be defended against any objections which are made against a favored alternative.

I will now briefly discuss how a person may elaborate the representation of a decision situation by finding alternative anchors for his/her evaluative judgments. Obviously, searching for suitable anchors may be a way of obtaining a dominance structure. Choosing a job with a low salary may be experienced as less painful if the decision maker has friends having jobs with still lower salaries, or has had earlier jobs with the same or lower or salaries. In such a case the evaluation of disadantages will be de-emphasized. Similarily, selection of anchors may also be used for bolstering advantages of a promising alternative. Little seems to be known about how selection of anchors is used in dominance structuring (See, however, Montgomery, 1989, for a discussion of verbal protocol data that support the idea that anchoring is used for creating dominance structures.)

5. CONCLUDING COMMENT

In which situations do decision makers simplify and when do they elaborate on given information? It may be speculated that unimportant and/or routine decisions are associated with simplification whereas important and/or unique decisions promote elaborative activities. It might be an interesting task for future research to study the relationship between situational factors and the use of simplification versus elaboration in decision making. Research along these lines may also indicate the usefulness of the dominance search model as a tool for the description of human decision making.

ACKNOWLEDGMENTS

This paper was supported by a grant from The Swedish Council for Research in the Humanities and Social Sciences. The paper has benefitted from discussions with Tommy Gärling, Eric Lindberg, and Ola Svenson and from comments made by Tommy Gärling on a previous version of the paper.

Correspondence should be addressed to Henry Montgomery Department of Psychology University of Göteborg Box 14158 S-400 20 Göteborg, Sweden

REFERENCES

Beach, L.R., & Mitchell, T.R. (1987). Image theory: principles, goals, and plans in decision making. Acta Psychologica, 66, 201-220.

Biel, A., & Montgomery, H. (1986). Scenarios in energy planning. In B. Brehmer, H. Jungermann, P. Lourens, & G. Sevon (Eds.), New directions in research on decision making (pp. 205-218). Amsterdam: North-Holland.

Biel, A., & Montgomery, H. (1989). Scenario analysis and energy politics - the disclosure of causal structure in decision making. In H. Montgomery & O. Svenson (Eds.), Process and structure in human decision making (pp. 243-259). Chichester: Wiley.

Campbell, A., Converse, P.E., & Rogers, W.L. (1976). The quality of American life. New York: Russel Sage Foundation.

Dahlstrand, U., & Montgomery, H. (in press). Information search and evaluative processes in decision making: A computer based process tracing study. In H. Montgomery & O. Svenson (Eds.), Process and structure in human decision making (pp. 151-161). (Reprinted from Acta Psychologica, 1984, 56, 113-123.

Hellström, Å. (1984). The time-order error and its relatives: Mirrors of cognitive processes in comparing. Psychological Bulletin, 97, 35-61.

Helson, A. (1964). Adaptation-level theory. New York: Harper & Row.

Lindberg, E., Gärling, T., & Montgomery, H. (1987) Intra-urban residential mobility: Beliefs about the attainment of life values as determinants of subjective evaluations of housing alternatives. (Umeå Psychological Reports, No. 190). Umeå: University of Umeå, Department of Psychology.

Lindberg, E., Gärling, T., & Montgomery, H. (1988). Beliefs and values as determinants of residential preferences and choices. Scandinavian Journal of Housing and Planning Research.

Lindberg, E., Gärling, T., Montgomery, H., & Waara, R. (1987). People's evaluation of housing attributes. Scandinavian Housing and Planning Research, 4, 81-103.

Montgomery, H. (1983). Decision rules and the search for a dominance structure: Towards a process model of decision making. In P. Humphreys, O. Svenson, & A. Vari (Eds.), Analyzing and aiding decision processes (pp. 343-369). Amsterdam/Budapest: North-Holland and Hungarian Academic Press.

Montgomery, H. (1984). Cognitive and affective aspects of life values as determinants of well-being: A pilot study (Göteborg Psychological Reports, 14, No. 3). Göteborg: University of Göteborg, Department of Psychology.

Montgomery, H. (1987). Image theory and dominance search theory: How is decision making actually done? Acta Psychologica, 66, 221-224.

Montgomery, H. (1989). From cognition to action: The search for dominance in decision making. In H. Montgomery and O. Svenson (Eds.), Process and structure in human decision making (pp. 23-49). Chichester: Wilery.

Montgomery, H., & Biel, A. (1984, April). Scenarios and causal models in political decision making. Paper presented at the annual conference of the British Psychological Society, Warwick.

Montgomery, H., & Svenson, O. (1976). On decision rules and information processing strategies for choices among multi-attribute alternatives. Scandinavian Journal of Psychology, 17, 283-291.

Montgomery, H. & Svenson, O. (1989). A think-aloud study of dominance structuring in decision makling. In H. Montgomery & O. Svenson (Eds.), Process and structure in human decision making (pp. 135-150). (Reprinted from Tietz R., (Ed.). (1983). Aspiration levels in bargaining and economic decision making (pp. 366-383). Berlin: Springer Verlag).

Parducci, A. (1965). Category judgment: A range-frequency model. Psychological Review, 72, 407-418.

Parducci, A. (1968). The relativism of absolute judgments. Scientific American, 219, 84-90.

Payne, J.W. (1976). Task complexity and contingent processing in decision making: An information search and protocol analysis. Organizational Behavior and Human Performance, 16, 366-387.

Simon, H. (1955). A behavioral model of rational choice. Quarterly Journal of Economics, 68, 99-118.

Svenson, O. (1979). Process descriptions of decisions. Organizational Behavior and Human Performance, 23, 86-112.

Thüring, M., & Jungermann, H. (1986). Constructing and running mental models for inferences about the future. In B. Brehmer, H. Jungermann, P. Lourens, & G. Sevon (Eds.), New directions in research on decision making, Amsterdam: North- Holland.

Tversky, A. (1969). Intransitivity of preferences. Psychological Review, 76, 133-155.

Tversky, A. (1972). Elimination by aspects: A theory of choice. Psychological Review, 79, 31-48.

Wright, P., & Barbour, F. (1977). Phased decision strategies: Sequels to an initial screening. (Research Paper no. 353). Stanford: Stanford University, Graduate School of Business.

SECTION 8

**MEASURES OF INDIVIDUAL DIFFERENCES
IN INTELLECTUAL ABILITY**

Human Information Processing: Measures,
Mechanisms, and Models, *D. Vickers and P.L. Smith (eds.)*
© *Elsevier Science Publishers B.V. (North-Holland), 1989*

INSPECTION TIME IS RELATED TO INTELLIGENCE IN SOME SUBJECTS BUT NOT IN ALL

Brian Mackenzie, Elizabeth Bingham, Steven Cumming, Philip Doyle, Catherine Turner, Elizabeth Molloy, Frances Martin, James Alexander

University of Tasmania

William Lovegrove

University of Wollongong

Approximately half the subjects in typical inspection time experiments report perceiving apparent motion in the stimulus display. That is, they see the target lines seem to move or stretch to the length of the longer, overlaying, masking lines. The remaining subjects do not report perceiving anything like apparent motion. The distinction between the two groups of subjects is important, because in the 'non-perceivers', inspection time is significantly correlated with nonverbal IQ. In the 'perceivers', there is no significant correlation. This paper reports five experiments that show the distinction between perceivers and non-perceivers. The experiments attempt to relate these sample differences to differences in cognitive and perceptual characteristics of perceivers and non-perceivers, but with only limited success. Finally, the paper proposes experiments to determine whether the distinction between perceivers and non-perceivers is a methodological artifact, or whether it has important implications for understanding the cognitive processes tapped by measures of inspection time.

1. INTRODUCTION

This paper is the story of an idiosyncratic quest. Over the past four or five years a number of us, including the first author continuously and most of the others at various times, have been troubled by a particular issue in inspection time (IT) research, an issue that many researchers in the field have noticed but few have been seriously concerned about. This issue has to do with the perception of apparent motion in the standard two-line IT task, and the implications of perceiving it.

In the standard task as used in our laboratory, the subject is shown two horizontal target lines of different lengths, one lying two cm above the other. After a variable exposure period, usually between 20 and 100 msec, the target lines are overlaid by longer masking lines. The subject's task is to say which of the two target lines was longer. Many subjects, amounting to half or slightly more, report a similar perceptual experience when the masking lines overlay the target lines. They report that they do not see the mask replace the target; instead they see the target lines grow or stretch to the length of the masking lines. Typical reports from the grade seven children in some of our experiments have been that the two lines had a race to the right hand side of the screen and the longer one won, or that the longer one moved faster than the shorter one (occasionally but not often that the shorter one moved faster). The remaining subjects do not report any such movement when asked what they saw. Some of these subjects say that they saw either bright flashes or dark spaces at the ends of the two target lines, or that they saw the target lines outlined more brightly for an instant when the masking lines covered them, and many say that they didn't see anything in particular at all.

Quite reliably and regularly, subjects divide themselves into those who perceive apparent motion in the inspection time display, whom we will call the 'perceivers', and those who do not, whom we will call the 'non-perceivers'. The perceivers are usually a little faster on the inspection time task than the non-perceivers, and they sometimes have marginally higher scores on the non-verbal IQ tests we use (age appropriate versions of the Wechsler or Raven's Progressive Matrices tests), but neither difference has typically been significant.

So why does it matter? The perceivers and non-perceivers do differ in one important respect: in every study in which we have been able to measure all the variables, inspection time has been significantly correlated with nonverbal IQ in the non-perceivers, but not in the perceivers. In those subjects who report apparent motion, the correlation with IQ has always been non-significant, lying between 0 and -0.2, and averaging -0.16. In those who do not report apparent motion, the correlation has always been significant, lying between -0.4 and -0.7 and averaging -0.62. In every experiment, the difference between the correlations has been either statistically significant or nearly so, and when we combine the comparisons across the five experiments to be described here, the difference between the perceivers and the non-perceivers in the size of the IT-IQ correlation is significant at the .001 level. The consistency in results is strong, despite the fact that the methods of IQ measurement and the sample composition have varied substantially across experiments.

This consistent pattern of subsample differences is a puzzle that we believe it is important to solve. It is important because it is likely that only one of these sets of subsample correlations represents the 'true' correlation between inspection time and IQ. Either the 'true' correlation is approximately an impressively high -0.6, and is somehow blocked in the apparent motion perceivers, or the 'true' correlation is approximately a trivial -0.15, and is artificially boosted in the non-perceivers. The former could be the case, for instance, if the perceivers had discovered some perceptual strategy that enabled them to overcome the effects of the mask (as implied by Nettelbeck, 1982); use of that strategy would prevent the inspection time procedure from measuring whatever processes it would measure otherwise. The latter could be the case if all subjects eventually discovered such strategies, but the higher IQ subjects tended to discover them sooner; in that case the IT procedure would not necessarily measure any processes of particular interest at all. It is conceivable, of course, that the inspection time procedure accurately indexes the same low level cognitive processes in both perceivers and non-perceivers, and that the difference between them is a fundamental processing difference in the relationship between basic cognitive processes and intellectual potential in the two groups. It is conceivable, but implausible. For now, we prefer the more parsimonious hypothesis that one of these correlations, at least, is an artifact. Another way of describing the puzzle, therefore, is to ask which of these correlations we can believe.

We will now outline five studies conducted in the Cognition Laboratory at the University of Tasmania, to review what progress we have made in solving the puzzle. All of these studies had other purposes apart from the investigation of apparent motion, but all included results that bear on the question of apparent motion. The outcomes are summarized in Table 1.2.

2. EXPERIMENTAL STUDIES

2.1 Experiment 1

Our first inspection time experiment used first year university students as subjects, and the Wechsler Adult Intelligence Scale (WAIS) for intellectual assessment. The correlation between IT and Performance IQ on the WAIS was -.72 for the non-perceivers, dropping to -.20 for the perceivers. As it happened, both of us who were responsible for this study (previously reported as Mackenzie & Bingham, 1985) were perceivers, both had very short inspection times, and both were markedly over-confident. When we first noted the apparent motion on the video display, we reasoned that if we could teach everybody to use it as the basis for making their length discriminations, they would all come to have very short inspection times and the correlation with IQ would vanish. To our surprise, however, the non-perceivers insisted that they could not see any apparent motion no matter how hard they tried, and we were quite unsuccessful in teaching them to do so. This first experiment made inspection time a serious topic of research for the laboratory, and did much to cure the experimenters of their over-confidence. The conclusion from the study: attending to apparent motion cues does not seem to be a teachable, or at least a readily teachable, strategy.

Table 1

Comparison of Apparent Motion Perceivers and Non-Perceivers: Results over Five Studies

Psychological test	N	Apparent Motion Perceivers			N	Apparent Motion Non-Perceivers		
		Test Mean (S.D.)	IT Mean (S.D.)	IT-IQ Correl.		Test Mean (S.D.)	IT Mean (S.D.)	IT-IQ Correl.
1. WAIS PIQ	16	112.0 (11.4)	68.0 (35.2)	-0.20	13	107.0 (9.2)	89.6 (43.3)	-0.72
2. Advanced Prog.Matrices	22	26.6 (4.2)	49.4 (15.4)	-0.19	15	26.2 (4.9)	97.0 (50.8)	-0.66
3. WISC-R PIQ	16	109.9 (8.6)	67.7 (40.1)	-0.24	22	105.6 (12.7)	78.5 (55.0)	-0.60
4. Standard & Adv Matrices	20	69.4 (11.0)	33.3 (28.9)	-0.01	18	62.0 (9.3)	55.4 (37.7)	-0.66
5. Standard Prog.Matrices	32	107.1 (7.7)	91.8 (71.6)	-0.01	27	109.0 (6.4)	57.4 (35.8)	-0.42
Total (RMS)	106			-0.16	95			-0.62

2.2 Experiment 2

This experiment used a variety of male university student volunteers as subjects, and the Advanced Progressive Matrices (APM) for intellectual assessment. The correlation between IT and APM score was -.66 for the non-perceivers, dropping to -.19 for the perceivers. In this experiment (previously reported as Mackenzie & Cumming, 1986), we took four separate measurements of inspection time and asked carefully graded non-directive questions after each one about what the subjects saw in the display. The perceivers responded consistently that they saw the lines move. The non-perceivers often seemed confused by the question and gave a variety of answers without ever referring to anything that could be interpreted as apparent motion. The other relevant feature of this experiment was that half the subjects were regular video games players and half were almost complete non-players. This selection variable was introduced because a number of subjects in the first experiment had commented that the inspection time task on the video screen was like a simple video game; selection of games players might, we felt, yield a sample with a high degree of relevant previous experience. As it happened, the video games players had significantly faster inspection times than the non-players, but they also had higher APM scores; when we corrected statistically for the difference in one, the difference in the other vanished also. The games players were no more likely than the non-players to report seeing or making use of apparent motion. The conclusion from the study: perception or non-perception of apparent motion in the inspection time task is stable and consistent, but apparently not related to previous experience with fast moving video displays.

2.3 Experiment 3

Our third experiment used Grade 7 children (mean age 12.6) for subjects, and the Revised Wechsler Intelligence Scale for Children (WISC-R) for intellectual assessment. The correlation between Performance IQ and IT was -.60 in the non-perceivers, dropping to -.24 in the perceivers. This experiment was of interest because it replicated the distinction between the apparent motion perceivers and non-perceivers in a younger sample than we had used before. In addition, we undertook to see if the perceivers and non-perceivers differed in their degree of field dependence. The rationale was that if perception of apparent motion involved some kind of temporal integration of the elements of a rapidly shifting display, perhaps those subjects who perceived it were generally less tied to the individual details of the temporal array than those who did not. We thus estimated field dependence/independence with the Group Embedded Figures Test (Oltman, Raskin, & Witkin, 1971). However, there were no significant or near-significant differences between the perceivers and the non-perceivers in their field dependence as measured with this test. The conclusion from the study: the distinction between perceivers and non-perceivers could readily be made in 12-year-old children, but did not seem to be related to degree of field dependence.

2.4 Experiment 4

This experiment included both university students and students at a vocational training institute as subjects, and used the Standard Progressive Matrices and Advanced Progressive Matrices for intellectual assessment, summing the scores on the two tests. The correlation between the Progressive Matrices composite and IT was -.66 in the non-perceivers, falling to -.02 in the perceivers. In this experiment we tried to devise inspection time stimuli that did not stretch out in any one direction and thus would not afford any opportunity for seeing apparent motion; the reported correlations are with inspection time as measured with these new stimuli. (We also required subjects to perform the standard two-line task in order to assess perception of apparent motion). The stimuli we devised had a diamond and a square as the two targets, and a combination of the two as a mask. To the subjects, it seemed that one of the targets appeared first, and was then overlaid by the other. This technique of forming the mask from the combination of two targets was first used in inspection time research by Longstreth, Walsh, Alcorn, Szeszulski, & Manis (1986), and makes the discrimination task more of a Temporal Order Judgement (TOJ) than a shape or length discrimination. As it happened, the attempt to prevent perception of apparent motion with the new stimuli was only nominally successful. Many subjects who reported perceiving apparent motion in the original stimuli reported perceiving apparent depth in the new ones, such that the first shape seemed to float in space above the second one. A chi-square test confirmed a significant relationship (p < .001) between seeing apparent motion and seeing apparent depth. The conclusion from the study: the differences between perceivers and non-perceivers of apparent motion are replicable with at least some other perceptual phenomena, including one form of a Temporal Order Judgement.

2.5 Experiment 5

Our fifth experiment again used grade 7 children (mean age 12.5) as subjects, and the Standard Progressive Matrices (SPM) for intellectual assessment. The correlation between SPM score and IT was -.42 in the non-perceivers, dropping to -.01 in the perceivers. The correlation with SPM in the non-perceivers was lower than we had found before, but the SPM scores in this experiment were a year old, having come from a mass testing carried out in grade 6. In this experiment, we tried to build on the suggestive results of Experiment 4 by measuring known (or at least widely accepted) perceptual mechanisms, and testing for differences in these mechanisms between perceivers and non-perceivers. Specifically, we attempted to index the functioning of the transient and sustained systems in visual perception (Breitmeyer & Ganz, 1976; Breitmeyer, 1984). To measure this we used a Tektronix X-Y display to show subjects counterphase flickering gratings of two cycles per degree (c/d) (where 1 c/d refers to one dark and one light bar subtended through one degree of visual angle), with a sinusoidal luminance distribution. The dependent variable was contrast sensitivity, the inverse of contrast threshold. Contrast threshold is the difference in brightness between the light and the dark bands needed for the subjects to be able to discriminate the flickering grating from a blank field of equal average brightness. The gratings had a counterphase flicker (that is, the light and dark bands alternated) at either a fast rate of 20 times a second (20 Hz) or a slow rate of 6 times a second (6 Hz). The theory (Breitmeyer & Ganz, 1976) is that the contrast needed to perceive the grating which is flickering at the 20 Hz rate will index the sensitivity of the transient system, responsible for rapid visual response to movement of general shapes. The contrast needed to perceive the grating flickering at the 6 Hz rate will be influenced more by the sustained system, responsible for much slower visual responses to fine details. In current theory, backward masking involves inhibition of the slow sustained response to the target by the fast transient response to the mask. If the perceivers had either a stronger transient or a weaker sustained response to the stimuli than the non-perceivers did, then their overall visual response would be dominated by the transient system which is optimized for detection of rapid changes. Their perception of apparent motion, and by inference the blocking of any relationship between inspection time and IQ, could thus be referred to transient system performance.

As it happened, there were significant differences between perceivers and non-perceivers in contrast sensitivity, but not quite as hypothesized. The perceivers displayed higher sensitivity at both fast and slow flicker rates, with the difference slightly greater at the slow flicker rate. However, the division between transient and sustained functioning is not as clear as was once thought, and it is possible that transient functioning is responsible to a significant degree for contrast sensitivity at low flicker rates, also (e.g., Watson & Robson, 1981). The conclusion from the study: perceptual mechanisms seem clearly to be implicated in the differences between perceivers and non-perceivers, but those mechanisms cannot be identified simply as efficiency of either the transient or sustained system. This conclusion is a limited one, but is the first systematic demonstration of differences between apparent motion perceivers and non-perceivers, other than differences in the perception of the targets themselves.

3. DISCUSSION

Our attempts to discover the role of apparent motion in inspection time experiments have had limited but real success. We have replicated the difference between perceivers and non-perceivers of apparent motion four times since the initial experiment, and regard it as being just about as robust as the overall relationship between inspection time and IQ. We have found that the distinction, and its functional significance in establishing different subsamples, holds for children as well as adults and for stimuli other than the original two-line target stimuli. Finally, we have made a beginning on the task of relating the difference to specific differences in the perceptual systems of perceivers and non-perceivers.

We do not yet know whether it is the high or the low correlation between IT and IQ that is the 'true' one, but we think that extensions to Experiment 4 may provide the answer at last. Perception of apparent motion in the IT display can be reduced by using masking stimuli that cut across the contours of the target stimuli, and Nettelbeck (personal communication to B.Mackenzie) has devised masks that are more effective for the purpose than those used in Experiment 4. An appropriate further experiment, therefore, is to divide a sample of subjects into apparent motion perceivers and non-perceivers on the basis of their experience with the original two-line task, and then to measure their IT with a mask that effectively eliminates any apparent motion. If the perceivers thereupon show as high a correlation between IT and IQ as the non-perceivers did previously, then we can conclude that the high correlation was the true one all along, and that perception of apparent motion simply got in the way of assessing it. If the non-perceivers show as low a correlation as the perceivers always did, then we can conclude that the low correlation was the true one all along, and that the IT-IQ relationship is artifactual. However, if the perceivers and non-perceivers continue to differ in how closely their ITs are related to their IQs, then we will have to take more seriously the hypothesis that perception or non-perception of apparent motion indexes some possibly fundamental processing differences in the two groups. Extensions of Experiment 5 may then throw light on the nature of these differences.

CORRESPONDENCE

Correspondence should be addressed to Dr Brian Mackenzie, Department of Psychology, University of Tasmania, G.P.O Box 252 C, Hobart, Tasmania, 7001, Australia.

REFERENCES.

Breitmeyer, B. (1984). Visual masking: An integrative approach. New York: Oxford University Press.

Breitmeyer, B., & Ganz, L. (1976). Implications of sustained and transient channels for theories of visual pattern masking, saccadic suppression, and information processing. Psychological Review, 83, 1-36.

Longstreth, L. E., Walsh, D. A., Alcorn, M. B., Szeszulski, P. A., & Manis, F. R. (1986). Backward masking, IQ, SAT, and reaction time: Inter-relationships and theory. Personality and Individual Differences, 5, 643-651.

Mackenzie, B., & Bingham, E. (1985). IQ, inspection time, and response strategies in a university population. Australian Journal of Psychology, 37, 257-268.

Mackenzie, B., & Cumming, S. (1986). How fragile is the relationship between inspection time and intelligence: The effects of apparent-motion cues and previous experience. Personality and Individual Differences, 5, 721-729.

Nettelbeck, T. (1982). Inspection time: An index for intelligence? Quarterly Journal of Experimental Psychology, 34A, 299-312.

Oltman, P. K., Raskin, E., & Witkin, H. A. (1971). Group Embedded Figures Test. Palo Alto, Calif.: Consulting Psychologists Press.

Watson, A. B., & Robson, J. G. (1981). Discrimination at threshold: Labelled detectors in human vision. Vision Research, 21, 1115-1122.

Human Information Processing: Measures,
Mechanisms, and Models, D. Vickers and P.L. Smith (eds.)
© Elsevier Science Publishers B.V. (North-Holland), 1989

AUDITORY INSPECTION TIME: REVIEW, RECENT RESEARCH AND REASSESSMENT

Ian J. Deary

University of Edinburgh

This study examined the hypothesis that individual differences in auditory inspection time (AIT) are largely due to differences in pitch discrimination ability. We tested 120 schoolchildren (60 boys, 60 girls) of mean age 11.5 years on two verbal and non-verbal ability tests and on the Bentley tests of Musical Ability. Subjects were also tested on a novel form of the AIT test which was devised in response to the criticisms of an earlier version of the test (Irwin, 1984). About 50 % of schoolchildren (compared with 67 % of undergraduates) were able to perform the AIT task. In the boy's group, all ability tests correlated at about -.35 with AIT durations. In the girl's group, AIT durations and verbal ability tests correlated at about -.4, while non-verbal tests showed much lower correlations with AIT. Pitch perception ability correlated at about -.2 with all ability tests and with AIT. Partial correlations between AIT and ability tests, controlling for pitch perception, achieve levels of about -.3. Factor analysis reveals that AIT variance shared with pitch perception may be attributed to g.

1. INTRODUCTION

The perceptual index known as 'inspection time' (IT) was developed in the early 1970s as one aspect of an accumulator model of visual perception (Vickers, Nettelbeck and Willson, 1972). An individual's IT is the minimum stimulus presentation time that allows him to reach a predetermined level of accuracy in a decision task. The decision task is usually simple, and it often involves deciding which of two lines of markedly different length is longer. Any one of a number of psychophysical procedures (e.g., adaptive staircase, method of limits, or method of constant stimuli) may reliably be used to estimate the duration required by a subject in order to make, say, 85% correct decisions in a two choice task. IT must be distinguished from reaction time: its measurement does not involve the subject responding rapidly. In the estimation procedure only the correctness of the responses is recorded;

subjects respond at leisure and accuracy is stressed over speed of response.

In the eleven years after Nettelbeck and Lally (1976) first reported a significant correlation between IT and psychometric measures of intelligence, there were over 20 attempted replications of the result. Others have reviewed these studies (Brand and Deary, 1982; Vernon, 1986; Nettelbeck, 1987), and I shall not replicate these efforts here. Briefly, the mean uncorrected correlation between IT and IQ-type scores in all studies to date is -.35. However, these studies include a preponderance of samples where the mean IQ is high and the range of ability is restricted (because undergraduates are a convenient source of subjects), and the mean disattenuated IT-IQ correlation is about -.50 (Nettelbeck, 1987). The relationship between IT and IQ holds for both verbal and non-verbal tests of intelligence; and it holds in many different sample types, including the mentally handicapped, young children, the elderly and college students. Given that a moderate relationship between IT and IQ exists, the main focus of recent efforts has been to discover the reason for this correlation.

There are two broad views with regard to explanation: IT is either a cause of or a consequence of high intelligence. Take the latter position first. It may be argued that there are aspects of the visual IT task that make it easier for those with high IQs. Some have investigated the possibility that successful completion of IT tasks involves using strategies to penetrate apparent movement cues which result in artefactual fast ITs (MacKenzie and Bingham, 1985; MacKenzie and Cumming, 1986). Another 'consequence' hypothesis is that high IQ subjects are more able and/or willing to comply with boring tasks like IT, RT and evoked potential stimuli (Mackintosh, 1986) and to maintain attention during them. Both of these views interpret IT as an uninteresting consequence of high IQ and, if either is correct, then IT cannot be offered as the basis for a substantial part of IQ variance.

The second hypothesis has it that IT is an index of mental speed which may explain some of the variance in IQ-type test scores. Brand (1984), Brand and Deary (1982) and Deary (in press) have argued that a fast inspection time is ontogenetically related to high levels of intelligence: the quicker completion of processing any one discriminandum leaves the subject more time to make more discriminations or enables him to make more detailed discriminations of the same stimulus, and this leads to the building up of greater levels of stored knowledge. The nature of this mental speed has been debated. Brand and Deary (1982) tended to interpret the IT as an index of general mental speed, perhaps reflecting a general neural efficiency or fidelity of information transfer, while others (see Nettelbeck, 1987) have hypothesised that IT reflects the speed of information input processes, particularly that stage of processing where information is passed from sensory registers to short term memory.

This is the background of empirical evidence and theory which drives current experimental work on IT. In Edinburgh, we have investigated IT along four fronts. We have examined the brain potentials which are evoked by the IT stimuli and we have found some reliable correlations among IT, IQ and AEP indices (Zhang, Caryl and Deary, in press). Second, we are currently investigating the effects of blocking or enhancing various neurotransmitter pathways on the performance of IT tasks (Petrie, 1988). Third, we have attempted to test various hypotheses put forward by those who see strategies as the key to performing the IT task (Egan, 1986). Fourth, we have developed an auditory version of the IT task in order to extend the IT studies into a modality other than vision.

It is the auditory IT work which will be discussed in detail in this paper. The reason for devising the auditory IT (AIT) task was that, if the visual task was more than a modality-specific perceptual trick, and if IT was a measure of general mental speed, then two hypotheses follow. First, AIT should correlate with IQ. Second, AIT should correlate with visual IT (VIT).

2. EARLY AUDITORY INSPECTION TIME STUDIES

Deary (1980, reported in Brand and Deary, 1982) devised an AIT task with the intention of indexing mental speed in a way that was analogous with VIT. The auditory discrimination was simple: which of two square wave tones of markedly different pitch, and presented one after the other, was presented first. Subjects were alerted by a cue, heard the first tone (either 770 or 880 Hz), heard white noise for 500 ms and then heard the second tone (880 or 770 Hz). Each tone was played for the same duration, ranging from 200ms, to 2.7ms. Both tones were forward and backward masked using white noise. The test was presented as blocks of trials, beginning with blocks of stimuli of long duration and proceeding to shorter and more difficult durations. AIT represented that part of the performance curve where subjects were 90% correct in their judgements regarding the order of the stimuli. AIT correlated at -.70 with Raven's Progressive Matrices and at -.66 with Mill Hill Vocabulary scores (n=13; two subjects were mentally handicapped). In Deary's (1980) study AIT and VIT were correlated at a level near to unity, but the correlation was dependent upon the inclusion of the mentally handicapped subjects.

Two independent attempts to replicate this result followed in the next six years. Irwin (1984) used a task very similar to that of Deary

(1980). He tested 50 twelve year old children and obtained correlations between the AIT, the Raven's Matrices and the Mill Hill Vocabulary scores of -.23 and -.32, respectively. While these were significant, Irwin failed to replicate the significant AIT-VIT correlation. Nettelbeck, Edwards and Vreugdenhil (1986) improved the AIT task by replacing the white noise mask with a mask consisting of 15ms alternating bursts of both target tones. Their new mask was used before, between and after the tones, for 1000ms in each case. IQ was tested in 30 subjects using Raven's Advanced Progressive Matrices and the AIT-IQ correlation was -.38, while the VIT-AIT correlation was .39.

3. PROBLEMS WITH, AND IMPROVEMENTS IN, THE AIT TASK

Although the AIT task had the advantage of not being penetrable by strategies, which remain a possibility with those VIT stimuli which produce apparent movement effects, the AIT task, as devised by Deary (1980) and developed by Nettelbeck et al. (1986), had some obvious problems which did not occur with the VIT task. First, the AIT testing tended to result in a skewed distribution of scores, with most subjects obtaining very short AITs and a few obtaining very long AITs. Typical of the results are those of Deary (1980), where the range of AITs was 6 to 160ms, but where the median was 10ms. There were at least three factors contributing to this type of distribution. First, the inclusion of mentally handicapped subjects tended to result in those subjects obtaining very long AITs. Second, white noise was an ineffective mask and allowed subjects to continue to extract stimulus information from the sensory representation of the stimulus, even after the mask had begun. Third, although subjects were being pre-tested for pitch discrimination ability, those subjects who found the basic discrimination in the AIT task very difficult were not always being left out of the later analyses. This amounts to something like allowing subjects with very poor visual acuity to proceed with the visual IT task: it introduces pitch discrimination variance into a task which is supposed to be measuring speed of processing only. A second problem with the original AIT task was the overlap in frequency spectra at very short tone durations. Irwin (1984) provided evidence which demonstrated that, at durations of about 10ms (a region where many subjects were able to make correct AIT discriminations), the target tones had large overlaps in their frequency spectra, a phenomenon not found when the target tones were played for, say, 75ms. Thus, as the duration of the tone pairs became shorter, the AIT task might have been an amalgam of both a perceptual speed and a pitch discrimination task. Finally, the AIT task was not analogous with the VIT task, because it allowed the subject some time between the two stimuli: subjects were able to rehearse the first of the two tones in short term memory in the 500 or 1000ms between the tones, and the task may have allowed rehearsal of the second tone because the mask was not effective.

In view of these problems, Deary, Caryl, Egan and Wight (in press) devised a new auditory IT task. As before, subjects made a decision about the order of two tones which were of markedly different pitch (880 and 784 Hz). The mask came on immediately after the second tone had ended, and took the form of a series of alternating 10ms bursts of the two target tones. There was no space between the two target tones. Subjects were trained on the new task, and those who were unable to make reliable decisions at long tone durations were excluded from further analysis. (In fact, we allowed these subjects to complete all blocks of AIT trials, but we found that they formed a group whose scores had no overlap with those subjects who were able to respond reliably to longer durations on the task.) This task appears to have ended the problem of very short AITs: our first testing on 80 undergraduates resulted in a mean AIT of 75.8ms (SD 27.5) and no individual had an AIT of less than 30ms. The same mean level and distribution of AIT durations was found in the studies which follow.

In the first study using this new AIT task, we tested various subgroups of 120 undergraduates on AIT, the three most commonly used versions of the VIT task (vertical lines, horizontal lines, and the stimuli used by Longstreth et al. (1986)), the Alice Heim 5 IQ test, Mill Hill Vocabulary and Raven's Advanced Progressive Matrices (Deary et al., in press). With the exception of the AH5, the standard deviations on the IQ tests, were very small. The AH5-IT correlations, for the three visual tasks, ranged from -.29 to -.33. The AH5-AIT correlation was -.31. Correlations between AIT and the three VIT tasks ranged from .24 to .53. We have replicated the AIT-IQ correlation using this new task on two further samples (Deary, Head and Egan, in press). In a sample of 34 undergraduates the Alice Heim 6-AIT correlation was -.39 (the AIT and the verbal IQ component of the AH6 correlation was -.45); and in a sample of 53 twelve year old schoolchildren the correlations between AIT and Mill Hill Vocabulary and Raven's Matrices scores were -.36 and -.26 respectively.

4. SENSORY DISCRIMINATION OR PROCESSING SPEED?

While the new AIT task has taken the AIT durations away from the region where pitch discrimination probably confounds duration as the key variable, the question as to whether some AIT variance is attributable to individual differences in pitch discrimination remains to be addressed directly. Irwin (1984) found that AITs correlated at -.51 with scores on the Seashore test of pitch discrimination. But, recall that Irwin was using the white noise-masked task, and that he did not report excluding those subjects unable reliably to perform the AIT task at long durations before analysing his data. Deary et al. (in press) included the Seashore test for the undergraduate sample and tested the schoolchildren sample twice on the shorter Bentley pitch discrimination test. In the undergraduate sample pitch discrimination did not correlate significantly with either IQ measures or AIT, and when pitch discrimination ability was partialled out of the AIT-IQ correlation there was almost no change. In the schoolchildren, pitch discrimination correlated at about -.2 with a test of verbal ability, but at non-significant levels with Raven's IQ and mathematical ability. Also in schoolchildren, pitch discrimination correlated at -.18 with AIT, but, when pitch discrimination was partialled out of the AIT-IQ correlations, they remained almost the same as before.

From our studies, then, it appears that pitch discrimination does correlate at low levels with both AIT and verbal IQ in children, but not in high ability adults. In fact, there are several reports in the literature where measures of pitch discrimination correlate with measures of intelligence, especially in schoolchildren (this was the subject of a recent historical review and reanalysis by Deary (in press b)).

Interestingly, there has been a similar discussion of the interplay between processing speed and sensory discrimination in a separate series of studies. Raz, et al., (1983) and Raz and Willerman (1985) used a backward recognition masking test to estimate undergraduates' speed of auditory processing. This is done by playing a single target tone, either 770 or 870 Hz, for 20ms, leaving a variable interval between the tone and a mask, and masking with a tone which is intermediate in pitch between the two possible targets. Subjects indicate whether the target was high or low. Tone to mask interval may take one of the following values: 0, 20, 30, 60, 120 or 480ms. The number of correct identifications of target tones may be seen as a measure of auditory processing speed, and the correlation between ability on this task and IQ scores ranged from -.37 to -.49 in their 1983 study and from -.37 to -.53 in the 1985 study (n=36).

These results may be interpreted as straightforward corroboration of the AIT-IQ correlations, but a more recent study by Raz, Willerman and Yama (1987) raises the issue of pitch perception once again. Using an adaptive staircase procedure, they played subjects two 20ms tones which were 850ms apart and unmasked. Subjects were asked to indicate whether the high tone came first or second. The algorithm sought the smallest pitch difference where subjects could make accurate discriminations. At the outset, the two tones were 100Hz apart and, in some cases, this was reduced to 2 to 3 Hz. In their first experiment, IQ was correlated with frequency discrimination ability for two signal ramps at -.42 and -.54 (n=25). The correlation was not caused by individual differences in practice, stimulus spectral composition, musical experience or demographic characteristics. In a second sample, using undergraduates pre-selected to provide a wide range of IQs, IQ correlated at -.50 and -.52 with two discrimination indices. Again, the correlations were almost unchanged when musical experience was partialled out. In their third experiment, Raz, Willerman and Yama (1987) devised a signal detection task which was just as complicated as the previous discrimination task, but found no correlation between signal detection threshold and cognitive ability. They concluded that, while signal recognition correlates with ability, signal detection does not.

It is also interesting to note that the third experiment of Raz, Willerman and Yama (1987) was designed to test the hypothesis that the high IQ subject simply does better on any novel 'non-entrenched' task, and that it is this fast adaptation to the strange situation in the laboratory that explains the typical IQ-IT correlation. This, they argued, was a suggestion put forward by many cognitive psychologists, and it was refuted by their findings. However, note that this hypothesis is almost the opposite of that thought up by MacIntosh (1986), who suggests that the high IQ subject performs better given the boring nature of laboratory tasks, such as IT. It appears that attempts to explain away the IT-IQ correlation in cognitive terms can be extremely flexible.

5. CONCLUSIONS

If the many VIT studies, the AIT studies mentioned here and the studies of Raz and his co-workers are taken together we may make some tentative conclusions. There is much evidence to indicate that both visual and auditory processing speed correlate at moderate levels with psychometric measures of intelligence. Also, in three out of four studies, VIT and AIT have a moderate intercorrelation. Our recent studies appear to indicate that AIT is more closely related to verbal IQ than to non-verbal IQ, indicating that processing speed advantages in one modality may provide the basis for advantages in specific types of cognitive ability. The moderate intercorrelations of various forms of the VIT task (Deary, et al., (in press)) suggest that each task has a degree of task-specific variance, as well as general processing speed variance. Our evoked potential studies suggest that these two sources of variance have separate correlates. The general speed factor appears to be related to IQ, whereas the more task-specific variance is correlated with evoked potential indices of the early stages of information intake or pattern recognition (P200 rise time particularly) (Deary and Caryl, 1988; Hall, 1988).

Although our studies appear to have ruled out the involvement of pitch discrimination as a confounding variable in the AIT task, the results of Raz, Willerman and Yama (1987) indicate that, with briefly presented auditory stimuli, high IQ subjects make finer pitch discrimination judgements. This should make us wary of prematurely concluding that speed of processing is the key variable, even in tasks which appear to index speed of processing only. Raz and his colleagues (1987) argue that the IT-IQ correlations may be explained by the high IQ subject having: faster feature extraction; better sensory representation of stimuli; faster decision time; less bias in responding; or a combination of the above. The decision time and response bias differences were ruled out by Nettelbeck and Lally (1976) and Lally and Nettelbeck (1977). The remaining novel suggestion, therefore, is that the high IQ subject has a better representation of sensory stimuli. Raz and colleagues remind us that, "quality of signal representation rather than speed of processing may be the key feature of an intelligent brain." However, speed of processing and quality of representations are probably neither alternatives nor explanations at the same level.

If we go back to the theory of Vickers, et al. (1972), it states that individuals, when making decisions about a stimulus in a two-choice decision task, must accumulate evidence for the two options against a background of noise. Evidence accumulates by the subject making inspections of the stimulus, each inspection takes a minimum amount of time, and a decision is made when the evidence for one of the alternatives passes some threshold. In the IT task, the stimulus presentation time is manipulated and, at very brief durations, the subject has not been able to accumulate sufficient evidence from the stimulus to make reliably correct decisions. However, for any given stimulus duration, because of individual differences in IT, some subjects will make more inspections than others, and a subject with a very short IT will achieve a faithful representation of a brief stimulus, whereas a subject with a long it will have a poor representation. Therefore, a fast IT may cause better representation of stimuli, and Raz's finding that high IQ subjects make better pitch discriminations to briefly presented tone pairs may be explained by the fact that, given a constant presentation time, as the pitch discrimination becomes more difficult, more inspections of the stimuli need to be taken in order to make reliable discriminations. This is unlikely to be a factor in the Seashore test, where the stimuli are presented for 500ms (which is far longer than any AITs reported in the above studies) and are unmasked. However, with 20ms tones of very similar pitch, even when they are unmasked and separated by 850ms, it is likely that the subject with superior IT will have an advantage.

In summary, the argument which pits processing speed against fidelity of stimulus representation may well be a non-argument: the experiments reported here are congruent with an explanation which states that a fast inspection time is primarily an advantage in information processing speed, and that this results in more faithful representation of briefly presented stimuli.

CORRESPONDENCE

Correspondence concerning this paper should be addressed to Dr Ian Deary, Department of Psychology, University of Edinburgh, 7 George Square, Edinburgh EH8 9JZ U.K.

REFERENCES

Brand, C.R. (1984) Intelligence and inspection time: an ontogenetic relationship? In C.J. Turner and H.B. Miles (Eds), The Biology of Human Intelligence. Nafferton, North Humberside: Nafferton Books.

Brand, C.R. and Deary, I.J. (1982) Intelligence and 'inspection time'. In H.J. Eysenck (Ed.), A Model for Intelligence. New York:Springer Verlag.

Deary, I.J. (1980) How general is the mental speed factor in 'general' intelligence: an attempt to extend inspection time to the auditory modality. B.Sc.(Hons) Thesis, University of Edinburgh.

Deary, I.J. Intelligence and encoding speed in infants, adults and children. C.P.C. : Cahiers de Psychologie Cognitive / European Bulletin of Cognitive Psychology, 8, 462-468.

Deary, I.J. The nature of intelligence: simplicity to complexity and back again. In D. Forshaw and M. Shepherd (Eds), Maudsley Essay Series in the History of Psychiatry and Psychology (in press).

Deary, I.J. and Caryl, P.G. (1988) Inspection time and cognitive ability. Paper presented at the International Conference on Thinking, Aberdeen.

Deary, I.J., Caryl, P.G., Egan, V. and Wight, D. Visual and auditory inspection time: their interrelationship and correlation with intelligence in high ability subjects. Personality and Individual Differences, (in press).

Deary, I.J., Head, B. and Egan, V. Auditory inspection time, intelligence and pitch perception. Intelligence, in press.

Egan, V. (1986) Intelligence and inspection time: do high-IQ subjects use cognitive strategies? Personality and Individual Differences, 7, 695-700.

Hall, B. (1988) Evoked potentials, auditory inspection time and intelligence. M.A.(Hons) Thesis, University of Edinburgh.

Irwin, R.J. (1984) Inspection time and its relation to intelligence. Intelligence, 8, 47-65.

Lally, M. and Nettelbeck, T. (1977) Intelligence, reaction time and inspection time. American Journal of Mental Deficiency, 82, 273-281.

Longstreth, L.E., Walsh, D.A., Alcorn, M.B., Szeszulski, P.A. and Manis, F.R. (1986) Backward masking, IQ, SAT and reaction time: interrelationships and theory. Personality and Individual Differences, 7, 643-652.

MacIntosh, N.J. (1986) The biology of intelligence? British Journal of Psychology, 77, 1-18.

Mackenzie, B. and Bingham, E. (1985) IQ, inspection time and response strategies in a university population. Australian Journal of Psychology, 7, 257-268.

Mackenzie, B. and Cumming, S. (1986) How fragile is the relationship between inspection time and intelligence: the effects of apparent motion cues and previous experience. Personality and Individual Differences, 7, 721-729.

Nettelbeck, T. (1987) Inspection time and intelligence. In P.A.Vernon (Ed.), Speed of Information Processing and Intelligence. New Jersey: Ablex.

Nettelbeck, T., Edwards, C. and Vreugdenhil, A. (1986) Inspection time and IQ: evidence for a mental speed-ability association. Personality and Individual Differences, 7, 633-642.

Nettelbeck, T. and Lally, M. (1976) Inspection time and measured intelligence. British Journal of Psychology, 67, 17-22.

Petrie, R. (1988) The effect of smoking on human information processing. B.Sc.(Hons) Thesis, University of Edinburgh.

Raz, N. and Willerman, L. (1985) Aptitude-related differences in auditory information processing: effects of selective attention and tone duration. Personality and Individual Differences, 6, 299-304.

Raz, N., Willerman, L., Ingmundson, P. and Hanlon, M. (1983) Aptitude-related differences in auditory recognition masking. Intelligence, 7, 71-90.

Raz, N., Willerman, L. and Yama, M. (1987) On sense and senses: intelligence and auditory information processing. Personality and Individual Differences, 8, 201-210.

Vernon, P.A. (1986) Inspection time: does it measure intelligence? Personality and Individual Differences, 7, 715-720.

Vickers, D., Nettelbeck, T. and Willson, R.J. (1972) Perceptual indices of performance: the measurement of 'inspection time' and 'noise' in the visual system. Perception, 1, 263-295.

Zhang, Y., Caryl, P.G. and Deary, I.J. Evoked potential correlates of inspection time. Personality and Individual Differences (in press).

Human Information Processing: Measures,
Mechanisms, and Models, D. Vickers and P.L. Smith (eds.)
Elsevier Science Publishers B.V. (North-Holland), 1989

INSPECTION TIME AND THE RELATIONSHIP BETWEEN STIMULUS ENCODING AND RESPONSE SELECTION FACTORS IN DEVELOPMENT

Michael Anderson

University of Edinburgh

Inspection time (IT), postulated as a measure of an individual's speed of perceptual encoding, has been shown to relate to differences in IQ in adults but to differences in mental age (MA) in children, suggesting that speed of perceptual encoding undergoes developmental change. I have argued, on the contrary, that speed of encoding remains relatively unchanged throughout development (relating to IQ over a wide age range), and that apparent decreases in estimated IT with age are due to factors other than an increase in the speed of processing. The experiment reported here investigates whether changing the stimulus encoding demands, or changing the response selection requirements, interacts with any age differences found. Measures of IT are taken using a video game task, where the children have to identify a space invader. The stimulus encoding and response selection factors are systematically varied. Sixteen children in each group of eight and twelve year-olds were tested. The IT measure was found to increase when the stimulus encoding load was increased, but did so equally for both groups. In contrast, increasing response selection factors increased IT much more for the younger group. This is seen as tentative support for the possibility that observed age differences in IT may be due to factors other than differences in speed of processing.

1. INTRODUCTION

Inspection time (IT) has been proposed as a measure of the minimum time required to make a single inspection of sensory input (Vickers 1979). The fact that inspection time correlates -0.5 with IQ in adult populations (Nettelbeck 1987) has given considerable impetus to theories which postulate that individual differences in intelligence are based on differences in speed, or efficiency, of processing (Jensen 1982, Eysenck 1986). Studies that have looked at IT during development have found that IT decreases with increasing age (Nettelbeck and Wilson 1985,

Wilson and Nettelbeck 1986), which may indicate that increasing speed of processing may be the causal agent in cognitive development. In this way, individual differences in adult IQ, and developmental changes in cognitive ability, would be a reflection of the same underlying process (Brand 1984). On the contrary, I have argued that individual differences in intelligence and developmental change reflect quite different processes (Anderson 1988, and in preparation). Taking the position that development is characterised by increasing knowledge, while individual differences reflect variations in speed of processing, I have hypothesized that speed of processing would remain relatively unchanged throughout development. If this is so, then high intelligence, or IQ, should predict processing speed, irrespective of the child's age. This was confirmed for children from six to ten years old (Anderson 1986). A subsequent experiment extended this idea by showing that reaction time (RT), being more influenced than IT by knowledge and strategic processes, was related to chronological and mental ages during development, and not at all to IQ, whereas IT was again related to IQ, irrespective of the child's age (Anderson 1988).

Although the predicted relationship was found between IT and IQ during development, it was also the case that IT correlated higher with mental age (MA), in both these studies. To explain why IT should correlate better with MA than with IQ, I proposed that the decrease in IT with age is due to changes in the ability of the child to handle aspects of the task not directly related to processing speed. Thus MA, being correlated with IQ, picks up some of the speed of processing variance, and, in addition, it picks up developmental changes in knowledge, or task sophistication, that aid performance in an IT task. To support this hypothesis it is necessary to show that there are factors, unrelated to differences in speed of processing, which influence IT and are subject to developmental change.

The experiment presented here investigates the possibility that age-related differences in IT may be due to changes in the facility with which responses are selected after the stimulus has been encoded. The perceptual encoding and response selection requirements of an IT task are manipulated, and the relative effect on age differences is observed. The hypothesis is that if speed of perceptual encoding changes in development, then any change in stimulus encoding parameters that leads to a decrease in IT should interact with age differences. If the stimulus encoding parameters are held constant, but the response requirements change, then any interaction with age would be indicative of a differential contribution of response selection factors to younger children's IT.

2. METHOD

2.1 Subjects

Thirty two subjects, sixteen 12-year-olds and sixteen 8-year olds, were tested on Standard Raven Progressive Matrices (mean score 31.3, range 6 to 49; IQ equivalent mean of 103, sd = 13.4, with a range of 78 to 125). All attended a normal county middle school. Any subjects who required glasses wore them during testing. All the subjects had taken part in previous inspection time studies.

2.2 Apparatus

The IT task is embedded in a computer-controlled video game, described extensively in Anderson (1988), in which the stimuli are presented in the form of space invaders. The space invaders have four, instead of the more usual two, antennae. This created five kinds of invaders, one where the antennae were all the same length (5 mm), and four where one of the four antennae was half the size of the other three (2.5 mm, subtending a visual angle of 0.57 deg., at a viewing distance of 25 cm). There were two sets of response keys appropriate for different response conditions (see below). One set contained two keys for the conditions where subjects had to make a same-different discrimination, and one contained five keys for the other conditions where the individual invader had to be identified.

2.3 Procedure

The task was to identify a briefly presented space invader and to 'shoot' it by pressing the key appropriate to that invader. The invader was hidden from view by a wall (mask) which disappeared, on pressing a button, to reveal the invader. The wall would then reappear to mask the stimulus after a pre-set exposure duration. This task procedure is described fully in Anderson (1986, 1988). The subjects were all given practice in discriminating the invaders according the appropriate condition instruction (see below), and were then tested on 60 exposures, with 12 at each of five different durations (100, 80, 60, 40 and 20 msecs), as in the standard method of constant stimuli procedure.

There were four experimental conditions. In condition 1 there were three stimuli, with two responses (S3-R2). The three invaders used were: one with all four antennae the same size; one with the second antennae shorter than the others; and one with the third antennae shorter than the others. In this condition there were only two responses. Subjects had to decide whether the invader had antennae all of which were the same size, or one of which was different. Objectively, 50% were the same and 50% were different. This is the IT paradigm used in previous experiments (Anderson 1986, 1988). In condition 2 there were three stimuli and three responses (S3-R3). The same three space invaders as used in condition 1 had to be individually identified, instead of simply being classified as same or different. As before, 50% of the stimuli presented at each exposure duration had all antennae the same length. In condition 3 (S5-R2) all five stimuli were used, but the subjects had to make a same-different discrimination, as in condition 1. Again, the stimulus with equal antennae was presented on 50% of the trials at each exposure duration. In condition 4 (S5-R5) all five stimuli were again used, but, this time, as in condition 2, each one had to be identified individually. Again, at each exposure duration, the stimulus with equal antennae was presented on 50% of the trials.

All subjects completed all conditions, with testing on conditions 1 and 3 (same-different judgement) and conditions 2 and 4 (identity judgement) confined to separate days to minimise any possible interference from alternative response requirements. The subjects were given practice before each condition. An estimate of IT was obtained for each subject, in each condition, by calculating d' values at each exposure duration and extrapolating to an estimated IT equivalent to a d' of 3.94, or 97.5% accuracy.

3. RESULTS

Mean ITs in the four conditions are set out in Table 1.

Table 1

Mean IT (msec) in the four Conditions

	1 S3-R2	2 S3-R3	3 S5-R2	4 S5-R5
8-year olds				
Means	37	60	53	76
S.Ds	30	46	37	38
12-year olds				
Means	25	28	46	34
S.Ds	12	12	19	16

Comparing Age and Condition in an ANOVA produced a main effect of Age ($F= 7.57$, df 1,30 $p<.05$) with older children having, in general, shorter ITs than younger children. There was an effect of Conditions (F= 8.93, df 3,90 p<.001) and an Age x Conditions interaction (F= 5.71, df 3,90 p<.01). Thus, the experimental manipulations influenced the estimation of IT in different ways for different age groups. Comparing S3-R2 with S5-R2, where the response requirements remain the same (same-different discrimination), but where the number of potential stimuli that must be encoded increases (from 3 to five), we find an increase in IT for both groups (F= 21.21, df 1,30 p<.001), but a non-significant interaction with Age (F= 0.24). This contrasts with what happens when we change the response selection demands while holding the number of stimuli constant. Comparing S3-R2 with S3-R3, and comparing S5-R2 with S5-R5, produces significant Age x Condition interactions (F= 4.61, df 1,30 p<.05) and F=15.24, df 1,30 p<.001, respectively).

The correlations between IT and IQ, mental age (MA) and chronological age (CA) are presented in Table 2.

Table 2

Correlations of IQ, MA, and CA with IT in the four conditions

		1 S3-R2	2 S3-R3	3 S5-R2	4 S5-R5
All Subjects (n=32)	IQ	-.38**	-.38**	-.38**	-.14
	MA	-.47***	-.62***	-.39**	-.59***
	CA	-.24	-.44**	-.16	-.62***
12-year-olds (n=16)	IQ	-.11	.08	.06	.18
	MA	-.12	.06	.10	.12
	CA	.02	-.12	-.35	-.33
8 year-olds (n=16)	IQ	-.52**	-.60***	-.59**	-.35
	MA	-.55**	-.65***	-.65***	-.40
	CA	.03	-.18	-.19	-.32

Over all subjects, the correlation with IQ is significant, except for condition 4, but still remains lower than that found for MA. For the first time using this task (see Anderson, 1986; 1988) there are large chronological age correlations with IT, although they are confined to conditions 2 and 4, i.e. the ones where the response selection demands were increased. A closer look reveals that there are no significant relationships within the older group, although the IQ effect is particularly strong for all conditions, except condition 4, within the younger age group.

4. DISCUSSION

In this experiment, condition 1 (S3-R2) is the same as the IT task used in previous studies, and it produces the familiar age difference in estimated IT. If the speed of processing of stimulus information increases during development, then it might be expected that increasing the stimulus processing demands would interact with any age effect. This does not appear to happen. Increasing the number of possible stimuli, but keeping the same response requirement (same-different discrimination), leads to an increase in estimated IT which is similar for both groups. This suggests that the original group difference may not be based on differences in speed of perceptual encoding differences. In contrast, increasing the response demands, within both the three and five stimuli conditions, interacts with Age, with younger children's IT increasing significantly more than older children's. This suggests that Age differences may reflect changes in the ability to select the appropriate response accurately after the stimulus has been encoded, rather than changes in the speed of perceptual encoding.

It could be argued that changing the response requirements, from a same-different to an identity judgement, may also change the perceptual encoding strategies of the children, thereby confounding response selection and stimulus encoding factors. For example, it may be that the difference between the condition where one of five responses have to be selected (S5-R5) and the condition where one of two responses have to be selected (S5-R2), is that the latter requires only two perceptual categories to be discriminated instead of five stimuli. If this were the case, then, at the very least, we would have to suppose that encoding strategies are different at different ages. This would still imply that developmental differences in IT may be due to changes unrelated to changes in processing speed per se. In any case, it seems unlikely that strategic differences in encoding could explain these results. First, younger children show a marked advantage when making a same-different, as opposed to an identity judgement, but older children do not. It would be strange to suppose that younger children, being able to take advantage of the option of searching for a single feature to discriminate two categories, are strategically more proficient than older children. Second, the differences between the response conditions are greater for the three stimuli than for the five stimuli conditions. The strategic hypothesis would surely predict the opposite, with the greatest saving being made when there are more stimuli to be individually identified.

The correlations of IT with IQ, MA and CA in the different conditions are consistent with the hypothesis that the higher MA/IT, as opposed to the IQ/IT correlations reported in development, may be due to changes in the child's ability to handle speed-irrelevant aspects of the task, rather than to real changes in processing speed. Thus, as the response selection requirements of the task increase, so does the correlation with MA and CA, whereas the correlations with IQ (being due ex hypothesi, to the shared variance with processing speed) are relatively unchanging across conditions. Where the response selection requirements are greatest (Condition 4), the correlation with IQ all but disappears. In this condition a high IQ cannot compensate for being young. It seems likely, then, that high response selection demands put a higher premium on developmental differences. Within the older group, none of the correlations is significant. This is disquieting, but consistent with other studies which have found that, when subject are highly practised (all were very familiar with the paradigm, having participated in a number of IT experiments), or when there is more opportunity for strategies to influence performance, the task no longer correlates with intelligence (MacKenzie & Bingham 1985, Egan 1986). For the younger group, high correlations between IT and IQ are found in all conditions, except condition 4. Again, when there is a greater opportunity for variation in response strategies to influence IT, the correlation with IQ decreases.

In conclusion, it is clear that younger children are more affected by changes in response requirements than are older children, but can meet increased encoding demands with equal facility. This may indicate that the decrease in IT during development may be due to changes in the ability to handle the response requirements of the task, rather than to changes in speed of processing.

CORRESPONDENCE

Correspondence concerning this paper should be sent to Dr M. Anderson, Psychology Department, University of Edinburgh, George Square, Edinburgh. U.K

REFERENCES

Anderson, M. (1988) Inspection time, information processing, and the development of intelligence. British Journal of Developmental Psychology, 6, 43-57.

Anderson, M. (1986) Inspection time and IQ in young children. Personality and
    Individual Differences, 7, 677-686.

Anderson, M. (in preparation) Intelligence and Development: a Cognitive Theory.
    Oxford: Blackwell.

Brand, C. (1984) Intelligence and inspection time: an ontogenetic relationship? In
    Turner, C.J. (Ed) The Biology of Human Intelligence. Humberside: Nafferton
    Books.

Egan, V. (1986) Intelligence and inspection time: do high-IQ subjects use cognitive
    strategies? Personality and Individual Differences, 7, 695-700.

Eysenck, H.J. (1986) The theory of intelligence and the psychophysiology of cognition.
    In, Advances in the Psychology of Human Intelligence, Sternberg, R.J. (Ed).
    New Jersey: Erlbaum.

Jensen, A.R. (1982) Reaction time and psychometric g. In Eysenck, H.J. (Ed) A Model
    for Intelligence. Berlin: Springer-Verlag.

Mackenzie, B., and Bingham, E. (1985) IQ, inspection time and response strategies in a
    University population. Australian Journal of Psychology, 37, 257-268.

Nettelbeck, T. (1987) Inspection time and intelligence. In Vernon, P.A. (Ed) Speed of
    Information Processing and Intelligence. New York: Ablex.

Nettelbeck, T., and Wilson, C. (1985) A cross sequential analysis of developmental
    differences in speed of visual information processing. Journal of Experimental
    Child Psychology, 40, 1-22.

Vickers, D. (1979) Decision Processes in Visual Perception. London: Academic Press.

Wilson, C. and Nettelbeck, T. (1986) Inspection time and the mental age deviation
    hypothesis. personality and Individual Differences, 7, 669-675.

Human Information Processing: Measures,
Mechanisms, and Models, D. Vickers and P. L. Smith (eds.)
©Elsevier Science Publishers B. V. (North-Holland), 1989

INSPECTION TIME AND IQ IN CHILDREN

T. Nettelbeck

University of Adelaide

An estimate of inspection time (IT) usually involves a very simple visual discrimination, with viewing time for the target figure being restricted by a backward mask. In the past decade IT has attracted considerable research interest, as a possible index of speed of information processing, and as providing a test of the perennial idea that an association exists between mental speed and intelligence. Although research has suggested that there is a reliable and moderately strong correlation between IT and adult IQ, results to date from work involving children have been problematic. In our study, we have obtained a correlation of -.5 between IT and IQ, for a sample of 47 six-year-old children. This largely reflected performance on 'catch' unmasked trials, included as a check on the appropriate directedness of attention. These results were replicated 12 months later with a sub-sample of 20 of these children. A second study tested the hypothesis that a reduction in IT with maturation is predominantly attributable to knowledge about task demands. This prediction was not supported since substantial practice to asymptotic performance failed to eradicate differences in mean IT between 11 five-year-olds and 13 eleven-year-olds.

1. INTRODUCTION

Although the notion of a significant association between "mental speed" and "mental ability" has a long history in psychology, research findings in this area have not, until recently, generally suggested that speed could account for more than about 10 percent of variance in intelligence. (Jensen 1982). Over the past decade, however, there have been a number of reports of more appreciable correlations between various measures of timed performance and a variety of IQ tests (Eysenck, 1987).

One such measure is inspection time (IT), assumed to be the minimum time required by an individual to make a single sample from sensory input, and interpreted therefore as an index of basic limitations on the efficiency of information processing (Vickers, Nettelbeck and Willson, 1972). At least as far as normal young adults are concerned, most recent evidence suggests that IT correlates around -.50 with IQ, an outcome not dependent on the inclusion of intellectually disabled participants (Nettelbeck, 1987).

Procedures for estimating IT have commonly required a very simple discriminative judgement, with the availability of critical information being restricted to a brief exposure. The duration of the exposure is varied, to determine the time necessary for a subject to achieve some predetermined level of accuracy. Despite wide variation across studies in procedural details, most investigators have reported moderate to high reliability in IT, even across several successive measures and over periods of time up to two years (Nettelbeck, 1987). The absolute stability of IT has been found to be less impressive, however, with evidence of substantial practice effects, thought to be due at least in part to the ability of subjects to spontaneously adopt strategies which negate the effectiveness of the backward masking procedure (Mackenzie and Cumming, 1986: Nettelbeck, 1982). Although there is as yet no evidence that the use of these strategies is a direct consequence of higher IQ, any IT-IQ correlation is generally severely reduced among those subjects identified as strategy users. This is a troublesome shortcoming in a method conceived initially as having advantages over measures of reaction times, which are widely acknowledged to reflect aspects of complex cognitive performance over which a subject retains control (Nettelbeck, 1985; Rabbitt, 1985). However, until a satisfactory, alternative procedure is developed, we have continued to use backward masking, while attempting to identify strategy users, following Mackenzie and Bingham (1985).

As demonstrated by dichoptic presentation procedures, IT limitations are located centrally (Nettelbeck, 1987), and my working hypothesis is that the mental speed indexed by IT reflects what Horn (1968) terms "anlage functioning" - i.e. the operation of elementary central neural capacities which provide a basis for the development of later intelligence.[1] No assumption is made about what, or how many basic processes are tapped by IT, nor about whether individual differences in mental speed are better regarded as a primary characteristic of encoding and storage activities (Brand & Deary, 1982; Jensen, 1982) or as a secondary consequence of the reliability of neural transmission (Eysenck, 1984). However, if both IT and IQ measures reflect speed of information processing, then these variables should be found to be correlated within childhood age cohorts.

2. CORRELATIONS BETWEEN IT AND IQ IN CHILDHOOD

Only a small number of IT-IQ studies have involved young children and results have been contradictory, ranging from a strong correlation between IT and IQ of -.78 (Hosier, 1979; 12 four-year-olds) to low, near zero results (Hulme and Turnbull, 1983; 65 six to seven-year-olds). (A review of these studies is given by Nettelbeck and Young, in press). In our most recent investigation, however, we have obtained uncorrected correlations of -.57 between IT and WISC-R raw scores. Using a sample of 47 children, aged between 6 years, 0 months and 6 years, 11 months, whose IQ scores ranged from 86 to 136, we have obtained an uncorrected correlation of -.50 between IT and standardized Full Scale IQ (Nettelbeck and Young, in press). Thus, our result runs counter to Hulme and Turnbull's (1983) conclusion that a strong correlation between IT and IQ would be found only when intellectually disabled children were included in the sample.

3. INTERPRETING THE IT-IQ CORRELATION

Principal components analysis of IT and WISC-R subtest scores identified three components, the first being a general ability component which included IT, with the second and third being interpretable as spatial and reasoning components, respectively. This result was therefore consistent with a previous conclusion based on adult subjects, namely, that IT affects some function underlying a broad range of cognitive activities (Nettelbeck, Edwards and Vreugdenhil, 1986). Further, various follow-up analyses converged to suggest that an ability to control attention was a critical consideration, the major finding being that among a sub-group of children (n=12), assumed to have poorer attention on the basis of errors made to unmasked trials, average IT was significantly longer and correlations with IQ measures were also stronger, than among the larger subgroup of children who did not make any errors of this kind.

We have now remeasured IT and IQ for 20 of the 47 children, 12 months following the first measures. Results from the longitudinal study were substantially the same as on the first occasion, with the correlation between IT and Full Scale IQ being -.63 (compared with -.52 for initial measures from this sample), and the principal components solution linking IT to a general function. Once again, we have found evidence consistent with the conclusion that attention is involved, the correlation between IT and the number of errors made on unmasked trials being .51.

Retest reliabilities for WISC-R and IT were .66 and .68 respectively. The cross-lagged panel correlations between initial ITs and the second WISC-R scores and between initial WISC-R scores and second ITs were -.32 and -.63, respectively. While the difference between these two coefficients was not statistically significant because of the small sample involved, the direction of this difference was not consistent with a proposition that processes indexed by IT are responsible for the development of IQ.

4. CHANGES IN IT IN CHILDHOOD

Backward masking has been widely applied to the investigation of speed of visual information processing in children (Hoving, Spencer, Robb and Schulte, 1978). Generally, masking effects have been found to become progressively less pronounced throughout childhood, at least up to about 10-12 years of age. However, while this outcome is consistent with the hypothesis that speed of processing improves with maturation, there has been extensive debate about the extent to which this is the consequence of fundamental structural changes, as opposed to the development of higher order cognitive functions.

Nettelbeck and Wilson (1985) have found that IT decreased with normal development between the ages of 6 and about 11 - 13 years. Seven cohorts (each with n=10) were tested in a cross-sectional design, with longitudinal follow-up over two years, which established significant maturation effects on IT, over and above the influence of practice. Individual differences in IT were generally stable across time, in that a measure at one age reliably predicted later measures from the same individuals when they were one and two years older. Nettelbeck and Wilson therefore concluded that, while improved performance may reflect increasing strategic efficiency associated with general learning processes, this development may itself be structurally dependent, and improvement could not plausibly be attributed simply to task-specific knowledge.

However, while obtaining generally significant, though rather low correlations between IT and IQ, Anderson (1988) has found little evidence for a decreasing trend in IT over a similar age range, in a study employing a version in which the IT paradigm is embedded in a video game. He has concluded that processing efficiency does not change with maturation, and that any such change in IT is the consequence of task demands which are influenced by the general level of knowledge which the child has acquired during maturation.

We have attempted to test this suggestion by measuring IT among children and adults under conditions permitting practice to asymptotic performance.[2] The rationale was that such extended practice would permit children to develop maximum strategic efficiency, so that a difference in asymptotic levels should reflect a difference in structural sophistication. Eleven five-year-olds, 13 eleven-year-olds and 20 university undergraduates took part. Following extensive preliminary practice, 26, 20 and 15 successive measures of IT were made from the 5-year-olds, 11-year-olds and undergraduates, respectively. Children were also tested on Raven's Coloured Progressive Matrices (CPM) but the abilities of undergraduates were not tested in any way. Results can be summarized as follows:

    1. The average performance of 11-year-olds and undergraduates was virtually identical, both with regards to the initial measure of IT and to subsequent improvement.

    2. An initially large difference between 5-year-olds and 11-year-olds was substantially reduced by practice but asymptotic performance remained statistically significantly different.

    3. This difference was not attributable to IQ differences between the two groups of children since CPM scores corrected for age suggested comparable age-related abilities in 5 and 11-year-olds. (Mean IQ = 114 and 109 respectively, with an equal range of raw scores).

    4. For both groups of children, correlations between IT and CPM scores were moderately high initially, averaging -.59 and -.54 across the first four measures of IT for 5 and 11-year-olds respectively. However, correlations between CPM and asymptotic IT were reduced to near zero, being -.23 and -.02 for 5 and 11-year-olds.

    Arguably, this outcome reflected no more than a correlation between IQ and rate of learning in a simple discrimination task. There was, however, evidence for a different kind of explanation, since repeated questions to the children about how they made their decisions revealed that an increasing number of children in both groups eventually found ways of penetrating the backward mask and rendering it ineffective. Consistent with this finding, variability in IT within both groups of children reduced markedly to about the same extent, with SDs falling from 63 to 14 ms among 5-year-olds and from 29 to 7 ms among 11-year-olds.

5. CONCLUSIONS

    There are grounds for dissatisfaction with the procedures followed, particularly in view of evidence that, when repeated measures are involved, the estimates of IT obtained from many subjects reflect some floor level of unmasked performance. Extensive endeavours to overcome this shortcoming have failed to establish a guaranteed, viable backward masking procedure and we have therefore concluded that some alternative method which avoids masking altogether is required to further investigate IT-IQ differences.

Nevertheless, taken together, these results are consistent with the proposition that the speed of processes reflected in initial IT measures increases during childhood development until around the age of 11, after which it remains relatively stable into early adulthood. This interpretation does not exclude the influence of strategic efficiency on performance but does suggest that access to increasingly efficient strategies is age-dependent. Increasing speed is therefore interpretable as a function of mental age and, consistent with this suggestion, faster IT is associated with higher IQ within age cohorts. The function shared by IT and IQ appears to involve an ability to concentrate attention, an outcome which contradicts Brand and Deary's (1982) suggestion that IT is not dependent on attentional considerations.

FOOTNOTES

1. The nature of intelligence is not addressed here, but the views expressed are consistent with the theory of orthogonal variables proposed by Detterman (1982).

2. The children were tested by P. Vita, as part of a Psychology Honours research project, University of Adelaide, 1988. Adult data were collected by R. Young.

ACKNOWLEDGEMENTS

Preparation of this chapter was supported by ARC grant A78715070.

Address correspondence to Ted Nettelbeck, Department of Psychology, University of Adelaide, G.P.O. Box 498, Adelaide, South Australia, 5001

REFERENCES

Anderson, M. (1988). Inspection time, information processing and the development of intelligence. British Journal of Developmental Psychology, 6, 43-57.

Brand, C.R. and Deary, I.J. (1982). Intelligence and 'inspection time'. In H.J. Eysenck (Ed)., A model for intelligence, (pp. 133-148). Springer-Verlag, New York.

Detterman, D.K. (1982). Does "g" exist? Intelligence, 6, 99-108.

Eysenck, H.J. (1984). Intelligence versus behaviour. The behavioural and brain sciences, 7, 290-291.

Eysenck, H.J. (1987). Speed of information processing, reaction time, and the theory of intelligence. In P.A. Vernon (Ed.) Speed of information-processing, and intelligence, (pp.21-67). Ablex, Norwood, N.J.

Horn, J.I. (1968). Organization of abilities and the development of intelligence. Psychological Review, 75, 242-259.

Hosie, B.M. (1979). Mental speed and intelligence: Their relationship and development in 4-year-old children. Unpublished thesis for the Honours Degree in Psychology, University of Edinburgh.

Hoving, K.L., Spencer, T., Robb, K.Y., & Schulte, D. (1978). Developmental changes in visual information processing. In P.A. Ornstein (Ed.), Memory development in children (pp.21-67). New York: Erlbaum.

Hulme, C. and Turnbull, J. (1983) Intelligence and inspection time in normal and mentally retarded subjects. British Journal of Psychology 74, 365-370.

Jensen, A.R. (1982). Reaction time and psychometric g. In H.J. Eysenck (Ed.), A model for intelligence (pp. 93-132). Berlin and New York: Springer-Verlag.

Mackenzie, B. and Bingham, E. (1985). IQ, inspection time, and response strategies in a university population. Australian Journal of Psychology, 37, 257-268.

Mackenzie, B. and Cumming, S. (1986). How fragile is the relationship between inspection time and intelligence: The effects of apparent motion cues and previous experience. Journal of Personality and Individual Differences, 7, 721-729

Nettelbeck, T., Edwards, C., & Vreugdenhil, A. (1986). Inspection time and IQ: Evidence for a mental speed-ability association. Personality and individual differences, 7, 633-641.

Nettelbeck, T. (1982). Inspection time: An index for intelligence? Quarterly Journal of Experimental Psychology, 34A, 299-312.

Nettelbeck, T. (1985). What reaction times time. The behavioural and brain sciences, 8, 235.

Nettelbeck, T. (1987). Inspection time and intelligence. In P.A. Vernon (Ed.), Speed of information-processing and intelligence, (pp. 295-346). Ablex, Norwood, N.J.

Nettelbeck, T. and Wilson, C. (1985). A cross-sequential analysis of developmental differences in speed of visual information processing. Journal of Experimental Child Psychology, 40, 1-22.

Nettelbeck, T., & Young, R. (in press). Inspection time and intelligence in 6-year-old children. Personality and individual differences.

Rabbitt, P.M.A. (1985). Oh g Dr. Jensen! or, g-ing up cognitive psychology? The behavioural and brain sciences, 8, 238-239.

Vickers, D., Nettelbeck, T. and Willson, R.J. (1972). Perceptual indices of performance: the measurement of 'inspection time' and 'noise' in the visual system. Perception, 1, 263-295.

Human Information Processing: Measures,
Mechanisms, and Models, D. Vickers and P. L. Smith (eds.)
© Elsevier Science Publishers B.V. (North-Holland), 1989

STRESS, ANXIETY AND INTELLIGENT PERFORMANCE

Michael W. Eysenck

University of London

Different theoretical perspectives on the effects of anxiety and stress on intelligent performance are evaluated, and a new theoretical account is proposed. According to this account, anxiety and stress generally impair intelligent performance via their effects on attentional functioning. These effects include increased susceptibility to distraction, greater attentional selectivity, and reduced available working memory capacity (especially of the central executive). Adverse effects of anxiety and stress on performance are counteracted by the more active executive control system in high anxious individuals. As a consequence, anxiety more frequently has an adverse effect on processing efficiency than on performance effectiveness. Recent experimental evidence supporting these theoretical assumptions is reported.

1. INTRODUCTION

The literature concerning stress, anxiety, and intelligent performance has been reviewed by Eysenck (1982, 1984). One of the more robust findings is that the effects of stress and anxiety on performance depend importantly on the cognitive demands of the task. In general terms, tasks which are complex and place substantial demands on intelligence are more adversely affected by stress and by anxiety than are tasks which are simple and relatively undemanding. For example, Mayer (1977) compared groups high and low in trait anxiety on various straightforward rote problems (e.g. visual search, simple mathematical operations) and on complex intellectually demanding tasks correlating highly with I.Q. (e.g., anagrams, water-jar problems). The two groups did not differ in their performance of the rote problems. However, the low anxious group solved approximately 80% of the complex problems, whereas the high anxious group solved only just over 40%.

At a superficial level, these findings are consistent with the Yerkes-Dodson Law (Yerkes & Dodson, 1908), according to which the optimal level of arousal varies inversely with task difficulty. However, there are serious limitations with the Yerkes-Dodson Law. Firstly, the notion of 'task difficulty' is an amorphous one. Secondly, and more importantly, the Yerkes-Dodson Law describes the relationship between arousal or anxiety and performance, but fails to provide an explanation for this relationship. Therefore, we must look elsewhere for a theoretical account.

2. HUMPHREYS AND REVELLE (1984)

One of the most developed theoretical frameworks in this area was proposed by Humphreys and Revelle (1984). They argued that the level of state anxiety is determined jointly by an individual's level of trait anxiety and by situational stress. High state anxiety leads to avoidance motivation, which reduces on-task effort. Reduced on-task effort in turn leads to reduced sustained information transfer, which they define as involving the processing of a stimulus, the association of an arbitrary response to that stimulus, and the execution of that response. State anxiety also leads to an increase in arousal (defined as "the state of the organism that in everyday terms is called alertness, vigor, peppiness, and activation" p.157). This increased arousal leads to increased sustained information transfer and to impaired short-term memory.

According to Humphreys and Revelle (1984), it is possible to predict the effects of anxiety and stress on task performance by considering the involvement of sustained information transfer and/or short-term memory in the task. By definition, complex or intellectually demanding tasks involve both sustained information transfer and short-term memory. High state anxiety may increase or decrease sustained information transfer, depending on the extent to which anxiety affects on-task effort and arousal. However, high state anxiety always impairs short-term memory, and this is the main reason why high anxiety produces detrimental effects on complex tasks.

The theory proposed by Humphreys and Revelle (1984) is an interesting one, and they are surely correct in assuming that adverse effects of anxiety and stress on short-term memory capacity play an important role in impairing complex cognitive performance. However, there are two major deficiencies in their theoretical perspective. Firstly, their theory does not include a control system which can be used to compensate for the adverse effects of anxiety on aspects of information processing. As we will see later, it is probably essential to assume that anxiety affects the functioning of a control system in order to understand the effects of anxiety on intelligent performance. Secondly, some of the theoretical constructs which they make use of are imprecise. Two examples are 'arousal' and 'short-term memory, both of which are defined in uni-dimensional terms which have been generally abandoned by other theorists.

3. PROPOSED THEORETICAL FRAMEWORK

The available evidence indicates that stress and anxiety have several different effects on the information-processing system during the performance of cognitively demanding tasks. One of the most important of these effects is that high levels of state anxiety reduce the amount of working memory capacity available for task performance, perhaps because of worry, self-concern, and other task-irrelevant activities. The essence of a working memory system is that it permits concurrent active processing and transient storage of information, functions which are crucial in the performance of most cognitively demanding tasks. In the recent formulation of Baddeley (1986), the working memory system consists of a central executive resembling attention, as well as an articulatory loop involved in verbal rehearsal and a visuo-spatial sketch pad.

The notion that high anxiety reduces the available capacity of working memory may be of use in accounting for the typical interaction between anxiety and task difficulty, if the reasonable assumption is made that the demands on working memory capacity generally increase in line with task difficulty or complexity. However, the working memory hypothesis has been tested more directly in studies by Darke (1987) and by Eysenck (1985), both of which are discussed below.

In addition to the effects of anxiety and stress on available working memory capacity, there are also effects on other aspects of attentional functioning. For example, Easterbrook (1959) argued that states of high emotionality, arousal, and anxiety all produce comparable effects on cue utilization. The range of cues used (i.e. breadth of attention) reduces as anxiety or arousal increases, which "will reduce the proportion of irrelevant cues employed, and so improve performance. When all irrelevant cues have been excluded, however, ...further reduction in the number of cues employed can only affect relevant cues, and proficiency will fall" (p.193). The evidence generally supports the notion that high anxiety leads to greater attentional selectivity (Eysenck, 1982), but the proper interpretation of this result is in doubt. Easterbrook (1959) claimed that a relatively passive and automatic process was involved, but this is unlikely. In view of the reduced available working memory capacity in high anxiety, it is probable that one consequence is an active restriction of the limited available attentional and other stimuli.

One of the implications of Easterbrook's (1959) theoretical position is that high anxiety should be associated with reduced distractibility. In contrast, Wachtel (1967) argued that anxiety leads to greater attentional lability, which implies that anxiety actually increases susceptibility to distraction. The evidence tends to indicate that those high in trait anxiety are more distractible than those low in trait anxiety (e.g., Dornic, 1977; Dornic & Fernaeus, 1981), but the evidence is by no means consistent (see Eysenck, 1982, for a review). Additional unpublished evidence is discussed below.

It has been assumed so far that high levels of anxiety and stress might impair intelligent performance for a variety of reasons. High anxiety reduces the available capacity of working memory, it increases attentional selectivity, and it increases susceptibility to distraction. This approach can be regarded as illustrating a one-stage model, in which high anxiety impairs or enhances components of information processing, and this impairment or enhancement then affects performance. However, it is becoming increasingly clear that a more complex theoretical approach is required. According to a two-stage model (Eysenck, 1979, 1982), the effects of anxiety on aspects of information processing and performance are monitored and altered by an executive control system, which may compensate for adverse effects of anxiety on information processing.

According to the two-stage model presented by Eysenck (1982), it is important to distinguish between performance effectiveness and processing efficiency. Performance effectiveness is imply a measure of the quality of performance. In contrast, processing efficiency refers to the relationship between the effectiveness of performance and the effort or processing resources invested in it. It is assumed that those high in trait anxiety generally have a more active control system than those low in trait anxiety. As a consequence, anxiety is more likely to reduce processing efficiency than to impair performance effectiveness. One of the clearest predictions from this theoretical position is that non-significant effects of anxiety on performance effectiveness will often camouflage adverse effects of anxiety on processing efficiency.

4. EXPERIMENTAL EVIDENCE

Darke (1987) has tested the hypothesis that high anxiety reduces available working memory capacity. He used a task specifically designed by Daneman and Carpenter (1980) to measure working memory capacity. In this task, several sentences are presented for comprehension, followed by the instruction to recall the last word in each sentence. Working memory capacity was indexed by the reading span, which is the greatest number of sentences which can be read with perfect recall of their last words. There was a substantial effect of trait anxiety, with those low in trait anxiety having a reading span approximately 80% greater than that of those high in trait anxiety. In contrast, there was only a 20% effect of trait anxiety on digit span.

This difference between the effects of trait anxiety on reading span and on digit span is of theoretical interest. Despite some superficial similarities between the two measures, they differ greatly in terms of the involvement of the working memory system. Reading span is combined with a comprehension task, and thus places great demands on both the central executive and the articulatory loop. Digit span mainly involves the articulatory loop, plus a partial involvement of the central executive. An implication of these findings is that anxiety has its greatest adverse effect on the central executive component of working memory. .

The theoretical views discussed above have also been tested using the letter-transformation task originally proposed by Hamilton, Hockey, and Rejman (1977). In essence, this task requires the task to transform between one and four letters by moving through the alphabet a specified distance. Thus, for example, the answer to G + 3 is J, and the answer to JTE + 4 is NXI. This letter-transformation task is of interest for a number of reasons. Firstly, it provides a set of tasks ranging from very simple to extremely complex. Secondly, it has been established that performance on the letter-transformation task correlates highly (approximately +.65) with I.Q. (Lambert, unpublished). Thirdly, as the number of letters in the task increases, the demands on the working memory system increase proportionately.

A fourth, and especially important, characteristic of the letter-transformation task is that it is possible to assess the microstructure of performance. Most of the studies investigating the effects of anxiety and stress on complex task performance have used tasks which permit only global measures of overall performance. In contrast, detailed timings of the various component processes involved in the letter-transformation task are possible if a computer-based version of the task is used. In essence, it is claimed that three different stages of processing occur with each letter: (1) access to long-term memory and to the appropriate part of the alphabet; (2) performance of the transformation itself; and (3) rehearsal and storage of the accumulating answer. These stages can be timed if the subjects are required to press a button to present the letter, the transformation is performed aloud, and a button is pressed to present the next letter. The time between the onset of the letter and the onset of the transformation is the access time, the duration of speech is the transformation time, and the interval between the cessation of speech and the onset of the next letter is the rehearsal and storage time. Therefore, for a four-letter problem, it is possible to sub-divide the total solution time into 12 component times (three stages x four letters).

The letter transformation task has been used in several experiments, two of which were reported by Eysenck (1985), but most of which remain unpublished. In all of the experiments, subjects received a considerable amount of practice, and any subjects failing to meet fairly stringent criteria for accurate performance on the task were eliminated. As a consequence, error rates on the main trials were typically under 5%, and the main measures taken were times to perform the component stages. A further characteristic of all of the experiments is that mild stress in the form of ego-involving instructions was induced.

In the first experiment (Eysenck, 1985), subjects were run under monetary incentive or neutral conditions on one, two, three, and four letter conditions with instructions to work two or four letters through the alphabet (e.g. the answer to C + 4 is G). Only the solution time for each problem was recorded. There was a highly significant interaction between trait anxiety and task complexity in the form of the number of letters in the problem. This is consistent with the numerous interactions between anxiety and task complexity in the literature, and indicates that adverse effects of anxiety on task performance occur when the demands on working memory are great. In addition, there was a significant interaction between trait anxiety and incentive. Incentive improved the performance of the low anxious group but had no effect on the performance of the high anxious group. This is consistent with the notion that those high in trait anxiety tend to have a more active control system than those low in trait anxiety. This control system compensates for the adverse effects of anxiety on performance, and means that those high in trait anxiety are closer than those low in trait anxiety to maximum resource allocation or effort under control conditions.

Similar results were reported by Calvo (1985). He administered a test of non-verbal inductive reasoning containing items of various difficulty levels. Incentive was offered for good performance. Trait anxiety interacted significantly with incentive conditions: the performance of those low in trait anxiety was improved by incentive, whereas that of high anxious subjects was impaired.

The major limitation of the first experiment was that it did not permit unequivocal identification of the specific component or components of three- and four-letter problems adversely affected by anxiety. This limitation was overcome in the second experiment, in which only four-letter problems were used under incentive conditions, and the subjects always had to work four letters through the alphabet. As before, the high anxious group performed significantly slower than the low anxious group on the four-letter problems. Detailed analysis of times on the 12 components involved indicated that high anxiety slowed performance on only three: the rehearsal and storage times associated with the second, third, and fourth letters. Since the access component involves a relatively over-learned and automatic process and the transformation component involves largely the articulatory loop, the rehearsal and storage component is the one placing greatest demands on the central executive of the working memory system. It may thus tentatively be concluded that the adverse effects of trait anxiety on four-letter problems occur primarily within the central executive rather than within the articulatory loop.

The non-significant findings from the second experiment are also of theoretical interest. For example, the lack of effect of trait anxiety on transformation times for all four letters indicates that anxiety has little or no effect on the articulatory loop even when there is concurrent rehearsal and storage of part of the accumulating answer.

The third experiment in the series (unpublished) focussed specifically on one- and two- letter problems. Experiment one had indicated that there were no effects of trait anxiety on solution times to such problems, but the theoretical framework described above suggests that non-significant effects of anxiety on performance often camouflage underlying differences. Accordingly, performance on such problems was considered either on its own or with a concurrent reaction-time task. This reaction-time task consisted of irregularly spaced tones (with a mean interval of 5 s) presented via headphones and requiring a rapid motor response. Subjects were instructed to ensure that performance on the letter-transformation task was maintained at as high a level as possible, with only spare processing resources being applied to the subsidiary reaction-time task.

The findings for the letter-transformation task replicated those from the first experiment, in that there was no effect of trait anxiety on the performance of either one- or two-letter problems. In addition, performance on these problems was unaffected by the presence or absence of the concurrent reaction-time task. This indicates that the subjects had followed the instructions. The crucial finding from the latency data on the reaction-time task was that there was a significant interaction between trait anxiety and the number of letters in the problem, $F(1,18) = 5.58$, $p < .05$. The high and low anxious groups did not differ in reaction time when one-letter problems were being presented, but the high anxious group was significantly slower than the low anxious group when two-letter problems were being presented. This suggests that the comparable performance of the two anxiety groups on the two-letter problems was obtained at greater 'cost' to the high anxious group in terms of effort expenditure. As a consequence, the high anxious subjects had fewer spare processing resources available for handling the reaction-time task. In other words, while the high and low anxious groups exhibited equal performance effectiveness on two-letter problems, the high anxious group was actually performing with lower processing efficiency.

The distinction between processing effectiveness and processing efficiency has been used only rarely in the experimental literature. Despite this, there are various studies in which trait anxiety and/or stress had no effect on task performance, but ancillary measures suggested that processing efficiency was lower in the high anxious group than in the low anxious one (see Eysenck, 1982, for a review).

The fourth experiment on the letter-transformation task was conducted with the assistance of Jan Graydon, and is unpublished. Four-letter problems requiring subjects to work either two or four letters through the alphabet were presented. There were three distraction conditions: letters; meaningless blips; and control (no distraction). Both forms of distraction were presented at 80 dB(A) with a mean of 10 s between stimuli and a range of 8 to 12 s. The high anxious group consisted of those subjects who were high in neuroticism and low in extraversion, whereas the low anxious group consisted of those subjects who were low in neuroticism and high in extraversion.

The data used were the mean correct solution times on the letter-transformation task. Anxiety interacted significantly with distraction conditions, $F (2,20) = 3.72$ p<.05. An analysis of the simple main effects revealed that the high anxious group was affected by the distraction conditions, $F (2,20) = 9.43$, p<.01, whereas the low anxious group was not, $F (2,20) = 1.48$. More specifically, the two groups did not differ in the effects of the blip distracting stimuli, but the high anxious group performed 10.73% slower in the presence of letter distracting stimuli than in the no distraction control condition, whereas the low anxious group were 0.8% faster with letter distracting stimuli than in the control condition.

In sum, the empirical evidence indicates that a two-stage model incorporating the distinction between performance effectiveness and processing efficiency is preferable to previous one-stage models. In addition, there is support for the notion that a two-stage model incorporating the distinction between performance effectiveness and processing efficiency is preferable to previous one-stage models. In addition, there is support for the notion that anxiety affects the functioning of the attentional system in various ways. These effects on attention are probably mainly responsible for adverse effects of anxiety and stress on intelligent performance.

5. CONCLUSIONS

Several factors combine to determine the effects of anxiety and stress on intelligent performance. The evidence is strongest that anxiety and stress affect the functioning of the attentional system by reducing the available capacity of working memory, by increasing attentional selectivity, and by increasing susceptibility to distraction. While all of these aspects of attentional functioning are conceptually distinct, they may in practice be dynamically inter-related. For example, reduced working memory capacity might mean that there were insufficient processing resources available to inhibit the distracting effects of extraneous, non-task stimuli, and that greater attentional selectivity was needed in order to maintain performance. Alternatively, anxiety and stress may produce increased distractibility, with this in turn reducing available working memory capacity.

The evidence also indicates that those high in anxiety have a more active executive control system which compensates for adverse effects of anxiety on information processing. As a consequence, high anxious individuals often exhibit lower processing efficiency than low anxious individuals despite having comparable performance effectiveness.

CORRESPONDENCE

Correspondence concerning this paper should be addressed to Prof. Michael W. Eysenck, Department of Psychology, Royal Holloway and Bedford New College, University of London, Egham Hill, Egham, Surrey, TW20 0EX England.

REFERENCES

Baddeley, A.D. (1986). Working memory. Oxford: Oxford University Press

Calvo, M.G. (1985). Effort, aversive representations and performance in text anxiety. Personality and Individual Differences, 6, 563-571.

Daneman, M. & Carpenter, P.A. (1980). Individual differences in working memory and reading. Journal of Verbal Learning and Verbal Behavior, 19, 450-466.

Darke, S.G. (1987). The relationship between test anxiety and cognitive task performance. Unpublished Ph.D. thesis, University of Sydney, Australia.

Dornic, S. (1977). Mental load, effort, and individual differences. Reports of the Department of Psychology, University of Stockholm, No. 509.

Dornic, S. & Fernaeus, S.-E. (1981). Individual differences in high-load tasks: The effect of verbal distraction. Reports from the Department of Psychology, University of Stockholm. No. 568.

Easterbrook, J.A. (1959). The effect of emotion on cue utilisation and the organization of behavior. Psychological Review, 66, 183-201.

Eysenck, M.W. (1979). Anxiety, learning, and memory: A reconceptualization. Journal of Research in Personality, 13, 363-385.

Eysenck, M.W. (1982). Attention and arousal: Cognition and performance. Berlin: Springer.

Eysenck, M.W. (1984). A handbook of cognitive psychology. London: Erlbaum.

Hamilton, P., Hockey, G.R.J., & Rejman, M. (1977). The place of the concept of activation in human information processing theory: An integrative approach. In S. Dornic (Ed.), Attention and performance, Vol. V1. Hillsdale, N.J: Erlbaum.

Humphreys, M.S. & Revelle, W. (1984). Personality, motivation, and performance: A theory of the relationship between individual differences and information processing. Psychological Review, 91, 153-184.

Mayer, R.E. (1977). Problem-solving performance with task overload: Effects of self-pacing and trait anxiety. Bulletin of the Psychonomic Society, 9, 283-286.

Wachtel, P.L. (1967). Conceptions of broad and narrow attention. Psychological Bulletin, 68, 417-429.

Yerkes, R.M. & Dodson, J.D. (1908). The relation of strength of stimulus of rapidity of habit-formation. Journal of Comparative Neurology and Psychology, 18, 459-482.

Human Information Processing: Measures,
Mechanisms, and Models. D. Vickers and P. L. Smith (eds.)
© Elsevier Science Publishers B. V. (North-Holland), 1989

A SYSTEM OF COGNITIVE ASSESSMENT AND ITS ADVANTAGE OVER I.Q.

J. P. Das

University of Alberta

A theory of cognitive processing and a system for assessment of those functions are described in the first part of the paper. The theory alludes to brain functions organized by Luria. Empirical and statistical research for operationalizing the theory are also presented. In the second part, some examples of the application of the theory and assessment are provided. The examples show the distinct advantage of a process-based approach over a 'g' or general assessment of intelligence for understanding the cognitive functions of mentally retarded, learning disabled and brain-damaged individuals.

1. INTRODUCTION

Over the past 20 years, there has been a significant shift away from the definition of abilities toward an interest in understanding cognitive processes (Glaser, 1972; Messick, 1973). In response to this shift from ability to process, some psychologists have turned to information processing approaches to intelligence (e.g. Hunt, 1980; Simon, 1981) because the broad framework provided by information processing can accommodate disparate theories of intelligence such as computer-based and neuropsychological models. Understanding how information is processed may require some attempt to comprehend how it occurs in the brain. The aim of understanding the proverbial 'black box' is shared by intelligence theorists such as Eysenck (1981) and Jensen (1981), and is especially evidenced in their attempts to discover a biological foundation for intelligence.

The information-integration model developed by Das (1972, 1973, 1984a, 1984b) and recently expanded by Ashman, Kirby and Naglieri (see Das & Varnhagen, 1986; Naglieri & Das, 1988) is based upon the desire to know how information is processed in the brain. The model follows the neuropsychological research of Luria (1966a, 1966b, 1973). It expands on Luria's conceptualization by operationalizing his notions of the organization of cognitive functions. It also incorporates concepts from other research in cognitive psychology (e.g. Atkinson & Shiffrin, 1968; Broadbent, 1981; Hunt, 1980).

Such a model of intelligence has a base in both cognitive psychology as well as in neuropsychology. By choosing this combined foundation, we hope that we have moved away from two recent trends which currently characterize some theories of intelligence. These are (a) a trend towards formalizing intelligence without a reference to the realities of brain-function and (b) an unintended disregard for metaphysical implications of such 'explanatory' concepts as "executive" processes and the "componential analysis" of mental functions. The notion of an 'executive' is reminiscent of the homunculus sitting in the mind or whispering in the ear, and should be rejected. The foundations of cognitive strategy training aimed at strengthening the powers of an executive need rebuilding if the implication of a homunculus is to be avoided. Likewise, although mental operations need to be broken down into components, and these in turn into numerous subcomponents, we should not lose sight of the unity of mental functioning. If there is no underlying "structure" unifying the various components which have been logically derived by analyzing the performance of an individual, then a study of these components will not advance our understanding of intelligence.

Perhaps because of the past history of intelligence research, which is associated with the development of "IQ" tests, it is desirable to refocus our efforts on an understanding of cognitive processes rather than intelligence. This will be attempted in the first part of the paper which will include a brief description of the theory and the measurement of cognitive functions following from the theory. In the second and final section, I shall show the advantages of cognitive process measures in understanding mental retardation, learning disabilities, hyperactivity, and the cognitive deficits following mild head injury.

2. OUTLINE OF THE THEORY

The basic statement of the theory is that cognition can be understood as the result of the interdependent functioning of three neurological systems: those responsible for arousal (and attention); coding (or processing); and planning. In reviews of the theory in 1975 and 1979 (Das, Kirby & Jarman, 1975, 1979), we concentrated almost exclusively upon the second system, arguing that this system engages basically in two forms of information processing. Following Luria, we called these simultaneous and successive processes. Because of the concentration upon two aspects of information integration, the theory became known as simultaneous and successive processing theory. In recent years we have tried to complete the theory by describing the arousal and planning system as well (Naglieri & Das, 1988).

3. THE AROUSAL SYSTEM

The arousal system is located in the brain stem and lower cortex, and includes the reticular activating system. This system is responsible for maintaining an appropriate degree of alertness in the cortex, and for "energizing" the cortex when needed (for instance in an orienting response). Arousal is involved in the maintenance of attention as well as in selective attention. In fact, sometimes it is difficult to separate arousal from attention in tasks that measure either sustained attention (vigilance) or selective attention (tasks which have built-in distractors).

Attention and arousal are therefore linked as determinants of task performance. This is a basic function which influences the individual's competence in coding of information and in planning, and which in turn, is influenced by coding and planning.

4. SIMULTANEOUS-SUCCESSIVE CODING

Coding includes reception, interpreting, transforming (recoding), and storage of information. As such, the functions are much broader than the label "coding" would suggest. It is located in the posterior cortex (temporal, occipital, and parietal lobes, as well as the rear portions of the frontal lobes).

The functioning of this information processing system can be described in many ways; in fact, much of cognitive psychology is devoted to this system. The distinction which we have emphasized concerns the "types" of processing in which the system engages, which we argue to be two in number, either simultaneous or successive. It is important to realize first of all that these are intended as "categories" of processes and not as an exhaustive list of actual processes, and secondly that there are many other distinctions relevant to the functioning of the coding system. For example, other dimensions relevant to the processing system would include the type of code content (e.g. verbal vs. spatial), the complexity of the codes involved, and the type of memory addressed (working vs. long-term memory).

The basic distinction between simultaneous and successive types of processing is that in simultaneous processing the units of information are related in a quasi-spatial manner, whereas in successive they are held in temporal order. In either case the units involved can, in principle, be of any level of complexity and can involve any type of content. So, for example, successive processing can occur with respect to lower level units, such as sounds, or higher level units, such as concepts, and similarly can involve verbal content (sounds or words) or spatial content (non-verbalizable line patterns). Material for processing can be presented visually, auditorily or through other sensory modalities; thus, it is the type of processing required for the material, not the modality, which is important for distinguishing between the two processes.

5. PLANNING

The third of the three interdependent cognitive systems is responsible for "planning", by which I refer to generation of plans or problems as well as to goal setting, strategy selection or construction, and performance monitoring. Considerable evidence suggests that this system is located in the pre-frontal areas of the brain (Luria, 1966a, 1966b, 1973).

Planning can be observed in many different forms and at many different levels of task. For example, many of the commonly-used planning tasks are perceptual tasks in which the subject must scan a visual display for a particular target; in this case, an efficient strategy results in quicker and more accurate performance. At a much higher level, such as in problem solving tasks, in which no simple strategy is immediately evident, a program of action needs to be first formulated and then followed.

6. INTEGRATED FUNCTIONING AND INDIVIDUAL DIFFERENCES

At first glance, the notions of integrated functioning (i.e. the interdependence of the cognitive systems, and the involvement of all systems in virtually all tasks) may seem inconsistent with the use of tests to identify stable individual difference factors representing the various cognitive processes. For example, if both simultaneous and successive processing are involved in all tasks, how can we obtain simultaneous and successive factors in a factor analysis?

The answer, not unique to the information integration model, is that individual differences are due to those aspects of the task which are most difficult. For example, in Digit Span, the difficulty is usually associated with remembering the sequence of numbers (successive), and not with the identification of the individual numbers (simultaneous). If the nature of task were altered so that number identification became preeminently important (for instance by using the numbers from an unfamiliar language), then we would expect the loading of the task to change from successive to simultaneous. Similarly, a change in strategy could produce a change in factor loadings. For example, if the responses to the list of numbers are to be written down, and the missing numbers are identified by blanks to be filled in later during revision, the procedure should produce a loading upon simultaneous processing.

More vexing is the question of whether we should be very concerned about factor loadings at all. The vast majority of the early work on simultaneous and successive processing has been factor analytic in nature (see Das, Kirby, & Jarman, 1975, 1979). The goal of this research has been to demonstrate that the two factors could be observed in various normal populations, thus confirming Luria's observations on clinical cases. Similar efforts were devoted to showing that a planning factor could be differentiated (Ashman & Das, 1980; Das, 1980). Each of these three categories of process is sufficiently complex that some combinations of tests will not yield the expected factor structure. Consider factor analyzing 4 tests of simultaneous processing and 4 of successive processing as determined by the constructs. But 6 of the tests are verbal, and the remaining nonverbal. Because the theory does not deny the validity of distinguishing between verbal and spatial task content, it is really not challenged by a finding that verbal and spatial factors emerge rather than simultaneous and successive. We obtain what we put into factor analysis, which describes the correlations rather than tests a theory. In fact, due to the involvement of other skills and knowledge bases, the actual correlation between two tests of the same process may be quite low.

7. MEASUREMENT OF AROUSAL-ATTENTION

Arousal is a reflexive response to a stimulus input and can be described as an orienting reaction involving a set of physiological and behavioral changes occurring to a novel stimulus (e.g. head turning). Arousal levels also influence "selective attention" as in prolonged execution of some activity. During periods of low alertness caused by sleep deprivation and monotony, our attention is low, and our ability to react with accuracy and swiftness decreases substantially. Performance on vigilance tasks is a conventional method of demonstrating this (Parasuraman & Davies, 1984).

Both arousal and attention constructs have face validity as components of intelligence because a weakness in either one of them should be expected to result in reduced cognitive competence. Geschwind (1982) showed how failure to comprehend, learn or memorize may be due to a lack of attention. He further implied that selective attention has to be maintained over a period of time in order to achieve coherence in thought and action.

To conclude, these observations on attention and arousal imply that a comprehensive assessment of cognitive functions must include measures of attention (see Hunt, 1980). In assessing normal as well as special children (such as the mentally retarded, the learning disabled, and those who are suffering from attentional deficits), both sustained and selective attention should be measured.

8. MEASUREMENT OF CODING

Measurement of coding, in the two forms of simultaneous and successive processing has been examined by Das since the early 1970's and Luria (1966a, 1966b) prior to that time. The major difference between two researchers' approaches to an evaluation of these constructs has been that Luria used the method of syndrome analysis (Luria & Artem'eva, 1970) while Das (1972, 1973) and others (e.g. Das, Kirby & Jarman, 1979; Naglieri & Das, 1988) have used factor analytic techniques. These factor analytic studies have uncovered planning, simultaneous, and successive factors for both normal and exceptional children (the mentally retarded and learning disabled), as well as individuals from different age groups and cultures.

The tests used to measure simultaneous and successive processing have been varied in terms of form and content. For example, while Raven's matrices (Raven, 1958) involve nonverbal analogical reasoning, figure copying requires drawing a design, and Graham & Kendall's (1960) memory for design task requires recall and reproduction of a figure exposed for a brief period of time. Simultaneous processing is not to be confused with non-verbal processing. A verbal test like the Token Test (Naglieri & Das, 1988), as well as a nonverbal test such as the WISC-R Block Design (Wachs & Harris, 1986) have been shown to load on a simultaneous factor. Similarly, successive processing factors have been found using tasks of serial recall of words and digits (Das, Kirby & Jarman, 1979), successive hand movements (Naglieri & Das, 1988), a test of syntax involving sentences presented orally, Wepman's auditory discrimination test (Ryckman, 1981), and sound-blending from the Goldman, Fristoe, Woodcock tests (Wachs & Harris, 1984).

9. MEASUREMENT OF PLANNING

Planning behavior is the most difficult of the three functions to measure for two reasons. First, since all behavior must involve plans, conscious or unconscious, how can planning be measured apart from coding? The answer must be found in designing tasks in such a manner as to highlight planning by using tasks with minimal coding requirements. A second problem is to measure planning in a relatively brief amount of time without making the task appear to be simply a test of speed. This problem has been addressed by the careful selection of planning tasks and the use of tests that require efficient rather than speedy performance.

The tasks used to measure planning have been varied in both form and content. A list of the different tests include a verbal test requiring the writing of a composition about a picture, a problem solving task such as the game Mastermind (Das & Heemsbergen, 1983). Both tasks can be classed as 'conceptual' compared to Trail making (memory) and Visual Search (perceptual) (Das, 1984a, 1984b). Other tasks involving working memory such as matching numbers (Naglieri & Das, 1988), and clustering (Schofield & Ashman, 1986), have also loaded on a planning factor. It is evident that these tasks vary sufficiently to demonstrate that planning involves organization, direction of actions, and in general, efficient solutions of problems, not simply speed, and are examples of how tasks with minimal coding requirements can be used to measure planning processes.

10. ADVANTAGES OVER IQ

No one doubts that a measure of 'general' intellectual functioning is useful; in this sense IQ may be compared to the general depth of a river near a village. However, if I am a new swimmer, I ought to know which parts are just too deep and hence risky for me. Similarly, if I am a fisherman, I need to know the depth of the riverbed in specific parts so that I may expect shrimps to live in one and carps in another. Knowledge about the general depth of the river has limited use. In the same sense, IQs are not useful for understanding the cognitive processes of general or special populations, but specific cognitive measures relating to coding, planning and attention are.

For example, consider a study on retarded individuals with Down's syndrome who are comparable with other retarded individuals of equal IQs. But the Down's syndrome individuals have been suspected to have a 'verbal deficit' in comparison with other retarded individuals. In a pilot study, we had specified the deficit as one located in successive process. In a subsequent study, we wished to examine this further (Varnhagen, Das, & Varnhagen, 1987). Auditory and visual memory span for letters and component memory processes of trainable mentally retarded young adults with Down's syndrome and of other etiologies were compared. Component processes of the span task included long-term memory access for labels for the stimuli, and memory for the order in which the stimuli were presented; in other words, successive processing tasks comprising both item and order memory components. Results indicated that although all subjects had relatively poor auditory memory spans, the Down syndrome group was especially poor at long-term memory access for letter identification (item memory) and at short-term storage and processing of auditory information. Lexical storage and retrieval deficiencies were isolated in the study. As a result, it was possible to account for the 'verbal difficulties' experienced by the individuals with Down's syndrome in terms of slow access to long-term memory for letters, which was a major factor contributing to their deficiency in processing lexical information.

The learning disabled children present a frustrating problem for the psychologists who are concerned with IQ in that they seem to have a generally average to good IQ, but have significant difficulty in reading. It was concluded from applying the tests for the cognitive processes, that when specific reading disability is severe (more than 2 years delay in reading), the children are found to be clearly behind the average readers both in successive tasks and in simultaneous and planning tasks. However, when less severely disabled children are chosen, they are found to be poor in some (e.g., those that require proficient phonological coding), but not all, successive processing tasks (Das, 1988). The above results are examples of the advantage which process-based testing has over tests of general intelligence.

Furthermore, research with process-based tests on reading-disabled children suggests that these children may suffer more from "deficient planning" for applying simultaneous and successive strategies to reading tasks. Robinson (1983) examined the specific relationships between simultaneous and successive processes, syntactic and semantic language skills, and the use of these grammatical relations in word-attack and comprehension tasks. Robinson confirmed the predicted finding of an association between simultaneous processing and semantic skills. However, no confirmation of the relationship between successive processing and syntactic skills was obtained. On the other hand, Robinson observed that the reading-disabled children tended to use simultaneous modes of processing where successive modes would have been more appropriate. Das and Snart (1982) and Naglieri and Das (Das, 1988) also report studies which they did to show a close relationship between planning process and reading disability. Thus, reading disability may result from a combination of deficient information-processing skills and inappropriate selection of processing strategies.

The next example is drawn from the processing deficit of a brain damaged patient. Examining the intellectual dysfunctions of brain-damaged patients typically begins with the taking of General intelligence measures. However, the tests for cognitive processes of attention, coding and planning are especially appropriate for evaluation of cases of neurological impairment which may be either mild or involve specific deficit in one of the three broad functions. I would like to give an example of a case of a lady who was involved in a minor car accident, and hence was not considered even for a routine CAT scan. She was an extremely articulate person when examined a few months following the accident, and was found to have an above average IQ . In the Planning test, however, she performed like a 9 year old. Much more interesting, however, was her utter inability to find alternative answers to a planning problem in which there were two correct solutions. She was asked to find the other when she had just given one of the solutions. She not only took a very long time to solve the problem again, but repeated the earlier solution without any awareness that she had given it a few minutes before. In another planning task, she was asked to write a brief one-page story after seeing TAT card #2 (the scene involves a man ploughing the field and a woman looking on). She utterly failed in this task, kept looking back at the picture and finally wrote 3 sentences. Planning Composition is one of the frontal lobe functions which was obviously impaired in her case.

11. CONCLUDING REMARKS

The models of intelligence within the information processing framework can be divided into those which are based on neuropsychological notions and those which are not; an example of the former is presented in this paper. By viewing cognitive functions as three distinct but interdependent processes, the model goes beyond 'g' or general intelligence. Previous research on the statistical and empirical aspects of the model were reviewed to show that it is a viable approach. Examples of the model's advantage over 'general' intelligence are many. The three examples given here illustrate how an estimate of general intelligence is inadequate for the conceptualization of problems such as 'verbal deficit' in Down's syndrome, processing deficits in the learning disabled, or the planning dysfunctions in an otherwise intelligent victim of a minor traffic accident. General intelligence is as valid as the 'strength of soil' concept is for plant growers. It is not wrong but archaic, and needs to be superseded. A diagnosis of intellectual strengths and weaknesses is the purpose of all tests of general intelligence. It is argued here that the IQ tests are typically disadvantaged in fulfilling this need.

ACKNOWLEDGEMENTS

Correspondence concerning this paper should be addressed to J. P. Das, 6-123c Education North, Developmental Disabilities Centre, University of Alberta, Edmonton, Alberta T6G 2G5.

The author acknowledges the contributions of Drs. J. Kirby & J. Naglieri to this paper.

REFERENCES

Ashman, A. F. & Das, J. P. (1980). Relation between planning and simultaneous and successive processing. Perceptual and Motor Skills, 51, 371-382.

Atkinson, R. C. & Shiffrin, R. M. (1968). Human memory. In K. W. Spence & J. T. Spence (Eds.), Advances in the psychology of learning and motivation research and theory, Vol. 2. New York: Academic Press.

Broadbent, D. E. (1981). From the percept to the cognitive structure. In J. Long & A. Baddeley (Eds.), Attention and Performance, Vol. 9. Hillsdale, N.J.: Erlbaum, 1-26.

Das, J. P. (1972). Patterns of cognitive ability in nonretarded and retarded children. American Journal of Mental Deficiency, 77, 6-12.

Das, J. P. (1973). Cultural deprivation and cognitive competence. In N. R. Ellis (Ed.), International review of research in mental retardation, Vol. 6. New York: Academic Press.

Das, J. P. (1980). Planning: Theoretical considerations and empirical evidence. Psychological Research (W. Germany), 41, 141-151.

Das, J. P. (1984a). Aspects of planning. In J. R. Kirby (Ed.), Cognitive strategies and educational performance. Orlando, Fl.: Academic Press.

Das, J. P. (1984b). Intelligence and information integration. In J. R. Kirby (Ed.), Cognitive strategies and educational performance. Orlando, Fl: Academic Press.

Das, J. P. & Heemsbergen, D. B. (1983). Planning as a factor in the assessment of cognitive processes. Journal of Psychoeducational Assessment, 1, 1-15.

Das, J. P., Kirby, J., & Jarman, R. F. (1975). Simultaneous and successive synthesis: An alternative model for cognitive abilities. Psychological Bulletin, 82 (1), 87-103.

Das, J. P., Kirby, J. E., & Jarman, R. (1979). Simultaneous and successive cognitive processes. New York: Academic Press.

Das, J. P. & Naglieri, J. A. (1987). Cognitive Assessment System. San Antonio: The Psychological Corporation.

Das, J. P. & Snart, F. (1982). Coding and planning functions of normal and disabled readers. Paper presented at the annual meeting of the Canadian Psychological Association.

Das, J. P., & Varnhagen, C. K. (1986). Neuropsychological functioning and cognitive processing. Child Neuropsychology, Vol. 1. 117-140.

Eysenck, H.J. (1981). The Nature of Intelligence. In M.P. Friedman, J.P. Das and N. O'Connor (Eds.), Intelligence and Learning, 67-85.

Geschwind, N. (1982). Disorders of attention: A frontier in neuropsychology. In D. E. Broadbent & L. Weiskrantz (Eds.), The neuropsychology of cognitive function, Philosophical Transactions of the Royal Society of London, 173-185.

Glaser, R. (1972). The new aptitudes. Educational Researcher, 1, 5-13.

Graham, F. K., & Kendall, B. S. (1960). Memory-for-Designs Test: Revised general manual. Perceptual and Motor Skills, 11, 147-188.

Hunt, E. B. (1980). Intelligence as an information processing concept. British Journal of Psychology, 71, 449-474.

Jensen, A. (1981). Reaction Time and Intelligence. In M.P. Friedman, J.P. Das and N. O'Connor (Eds.), Intelligence and Learning, 39-50. New York: Plenum.

Luria, A. R. (1966a). Higher cortical functions in man. New York: Basic Books.

Luria, A. R. (1966b). Human brain and psychological processes. New York: Harper and Row.

Luria, A. R. (1973). The working brain. Middlesex, England: Penguin Books Limited.

Luria, A. R., & Artem'eva, E. Y. (1970). Two approaches to an evaluation of the reliability of psychological investigations. Soviet Psychology, 8, 271-282.

Messick, S. (1973). Multivariate models of cognition and personality: The need for both process and structure in psychological theory and measurement. In J. Royce (Ed.), Contributions of multivariate analysis to theoretical psychology. New York: Academic Press.

Naglieri, J., & Das, J. P. (1988). Planning-Arousal-Simultaneous-Successive (PASS): A Model for Assessment. Journal of School Psychology, 26, 35-48.

Parasuraman, R., & Davies, D.R. (Eds.), (1984). Varieties of Attention. New York: Academic Press.

Raven, John C. (1958). Standard Progressive Matrices Sets, A, B, C, D and E. London: H.K. Lewis & Co. Ltd.

Robinson, G.L.W. (1983). Simultaneous and successive information processing, language, and reading processes in reading disabled children. Unpublished doctoral dissertation, University of Newcastle, Newcastle, Australia.

Ryckman, D.B. (1981). Reading achievement, IQ, and simultaneous-successive processing among normal and learning disabled children. Alberta Journal of Educational Research, 27, 74-83.

Schofield, N.J., & Ashman, A.F. (1986). The relationship between digit span and cognitive processing across ability groups. Intelligence, 10, 1-8.

Simon, H.A. (1981). Studying human intelligence by creating artificial intelligence. American Scientist, 69 (3), 300-309.

Wachs, M., & Harris, M. (1986). Simultaneous and successive processing in university students: expanding the limits. Journal of Psychoeducational Assessment, 4, 103-112.

AUTHOR INDEX

COMMITTEES OF THE XXIV INTERNATIONAL CONGRESS OF PSYCHOLOGY

MANAGEMENT AND CONGRESS COMMITTEE

P. W. Sheehan, President

R. C. King, Chair

J. K. Collins, Director

H. P. Pfister, Secretary-General

B. J. Fallon, Treasurer

S. H. Lovibond, Director, Scientific Program

A. F. Bennett, Deputy Director, Scientific Program

K. M. McConkey, Secretary, Scientific Program

D. J. Kavanagh, Information Services

J. A. Antill, APS Treasurer

R. A. Cummins, APS Executive Officer

M. C. Knowles

L. Mann, APS President

D. McNicol, APS Vice-President

R. W. Russell, IUPsyS Liaison

G. V. Stanley, APS President-Elect

R. Taft

C. Williams

PREVIOUS MEMBERS:

J. A. Boughton; D. G. Cross; P. M. Lahy; D. M. Keats; D. Kiellerup; M. Macmillan; F. D. Naylor; P. G. Power; J. P. Young; I. K. Waterhouse

SCIENTIFIC PROGRAM COMMITTEE

S. H. Lovibond, Director,   A. F. Bennett, Deputy Director

Conveners:

N. W. Bond, Timetable

D. G. Cross, Young Psychologists' Program

J. A. Keats, Symposia

R H. Markham, Handbooks

P. W. Sheehan, Keynote/Invited Speakers

D. A. T. Siddle, Individual Papers

R. Taft, Satellite Program

D. Vickers, Publications

C. Williams, Workshops

APS Division of Professional Affairs Representatives:

R. Bradbury-Little;   D. P. Brunt

INTERNATIONAL UNION OF PSYCHOLOGICAL SCIENCE

Executive Committee 1984-1988

President	W. Holtzman (U.S.A.)
Vice Presidents	R. Diaz-Guerrero (Mexico)
	B. Lomov (U.S.S.R.)
Secretary-General	K. Pawlik (F.R.G.)
Treasurer	D. Belanger (Canada)

H. Azuma (Japan)   F. Klix (G.D.R.)
G. de Montmollin (France)   M. Rozenzweig (U.S.A.)
M. O. A. Durojaiye (Nigeria) D. Sinha (India)
G. d'Ydewalle (Belgium)   R. Taft (Australia)
Q. Jing (China)   M. Takala (Finland)

Executive Committee (1988-1992)

President	M. Rosenzweig (U.S.A.)
Past President	W. Holtzman (U.S.A.)
Vice Presidents	H. Azuma (Japan)
	M. Takala (Finland)
Secretary-General	K. Pawlik (F.R.G.)
Deputy Secretary-General	G. d'Ydewalle (Belgium)
Treasurer	D. Belanger (Canada)

R. Diaz-Guerrero (Mexico)   F. Klix (G.D.R.)
R. Gelman (U.S.A.   B. Lomov (U.S.S.R.)
T. Hogan (Canada)   L. Nilsson (Sweden)
Q. Jing (China)   P. Sheehan (Australia)
C. Kagitcibasi (Turkey)   D. Sinha (India)